A

CRITICAL AND EXEGETICAL

# COMMENTARY

ON

# THE BOOK OF EXODUS,

WITH A

## NEW TRANSLATION.

BY

JAMES G. MURPHY, D.D., T.C.D.,

PROFESSOR OF HEBREW, BELFAST.

Wipf & Stock
PUBLISHERS
Eugene, Oregon

Wipf and Stock Publishers
199 W 8th Ave, Suite 3
Eugene, OR 97401

A Critical and Exegetical Commentary on the Book of Exodus
By Murphy, James G.
ISBN: 1-57910-074-0
Publication date 11/12/1997
Previously published by Warren Draper, 1998

# PREFACE.

If the one God make a world and write a book, it is to be expected that nature and Scripture will agree. But their interpreters may differ. It is notorious that there has been a philosophy that was only vain deceit — a science, falsely so called. This was simply a false interpretation of nature. It could not be presumed that such would agree with the Bible. It is equally well known that false principles of interpretation have been applied to the Scripture, the results of which have also been at variance with nature. Admitting, however, the word and the work to come both from God, men, with the narrow and partially erroneous philosophy of their day, have endeavored to harmonize them. In doing so, they have in some instances imposed a sense upon Scripture which has eventually turned out to be incongruous with the conclusions of a wider and more exact philosophy. But while the former results of speculative and scientific inquiry have been modified or reversed, it has been generally taken for granted that the old meanings attached to those portions of Scripture that touch upon physical or metaphysical phenomena remain true and incontrovertible.

It is to be remembered, however, that these meanings flowed from minds otherwise well cultivated, but at the same time imbued with the errors of their day on physical and other questions. Their mistaken preconceptions insensibly guided their interpretation; and hence they found in Scripture, and fixed upon it, the prejudices of a dogmatic science. And there are actually men of critical and cultivated minds, open to the advancing and astonishing disclosures of modern science, who reject with impatience, and pronounce to be ingenious trifling, any attempt at an interpretation of Scripture free from the prejudices of the past and in harmony with the science of the present. They assume that the interpreter has already done all justice to these parts of Scripture, and regard it as a settled point that this venerable record of the past is, and must have been, out of harmony with the present state of science.

If the Scripture was a book of merely human origin we might acquiesce in this conclusion. In that case, being composed, most of it long before the Christian era, and all of it long before the era of physical science, it must have partaken of the errors of its age. And the wonder would be, not that it contains the few errors on physical questions which some interpreters find in it, but that it does not contain a multitude of others common to the ages in which it was produced. The Mosaic cosmogony, history, and philology, even according to the common interpretation, solve questions, which without their aid speculation and science have attempted in vain. It need scarcely be added that the theology and ethics of the Pentateuch, not to speak of the New Testament, far transcend all the attainments of unassisted human reason. The appearance of such a volume in such an age is simply unaccountable on the hypothesis of its human origin.

The Scripture, however claiming and proving itself in so many ways to be of divine origin and authority, is clearly as liable to be misinterpreted as nature. It is positively more so. Nature comes directly from the hand of God, and shows no traces of a human hand, except what havoc sin has wrought in man. Yet it has been long and grievously misapprehended by the haste or pride of its interpreters. But Scripture comes from God through the minds and utterances of men. Hence it expresses the revelations of God in the phraseology of untutored or misinformed man. It presents, therefore, an incidental element of relative imperfection in the mode of expression. How much more, then, is it liable to be misunderstood by an interpreter, who is himself led astray by the errors of his own or past times?

A free and fair thinker will feel that a divine communication, if such may be, must achieve the difficult, and to man impossible, task of conveying a system of truth in the imperfect vehicle of human language, without coming into real conflict with the facts of nature. Now it is plain that a communication so expressed, though it be in fundamental harmony with nature, may appear not to be so from casual phrases, which convey a fact, indeed, plainly enough, but in terms which involve an old or popular misconception regarding it. Thus when we say, "the sun sets," the event intended is adequately expressed, and perfectly understood, though the terms fail to give a strictly accurate account of what actually takes place. And only when we have succeeded in disentangling the error unavoidably belonging to the medium of communication are we at liberty to regard the meaning remaining in the words as the statement intended by the sacred record. Hence, in receiving a divine revelation couched in human words, it is only fair that we discount any error that may incidentally lurk in the ordinary phraseology of the time.

This law for the exposition of a divine record, though evident in itself, and demanded by equity, has yet had to force its way in all ages to acceptance and authority. When Galileo, in the seventeenth century, proclaimed that the earth had a diurnal motion on its axis, and an annual motion round the sun, he was condemned for teaching what was contradictory to the assertions of the Bible. His judges were not aware, or did not admit, of the fair and obvious principle of interpretation which has now received a partial recognition. No one now maintains that the Scriptures assert that the earth stands still, while the sun performs a diurnal revolution in twenty-four hours. Yet there are men in this nineteenth century who regard with hesitation, if they do not turn away with undisguised distrust, from any attempt to apply this or any other equally fair rule of hermeneutics to those portions of the Bible which are presumed to be repugnant to the conclusions of physical science. We could understand this, if its divine authority were to be abandoned. But with its claim to be given by inspiration of God before us, we submit that it is as well entitled to an amended interpretation as nature itself. Natural science receives a constant readjustment as new facts disclose themselves to the enlightened observer. Biblical science has a still more pressing claim to a similar reconstruction, inasmuch as it has long suffered from a defective mode of elucidation, not based on a fair estimate of itself, but biassed by a false view of nature. The interpreter of nature amends his method under the force of accumulated experience. Let the interpreter of Scripture enjoy the same right. Especially let him be released from the bondage which the vain philosophy of a bygone age has imposed upon him. Liberated from the prejudices of the past, and standing in the light of present science, let him at least make the attempt to interpret Scripture as the word of God, that must be in real harmony with the works of God. It will be time enough to abandon the theory of divine inspiration when right principles of hermeneutics, freely and fairly applied, fail to bring out a meaning that will be in harmony with the indubitable facts of nature.

The same line of reasoning applies to moral and metaphysical questions as to physical. Let us fully apprehend the foundations of our mental philosophy before we make it the standard by which we are to test the morals of Scripture. And let us be scrupulously faithful in ascertaining what is the precise meaning of Scripture, before we pronounce it to be at variance with any first principle of ethical or metaphysical truth.

The interpretation of the Book of Genesis, offered by the present writer to the public in 1863, was the issue of an attempt to ascertain the meaning of that venerable portion of holy writ according to exegetical rules, which reviewers have admitted to be just, and one has even pronounced it to be a series of truisms. Some results of this interpretation were, if not new, yet sufficiently remarkable. The record of the primeval creation was found to be contained in the first verse of Genesis. The state of at least a portion of the surface of the earth antecedent to the six days of creative effort is described in the second verse. The creation narrated in the remainder of the first chapter is partial in regard both to time and place, being accomplished in six literal days, and confined in range to that portion of the earth's surface which was declared in the second verse to be waste, void, and dark. The deluge is limited to a still narrower area, extending only to the region inhabited by man. The ark was designed and constructed to preserve only such animals of a domestic and harmless kind as might have become extinct, because they were limited in range. It did not, therefore, receive animals residing in more distant regions, or belonging to an earlier creation. The six days' creation, moreover, furnishes an instance of a local centre of creation, and consequently favors the presumption of other local and previous centres of creation for different orders of animal and vegetable life. These, and other similar results, are elicited from the text, it is submitted, by a natural and unstrained interpretation.

It may be said that in both these cases the terms of the descriptions are universal, and the interpretation has been uniformly so. But it is to be remembered that there was a universality at first both in regard to man and the objects known to him. And hence the terms of the text agree with the orignal compass of human experience. But when the terms land, animal, etc., come to have an extent of meaning beyond what was known or contemplated in primeval times, it is manifest that an error may be insensibly imported into the sense; because what applied to these terms in their original extension may not be true of the new parts of their extension. And this error will progressively increase in amount until the land becomes the terraqueous globe, and the animals comprise all the species existing thereupon.

The present volume on Exodus is a second contribution to the exposition of the Old Testament, and to the practical demonstration that a just interpretation of the volume of inspiration will obviate supposed difficulties, which have arisen mainly from misapprehension, and bring out more strikingly and uniformly its essential harmony with science, reason, and history. It removes, in the author's apprehension, any impossibilities that may have seemed to lie in the natural events that are recorded in the narrative. This is a matter of the first importance, not only in regard to the credibility of the history, but in reference to the origin and structure of the whole Pentateuch. For while the historical validity of the document stands, the free handling, by which the text is parcelled out and distributed among a succession of authors, the earliest of whom lived centuries after the events occurred, loses the basis on which alone it can be securely erected; and the evidence for its Mosaic authorship rests upon a foundation which cannot be moved.

The resources for the vindication of the historical veracity of the narrative in Exodus are far from being exhausted. The elucidation of Egyptian history by the labors of Lepsius, Rawlinson, Hincks, Talbot, and others; the restoration of its chronology, to which Dr. Hincks has contributed some most interesting and valuable papers; the investigation of the historical and anthropological traces which remain of the migrations of ancient tribes; and the conclusions of a thoroughly discussed theory of national and social economy, will yet throw a flood of light on the exodus of Israel and the events consequent upon it. The profounder investigations of ethical and political questions, and the prosecution of the abstruse but important and practical inquiry into the mode of training families and nations in the conception, reception, and perpetuation of true ideas, beliefs, and cognitions respecting God, and their practical relation to him, will also open the way for a juster comprehension of the meaning of Exodus, as well as the other books of the Pentateuch.

Such, indeed, is the apologetic view of the bearing of those studies on the book. But the real character of the books of Moses, as the primeval portion of the word of God, precisely reverses this bearing. The Pentateuch is the light of revelation shedding its salubrious beams on those questionings of the spirit of man, on those themes which have been darkened and confused by the entrance of sin. And when men come to acknowledge the divine authority, and penetrate into the true meaning of this second book of it, this book of moral resolvings and teachings and doings, they will find in it a safe guide to new and sound views of ethical, political, and educational science. It would not be easy to exaggerate the importance of that book which recounts the separation of the chosen people of God from the world, the giving of the moral law, and the setting up of the tabernacle, which symbolizes the way of reconciliation and communion with God.

The method of exposition pursued in this volume, as well as in that in Genesis, is the following: First, the general arrangement and division of topics in the book are brought under notice. Next, at the head of each section, a few prominent words are quoted and briefly expounded, for the sake of readers acquainted with Hebrew, who are supposed to peruse the section in the original. Then follows a translation of the section, which is designed to be a mere revision of the Authorized Version. This the reader will compare with the original, or with the corresponding portion of his English Bible. The commentary then appended is designed to explain the momentous import of the historical facts recorded, to mark their bearing on the highest interests of man, and to unfold the great principles of ethical and theological truth which are stated for his guidance and comfort. These are obviously the weightiest questions that can engage the attention of man. Certain and definite answers on these all-important topics are to be found in the books of revelation, and in no other quarter. We have, therefore, the strongest motives to examine the Scriptures, to make ourselves acquainted with their profoundly interesting contents, and to avail ourselves of the information they convey to escape the penal consequences of sin and enter upon the path of everlasting life.

In pursuing such investigations as these, the writer has not occupied much space with those questions of literary criticism which are now ably discussed in introductions to the Bible and in Biblical dictionaries. He has refrained in general from bewildering the reader with the enumeration of a series of incongruous opinions, and has been sparing in the quotation of authorities for every particular statement made. In this way he has endeavored to economise space for a more full discussion, though in as concise a form as possible, of all that bears upon the ways of God with man. The difficulties that are started in the publications of the day have received a large share of attention; and whatever seemed to be the best mode of obviating their force has been uniformly indicated in an incidental way. And, at the risk of some appearance of dogmatism, it has been made a point in all important cases if possible to arrive at and to offer to the reader a decided opinion.

The author has made some contributions towards a formal and direct reply to recent objections to the Pentateuch. But he is content for the present with offering to the reader a second instalment of the positive argument for the authority and historical validity of that venerable document in this attempt at the exegetical elucidation of the book of Exodus. The right understanding of the Book of God is all the vindication it needs with the earnest reader.

# INTRODUCTION.

## IX. EXODUS.

THE Book of Exodus is the record of a new development in the ways of God with man. This is the departure of the chosen people out of Egypt. They went into that land a family; they came out a people. They entered as the honored and independent relatives of the Prime Minister of State; they departed as the fugitive serfs of a despotic and oppressive government. They took up their abode in Goshen at a time when the nations still retained some knowledge of the true God, some remembrance of his covenant with man, and some sense of his claim upon their reverence; they marched forth from the land of their sojourning at an epoch when the iniquity of the Amorites was full, when, whatever might be the case with a rare individual or tribe, the nations had corrupted the knowledge of God, disregarded his covenant, and wandered into the devious paths of will-worship. Apostasy from the truth on the loftiest themes of history had become the characteristic of the nations, when God brought forth from the bondage of Egypt into the sphere of conspicuous observation the nation whom he foreknew, to be the keepers of his sacred oracles and ordinances, the accepted parties to his holy and gracious covenant, and the maintainers and eventual disseminators of his pure and spiritual worship on earth. This great act is the topic of the Book of Exodus.

From this glance at its contents, it is manifest that it is not the full counterpart of Genesis. That venerable document is matched in grandeur of scope not even by the rest of the Pentateuch, but only by the remainder of the volume of revelation. It opens with a creation, of which man forms the prominent object; the Old Testament closes with the anticipation of a new creation (Isa. lxv. 17), in which also man will hold the conspicuous place; and the New Testament records the atoning obedience of Christ and the quickening work of the Holy Ghost, as the guarantee and earnest of that new creation, the consummation of which it again announces to the church (2 Pet. iii. 13). Genesis also touches upon the history of the whole race of man, and even after the call of Abraham traces the peaceful intercourse subsisting between the chosen family and the rest of mankind. Exodus marks the full-grown antagonism between the chosen nation and the heathen world, records the violent separation between the two, and then confines itself mainly to the history of the party that remained in communion with God. Its distinguishing event, the exodus, is accordingly the prōtotype of that great event in the experience of the individual in which he comes out from the bondage of the flesh into the freedom of the Spirit, as well as of those great occasions in the history of the church in which it reasserts its spiritual life and liberty, and passes with all the determination of new-born principle from the wilful service of sin into the conscientious obedience of holiness. This coming out is a process continually going on during the history of the church until all have come out, and the doomed world is given over to everlasting destruction.

It is the manner of Scripture to signalise the primary event in any given series as a lesson and example to all future generations. In Genesis are recorded all kinds of origins or births, and among others, the birth of Isaac, the seed of promise. In Exodus is recounted the deliberate action of the new-born, in coming out of the land of bondage. The wilderness between this land and the land of promise, the troubles, temptations, and failings of such a state of life, the giving of the law to a new-born and emancipated people, the setting up of the ordinances of a holy religion, are all typical events, prefiguring others of a like nature, but of still grander and grander import. They do not stand alone on memory's tablet, but embody a principle of constant value, which comes out in a series of analogous events in the course of human affairs. They are standing monuments in the great field of the past, written in legible characters on the page of history for the instruction of coming days. They lodge in the mind of man the principles which they exemplify, never afterwards to be dislodged from the hereditary wisdom of the race. History has been said to be philosophy teaching by examples, and this is nowhere so true as in that history which describes events from a heavenly point of view, selects them with a divine intuition of their exemplary character, and places them on record for the express purpose of instilling into men's hearts the great principles of sacred truth.

The scope of the Book of Exodus, however, is not to be limited to the mere fortunes of the chosen people. Even if it stood alone, its communications could not be confined to so narrow an area. But preceded by the Book of Genesis, and forming a continuation of that work, it has an essential and important bearing on the destinies of the whole race of man. It details a certain stage of that momentous process, by which the covenant of God with man is to be upheld, and its benefits secured for a growing proportion of our fallen race, until at length the main body, at least, of all kindreds and tongues returns to God. This imparts a new dignity to the record now before us, and imposes a higher significance on the characteristic events which it celebrates. The chosen nation are interesting no longer merely on account of themselves as an end contemplated by the Great Designer, but on account of their paramount importance as a means of incalculable blessing to the whole family of man. The oracles of God flow forth in gradual stream from the mouths of their prophets. The system of symbolic ordinances shadowing forth the way of salvation is set up and administered among them. The Messiah, who was revealed in these oracles and foreshadowed by these ordinances, is to be born of this people to make a propitiation not only for their sins, but for those of the whole world, fulfil the requirements of the ancient covenant on behalf of man, and so to receive the heathen for his inheritance, and the uttermost parts of the earth for his possession. In the exodus of this peculiar people out of Egypt, therefore, we are in the very pathway of that great transaction by which he with whom one day is as a thousand years, and a thousand years as one day, will eventually bring all the nations of man again into reconciliation with himself. This is the sublimest enterprise in which the interests of man can be concerned.

This book is a regular and orderly piece of composition. Hence it admits of easy analysis into its component parts. The exodus itself is the central event of the drama, and is embraced in six chapters (xiii.–xviii.) That which precedes naturally falls into two parts: the first of which recounts the bondage of Israel in Egypt, with the rise of the leader in this great movement, in six chapters (i.–vi.) ; the second narrates the ten plagues or momentous strokes of judgment, by which the opposition of the Egyptian monarch is overcome, and the way opened for the exodus of the liberated people, in other six chapters (vii.–xii.) The portion of the book which follows the main act is also divided between two important topics, the law-giving and the tabernacle. The former occupies six chapters more (xix.–xxiv.), and the latter extends over the remaining sixteen ; of which seven (xxv.–xxxi.) contain the specifications concerning the tabernacle, its furniture, and officials ; three (xxxii.–xxxiv.) relate a wild outbreak of will-worship among the people who had just escaped from bondage ; and the last six (xxxv.–xl.) record the construction of the tabernacle and the commencement of the divinely instituted national worship.

This book is composed in the customary style and method of the sacred writer. It forms a complete whole, and closes with a crowning event. The writer has this end in view throughout the work, and advances to it with undeviating tenacity of purpose. Hence he omits those collateral topics, which are not essential to the main thread of his narrative, and tend to disturb the unity and mar the effect of the whole. These he will take up hereafter in their appropriate connection.

The following table exhibits the arrangement of the book, as indicated above :

| | | | |
|---|---|---|---|
| EXODUS. | SECTION I. Bondage in Egypt. | I. Israel oppressed in Egypt, | i. |
| | | II. Moses born and bred, | ii. |
| | | III. Moses called and commissioned, | iii., iv. |
| | | IV. Moses enters on his office, | v., vi. |
| | SECTION II. The Ten Plagues. | V. The first three plagues, | vii., viii. 19. |
| | | VI. The second three plagues, | viii. 20 - ix. 12. |
| | | VII. The third three plagues, | ix. 13 - x. |
| | | VIII. The tenth plague. Passover, | xi., xii. |
| | SECTION III. The Exodus. | IX. The escape of Israel, | xiii. - xv. |
| | | X. Journey from Elim to Sinai, | xvi. - xviii. |
| | SECTION IV. The Lawgiving. | XI. The Moral Law, | xix., xx. |
| | | XII. The Civil Law, | xxi. - xxiv. |
| | SECTION V. The Tabernacle. | XIII. Plan of the Tabernacle, | xxv. - xxxi. |
| | | XIV. The first breach of the Covenant, | xxxii. - xxxiv. |
| | | XV. The Tabernacle made and set up, | xxxv. - xl. |

# COMMENTARY.

---

## PART III.

### SECTION I.—THE BONDAGE IN EGYPT.

#### I. ISRAEL OPPRESSED IN EGYPT.—Ex. i.

11. מַס *tribute, levy, task,* work done by a serf for his Lord. Keil understands by it the serf or socager himself. But Esther x. 1 is against this. פִּתֹם Pithom, Πειθὼ in Sept., is identified with Πάτουμος in Herod. ii. 158; or, omitting the Egyptian article, Θοῦμ in the later geographers. Brugsch derives it from *pa,* abode, and *Tum* or Atum, the sun after setting. רַעְמְסֵס Raamses, Ῥαμεσσῆ in Sept. It is rendered "son of Ra," the sun, who was worshipped at On or Heliopolis.

15. שִׁפְרָה Shiphrah, *brightness, beauty.* פּוּעָה Pu'ah for יְפוּעָה splendor (Simonis).

16. אָבְנַיִם *potter's wheel, birth-stool.* This word occurs only twice in Scripture. In Jer. xviii. 3 it denotes the potter's wheel. In the present passage it seems to signify the receptacle into which the new-born infant comes from the womb. Both these utensils may have been originally of stone (אֶבֶן). Gen. xxviii. 11.

21. וַיַּעַשׂ לָהֶם בָּתִּים *And made them houses,* gave them not only husbands, but children, who constitute families. The pronoun הֶם is masculine. But the plural masculine is occasionally applied to the female. (See Gen. xxxi. 9).

22. יְאֹר *a river,* in Memphitic *iaro,* in Sahidic *iero,* a term generally applied to the Nile.

I. 1. And these are the names of the sons of Israel, who
came into Mizraim; every man and his household came with
Jacob. 2. Reuben, Simon, Levi, and Judah, 3. Issakar, Zeb-

ulun, and Benjamin, 4. Dan and Naphtali, Gad and Asher.
5. And all the souls that came out of the thigh of Jacob were
seventy souls: and Joseph was already in Mizraim. 6. And
Joseph died, and all his brethren, and all that generation.
7. And the sons of Israel were fruitful, and increased and
multiplied, and waxed exceedingly mighty; and the land was
filled with them. ¶ 1.

8. Then arose a new king over Mizraim, who knew not
Joseph. 9. And he said unto his people, Behold, the people
of the sons of Israel are more and mightier than we. 10.
Come, let us deal wisely with them, lest they multiply, and it
come to pass that a war falleth out, and they also join with
those that hate us, and fight against us, and get up out of the
land. 11. And they set over them taskmasters to afflict them
with their burdens: and they built treasure-cities for Pharoh,
Pithom and Raamses. 12. And as they afflicted them, so
they multiplied and spread: and they were vexed because of
the sons of Israel. 13. And Mizraim made the sons of Israel
serve with rigor. 14. And they embittered their life with
hard service, in clay and in brick, and in all service in the
field; with all their service which they laid on them with
rigor.

15. And the king of Mizraim said to the Hebrew midwives,
of whom the name of the one was Shiphrah and the other
Puah. 16. And he said, When ye deliver the Hebrew women
and look upon the stool, if it be a son, then ye shall kill him,
and if it be a daughter, then she shall live. 17. And the mid-
wives feared God, and did not as the king of Mizraim spake
unto them, but saved the men-children alive. 18. And the
king of Mizraim called the midwives, and said unto them,
Why have ye done this thing, and saved the men-children
alive? 19. And the midwives said unto Pharoh, Because the

Hebrew women are not like the Mizrite women; for they are lively, and have brought forth ere the midwife comes in unto them. 20. And God dealt well with the midwives: and the people multiplied and waxed very mighty. 21. And it came to pass, because the midwives feared God, that he made them houses. 22. And Pharoh charged all his people, saying, Every son that is born ye shall cast into the river, and every daughter ye shall save alive. ¶ 2.

It is the custom of the sacred writer to note the great moments and turning-points in the history of God's dealings with man, and to pass lightly over the current of events that flow naturally from the tendency thus given. The entrance into Egypt was one of those leading movements; the departure from it is another. The intervening period of two hundred and ten years is summed up in the chapter before us, if we except certain events relative to Jacob and Joseph, which wind up the settlement of the chosen family in Egypt, and a few circumstances concerning Moses which are introductory to the national migration. The present chapter recounts the extraordinary increase of the family of Israel, and the ineffectual measures taken by the king of Egypt to check their growth.

1-7. The increase of the chosen seed. Here the historian, after the manner of Hebrew composition, goes back to the descent of Israel into Egypt as the starting-point of the new train of events about to be related. *And these are the names.* The recapitulation of the heads of houses in Jacob's family prepares the way for the vast augmentation about to be recorded. *Of Israel.* This word is here well chosen. The significance of the name, and the occasion of its application, still lived in the memory of the patriarch's posterity The outward privileges of the prince that had power with God and with man descended to them, and the inward character that corresponded with such a parentage was no doubt to be found in many of them. And now that the estrangement of the nations from the true God was become general and obvious, it was the more necessary that the chosen family should be reminded by this sacred name of the high destiny to which they were called. *Every man and his house.* They were already distributed into twelve houses, when they went down into Egypt. The sons of Leah are placed first, Benjamin son of Rachel next, and afterwards the four sons of the handmaids. *Seventy souls.* Jacob himself is included among the seventy souls, the natural head being essential to the unity and integrity of the family. The Sept. here has seventy-five, (see on Gen. xlvi. 27). Joseph is now mentioned apart from the others, because he had been in the country before them. 6. *And all that generation.* As some of those who descended with Jacob were mere infants, more than half of the two hundred and ten years would have elapsed before their decease. This would bring us within twenty years of the birth of Moses. 7. The rapid growth of Israel into a nation is the fact of this paragraph. It is expressed, as usual in Hebrew, by a climax of verbs: *were fruitful* is taken from the vegetable world, in which the increase varies from a small multiple to several hundreds-fold; *increased* (spawned, swarmed) is borrowed from the finny tribes, in which the rate of increase rises to many myriads; *multiplied* is a general word referring to number; and *waxed exceedingly mighty* is a similar phrase alluding to the strength which numbers confer, composed of a verb and an adverb repeated, and therefore well adapted to complete the climax. Then follows the result, *the land was filled with them.* It is quite evident that this statement implies a rate of increase amazingly higher than that which was usual in those days, and still higher than any that can be found in the present crowded state of the world. The circumstances were favourable for such an increase. They had scope and verge in a wide and thinly-peopled country; and they were placed in the best of the land (Gen. xlvii. 11). These advantages alone, however, could not account for their accelerated growth; for the Egyptians were not much less favored in these respects. But the blessing of Jehovah, the God of promise, was now realized to them. After a long delay the word came to Israel, the third patriarch: "I am God Almighty; be fruitful and multiply: a nation and a congregation of nations shall be of thee, and kings shall come out of thy loins" (Gen. xxxv. 11). We see also the effect of the migration into Egypt. In Kenaan the inevitable tendency was to lose all family distinction, and merge into the nations of that country. Only in a border land, on territory specially ceded to them by a people who had a national antipathy to their pursuits, could a select nation have grown up without coalescing in blood, in language, and in institutions with the surrounding tribes. Hence in Goshen the chosen family grows in two hundred and ten years into the chosen nation, destined to witness among the nations for the unity, spirituality, and mercy of the Creator of all.

8–22. The unwarrantable measures taken by the king of Egypt to check the growth of the people. These were three: to impose slave labor, to enjoin the midwives to slay the male children as soon as born, and to command his people to throw the male infants into the river. *A new king over Mizraim.* Joseph was thirty-nine years old when his kindred settled in Egypt, lived to the age of one hundred and ten, and therefore died seventy-one years after that settlement. We may suppose that all the generation that came down into Egypt died one hundred and ten years after the same event. In the interval between this and the birth of Moses arose this "new king over Mizraim." The chronology of the early period of Egyptian history has not yet been definitely settled. It is probable, however, that at the time in question there were two or more contemporary sovereigns reigning in different parts of what we now call Egypt: one at Thebes, the capital of Pathros, the land of the Pathrusim (Gen. x. 14), perhaps of the 17th dynasty of Manetho; another at Memphis, the capital of Mizraim proper, possibly of the 6th dynasty of the same author; and not impossibly a third at Xois, in the western part of the Delta. Other petty sovereignties, that may have existed, need not be considered. The Hyksos, or shepherd kings, not being designated by the seat of empire, may have been identical with the sovereigns of Xois or Memphis, or distinct, and even superior to both. In the last case the seat of this sovereignty may have been at On or Bubastis. The dynasty with which the Israelites now came into contact was either this last supposed one, or that of Memphis, which was convenient to On, and to the land of Goshen. *Who knew not Joseph.* This new king may have been the founder of the 7th dynasty, or a contemporary sovereign of the 16th. At all events, he came into power at least forty years after the death of Joseph, and about one hundred years after he ceased to take an active part in state affairs. This allows a sufficient time for Joseph and his services to be forgotten. "Not to know" is in scripture phrase to disregard. This new sovereign was not actuated by any sense of the benefits which that distinguished Israelite had conferred upon his country. 9. *The people of the sons of Israel.* They are now recognized as no longer a family, but a community. *More and mightier than we.* This marks out the speaker as the sovereign of a comparatively small principality, hampered, perhaps, on the northwest by one power, and on the south by another. Such a prince would feel himself embarrassed by the unparalleled growth of this foreign people within his borders, and might naturally express himself in the terms here employed, though the Israelites were only approaching to his own subjects in numbers and strength (vs. 10). *Join with those that hate us.* An intimation is here given that this king of Mizraim was by no means free from the dangers of rivalry and ambition, and was therefore far from being the sole monarch in the valley of the Nile. Those that hate him and his subjects are the other sovereigns in Xois, Thebes, and perhaps other parts of Egypt. He might be exposed also to attacks from the east, even though he were himself an invader from that quarter. *And get up out of the land.* Though he disregarded the political services rendered by Joseph, yet he is acquainted with the origin of the race, their claim to be free, and their expectation at some time to depart from Egypt. He found them valuable, whether as subjects or as serfs, and he does not wish to part with them. This incidental notice proves that the Israelites were still mindful of the God of their fathers, and cherished the hope of one day entering into possession of the promised land. We are elsewhere informed that Ezer and Elead, sons of Ephraim, were slain in a raid by the men of Gath, and that his granddaughter Sherah built Bethhoron, the nether and the upper, and Uzzen-sherah (1 Chron. vii. 21, 24). Whence it appears that in the days of their freedom, before this new king arose, they not only looked forward to a settlement in Palestine, but actually asserted a position in the country, at least for a time. This naturally connects itself with the share which Jacob had given to Joseph above his brethren (Gen. xlviii. 22). It is not unlikely that the district acquired by Jacob was actually claimed and taken possession of by Ephraim, for whom it was designed, and perhaps enlarged by conquest in that early period of the residence of Israel in Egypt. Whether the new king of Mizraim came from the region of Ephraim's early conquests history has not enabled us to say.

11. *Taskmasters* were superintendents of forced labor. This was customary among all ancient governments, and especially among the Egyptians, whose pyramids and other great works were mostly the product of slave labor. *Treasure-cities* were magazines for the storage of provisions and other commodities of war and police. *Pithom and Raamses* were situated on the borders of Egypt and Arabia. The former is called by Herodotus an Arabian town, and said to be near the eastern bank of the Nile, a little above Bubastis, at the commencement of the ancient canal in the valley of the Natron Lakes. The latter was in the same valley, farther to the east, near the site of Heroopolis, with which many identify it. Lepsius finds it in the ruins of Abu Kesheb and Heroopolis in Mukfar. Osborne endeavors to show that Pithom is Damietta, and Raamses Migdol, which he places at the head of the Gulf of Suez. These magazine cities on the border were well situated for troops making inroads into the eastern world from Egypt. The Sept. here adds On; but this was in existence in the time of Joseph (Gen. xli. 45), and the reading is not otherwise supported.

12–14. *So they multiplied,* The policy of the Egyptian king was ineffectual. The purpose of God was not set aside, but only promoted by these measures. *They were vexed.* These Egyptians were probably hard pressed on their southern frontier by a superior power. They had also a rooted aversion to the Israelites. *With rigor.* By compulsion they exacted hard service in clay, in brick, and in field labor. Agriculture was attended with considerable labor in the higher grounds of Egypt, on account of the necessity of watering them by artificial means. Bricks were the usual building material in Egypt. The monuments show that foreigners were employed in these servile works under native overseers.

15–21. Pharoh next applied to the Hebrew midwives to check the population by murdering the male infants. They are called Hebrew, a generic term applying to all the descendants of Heber (see on Gen. xiv. 13). Two midwives only are mentioned by name. About ninety years before the exodus, and therefore ten before the birth of Moses, the Israelites were about thirty thousand, and at the time of his birth about fifty thousand; as they doubled in about fifteen years, and the starting number, including wives, was about one hundred and twenty. From this we learn to moderate our estimate of the extent of that kingdom with which the Israelites were in contact. All Egypt, from the Mediterranean to the first Cataract, if united under one government, could not be afraid of thirty or fifty thousand men, women, and children. A petty state, having its centre at Heliopolis or Bubastis, and overshadowed by one or two southern powers, might feel some apprehension of a small people that was doubling itself in fifteen years. Of thirty or fifty thousand, much less than a third would be married women, and it may be that of these not more than a tenth would need or seek the aid of a professional midwife; and if on an average one birth in each family took place every two years, the two midwives would not have to attend more than one or two births every day, even if personal attendance were always given. But we may presume that they had a large number of deputies or assistants acting under their direction to meet all the demands on their services. 16. *The stool.* Some have supposed this to mean the mouth of the womb; but it seems more likely that it was the basin or vessel in which the new-born infant was received from the womb. 17. *God,* in the original the God,—the true, everlasting, almighty God, who was infinitely higher than Pharoh. 19. *For they are lively,* of a vigorous frame. This was quite true in point of fact. Among the Bedawin to this day, and others whose bodies are well developed by pastoral occupations and loose clothing, child-bearing is comparatively easy. The accompanying statement was also correct in the majority of cases, if not in all; especially if the mothers hearing the order of Pharoh did not admit the midwife, and she did not intrude, if possible, until the child was born. Of the exceptions the midwives, evading Pharoh's question, say nothing. 21. *And he made them houses,* gave them not only husbands, but also children, which were regarded as a boon and an honor by wives. It is conceivable that these women were unmarried, or if married, childless, and therefore at leisure to devote themselves to the aid of those who were bearing children. The word *them* is by some referred to the people in the previous verse. But this construction is harsh, and the verse in this sense adds nothing to what has been said before. Here, as usual, God requites like with like. The midwives save alive the offspring of the nation: God deals well with them in giving them offspring.

22. Being baffled by the midwives, Pharoh, as a last resort, commands all his people to cast the male infants into the Nile. This bloody mandate appears to have been given very shortly before the birth of Moses. These measures of the king, indeed, may have followed one another in rapid succession; and the magazine cities, though commenced before, may not have been completed till long after the issue of the last of them. The period of serfdom and oppression will in this case last not much longer than eighty or ninety years, namely from a few years before the birth of Moses to the exodus.

## II. MOSES BORN AND BROUGHT UP.—Ex. 2.

3. גֹּמֶא the *papyrus* of the Nile; r. *absorb, drink up*. Hence called *bibula papyrus* (Lucan iv. 136).

5. רָחַץ *wash* the body, or any part of it. כָּבַס *wash* clothes by treading with the feet.

10. מֹשֶׁה Mosheh. The word, if taken to be Hebrew, signifies *drawing*. By Josephus its Greek form Μωυσῆς is resolved into the Coptic μῶ water, and υσῆς saved from. *Mouu* water, and *sa* drag, may be the Coptic elements of the name. The corresponding Hebrew roots are probably contained in מַיִם water and נָשָׂא lift; though the Hebrew language does not deal freely in compounds. In explaining the origin of the name, however, the author employs a verb which contains the letters that are in the Hebrew form of the word. He either translates the name given by the princess, as Melanchthon from Schwarzerdt, or she spoke a dialect of Hebrew. The latter might be the case, if she was of the family of the Hyksos, who are supposed to have come from Phœnicia or Arabia.

18. רְעוּאֵל Re'uel, *friend of God*.

21. צִפֹּרָה Zipporah, *bird, sparrow*.

22. גֵּרְשֹׁם Gereshom, *stranger, exile;* r. גָּרַשׁ *drive out*, compounded

of גֵּר *stranger* and שׁם = שָׁם there. The latter is not necessary to warrant the expression of the text; as the native speakers of the language had a much freer and wider sense of the relation among roots than many of our philologers. Paronomasia plays a part in their etymology. They felt a relation between קַיִן and קָנָה Gen. iv. 1, בָּבֶל and בָּלַל Gen. xi. 9, גֵּר and גָּרַשׁ. The rules of philology, instead of correcting, should be gathered from these among other phenomena.

II. 1. Then went a man of the house of Levi, and took a daughter of Levi. 2. And the woman conceived and bare a son; and she saw that he was goodly, and hid him three months. 3. And she could not longer hide him, and she took for him an ark of rushes, and daubed it with asphalt and with pitch: and she put therein the child, and laid it in the flags by the river's brink. 4. And his sister stood afar off, to wit what would be done to him.

5. And the daughter of Pharoh went down to bathe in the river, and her maidens walked along by the river's side: and she saw the ark among the flags, and sent her handmaid, and she fetched it. 6. And she opened it, and saw the child, and lo the babe wept: and she had pity on him, and said, This is one of the Hebrew's children. 7. Then said his sister to Pharoh's daughter, Shall I go and call to thee a nurse of the Hebrew women, and she shall nurse the child for thee? 8. And Pharoh's daughter said to her, Go. And the maid, went and called the child's mother 9. And Pharoh's daughter said unto her, Take this child away and nurse him for me, and I will give thee thy wages. And the woman took the child and nursed him. 10. And the child grew, and she brought him to Pharoh's daughter, and he became her son, and she called his name Moses; and said, Because I drew him out of the water.

11. And it came to pass in those days, that Moses grew up and came out unto his brethren, and looked on their burdens: and he saw a Mizrite smiting a Hebrew, one of his brethren. 12. And he turned this way and that way, and saw that there was no man: and he smote the Mizrite, and hid him in the sand. 13. And he came out the second day, and lo two Hebrews were striving: and he said unto the wrong-doer, Why smitest thou thy neighbour? 14. And he said, Who made thee a ruler and a judge over us? Intendest thou to slay me, as thou slewest the Mizrite? And Moses feared, and said, Surely the thing is known. 15. And Pharoh heard this thing, and sought to slay Moses; and Moses fled from the face of Pharoh, and dwelt in the land of Midian; and he sat by the well.

16. Now the priest of Midian had seven daughters: and they came and drew, and filled the troughs to water their father's flock. 17. Then came the shepherds and drove them away: and Moses stood up and savėd them, and watered their flock. 18. And they went to Reuel their father; and he said Why are ye come so soon to-day? 19. And they said, A Mizrite delivered us out of the hand of the shepherds: and he also drew enough for us, and watered the flock. 20. And he said unto his daughters, And where is he? Why is it that ye have left the man? Call him, and let him eat bread. 21. And Moses was content to dwell with the man: and he gave Zipporah his daughter to Moses. 22. And she bare a son, and he called his name Gershom; for he said, I have been a stranger in a foreign land. ¶ 3.

23. And it came to pass many days after, that the king of Mizraim died: and the sons of Israel sighed by reason of the service, and cried; and their cry went up to God by reason of the service. 24. And God heard their groaning, and God

remembered his covenant with Abraham, with Isaac, and with Jacob. 25. And God saw the sons of Israel, and God had regard unto them. § 1.

In the preceding chapters is recorded the extremity of the chosen seed. This hard pressure of affliction was not unneeded. In the abundance and prosperity of Goshen they had well-nigh forgotten the absolute and exclusive claim of God on their homage and obedience. Nothing but the strong hand of oppression could bring them to a sense of their dependence and their duty. But they were a chosen race. Much is implied in this. The Most High does not allow them, as he might otherwise have done, to merge into the superstition and apostasy of the surrounding nations. He has, moreover, a purpose to serve by them, an end ulterior to their own spiritual benefit. He intends through them to perpetuate the knowledge of God, to bring in the Redeemer into the world, to effect a redemption that will be sufficient for all the nations of mankind, and finally to bring all the world into reconciliation with himself and with themselves. He will not be thwarted in this sublime and benign purpose. He has therefore laid the heavy hand of chastisement on this people to bring them to repentance. He will not, however, leave them to perish by the murderous devices of Pharoh. He will gradually prepare them to shake off the fetters of Egypt, and take their departure for the land of promise. And his providence is at work in another direction. Immediately after the issue of the bloody edict for the extermination of the people the deliverer is born who is to head the movement of national emancipation, and is preserved from destruction by the indirect influence of the hostile monarch himself.

In this chapter, accordingly, we have the parentage, birth, preservation, education, and exile of Moses, the coming deliverer of God's people. The historian reverts to a point of time anterior perhaps to any of the despotic measures of the sovereign, and enters upon another line of events.

1–4. The parentage and birth of Moses. *A man of the house of Levi*, Amram (Ex. vi. 20). *A daughter of Levi*, Jokebed. Hence it appears that Moses was a Hebrew of the Hebrews. Levi was forty-four years old when he came down to Egypt. We may suppose that Jokebed was born to him when he was one hundred years of age, and therefore sixty-six years after the immigration. Amram may have been born about the same time with his aunt, or even somewhat earlier. For his father Kohath (Ex. vi. 18) may have been twenty years old when he came to Egypt, and consequently eighty-six when Jokebed was born. About fifty years after, we may suppose, the nephew and aunt were married. There was not yet any law prohibiting the marriage of such relatives. A year after their marriage, the daughter mentioned in the narrative may have been born, and fourteen years after the same date Moses, who was eighty years old at the exodus. These numbers (66 + 50 + 14 + 80) make up two hundred and ten, the number of years during which the Israelites sojourned in Egypt.

2. *Goodly*, perfect, as if it had come directly from the hands of God without contracting any outward stain from its parents. Such is the force of Stephen's explanatory phrase, ἀστεῖος τῷ Θεῷ, beautiful before God. *And hid him three months.* Maternal affection, the beauty of the child, and hope in God, combined to produce this attempt at his preservation. 3. *An ark of rushes.* This reminds us of the ark of the flood (Gen. vi. 14). The rush was the papyrus, growing to the height of ten feet, and formerly abounding on the banks of the Nile. The root was used for fuel, the stem for making boats, and the bark or rind for making sails, shoes, garments, and paper. The papyrus rolls are found in the mummy-cases to this day, and may be unrolled and read. *Asphalt and pitch* — the former to fill up the interstices and make all smooth, the latter to make the little vessel water-tight. *Put therein the child.* This is a mother's last effort to save the doomed babe. It may appear feeble and hopeless; but it was done in faith, and it proved successful. 4. *His sister* is set to watch the result.

5–10. The rescue of Moses from a watery grave. The king's daughter, with her attendants, comes forth to bathe in the Nile, the waters of which were considered sacred and salutary. In a primitive state of society the females of the East enjoyed a greater degree of liberty than in after times, when they began to be guarded with jealous care in the seclusion of the harem, and concealed on a journey from the common gaze by the long and thick veil of the East. With all a female's fond affection she has pity on the weeping babe. Scripture is very choice in picking out the circumstances that give effect to the scene. *This is one of the Hebrews' children.* She is aware of the royal edict, and comprehends the whole affair at a glance. This tiny vessel is the last effort of a mother's affection to cast on Providence the care of her babe. 7. *His sister*, certainly, whether prompted or not, is equal to her task. She appears at the proper time, and puts the fitting question. 8. Pharoh's daughter is too glad to be relieved of her perplexity by saying, *Go. The maid*, the well-grown and marriageable virgin, as the term implies. This makes it probable that she was now about thirteen years of age at least, as we have supposed. 10. *And she called his name Moses.* His parents, most probably, had given him a name during the time he was with them, before he became the adopted son of Pharoh's daughter. But in ancient times the same individual often received different names from successive memorable incidents in his life (Gen. iii. 20, x. 25, xvii. 5, xxv. 30.) The adopter had a right to give a name to the adopted, and this name has prevailed over that which may have been given by his parents. Josephus calls Pharoh's daughter Thermuthis; Eusebius calls her Merrhis; but these determinations are founded on chronological combinations which have not yet been established.

It is quite evident that Pharoh's court was contiguous to the region occupied by the Israelites. This favors the notion of a small kingdom in the eastern part of the Delta, to the extent of which a tribe of thirty or fifty thousand would bear some notable relation. It is plain, too, that the royal residence was for the time being not far from the Nile. This will agree very well with Bubastis being at least the occasional abode of the royal family.

It is probable that the exterminating edict was withdrawn at or soon after the rescue of Moses. The caprice and passion of a despot might hastily issue such a decree. But after-thoughts would soon suggest the folly of cutting off this useful horde of serfs in a single generation. The debasement of the feelings by forced labor — which would render them more serviceable as slaves, and less formidable as rebels — is a much more satisfactory measure to an arbitrary government. Moreover, the natural feelings of humanity revolt against the indiscriminate and continued murder of male infants. The measure would be unpopular with his subjects, and with the members of his own family as soon as Moses appeared there, and would therefore soon be abandoned. Accordingly we hear no more of it.

11–15. The flight of Moses. *In those days.* This phrase here covers a space of forty years or more. *Moses grew up*, arrived at maturity. *He came out unto his brethren.* It is evident that the tie between Moses and his parents had never been broken. The charms of a court life for nearly forty years had not closed his ears against the cries of his afflicted people. His heart felt that the sufferers were his brethren. *He saw a Mizrite smiting a Hebrew* — one of the taskmasters correcting a serf under his charge, or, more probably, a private individual, in the mere arrogance of his political superiority, maltreating one of the inferior race whom he has chanced to meet. Moses, whose spirit had not been broken by the bondage common to the rest of his race, instantly taking the side of the oppressed, slays the Egyptian, and buries him in the sand. He may not have intended to deal a fatal blow, or he may not have been able to avoid it in self-defence; but no such explanation is offered in the text. We may not wish to stand over this deed in all its length and breadth; but we must not denounce it, as we might if it were done in our day. In a time and place where the wild will and the high hand have the rule, he that lifts the hand not for selfish ends, but for the defence of the weak, is not to be hastily condemned. He has much of the spirit of the magistrate, where the law and its administrator are wanting. 13. The next day he sees *two Hebrews striving.* He expostulates with the wrong-doer, who rudely repels his interference with the alarming question, "Intendest thou to slay me, as thou slewest the Mizrite?" These were the noticeable acts which decided Moses's future course. They tell much of what was working within his breast. For the last thirty years we may imagine him now and then stealing out of the royal precincts to look on the burdens of his people. Oft with a sore heart may the young patriot have returned to the palace, contrasted the freedom, luxury, and mental culture around him with the degradation of that race which he knew was chosen of God to hold the foremost rank and achieve the noblest ends for humanity.

The hope of their deliverance was cherished. The wish to take part in it was gathering strength with his years. He was at length precipitated into action by the scenes before him. But the rude question, "Who made thee a ruler and a judge over us?" prompted, perhaps, by his courtly guise and long isolation from his people, quenched his ardent aspirations. Having broken with Egypt, and been rejected by his kindred, he had no course for the present but exile. (See Acts vii. 21–29; Heb. xi. 24–26).

Moses was now forty years of age (Acts vii. 22, 23). This period of physical and intellectual growth he had spent at the court of Pharoh, and therefore had received the highest education the country could afford. The annual overflow of the Nile imparting a constant fertility to the soil rendered Egypt pre-eminently an agricultural country. The necessity of marking the time of its rise led to the study of astronomy and chronology. To determine the height to which it rose in successive years, and the boundaries of landed property which were liable to be obliterated by its waters, they were constrained to turn their attention to geometry. To the successful prosecution of mathematical science, and for the recording of the observations needful for its practical application, the art of writing was essential; and the papyrus reed afforded the ready material for such records. In these circumstances, the heavenly bodies, the Nile, and the animals of their country, became absorbing objects of attention, and eventually of worship. Music was also diligently cultivated in Egypt. Moses must have been familiar with the language, literature, and science of Egypt, as well as with the corruptions of its theology. This was the one side of his character. On the other side he was closely allied by intercourse and feeling with his kindred, and therefore intimately acquainted with the monuments of sacred history which were handed down to them, the elements of a pure theology, natural and revealed, which had been preserved by them, their present sufferings, and their future destiny. We cannot conceive a providential training more admirably adapted for the part he was to perform as the deliverer, legislator, and historian of the people of God.

15. Midian was the son of Abraham, and half-brother of Isaac. The Midianites were, therefore, the kinsfolk of Moses. A great part of Arabia, indeed, was occupied with descendants of Heber, the an-

cestor of Abraham and the Israelites. Thither it was natural for Moses to flee. The land of Midian lay partly southwest of Moab and partly on the coast of the Aelanitic Gulf, to the southwestern extremity of which the tribe seems to have penetrated. *And he sat by the well,* the well-known place of refreshment and rest for the traveller, and of common resort for the natives of the country.

16–22. The settlement and marriage of Moses in Midian. *The priest of Midian.* The ancient order of elders held a place in the polity of Midian (Num. xxii. 4). The supreme government seems to have been a commonwealth or confederacy, as there were five kings of Midian in the time of the entrance of Israel into the promised land (Num. xxxi. 8), and two princes and two kings are mentioned in the days of Gideon (Judg. viii 3, 5). As in primitive times the sacred and civil functions were generally united in one person, the priest of Midian was probably at least an elder in the state; but there is no reason to suppose that he was not a priest in the strict sense of the term, as the civil functionaries of Midian, we find, were designated by several other terms. We have already met with the early custom of daughters tending flocks (Gen. xxix. 6). They often needed defenders, as the weak are often wronged by the strong. *A Mizrite.* Moses is so regarded, as he probably wore the garb and spoke the language of Egypt, and may have stated that he was a fugitive from that country. *Why is it that ye have left the man?* A feeling of innate modesty, or a proper sense of their dependence as children, may have prevented the invitation proceeding immediately from themselves. *He gave Zipporah, his daughter, to Moses.* She was a descendant of Abraham, and so of the kindred of Moses. The connection was therefore suitable.

23–25. The sacred writer now resumes the general thread of the narrative, and describes with a few touches the crying oppression under which the people of Israel had now long labored. *Many days after.* The whole of the events following occurred during an interval of forty years, the period of Moses's sojourn in Midian. *The king of Mizraim died.* This may have taken place shortly after Moses left the country; but it did not abate the sufferings of the people. His successor pursued the same cruel policy. Their hard service commenced some time before the birth of Moses, and had now therefore lasted more than eighty years. *Sighed and cried.* The haughty spirit which denounced the defender and adviser as a self-constituted ruler and judge was now subdued. The wail of deep affliction ascended from broken hearts to heaven, to *the* living *God. God heard their groaning.* He hears all groanings. But he also remembered his covenant with their fathers (Gen. xvii. 2, 21, xlvi. 2–4). He not only heard, but saw the sons of Israel under the oppressor. He not only observed, as it were, with the outward senses, but knew with the inward mind, and acknowledged them to be the seed of the covenant. Such is the manner in which the narrator lays emphasis on the earnest attention with which the Lord regards the affliction of his people.

## III. MOSES CALLED AND COMMISSIONED.—Ex. iii., iv.

### CHAP. III.—MOSES CALLED.

1. יִתְרוֹ Jithro, *profit, pre-eminence ;* r. *be over and above.* חֹרֵב Choreb, *dry place ;* r. *drain.*

14. אֶהְיֶה אֲשֶׁר אֶהְיֶה Ehjeh, *for I am.* We approach with reverence to the discussion of this remarkable sentence. It has been rendered in two different ways: (1.) I am, because I am; and (2.) *I am that which I am.* The latter, we presume, is the meaning of the English version, I am that I am. There are three decisive objections to this rendering: 1st. It takes the whole sentence to be the name, like Shear-jashub (a remnant shall return), Maher-shalal-hash-baz (haste to the spoil, speed to the prey), the names of Isaiah's children. But the first word, Ehjeh, is the whole name, as is evident from the remainder of the verse: "Thus shalt thou say unto the sons of Israel, Ehjeh hath sent me unto you." 2d. It lays the emphasis on that which is not expressed in the name. It therefore conveys no information: for it states in words that God is that which he is; but does not tell what *that* is. It is not distinctive of God; for the saying, I am that I am, may be applied to any being whatever; and is, moreover, a mere triviality. It is, if anything, a mere intimation of the inscrutable mystery of the divine nature; yet it does not even affirm

that he is the Inconceivable, and therefore Ineffable. And even if it did, this bare thought is not fitted to implant confidence or induce persuasion in the minds of the Israelites. And 3d, the sentence thus rendered does not express the idea conveyed in the word Ehjeh, which is substituted for it in the latter part of the verse. The former is at best purely negative; the latter is purely positive. Hence the two forms of the name would be inconsistent in meaning.

The latter rendering being on these grounds untenable, the former must be regarded as correct. It agrees with the Vulg. *Ego sum, qui sum,* and the Sept. Ἐγώ ειμι ὁ ὤν, in making part of the sentence the name, though it differs from them in taking the first word, not the latter two, as the name. It affords a good sense. It finds in the answer of God the new name, and the reason of it, whether we translate אֲשֶׁר who, as, for, because, or since. I AM (is my name), for I am. It gives the same name in the two parts of the verse, and the same sense in each. It also agrees with the structure of the Hebrew and with the Masoretic pointing, in which there is a pause after the first word, thus: אֶהְיֶה. It only remains to ascertain what is the meaning of Ehjeh.

1st. The verb הָיָה refers not to the abstract existence of the schoolmen, but to the concrete being of the unsophisticated Hebrew mind, that is, being as active and obvious to the senses, (see on Gen. i. 2). This, when applied to the Eternal, means, therefore, not absolute beginning or essential change of being, but that eventual modification of being which is implied in engaging in a new course of action manifesting the agent to have being. To be, in a word, is to act in such a way as to manifest one's being to a competent observer. 2d. אֶהְיֶה is that form of the verb which denotes the incipient stage of an action or event. It means, therefore, *I go to be*, I am on the point of proving myself to be by a noticeable action. In regard to the chosen seed I have heretofore mainly promised; I am now about to appear in performance of my promise. 3d. The verb is in the first person, because the speaker is naming himself with all the emphasis of personal identification. It is obvious that this was a strikingly significant and appropriate name for Moses to bear to the people, as it announced a present God, come down to fulfil his covenant and perform his promise to the afflicted descendants of Abraham, Isaac, and Jacob.

III. 1. And Moses was keeping the flock of Jethro his
father-in-law, the priest of Midian: and he led the flock behind
the wilderness, and came to the mountain of God, to Horeb.
2. And the angel of the Lord appeared unto him in a flame of
fire out of the midst of the bush: and he looked, and, lo, the
bush burned with fire, and the bush was not consumed.
3. And Moses said, Let me now turn aside and see this great
sight, why the bush does not burn. 4. And the Lord saw
that he turned aside to see; and God called unto him out of
the midst of the bush, and said Moses, Moses. And he said,
Here am I. 5. And he said, Draw not nigh hither: put off
thy shoes from thy feet, for the place whereon thou standest
is holy ground.

6. And he said, I am the God of thy father, the God of
Abraham, the God of Isaac, and the God of Jacob. And
Moses hid his face, for he was afraid to look upon God.
7. And the Lord said, I have surely seen the affliction of my
people who are in Mizraim, and have heard their cry by
reason of their exactors; for I know their sorrows. 8. And
I came down to deliver them out of the hand of Mizraim, and
to bring them up out of that land unto a good and large land,
unto a land flowing with milk and honey; unto the place of
the Kenaanite, and the Hittite, and the Amorite, and the
Perizzite, and the Hivite, and the Jebusite. 9. And now,
behold, the cry of the sons of Israel is come unto me: and I
have also seen the oppression wherewith Mizraim oppresseth
them. 10. And now come, and I will send thee unto Pharoh:
and bring forth my people the sons of Israel out of Mizraim.

11. And Moses said unto God, Who am I, that I should go
unto Pharoh; and that I should bring forth the sons of Israel
out of Mizraim? 12. And He said, For I will be with thee,
and this shall be unto thee the token that I have sent thee:

when thou hast brought forth the people out of Mizraim ye
shall serve God upon this mountain.

13. And Moses said unto God, Lo, I shall go to the sons of
Israel and say unto them, The God of your fathers hath sent
me unto you; and they shall say to me, What is his name?
what shall I say unto them? 14. And God said unto Moses,
I AM, for I am. And he said, Thus shalt thou say unto the
sons of Israel, I AM hath sent me unto you.

15. And God said again unto Moses, Thus shalt thou say
unto the sons of Israel, The Lord, the God of your fathers,
the God of Abraham, the God of Isaac, and the God of Jacob,
hath sent me unto you: this is my name forever, and this is
my memorial unto all generations. 16. Go and gather the
elders of Israel and say unto them, The Lord, the God of
your fathers hath appeared to me, the God of Abraham, Isaac,
and Jacob, saying, I have surely visited you and seen that
which is done to you in Mizraim. 17. And I said, I will
bring you up out of the affliction of Mizraim unto the land of
the Kenaanite, and the Hittite, and the Amorite, and the
Perizzite, and Hivite, and the Jebusite; unto a land flowing
with milk and honey. 18. And they shall hearken to thy
voice; and thou shalt go, thou and the elders of Israel, unto
the king of Mizraim, and ye shall say unto him, The Lord, the
God of the Hebrews, hath met with us; and now let us go,
we pray, three days' journey into the wilderness, and sacrifice
to the Lord our God. 19. And I know that the king of
Mizraim will not let you go, but by a mighty hand. 20. And
I will stretch out my, hand and smite Mizraim with all my
wonders, which I will do in the midst thereof: and after that
he will let you go. 21. And I will give this people favor in
the eyes of Mizraim: and it shall come to pass that when ye
go, ye shall not go empty. 22. And every woman shall ask

of her neighbor, and of her that sojourneth in her house, jewels of silver, and jewels of gold, and garments, and ye shall put them on your sons and on your daughters, and ye shall spoil Mizraim.

Slowly and constantly for the last eighty years the oppression of Israel has been growing to a head, and now the Lord himself appears on the scene. He has not, indeed, been all that time an idle observer of their miseries. In the silence and secrecy of his providence the deliverer has been growing up, and is ripe for his task at the very hour of need. The Lord now comes to call him to his work.

The chronology of the interesting events about to be recorded is not minutely laid down. To give definiteness, however, to our conceptions of the course of things, it is desirable to fix approximately the shortest period in which they might have occurred. The earliest day for the full moon on the 15th of Nisan, the first day of unleavened bread, was the 22d of March. It is possible for the events between the vision at Horeb and the first passover to have taken place with some degree of probability in, at the least, eighty days. This number we obtain by allowing for the journey from Horeb to Midian and thence to Egypt thirteen days; for the first interviews with the people and with Pharoh seven days; for eight plagues, at seven days each, fifty-six days; and for the plague of darkness four days, The following table will make the arrangement plain

| | | | |
|---|---|---|---|
| Horeb to Egypt, till | Jan. 13 | Murrain, till | Feb. 24 |
| First Interview, | Jan. 20 | Boils, | Mar. 3 |
| Plague of Blood, | Jan. 27 | Hail, | Mar. 10 |
| Frogs, | Feb. 3 | Locusts, | Mar. 17 |
| Lice, | Feb. 10 | Darkness, | Mar. 21 |
| The Fly, | Feb. 17 | | |

The particulars of this presumptive arrangement will be noticed as we proceed. Some have protracted the interval to nearly ten months, in order to bring the first plague to the end of June, when the Nile begins to rise and assume a red and turbid appearance. But the first plague is of a nature entirely different from the periodical change of color at the swelling of the Nile; and moreover it is highly improbable that the ten plagues were spread over a period of nine months.

1–5. The Lord appears to Moses. *Jethro*, the pre-eminent. We have again and again to notice instances of the same individual having several names. He who was the eminent in one sense was in another the friend of God (ii. 18). The names are quite consistent. *Behind the wilderness*. Jethro's dwelling was doubtless east of Horeb, probably on the shore of the Gulf of Akabah ; but we cannot define it more closely. A wilderness lay between it and the springs and green valleys intersecting the range of Horeb, which was therefore behind the wilderness, because it was both on the other side from Jethro's home, and to the west of the intervening region. *The mountain of God*. This range of hills earned this name, if not from some previous manifestation of God, yet from the signal displays of his presence and power which are about to be narrated. 2, 3. *The angel of the Lord*. See on Gen. xvi. 7. *In a flame of fire*. The primary effect of the flame of fire is to consume; the secondary, to purify. When transferred to spiritual things, that which is fuel to the fire is moral evil (xxix. 14), and that which remains after its work is done is the pure, the holy (Num. xxxi. 23). Fire, however, does not make pure, but merely leaves the pure untouched. The Lord has often appeared in fire (xix. 18, xxiv. 17; Lev. ix. 24) *The bush*. This was a species of thorn. The hawthorn, according to Shaw and Pococke, abounds in the region of Horeb. *Was not consumed*. The fire was supernatural, and did not affect the vegetative life of the bush. This it was that arrested the attention of Moses. It was truly a "great sight," an unusual and notable phenomenon standing out from the ordinary course of nature. The mode of the divine appearance is not without design. It has a significance fitting the occasion. The bush that lives unscathed by the lambent flame that winds round all its leaves and branches, is an emblem of that which is pure and holy, and therefore of the true church of God in the furnace of affliction. The lowliness of the shrub comports well with the seeming feebleness and insignificance of the people of God, The flame of fire corresponds with the fiery trial through which they have had to pass, that the lusts of the flesh, which had grown up in Egypt, might be consumed, and faith and its kindred virtues be left behind in all their vigor and beauty.

4, 5. *The Lord saw ..... God called*. It would be the affectation of criticism to investigate in every case the ground for the distinctive use of these names Yet there is no doubt that the writer used them with a clear consciousness of their meaning. In mentioning that the "LORD saw" Moses turning aside to see, he regarded him, we must suppose, as the Great Being who has manifested himself and is present in the work of creation; and in adding that "God called" unto him, he had before his mind the supernatural, invisible sphere out of which the Eternal Omnipotent uttered his voice, *Moses, Moses,* as in Gen. xxii. 11. This is the personal call with which the commission of Moses begins. *Draw not nigh.* Do not intrude with daring heedlessness into the sacred presence of the divine majesty. *Put off thy shoes.* The custom of putting off the shoes before entering an apartment, lest they should defile the floor, passed in the East into a mark of respect, and then of reverence. Hence it becomes a habitual outward sign of an inward feeling of regard for the place and presence of a superior, or of the Supreme.

6–10. This passage closes with the commission to Moses. After the premonitory sentence comes the introduction. *I am the God of thy father.* "Thy father" is here used in a generic sense, to denote any ancestor from his immediate father up. The nations of the earth had now almost universally forsaken the God of their first father, the knowledge of whom had been clearly handed down to them by Noah, and betaken themselves to other gods, whom their fathers knew not, and who were no gods. Moses is here reminded of his holy ancestry, and apprised that he who now addresses him is the Great Being who made heaven and earth, and created man after his own image. But more particularly he is also the God of Abraham, Isaac, and Jacob, who entered into a special covenant of salvation with the fathers of Israel, by means of which the primeval covenant with man may be upheld, and all the Gentiles reconciled to God. *Hid his face.* The unexpected utterance of his name, the caution against too near an approach, the announcement of the divine presence, awakened a solemn awe in the mind of Moses, which discovered itself in hiding his face, lest he should be guilty of any profane gazing upon the apparition of the Holy One (Gen. xvi. 13).

7–10. After the introduction we have the commission. The preamble recounts the cause which moved the Lord to the present interposition. *I have surely seen.* I have been deeply concerned to observe the affliction of my people. *For I know their sorrow.* The *for* here is explanatory. I have not been inattentive to them, I have been cognizant of all that was taking place, and therefore I have seen and heard everything. *I came down* (Gen. xi. 5). God is personally interested and active in his people's cause. *A good and large land,* not inferior to Goshen in point of fertility, and affording scope for a growing population. *A land flowing with milk and honey,* a proverbial description of a choice land abounding in the grasses and flowering plants from which milk and honey come. *The place of the Kenaanite.* The Kenaanite and his derivative tribes originally amounted to twelve (Gen. x. 15–18). In the time of Abraham ten tribes occupied the land of promise, of which only five are known to be descendants of Kenaan (Gen. xv. 19–21). Of the six here enumerated, history traces five to Kenaan. Of the former list the Girgashite has now retired into obscurity, and the Hivite has recovered a prominent position. Of those not traceable to Kenaan only the Perizzite is mentioned. The others were probably beyond the boundary at present contemplated.

9, 10. *And now, behold, the cry of the sons of Israel.* It is noticeable that their oppression had lasted for eighty years. But now at length their cry indicated that affliction had done its work. In the anguish of their hearts they turned from man to God. They longed to be free from the bondage of Egypt, and they now saw no hope of escape but in God. Their cry goes up to heaven, and God appears on earth for their deliverance. *I will send thee unto Pharoh.* The purpose of the vision now unfolds itself to the mind of Moses.

11, 12. Moses puts in many pleas to be excused from this grave task. The Lord patiently and encouragingly hears all these scruples of his creature's mind, gives a satisfactory explanation, and applies a complete remedy to every difficulty, until there is nothing in the mind of Moses but an unreasonable shrinking from an arduous and honorable task. Even then he provides a full relief for the trembling heart in the eloquence and company of his brother Aaron. Thus gradually and tenderly he prepares the mind of his servant for acquiescing in, and then heartily devoting himself to, the high office to which he is called.

The first plea is his personal unworthiness. *Who am I?* He remembered the grandeur of the court and the haughtiness of the monarch. He was aware that the present sovereign was a stranger to him. He called to mind the rude reception he had met from one of his own kinsmen, when he formerly interfered in their behalf. All the difficulties of the enterprise crowded on his mind, and he felt himself inadequate to its achievement. *For I will be with thee.* The Lord is not moved from his purpose by the objection of Moses. He obviates it by an undeniable argument. I will be with thee. The power of God with us certainly surmounts all difficulties. This promise will hereafter be embodied in a name, IMMANUEL — God with us. Here it is framed in a sentence importing the active presence of the Almighty with his chosen servant. This has been the source of the church's life, strength, and hope in all ages. *This shall be the token.* To find himself and the rest of Israel serving God on this mountain will hereafter be to him a proof of his divine commission, and the assurance of this fact, which will undoubtedly follow the promise now given, is calculated to encourage him to undertake the task with cheerfulness and hope.

13, 14. Moses now starts a difficulty he might have with the people. They might ask him what is the name of him from whom he came. It is important to determine the real bearing of this question. (1.) We have repeatedly met with the custom in early times of giving several names to the same individual, as Jacob and Israel, Esau and Edom, Reuel and Jethro. This was not even peculiar to the East. Paris and Alexander, Lucumo and Tarquinius, Henry and Beauclerc, are familiar to us in other lands. The reason of this custom was that names were then significant, and served to mark out the individual by some peculiarity in his person, some trait in his character, or some event connected with his history. If several of these circumstances might occur in the case of a finite man, how much more may we expect them to come out in the contemplation of the infinite God. Accordingly, among a primitive people, his names grow in number as the manifold aspects of his all-perfect character break upon their view. He is called Elohim, the Everlasting, when his antecedent eternity and absolute independence are contemplated. He is termed Jehovah, the Self-existent, the Author of all existing things, when he is regarded as the free and personal God, manifesting his being to the intelligent universe by the works of his creative power. He is named El 'Elion, the Most High God, when his unattainable pre-eminence above all created things comes into view. He is designated El Shaddai, the Almighty God, when he wishes to set before the mind his unconquerable omnipotence. (2.) In the next place, Moses did not require to ask the name of God, if we mean by that the term by which he was commonly known. He was already familiar with his name. If the Book of Genesis was not yet before him in a written form, the traditions of his fathers were graven on his memory. Moreover, God had already announced himself to him as the God of his fathers. And, further, God does not present in his reply any one of all the names by which he had been previously known. Hence it is plain that the object of Moses in putting this question could not have been to ascertain any of the former names of God. (3.) The name, in the conception of Moses, was the title by which the present aspect of God to his people was to be designated. And the meaning of his question is, what is the principle of thy being or movement of thy will which is now to display itself to thy people?

The Lord is prompt in meeting this new difficulty of Moses. The immediate answer to his question is a new name, in some respect different in meaning from all his former designations. Ehjeh (Ehyeh), I AM, in the sense, I now proceed to make myself known *to be*, by giving being to my promise to Abraham of more than four hundred years' standing. Although the phrase I AM does not immediately convey all this to English ears, yet it is so brief and appropriate in its general sense, and so hallowed in our associations, that we would not venture to alter it. And even in this simple form, when coupled with a promise of deliverance such as Moses was commissioned to announce, it suggests the thought that his people will soon find that he *is* by the acts he performs. Still further, it is probable that the present tense of our English verb originally meant, and it is certain that it still retains among its meanings, the initial stage of an action or event, as in the phrase, I go to town. It is, therefore, the only form fit to express the Hebrew incipient. The use of the first person is a plain indication that the name is intended not merely to distinguish an individual, but to express a sentiment that will animate the people with hope and resolution. Such a form is strictly appropriate only in the mouth of the speaker; and, accordingly, it is not afterwards employed as a name of God. All this is in keeping, not with a mere name, but with a word of moral power fitted to stir the heart, and meet the present occasion.

Moses was now, therefore, armed with a name of potent significance by which to designate him by whose authority he was to approach the people. He could say, he in whose name I come is about to realize the promise of the land of Kenaan made to the seed of Abraham; and he has deigned to embody this fact in a significant name, indicating his present adherence to his covenant with your fathers.

15–22. Special directions are now given to Moses regarding his commission. First, the authority under which he acts is formally stated. The Lord, that is, Jehovah. We have already discussed the import of this name (Gen. ii. 4). It stands in relation to Ehjeh, as a habit of the active powers is to a particular volition. Jehovah is the author of reality in general; Ehjeh is he who is on the point of giving reality to a certain thing or event. The two names then refer to the same attribute of the divine nature, but in different points of view; the one presenting it as a potence in habitual exercise; the other as a potence passing into a new course of action. Hence we can understand how the Lord, after announcing himself to Moses by a new form of appellation, fitted to the special occasion, immediately reverts to the well-known and long-established name which involves the same property of his nature. In accordance with this identity of the quality signified by the two names, it is fitly added, "This is my name forever, and this my memorial unto all generations." The name refers to the objective and sensible sign; the memorial to the subjective and mental concept of the Divine Being. He that gives effect to his uttered resolve is the author of eternal life to his church.

16, 17. Next, the course he is to pursue with regard to the people of God is pointed out. *Gather the elders of Israel.* Officers of this class were common to all mankind in primeval times. We have already met with them in Egypt (Gen. l. 7). We here find them established in Israel antecedent to the legislation of Moses. Their name is derived from the quality of age, which confers experience and claims authority. They were perpetuated through all the variations of the commonwealth of Israel, and descended from them to the Christian church, in which they still maintain their place. *I have surely visited you,* personally come to see you, and all that is done to you, in order to take the proper steps for your deliverance.

18. The manner in which he is to approach the king of Egypt is next laid down. *They shall hearken to thy voice.* They have been chastened by the oppression of Egypt, and will now listen gladly to a duly accredited deliverer. Thus far Moses will find his reception encouraging. *Thou and the elders of Israel.* A venerable deputation of the heads of the people are to accompany Moses to Pharoh. *Jehovah, the God of the Hebrews.* To Israel this epithet of Jehovah would be encouraging; to Pharoh it is merely explanatory. We learn from it that the Shemites of the line of Heber continued to acknowledge the true God after the other nations had forsaken him. In other words, the revelation of God made to the common fathers of the human race remained in its purity among the Hebrews after it had been essentially corrupted among the other nations of the earth. It is plainly implied that the gods of Egypt were now essentially different from the God of the Hebrews; as will presently appear in the most conspicuous manner. *Hath met with us,* with Moses in the bush at Horeb, and with us in the signs he has wrought through him before us (vs. 30). *Let us go three day's journey in the wilderness.* This request seems at first to be put in a politic form, as if to secure a favorable answer. This, however, was quite unnecessary, since the Almighty was about to bring his people out of Egypt by a strong hand. It is merely expressed in a style of reserve and moderation. It was not requisite to reveal to Pharoh, who was in a hostile mood, all the intentions of God concerning his people. Hence Pharoh is merely informed that the God of the Hebrews has met with them; and their request is limited to the first step to be taken in obedience to his will. A three days' journey is mentioned, simply because this would take them clear out of Egypt, one day being employed in setting out, one in marching, and the third in coming to a resting-place. And a sacrifice is added, because this is the first act of obedience. The former involves their departure out of Egypt; the latter commences the perfect service of God. This is exactly the mode in which God trains his people. The immediate duty and the immediate blessing are set

before them, and these are pregnant with all further and higher duties and blessing. So he deals with Pharoh. But there is not only reserve, but moderation in the request. It makes the smallest demand consistent with actually leaving, and assigns the highest reason for taking this step, namely, the command of God. By sedulously avoiding everything harsh and extravagant in its terms, it affords the least possible occasion for Pharoh to harden his heart, and dismiss the petitioners with an obstinate refusal. At the same time it is a bold and open assertion of liberty. If the people had formed a secret plot to escape from the land of their bondage, we should have been slow to condemn, if not prompt to applaud. But this is not the Lord's way. If Pharoh had condescended to ask at once, "Who shall go? Will your wives and children go? Will your cattle and your other moveables be taken with you?" he would have received, as he eventually did, a ready and candid reply. But such questions were in reality superfluous. Pharoh was well aware that bondsmen who had marched three days out of the land of the oppressor, with their families and goods, would not return without compulsion.

19, 20. Moses is further forewarned of the unwillingness of Pharoh to grant the request of the people, and of the means by which this unwillingness is to be overcome. *And I know.* Fore-knowledge is as certain to God as after-knowledge. *But by a mighty hand,* the hand of God doing his wonders in the land of Ham. The servant of the Lord is therefore not to be discouraged by the unavailing opposition of Pharoh.

21, 22. The Israelites are not to go out empty-handed. The sojourn of Joseph in Egypt as a bond-slave had been the means of preserving the inhabitants of that country from extermination by a seven years' famine. The residence of his kindred in Goshen had always been a benefit, and not a burden, to Egypt. And for the last two or three generations the Israelites had been bond-slaves, toiling for the prosperity and aggrandisement of the nation. They had, therefore, an undoubted right to ask, and the Egyptians were eventually glad to give them, some aid for their journey. *Shall ask,* as a gift, if not a compensation for long unrequited services. The word cannot mean to borrow here, when the Egyptians were perfectly aware that the Israelites would not return. *Of her that sojourneth in her house*, either a visitor or a mistress whom she served, in any case her superior, and perhaps owner. *Spoil Mizraim.* The Egyptians would be so overcome by abject distress as to be ready to part with a considerable portion of their wealth, in order to get rid of a people whose presence menaced them with utter extermination.

### CHAP. IV. MOSES OBEYS THE CALL.

14. אַהֲרֹן Aharon, perhaps *bright* or *tall;* r. perhaps akin to אור *light*, or הַר *hill.*

18. יֶתֶר = יִתְרוֹ The latter is the reading of one MS. of the Sam., Syr., Vulg., and Arabic. The former, of the other MSS. and of the Sept.; of the latter in both parts of the verse. It seems an instance of diversity of language.

IV. 1. And Moses answered and said, But behold they will
not believe me, nor hearken unto my voice: for they will say,
The Lord hath not appeared unto thee. 2. And the Lord said
unto him, What is this in thy hand? And he said, A rod.
3. And he said, Cast it on the ground. And he cast it on the
ground, and it became a serpent; and Moses fled from before
it. 4. And the Lord said unto Moses, Put forth thy hand,
and catch it by the tail. And he put forth his hand and seized
it, and it became a rod in his hand. 5. That they may believe
that the Lord, the God of their fathers, the God of Abraham,
the God of Isaac, and the God of Jacob, hath appeared unto
thee. 6. And the Lord said unto him again, Put now thy
hand into thy bosom. And he put his hand into his bosom;
and he took it out, and lo his hand was leprous as snow.
7. And he said, Put thy hand again into thy bosom. And he
put his hand again into his bosom; and he took it out of his
bosom, and behold it was restored as his other flesh. 8. And
it shall be, if they will not believe thee, nor hearken to the

voice of the first sign, that they will believe the voice of the
latter sign. 9. And it shall be, if they will not believe even
these two signs, nor hearken unto thy voice, that thou shalt
take of the water of the river, and pour on the dry land: and
the water which thou takest out of the river shall become
blood upon the dry land.

10. And Moses said unto the Lord, O Lord, I am not
eloquent, neither heretofore, nor since thou hast spoken unto
thy servant; for I am slow of mouth and slow of tongue.
11. And the Lord said unto him, Who hath made man's
mouth, or who maketh dumb or deaf, or seeing or blind?
Do not I the Lord? 12. And now go, and I will be with
thy mouth, and teach thee what thou shalt speak. 13. And
he said, O Lord, send now by whomsoever thou wilt send.
14. And the anger of the Lord was kindled against Moses;
and he said, Is there not Aaron, thy brother, the Levite? I
know that he can speak well: and also behold he cometh forth
to meet thee, and he shall see thee, and be glad in his heart.
15. And thou shalt speak to him, and put words in his
mouth; and I will be with thy mouth and with his mouth,
and will teach you what ye shall do. 16. And he shall speak
for thee to the people, and it shall be that he shall be to thee
for a mouth, and thou shalt be to him for God. 17. And this
rod shalt thou take in thy hand, wherewith thou shalt do the
signs.

¶ 4.

18. And Moses went and returned to Jether his father-in-law, and said to him, Let me go now and return to my brethren who are in Mizraim, and see whether they be yet alive. And Jethro said unto Moses, Go in peace.

19. And the Lord said unto Moses in Midian, Go, return to
Mizraim, for all the men who sought thy life are dead.
20. And Moses took his wife and his sons, and set them upon

the ass, and returned to the land of Mizraim: and Moses took the rod of God in his hand.

21. And the Lord said unto Moses, When thou goest to return into Mizraim, behold all the wonders that I have put in thy hand, and do them before Pharoh; and I will harden his heart, and he shall not let the people go. 22. Then thou shalt say unto Pharoh, Thus saith the Lord, Israel is my son, my first-born. 23. And I said unto thee, Let my son go, and serve me, and thou didst refuse to let him go: behold, I will slay thy son, thy first-born.

24. And it came to pass by the way in the inn, that the Lord met him, and sought to kill him. 25. And Zipporah took a sharp stone, and cut off the foreskin of her son, and cast it at his feet: and she said, For a spouse of blood art thou to me. 26. And he left him: then she said, A spouse of blood, because of the circumcision. ¶ 5.

27. And the Lord said to Aaron, Go to meet Moses in the wilderness. And he went and met him in the mount of God, and kissed him. 28. And Moses told Aaron all the words of the Lord who had sent him, and all the signs which he had commanded him. 29. And Moses and Aaron went, and gathered all the elders of the sons of Israel. 30. And Aaron spake all the words which the Lord had spoken unto Moses; and did the signs in the eyes of the people. 31. And the people believed: and they heard that the Lord had visited the sons of Israel, and that he had looked on their affliction; and they bent their heads and bowed themselves down.

The Lord here obviates all the remaining difficulties of Moses, who then obtains leave of Jethro to return to Egypt (vs. 1–18). Setting out on his journey, he is met by Aaron, and on his arrival is well received by the people (vs. 19–31).

1–9. The third plea of Moses is the incredulity of the people.

There is no manifestation of God to Israel on record since he appeared to Jacob on the way to Egypt (Gen. xlvi. 2); and this was two hundred and ten years ago. And Moses had now been in exile forty years, and would be a comparative stranger to most of his nation The Lord meets this plea by supplying him with credentials that could not be gainsaid. These are in the form of certain supernatural wonders, of which the Lord now exhibits two in the sight of Moses for the confirmation of his own faith, and directs that along with these a third should be performed in Egypt to demonstrate to the people and to Pharoh that he was an ambassador from the God of the Hebrews. It has been generally felt that these wonders must have been selected with a due regard to the occasion, and are, therefore, not only miracles attesting a divine message, but signs shadowing forth pertinent truths to all the parties concerned. The early mind was peculiarly open to the figurative method of instruction. The hieroglyphic mode of writing was a most ingenious and elaborate application of symbols to the use of recording events.

2–5. The first sign given to Moses contains a plain allusion to his change of office. *A rod.* This is the instrument and symbol of his present condition,—the shepherd's crook. *Cast it on the ground*, an act symbolic of his abandonment of that condition. *It became a serpent*, a dangerous and formidable creature, from which Moses fled. There is no distant allusion here to the repugnance of Moses to the new office which was proposed to him. The serpent, moreover, was the ostensible tempter and traitor in the garden of Eden, and therefore the representative of the author and abettor of evil. And in particular the asp, a kind of serpent, played a conspicuous part in Egyptian mythology. It was the emblem of the goddess Ranno, the snake of Neph, the hieroglyphic of "goddess," and the sign of royalty. From this last use it was called Uraeus, from *ouro*, king, and *βασιλίσκος*, royal (Rawlinson's Herod. ii. 105). Egypt was, therefore, not obscurely pointed out, as the adversary of God and his people at this time. Moses shrunk from grappling with this hostile power. *Put forth thy hand and catch it.* This indicates Moses's reluctant acceptance of his new office. *It became a rod in his hand.* What was formidable to weak faith and hesitating obedience became a rod of power as soon as the decisive act was performed. The shepherd's rod is now the rod of God, with which he is to conduct the people of God from Egypt to the promised land. *That they may believe.* Moses is empowered to perform this miracle before the people, that they may believe his divine mission. Hence it appears that one end of a miracle is to authenticate a divine communication and be a warrant to faith.

6–8. The second sign points to a renewal of nature in Moses and the people. *Put now thy hand into thy bosom.* The hand is the emblem of power. The putting of it into the bosom is merely the withdrawing of it from action into rest and security. Taking it out is preparing to resume activity. *Leprous as snow.* Leprosy is a loathsome disease of the skin prevailing in Egypt and the southern parts of Asia. It appears in spots on different parts of the body, which sometimes become confluent and cover the whole body. It is called white from the color assumed by the part affected and the hair that grows on it. Hence the phrase, "leprous as snow." It is distinguished as *Lepra Mosaica,* from the notice taken of it by Moses in his legislation (Lev. xiii. 14). The leprosy is not employed in Scripture as a figure for sin as an act or habit. But the leper is declared unclean; and moral uncleanness is the consequence of such sin. The hand of Moses, when brought out for action is found to be leprous — not impotent, as in paralysis, but defiled, and defiling whatever it touches. This is a striking figure of the unclean or unhallowed power of fallen man, which works evil and not good. It is typical of the old man in Moses and in Israel, especially now when they are contaminated with the manners and customs of idolatrous Egypt. *Put thy hand again into thy bosom.* On drawing it forth from the bosom it is now found to be restored as the healthy flesh. The degenerate power of Moses was unfit for the work of God. Its sanctification is represented by the restoration of the leprous hand. And as Moses is consecrated to the task of leading the people out of Egypt, so are they to be consecrated to the Lord as a chosen generation to show forth his praise and accomplish his purpose. *The voice of the first sign.* By a beautiful figure these signs are described as having a voice, because they speak to the people of the presence and power of God with his messenger.

9. This sign evidently refers to Egypt. The Nile was venerated

as a divinity, under the name of Hapi — cognate, if not identical, with Apis. Its waters were therefore regarded as sacred, and highly esteemed as salubrious to the drinker and fertilizing to the soil. To change these waters into blood shed on the ground is to turn the stream of life into a pool of death. It speaks of disaster and death to Egypt and its gods. He that has power over the deified Nile may defy all the might of Pharoh. He is accredited as the minister of God, called to his office, qualified for his holy task, and armed with miraculous powers for the discomfiture of Egypt by the Lord, the most high God, founder of heaven and earth.

10–17. Moses comprehends all that is implied in this last sign, stands aghast at the deadly encounter with the powers of Egypt, and urges a fourth plea. *I am not eloquent*, a man of words, competent to lay before the mind of Pharoh the awful alternative of concession or compulsion. His powers of persuasion had not prevailed with his own countrymen. His present interview with the Almighty had not increased them, and he could not expect to maintain the argument worthily in this great cause before the haughty monarch of Egypt. 11. *Who hath made man's mouth?* The Lord is still patient with Moses, and meets his objection with an unanswerable rejoinder. In a series of interrogatories it is intimated that the Lord is an infallible judge of what amount of natural eloquence is requisite for the occasion, and is able and sure to supply the deficiency, if any such exist. 12. *I will be with thy mouth.* Here the requisite aid is expressly promised. 13. Notwithstanding this assuring reply, Moses prays the Lord to confer this honor on any other than himself. 14–17. This rather hasty and impatient expression of unwillingness provokes the Lord to anger. Yet, as this backwardness arose not from any unworthy motive, but from an absence of ambition, a love of retirement, or a deep feeling of humility, the Lord does not turn away from his purpose, but with a gentle firmness acquaints him with another relief he has provided for his slowness of speech. *Aaron, thy brother, the Levite.* This is put first, as the prominent object of thought. The words in apposition with Aaron are merely intended to designate him fully, according to the Hebrew manner. He is of the same parents and tribe as Moses, and therefore suitable as an associate in this arduous undertaking. And though he was the elder brother, yet the

Lord assures Moses that he will be glad to see him, and of course act under him. *Thou shalt speak to him.* Moses is to perform the higher part still, even in speaking, namely, to dictate the words which Aaron is to utter. The promise of divine aid is accordingly reiterated and extended to both. *He shall speak for thee to the people.* We learn from this that God does not needlessly alter the natural qualities of his highest servants. The characteristics of mind and will in the individual, though dedicated and adapted to a holy use, are still allowed to remain, and to peep out in all his sayings and doings. *And thou shalt be to him for God.* The figure here is as bold as it is expressive. What God is to Moses, that Moses is to Aaron in regard to the matter and the authority of his message. What Moses is to God, that Aaron is to be to Moses in regard to the delivery of it. *And this rod.* This wand of authority he recalls to the mind of Moses as another source of encouragement. *Wherewith thou shalt do the signs.* This staff was to be always with him as the badge of his office, if not the instrument of operation.

18–26. All his fears and scruples being at length overcome, Moses prepares for entering on his office. *Jether* here is Jethro in a subsequent part of this verse. We may learn from this that a mere variation in the orthography of a proper name may indicate a variety in pronunciation, and not a deviation from the autograph of the author. *Let me go now.* Moses asks leave of his father-in-law to depart. Not only common courtesy, but the benefits he had received from Jethro demand this. *See whether they be yet alive.* The private ends he had in view he is at liberty to disclose to Jethro. Other reaons it was not necessary to state, to warrant his departure. Jethro is just, as well as generous, and bids him go in peace.

19, 20. *In Midian.* This implies that the mount of God, west of the wilderness, where Moses saw the burning bush, was not in Midian. *For all the men who sought thy life are dead.* The present communication has reference, not to the heavenly mission of Moses, but to his personal relations with Egypt. The cause of flight from his kindred was the vengeance of the king and the kinsmen of him whom he had slain. They were now dead, and he was at liberty to return. The higher reasons for his return did not at present concern the Midianites. *His sons.* Though the birth of only one son has been recorded, yet we know from the subsequent narrative (Ex. xviii. 4) that a second son was born to him. *The ass.* This may mean either the single ass or the species of animal on which they rode. In the former case the two children must have been young. The ass is a much nobler animal in the East than with us. *The rod of the God,* the true and living God, in contrast with the gods of the heathen. The rod after having been transformed by the divine power into a serpent, and from a serpent into a staff of office, may justly be termed the rod of God.

21–23. The result of the application of Moses to Pharoh, and of the performance of all his wonders, will only be an obstinate refusal to let the people go. This is here again intimated, to prepare the way for the dread ultimatum which is to be finally announced to Pharoh. *Behold,* with the eye of remembrance and attention. *The wonders.* Works that are supernatural, or contravene the laws of nature. They are called signs in reference to their use, as attesting the presence, the message, or the messenger of God, or as symbolizing any fact or doctrine. "All" the wonders seem to refer, not merely to the three signs, but to the first nine plagues with which Egypt was visited. *In thy hand* in thy power by the rod in thy hand. *And I will harden his heart.* The hardening of Pharoh's heart is in this narrative ten times ascribed to the Lord. But it is also at least twice ascribed to Pharoh himself (viii. 28, ix. 34). In seven other passages it is stated simply as a fact, without assigning any cause. It is evident of itself that this fact is ascribed to God and to Pharoh in different respects; so that the two assertions are perfectly consistent with each other. It is equally plain that the act in question belongs to Pharoh, as the moral agent by whose intention it was performed. It belongs to God as the Designer, Creator, and Supreme Governor of the existing universe, of which free agents and their voluntary actings form a part. His absolute and universal dominion follows from the act of creation, and was constantly present to the minds of the children of God in ancient days. Its effect upon the mind was solemn and impressive, and never suggested the faintest presumption of injustice in God, even when the acts that were sinful in his creatures were traced in another sense to his holy and awful will. The Scripture, accordingly, never hesitates for a moment to ascribe absolute holiness to God, and all the guilt of a sinful act to the free agents. Further than this it becomes us not to define an administration which we are incompetent fully to conceive, or exactly to express. *Then thou shalt say unto Pharoh.* This is the ultimate message, when all feebler strokes had proved ineffectual. *Israel is my son,* adopted in sovereign mercy to the inheritance of privileges, which to those who appreciate and accept them will be perpetuated and enhanced. *My first-born,* and therefore most dear, but not exclusively dear. The first-born son suggests other sons born afterwards, and points in the distance to the calling of the Gentiles. *And I said unto thee.* This refers to the message again and again urged upon Pharoh, and hitherto obstinately rejected. *I will slay thy son.* This is the final stroke on him who persisted to the last in leaving all to the arbitrament of war, even with the Almighty. His first-born, the heir to his throne, and the first-born of all his people, must be slain before he can be induced to let Israel go.

24–26. The sacred narrative is not wont to notice incidents on the way, unless they come within the sphere of the spiritual. Thus Jacob travels from Beersheba to Haran, a distance of nearly five hundred miles, and only the occurrence at Bethel is mentioned. So here a single incident is taken up from the ordinary routine of the journey to Egypt, on account of its moral import. It contains an element of truth that is of present moment in elucidating the ways of God. *The Lord met him, and sought to kill him.* The Lord had been charging Moses with a menace of the gravest kind to Pharoh. It was well that Moses himself should feel acutely the pang of death, that he may comprehend the terrible meaning of this threat. It appears that his youngest son had not been circumcised through some unexplained fault of Moses. The neglect of the divinely appointed sign of the covenant of peace with God was a serious delinquency, especially in him who was to be the leader and lawgiver of the holy people. It was meet that the austere perfection of the divine holiness should be made known to Moses. It was necessary at this stage of his experience that he should learn that God is in earnest when he speaks, and will assuredly perform all that he has threatened. Hence the Lord sought to kill him, probably by some disease or sudden stroke, which threatened immediate death. *And Zipporah took.* It is probable from her spontaneous promptitude that Zipporah was in some way the cause of the delay in circumcising the child. *A sharp stone.* This was a stone or flint knife, such as was used afterwards by Joshua in circumcising the children of Israel on their entrance into the land of Kenaan (Jos. v. 2). We read that Tubal-cain, the eighth in descent from Adam, was a worker in brass and iron. Hence it appears that implements of stone were contemporaneous with those of the common metals. The use of them seems to have prevailed in rural or remote regions, into which the arts of smelting and forging metals had not penetrated. The theory, therefore, of the successive ages of stone, brass, and iron, may apply to particular localities, but not to the whole habitable earth. The arts of metallurgy flourished in certain races while the ruder ware, fashioned out of stone, bone, and wood, was prevalent among others. *And cast it at his feet.* This indicates that Moses had signified his wish that the child should be circumcised. *For a spouse of blood art thou to me.* The word *for* refers to the significant act of casting the foreskin at Moses's feet, which implied that her connection with him had necessitated this bloody rite. Her womanly tenderness shrunk from the painful operation. *And he left him.* The Lord, who sought to put him to death, remitted the penalty now that the neglected duty was performed. *Because of the circumcision.* This explains her accosting Moses as a spouse of blood, as it was to save him from death that she was constrained to do herself the masculine part of circumcising her child. This was a salutary and seasonable lesson to Zipporah as well as to Moses. The occurrence probably took place on the first night of their journey, as they had not reached the mount of God (vs. 27). The child was now unfit for travel, and it was easy for the mother to return with the two children to her father. It is most likely, therefore, that this was the point from which she was sent home by her husband (xviii. 2), in order to avoid the dangers and inconveniences which she was willing to brave on his account, had not this providential interposition ordered it otherwise.

Moses must have occupied at least a day in returning to Midian with the flock of Jethro, two or three days in making preparations, and a day in setting out with his wife and family. The distance from Midian to Egypt was probably not less than two hundred miles, for which we may allow seven days. Starting about the beginning of the year, according to our reckoning he would arrive in Egypt about the 13th of January.

27–31. We have here a summary of the reception which Moses met with from the people. *And the Lord said unto Aaron.* The narrative, as usual, goes back a little to take up another line of things. *In the wilderness,* the region between the gulfs of Suez and Akabah. *In the mount of the God* of heaven they met. *And kissed him,* the eastern mode of salutation. After receiving instructions from Moses, Aaron accompanied him to Egypt. They gathered the elders of the people (iii. 16). *And Aaron spake* (vs. 16). Aaron being eighty-three years of age, and having lived constantly among the people, now served to introduce Moses who had been an exile for forty years, and was therefore unknown to the rising generation. *And did the signs.* As Aaron did the signs before Pharoh, it is probable and accordant with the text that he should also be the performer before the people. This is in keeping with the relation between Moses and himself (vs. 16). It is also an example of the rule that a man is said to do what another does in his stead and by his authority (vs. 17). *Bowed themselves down.* Bent their bodies as well as their heads in reverence before God. So far all went well with Moses. His brother entered heartily into his mission, and the people acknowledged him as the messenger of God.

## IV. MOSES ENCOURAGED IN HIS OFFICE.—Ex. v., vi.

### CHAP. V.—MOSES APPEARS BEFORE PHAROH.

3. נִקְרָא. This form here signifies *to meet with,* as the verb does in several places (Gen xlii. 4; xlix. 1, and always in the form לִקְרַאת), and as the context proves (iii. 18). קָרָה is the more usual form of the verb with this meaning.

6. שֹׁטֵר γραμματεύς *a scribe,* prefect, officer, employed in duties involving the keeping of accounts, lists, and other records.

V. 1. And afterward Moses and Aaron went and said unto Pharoh, Thus saith the Lord, the God of Israel, let my people go and hold a feast unto me in the wilderness. 2. And Pharoh said, Who is the LORD, that I should hearken to his voice to let Israel go? I know not the LORD, neither will I let Israel go. 3. And they said, The God of the Hebrews hath met with us: let us go now three days' journey into the wilderness, and sacrifice unto the LORD our God, lest he fall upon us with pestilence or with the sword. 4. And the king of Mizraim said unto them, Wherefore do ye, Moses and Aaron, loose the people from their works? Get you to your burdens. 5. And Pharoh said, Lo, the people of the land are now many, and ye make them rest from their burdens.

6. And Pharoh commanded that day the taskmasters over the people and their officers, saying, 7. Ye shall not continue to give straw to the people to make brick, as heretofore; let them go and gather straw for themselves. 8. And the tale of the bricks which they made heretofore ye shall lay upon them; ye shall not take from it; for they are idle: therefore they cry, saying, Let us go sacrifice to our God. 9. Let the service be heavy on the men, and let them work therein; and let them not regard vain words. 10. Then went out the taskmasters of the people and their officers, and spake unto the people, saying, Thus saith Pharoh, I will not give you straw. 11. Go ye yourselves, get you straw where ye can find it; for not ought of your service shall be taken off.

12. And the people were scattered throughout all the land of Mizraim, to gather stubble for straw. 13. And the taskmasters hasted them, saying, Fulfil your works, the daily task, as when there was straw. 14. And the officers of the sons of Israel, whom Pharoh's taskmasters had set over them, were beaten, while it was said, Why have ye not fulfilled your task in making brick, as heretofore, both yesterday and to-day? 15. And the officers of the sons of Israel went in

and cried unto Pharoh, saying, Why dealest thou thus with
thy servants? 16. No straw is given unto thy servants, and
they say to us, Make brick: and behold thy servants are
beaten, and it is the fault of thy people. 17. And he said, Ye
are idle, ye are idle; therefore ye say, Let us go sacrifice to
the LORD. 18. And now go, work: and no straw shall be
given you, and the tale of bricks ye shall deliver.

19. And the officers of the sons of Israel saw that they were
in evil case, when it was said, Ye shall not take off from the
daily task of your bricks. 20. And they met Moses and
Aaron standing in the way as they came out from Pharoh.
21. And they said unto them, The LORD look upon you and
judge; because ye have made our savor to stink in the eyes
of Pharoh, and in the eyes of his servants, to put a sword in
their hand to slay us. 22. And Moses returned unto the LORD
and said, Lord, wherefore hast thou done evil to this people?
Why is this, that thou hast sent me? 23. And since I went
in to Pharoh to speak in thy name, he hath done evil to this
people; neither hast thou delivered thy people at all.

In further prosecution of their mission, Moses and Aaron now present themselves before Pharoh. But they are dismissed with contempt, and new hardships are imposed on the people and their officers. Moses returns to God disappointed and complaining.

1–5. The request made by Moses is contemptuously refused by Pharoh. *And afterward.* After the people had accepted his authority, Moses was prepared to go before Pharoh. *Moses and Aaron,* accompanied, no doubt, by the representatives of the people (iii. 18). *Thus saith Jehovah, the God of Israel.* Jehovah was the God of Adam (Gen. ii. 7, 16), the God of Noah (Gen. vi. 8, viii. 20, 21), and consequently of the whole race descended from him. He is here called the God of Israel, not as if he were one among the national gods, but because the other nations have corrupted the notion and worship of God, and because he has entered into a covenant of grace with Israel.

*Let my people go.* The request is peremptory, because it comes directly from God himself. And *hold a feast unto me in the wilderness.* To hold a feast, is the immediate object of the journey. This is according to the divine manner of teaching. God promises a present seed; but there is a future seed: a good land; but there is a better country: an earthly rest, beyond which there is a heavenly rest. He speaks to men of the near and the obvious, and those who hear he leads on to higher powers of understanding and nobler scenes of enjoyment. Besides Pharoh was not entitled to know, and he does not condescend to ask what were the ulterior purposes of God. *In the wilderness* simply means out of Egypt, beyond the jurisdiction of its sovereign and the interference of its people. A sequestered scene was often selected by ancient taste for a solemn festival. 2. *I know not the Lord.* Jehovah, the God of Israel, was not unknown to the predecessors of Pharoh (Gen. xii. 17, 41, xliii. 23). He could scarcely be ignorant that the Israelites had a God. But the import of the name here employed may have been unknown to him, and at all events he refuses to acknowledge the authority of Jehovah. Their reply is explanatory. *The God of the Hebrews,* of which well-known nation (Gen. x. 21, xiv. 13, xli. 15, xli. 12) the Israelites were a branch (i. 15–19), is he whose name is Jehovah. *Hath met with us,* has revealed himself to us in the miracles wrought in our presence, and the message communicated to us by Moses. *Three days' journey.* See on iii. 18. *Lest he fall on us with pestilence or with the sword.* The sword is under the control of Providence as well as the pestilence. This is added to bring out clearly the necessity of their departure. Pharoh will gain nothing by withholding his permission, as these bond slaves, whom he values so much, may be destroyed by a stroke from heaven, from which even his own subjects might not escape. There is a clear and unavoidable obligation, therefore, on the Israelites to make this demand. It dawns upon the mind of Pharoh that this departure involves the emancipation and independence of the Israelites. But he will not ask the question, or entertain the thought. He treats their demands with a haughty impatience. *Get you to your burdens.* This is meant for the representatives of the people, as the former part of his reply was addressed to Moses and Aaron. 5. *The people of the land.* They are called the people of the land with reference to

Goshen, where they were settled, in contrast with Pharoh himself, who belonged to the dominant race, which may have been of foreign extraction, or because they were engaged in rural occupations (i. 14). *Are now many.* They are already so numerous as to endanger the state. *And ye make them rest,* when they require to be kept down in numbers and in spirit by hard and constant labor. It is evident that Pharoh spurns the thought of letting the people go.

6–11. He determined to crush the nascent thought of freedom in the very bud. *That day.* The case is urgent, and no time is to be lost. *The taskmasters.* The Egyptian drivers, who had the management of the servile labor. *Their officers.* The Shoterim were orderlies or managers who kept an account of all matters that came under their charge. They appear to have been permanent officials in the state of Israel, as Moses makes express provision for their continuance (Deut. xvi. 18), and they are mentioned on various occasions in the subsequent history of the people (Num. xi. 16; Deut. i. 15 ; Judg. v. 14; 2 Chron. xxvi. 11). They occupied the highest rank among the people, for we find Moses selecting from among them members of the original Council or Sanhedrin of Israel (Num. xi. 16), and they are included among the representatives of the people in the public assembly (Deut. xxix. 10). The very name of this official indicates a literary people. It is judicious in a despotic sovereign, governing a conquered or enslaved tribe, to avail himself of certain parts of the political organization which they have adopted. 7. *Straw.* Straw cut into small pieces was mixed with the clay, apparently to give consistency to the brick until it was baked in the sun. The sun-dried bricks of Egypt are so durable that many still remain that were made many centuries before the Christian era. On being analyzed they are found to contain a portion of straw. *The tale of the bricks.* The same quantity of bricks was to be produced, though the straw had to be gathered, in addition to their former labors. *They are idle.* They have not enough to do, and so they have time to think about freedom. *Let them work therein,* be busy, fully employed. *Vain words.* Pharoh affects to regard the statement that their God had interposed as a falsehood invented by Moses and Aaron. 11. *Go ye,* for no other will any more supply you. *For not ought of your service shall be taken off.* Therefore bestir yourselves to find the straw.

12–18. After two days the Shoterim are beaten, because the appointed number of bricks is not supplied; and on complaining to Pharoh, obtain no redress. 13. *The daily task*, the rate of a day in its day. 16. *And it is the fault of thy people*, who do not supply us with straw as formerly. 17. *Ye are idle.* Pharoh has no new answer for the officers. The intolerable burden he will not remove.

19–23. The officers reproach Moses and Aaron for involving them and the people in this distress. Moses, deeply dejected, makes his appeal to God. 20. *They came upon*, encountered Moses and Aaron, who were standing in the way, probably awaiting the issue of their application to Pharoh. 21. *To put a sword in their hand to slay us*, to give a ground of offence, provoking Pharoh to such measures as will end in the destruction of the people. 22. *Moses returned unto the Lord.* His mission to Pharoh has entirely failed. It has only added to the misery of the people. He lays this before the Lord in very plain terms. The chapter is abruptly closed with the earnest expostulation of Moses. The sombre picture of wretchedness is thus left to make its full impression on the mind.

## VI. MOSES ENCOURAGED—HIS GENEALOGY.—Ex. vi.

17. לִבְנִי Libni, *white ;* r. *be white.* שִׁמְעִי Shimei, *hearing ;* r. *hear.*

18. עַמְרָם ʿAmram, *binding ;* r. *bind.* יִצְהָר Jitshar, *oil ;* r. *shine.* עֻזִּיאֵל Uzziel, *God my strength.*

19. מַחְלִי Machli, *sickness ;* r. *be sick.* מוּשִׁי Mushi, *yielding ;* r. *yield.*

20. יוֹכֶבֶד Jokebed, *glory to Jehovah.*

21. קֹרַח Qorach, *hail ;* r. *congeal.* נֶפֶג Nepheg, *sprig ;* r. u. *sprout.* זִכְרִי Zikri, *remembrance.*

22. מִישָׁאֵל Mishael, *who is what God is?* אֶלְצָפָן Eltsaphan, *God a hiding-place.* סִתְרִי Sithri, *hiding-place.*

23. אֱלִישֶׁבַע Elisheba', *God is my oath.* עַמִּינָדָב ʿAmminadab, *bounteous to my people.* נַחְשׁוֹן Nachshon, *serpentine.* נָדָב Nadab, *bounteous.* אֲבִיהוּא Abihu, *he a father.* אֶלְעָזָר El'azar, *God a help.* אִיתָמָר Ithamar, *where the palm.*

24. אַסִּיר Assir, *captive.* אֶלְקָנָה Elqanah, *gotten from God.* אֲבִיאָסָף Abiasaph, *father of gathering.*

25. פּוּטִיאֵל Putiel, *afflicted of God.* פִּינְחָס Pinechas, *brazen mouth.*

VI. 1. And the LORD said unto Moses, Now shalt thou see what I will do to Pharoh: for by a strong hand shall he let them go, and by a strong hand shall he drive them out of his land. 14. § § § 2.

2. And God spake unto Moses, and said unto him, I am the LORD. 3. And I appeared unto Abraham, unto Isaac, and unto Jacob as God Almighty; but by my name JEHOVAH was I not known to them. 4. And I have also established my covenant with them, to give them the land of Kenaan; the land of their sojournings wherein they sojourned. 5. And I have also heard the groaning of the sons of Israel, whom Mizraim keeps in bondage, and I remembered my covenant. 6. Wherefore say unto the sons of Israel, I am the LORD, and I will bring you out from under the burdens of Mizraim, and deliver you out of their service; and I will redeem you with a stretched-out arm and with great judgments. 7. And I will take you to me for a people, and I will be to you a God; and ye shall know that I am the LORD your God, who bringeth you out from under the burdens of Mizraim. 8. And I will bring you into the land, which I lifted up my hand to give to Abraham, to Isaac, and to Jacob; and I will give it to you for a possession: I am the LORD. 9. And Moses spake so unto the sons of Israel, and they hearkened not unto Moses from anguish of spirit and from hard service. ¶ 6.

10. And the LORD spake unto Moses, saying, 11. Go in, speak unto Pharoh king of Mizraim, that he let the sons of Israel go out of his land. 12. And Moses spake before the LORD, saying, Behold, the sons of Israel have not hearkened

unto me; and how shall Pharoh hearken unto me, who am uncircumcised of lips? ¶ 7.

13. And the Lord spake unto Moses and unto Aaron, and gave them a charge unto the sons of Israel, and unto Pharoh king of Mizraim, to bring the sons of Israel out of the land of Mizraim. § 3.

14. These are the heads of their fathers' houses: the sons of Reuben, the first-born of Israel; Henok and Pallu, Hezron and Karmi; these are the families of Reuben. 15. And the sons of Simon; Jemuel, and Jamin, and Ohad, and Jakin, and Zohar, and Saul, the son of a Kenaanitess; these are the families of Simon. 16. And these are the names of the sons of Levi, according to their generations; Gershon, and Kohath, and Merari. And the years of the life of Levi were seven and thirty and a hundred years. 17. The sons of Gershon; Libni and Shimi, according to their families. 18. And the sons of Kohath; Amram, and Izhar, and Hebron, and Uzziel. And the years of the life of Kohath were three and thirty and a hundred years. 19. And the sons of Merari; Mahli and Mushi. These are the families of Levi, according to their generations. 20. And Amram took him Jokebed, his aunt, to wife, and she bare him Aaron and Moses. And the years of the life of Amram were seven and thirty and a hundred years. 21. And the sons of Izhar; Korah, and Nepheg, and Zikri. 22. And the sons of Uzziel; Mishael, and Elzaphan, and Sithri. 23. And Aaron took Elisheba, daughter of Amminadab, sister of Nahshon, to wife; and she bare him Nadab and Abihu, Eleazar and Ithamar. 24. And the sons of Korah; Assir and Elkanah and Abiasaph. These are the families of the Korhites. 25. And Eleazar, Aaron's son, took him a wife of the daughters of Putiel; and she bare him Phinehas. These are the heads of the fathers of the

Levites, according to their families. 26. These are the Aaron and Moses, to whom the LORD had said, Bring out the sons of Israel from the land of Mizraim according to their hosts. 27. These are they who spake to Pharoh king of Mizraim, to bring out the sons of Israel from Mizraim. These are the Moses and Aaron. 28. And it was in the day when the LORD spake unto Moses in the land of Mizraim. § 4.

29. And the LORD spake unto Moses, saying, I am the LORD: speak unto Pharoh, king of Mizraim, all that I speak unto thee. 30. And Moses said before the LORD, Behold, I am uncircumcised of lips, and how shall Pharoh hearken unto me? ¶ 8.

The dejected Moses is reassured by a new assertion and exposition of the actual presence of God to perform his promise to his people (vs. 1–13). The pedigree of Moses and Aaron, and others who are to figure in the future scene is now given, preparatory to the commencement of Israel's deliverance (vs. 14–30).

1. The Lord's reply is directed not to the complaint of Moses, of which he takes no notice, but to the contemptuous refusal with which Pharoh had met his rightful demand. To receive a message from his Maker was an unspeakable honor. Even if he suspected the message to be a pretence, yet reverence for him in whose name the bearers of it professed to come should have led to the most cautious inquiry before he replied. He was not to act upon a surmise in any case, much less in a case of such moment. *Now.* In the very height of Pharoh's arrogance and oppression, and in the depth of the people's anguish and despair, will the Lord appear. *By a strong hand* (iii. 19). By the hand of the Almighty inflicting stroke upon stroke, until the spirit of Pharoh is broken. Thus will he be constrained not only to give them leave, but even to drive them out of his land. The second, "by a strong hand," for which the Sept. has "by a high arm" (ἐν βραχίονι ὑψηλῷ), is emphatic. The Sabbath lesson of the synagogue terminates here, after having given relief to the anxiety of the hearer by a new promise of God.

2–9. The reassurance of the preceding communication is now sustained by a recurrence to the cheering import of the name JEHOVAH, and a recapitulation of all the old promises to the patriarchs. *And God spake.* The Everlasting and Unchangeable One spake. *I am the* LORD, JEHOVAH. The Real, the Self-existent, the Author of all other existence, manifesting my being by my presence in and power over nature for the performance of my long-revealed purpose. This is a name of power and hope to cheer the darkest heart. 3. *As God Almighty.* The name Jehovah was made known to Adam by the stupendous works of the six days creation, which were unfolded in all their finished beauty and grandeur before his outward eyes and inmost soul (Gen. ii. 4, 16, 22, iv. 1). It was also revealed to Noah in the preservation of his own family, and the destruction of the old world by a flood, which were to the Most High but the waving of his hand, though to man they were the majestic doings of Jehovah. But in the matter of the promise made to Abraham and his seed of a land of habitation he was known to them yet only as a promiser, not yet as a performer. Hence he appeared to them as El Shaddai (Gen. xvii. 1), God Almighty, a name expressly fitted to awaken and warrant faith in a promise, inasmuch as it points to the attributes of unchangeableness and omnipotence, which are the guarantees of its ultimate fulfilment. *But by my name Jehovah was I not known to them.* As the performer of promise, the giver of existence to that purpose which he had expressed, he was not known, personally and practically known, to them. By the voice of history, by the records of the wondrous past, they were aware that he was the Lord, and this name was often actually on their lips (Gen. xii. 1, 7, 8, xiv. 22, xv. 2, 6, xvii. 1, xviii. 27, xxi. 33, xxii. 14, xxv. 21, xxviii. 13, 16, 21). But in their own experience, and in the matter of the special revelation made to them, and only now to be realized, he was not known to them as Jehovah the agent, but only as El Shaddai the potent. To know by personal observation is the primitive meaning of the verb יָדַע "know." This is evinced by the use of the perfect "I have perceived," to denote what we express by "I know," like *novi*, οἶδα, by the contrast of knowing with hearing, in such sentences as הֲלֹא תֵדְעוּ אִם לֹא תִשְׁמָעוּ (Isa. xl. 21), and by the frequent occurrence of the verb in this particular meaning (Gen. iii. 5, 7, 22, xviii. 21,

xxii. 12; Ex. v. 2). That "name" denotes the nature, the import of the name, the being to whom belongs the attribute signalized in the name, cannot be unknown to the attentive reader of the Bible. (See on Gen. i. 5, ii. 23, iii. 20, xxvii. 36; Ex. iii. 13). The meaning thus assigned to the important verse before us is, therefore, agreeable to the usage of Scripture. It vindicates the veracity and consistency of the sacred historian. And it is singularly pertinent to the context in which it occurs. It affords also a remarkable illustration of the custom exemplified in the names Bethel (Gen. xii. 8), Dan (Gen. xiv. 14), Jacob and Esau (Gen. xxv. 30), according to which a former name is renewed and perpetuated by a new occasion occurring for its application.

4, 5. These verses are a recapitulation of the past. 6–8. The promise now to be realized. *Say unto the sons of Israel, I am the* LORD. This is henceforth to be the word of encouragement, of authority, and of fellowship to Israel. It reminds them that God is now active on their behalf; that it is God who is thus active, and that he is present to dwell in the midst of them as a father among his adopted children. It guarantees the following promise. *A stretched-out arm*, a bold figure for the strenuous interposition of Jehovah. *Take you to me for a people.* This is a winning and persuasive argument to a down-trodden people. *Ye shall know that I am the* LORD. They shall know by actual experience that he is all that is implied in the name Jehovah, an actual, and therefore tried, deliverer. *I lifted up my hand* (Gen. xiv. 22), I sware, by lifting up, in solemn appeal to God as a witness, the hand, the emblem of power, to perform what is sworn. The phrase is transferred with a singular emphasis from the human gesture to the divine asseveration. *I am the* LORD. This sentence is here repeated for the third time in this message, enhanced by all the emphasis which the distinction made between the divine names (vs. 3) has added to its meaning. It is the seal of God thrice stamped upon his promise. 9. Notwithstanding the cheering effect of this new communication on Moses, the people were so heart-broken that they hearkened not to the comfortable words with which he addressed them.

10–12. With a heavy heart and sorely wounded spirit Moses must have turned from the people. Yet the Lord directs him to go again to Pharoh. Moses pleads his want of persuasive power. If his own people have not hearkened unto him, how will Pharoh hearken? *Uncircumcised of lips.* Circumcision is the sign of a renewal of nature. The uncircumcised is, therefore, by a natural figure, one who is still in the bondage of a corrupt heart, and incapable of holy doings. By a further turn of the metaphor, he is uncircumcised of lips who is incompetent to speak in a manner fitted to produce conviction and compliance.

13. It is here stated in summary terms that the Lord now gave a joint command or peremptory charge to Moses and Aaron, *unto*, that is, to go unto, the sons of Israel and unto Pharoh, and to bring Israel out of Egypt. Aaron is joined in the commission as before, to obviate the difficulty of Moses about his failure to persuade the people. The last symptom of reluctance on the part of Moses has now been overruled, and at this point the historian is conscious that it is due to the leaders of this great movement, and to the ends of history, to give an account of the relation in which Moses and Aaron, and some of their kindred, who take a part in the following transactions, stand to the other, and especially the elder, branches of the now great family of Israel. This is the very moment for introducing this statement, as these ministers of the Lord are on the eve of entering, without any more faltering, on the momentous conflict between the powers of light and darkness, which is to end in the deliverance of the children of Israel. Hence, after the summary notice of the positive command now laid upon Moses and Aaron, the genealogical notice is inserted.

14–28. The narrative here reverts to a point of time long passed in the general course of events related. *These are the heads of their fathers' houses.* The twelve tribes (שְׁבָטִים or מַטּוֹת) of Israel were now divided, each into families (מִשְׁפָּחוֹת), and the families into fathers' houses (בֵּית אָב, in the plural בֵּית אָבוֹת). It is evident that in a nation that had a set of officers whose business it was to keep written accounts of all matters coming under their charge, we may expect to find genealogical lists kept with care and accuracy. Moses, therefore, had no difficulty in finding the register of his family. In quoting from the public records, it was both respectful to the two elder tribes and essential to a clear statement of the relative position of Moses and Aaron in the nation to give at least the families contained in these tribes. Then follow what are, strictly speaking, *their*, that is, Moses and Aaron's fathers' houses. The ages of Levi, Kohath, and Amram, the lineal ancestors of the leaders of the people, are given. The second son of Levi is the father of Amram. *And Amram took him Jokebed, his aunt, to wife* (see on ii. 1). We are here brought to the parents of Moses and Aaron. 21. The sons of Izhar are introduced on account of Korah, who afterwards comes to a bad pre-eminence (Num. xvi.). 22. The sons of Uzziel are mentioned because they also recur in the narrative (Lev. x. 4). 23. Elisheba, sister of Nahshon, was the fifth (inclusive) in descent from Judah; while Aaron was only the fourth from Levi by his father's side, and the third by his mother's. This prepares us to expect great disparity in the number of generations in different lines. Aaron's sons will meet us in the narrative hereafter. 24. The sons of Korah were the survivors of their father, and became heads of families (Num. xxvi. 11). 25. Of Putiel we know nothing further. Phinehas is the sixth (inclusive) in descent from Levi, and the seventh from Judah. 26–28. *These are the Aaron and Moses.* The design of the preceding paragraph was to explain who Aaron and Moses were. They stand here in the order of seniority. At the end of the next verse they are placed in the order of rank. *To whom the Lord had said.* This refers to the commission he had given to them before their first interview with Pharoh. *These are they who spake to Pharoh* in the first interview, which is recorded in the fifth chapter. *And it was in the day.* This was the state of things at the time. This verse seems designed to date the time when the conjunction of circumstances described in the preceding passage regarding the family of Moses had taken place. In accordance with this, the closed section of the Masoretic text terminates with this verse. The connection of such a sentence with the preceding context is unusual; but it occurs in other instances (Deut. ii. 16; Zech. vi. 15). The phrase וַיְהִי it came to pass, simply indicates a point of time at which a preceding period terminates, and the following one begins. The prominent reference is usually to the latter; but it may be to the former (Gen. i. 7, 9, 11, 15, 24, 30). Sometimes the reference may be equal to both (Gen. iv. 8).

29, 30. These verses contain a recapitulation of verses 10–12, and therefore bring us up, in point of time, to the beginning of verse 13, which is itself a summary of what is given in detail in the beginning of the next chapter. The first seven verses of the seventh chapter might accordingly be regarded as the continuation of the sixth. But in the existing arrangement they form an appropriate introduction to the record of those ten strokes of judgments by which the resistance of Egypt was broken, and the way at length opened for the departure of Israel.

We have now perused the record of Israel's servitude in Egypt. It runs parallel with the early part of the life of the deliverer, or more precisely of Aaron, his senior by three years. It commences probably with a new dynasty in Egypt, at a time when the increase of the people was so marked as to become alarming to a sovereign not very firmly seated on the throne, and exposed to the hostility of neighboring powers. His policy, though it does not keep down the population, makes him aware of their value as servile laborers. He therefore persists in his arbitrary course until the cry of the oppressed people reaches heaven. The deliverer now appears; but his approach to the monarch is only the signal for a new outburst of violence and oppression. This casts the last shade of gloom and despondency over the scene.

## SECTION II.—THE TEN PLAGUES.

### V. THE FIRST THREE PLAGUES.—Ex. vii. 8–viii. 9.

#### CHAP. VII.—WATER CHANGED INTO BLOOD.

9. תַּנִּין *long creature, sea-monster, serpent, dragon.* It sometimes denotes the crocodile, Isa. xxvii. 1; li. 9. The Sept. give δράκων, which we have retained to distinguish it from נָחָשׁ *serpent,* which is a species of the more general term תַּנִּין. The crocodile might be included under either. But the asp or basilisk is more probable, though the term employed is perhaps designedly general.

11. מְכַשֵּׁף *sorcerer, magician, enchanter,* one who practises hidden or black arts; r. *hide.* These arts are called לְהָטִים = לָטִים *enchantments,* from לַהַט = לוּט *to hide.* Whether these arts were due to the light of experience or the powers of darkness, we have not the means of determining.

VII. 1. And the LORD said unto Moses, See, I have made
thee a god unto Pharoh; and Aaron thy brother shall be thy
prophet. 2. Thou shalt speak all that I command thee; and
Aaron thy brother shall speak unto Pharoh, that he send the
sons of Israel out of his land. 3. And I will harden Pha-
roh's heart; and multiply my signs and my wonders in the
land of Mizraim. 4. And Pharoh will not hearken unto you,
and I will lay my hand upon Mizraim: and I will bring forth
my hosts, my people, the sons of Israel, out of the land of Miz-
raim by great judgments. 5. And Mizraim shall know that I
am the LORD, when I stretch forth my hand upon Mizraim,
and bring out the sons of Israel from among them. 6. And
thus did Moses and Aaron; as the LORD commanded them, so

did they. 7. And Moses was eighty years old, and Aaron three and eighty years old, when they spake unto Pharoh.

8. And the LORD spake unto Moses and unto Aaron, saying: 9. When Pharoh shall speak unto you, saying, show for you a miracle; then thou shalt say unto Aaron, Take thy rod and cast it before Pharoh; let it become a dragon. 10. And Moses and Aaron went in unto Pharoh, and did so as the LORD had commanded; and Aaron cast down his rod before Pharoh and before his servants, and it became a dragon. 11. And Pharoh also called the sages and the sorcerers; and the scribes of Mizraim, they also did so with their enchantments. 12. And they cast down every man his rod, and they became dragons: and Aaron's rod swallowed up their rods. 13. And Pharoh's heart was hardened, and he hearkened not unto them, as the LORD had spoken. § 5.

14. And the LORD said unto Moses, Pharoh's heart is hard; he refuseth to let the people go. 15. Go unto Pharoh in the morning; lo, he goeth out unto the water, and thou shalt stand to meet him at the river's brink: and the rod which was turned to a serpent shalt thou take in thy hand. 16. And thou shalt say unto him, The LORD, the God of the Hebrews, hath sent me unto thee to say, Let my people go and serve me in the wilderness; and behold thou hast not hearkened hitherto. 17. Thus saith the LORD, In this thou shalt know that I am the LORD; behold I smite with the rod that is in my hand upon the water which is in the river, and it shall be turned into blood. 18. And the fish that is in the river shall die, and the river shall stink: and Mizraim shall loathe to drink the water of the river. § 6.

19. And the LORD said unto Moses, say unto Aaron, Take thy rod, and stretch out thy hand upon the waters of Mizraim, upon their rivers, upon their streams, and upon their ponds,

and upon every pool of their waters, and they shall become
blood: and there shall be blood in all the land of Mizraim,
both in wood and in stone. 20. And Moses and Aaron did so,
as the LORD commanded; and he lifted up the rod and smote
the water that was in the river, in the eyes of Pharoh, and in
the eyes of his servants; and all the water that was in the
river was turned into blood. 21. And the fish that was in the
river died; and the river stank, and Mizraim could not drink
water from the river: and the blood was in all the land of
Mizraim. 22. And the scribes of Mizraim did so with their
enchantments: and Pharoh's heart was hardened, neither did
he hearken unto them, as the LORD had spoken. 23. And
Pharoh turned and went into his house, neither did he set his
heart even to this. 24. And all Mizraim digged round about
the river for water to drink; for they could not drink of the
water of the river. 25. And seven days were fulfilled, after
the LORD had smitten the river. ¶ 10.

The problem to be solved in this section is the deliverance of a family, now grown into a nation, who have been unjustly reduced to a state of servitude, from a haughty despot who finds his advantage in retaining them by force in his service. Every man, we have no doubt, thinks he can easily solve it; and the solution proposed by each will depend very much on the character of the individual. All men will also, we conceive, acknowledge that the omniscient and omnipotent God could accomplish the end in question in a variety of ways, conceivable or inconceivable by man. It is certain, however, that the all-wise God can and will work this problem in one way. This will be the best way. He only knows what is the best way for all parties. He has respect in all his doings to the best interests of his rational creatures. This consists in the perfection and culture of their intellectual and moral nature, as the only solid foundation of complete and perpetual happiness. His method of procedure, therefore, will be exactly fitted not only to the nature of man, the chief rational party concerned, in general, but to the stage of development to which at the time he has attained. It is true and important in one sense that God giveth not account of any of his matters; but it is equally true and important that he takes account of all matters whatsoever in all his proceedings. Hence he has regard to Israel, to Egypt, to Kenaan, and to the whole human race in the manner in which he meets this great emergency. He has in view the present state of these parties, and adapts his measures to their instruction in spiritual things according to their several attainments in mental and moral truth. The result of the divine wisdom is the best plan of delivering Israel from Egypt, which is accordingly carried into effect, and is here delineated for our learning. Let us enter upon the study of it, hoping to be illuminated ourselves with many rays of that light which then broke upon the minds of Israel and his contemporaries.

We have already read the instructive account of the appointment of Moses to be the prime minister of Heaven in this great movement, and the deferential respect with which his credentials have been received by the people. Accompanied by the elders of Israel, he has approached Pharoh, and presented the authoritative message of the God of heaven and earth, requiring him to let Israel go and keep a feast to the Lord. In these facts we have striking instances of God's manner of proceeding. He does not appoint a servant without removing all his difficulties, and affording him the fullest instructions. He does not take a step in the emancipation of the people without obtaining their acceptance of the leader he has chosen and their concurrence in the measures he has devised. And, notwithstanding the absence of all equity, as well as gratitude, in the manner in which the Pharohs had degraded into serfs the free kinsmen of Joseph, he opens the negociations with the reigning sovereign by a simple and moderately worded, yet firm and frank, demand of the release of his people for the immediate purpose of a religious festival. It is obvious that so mild a request, so limited in its terms, in circumstances of so grave injustice, coming from the most high God, could not have been rejected by a right-minded man. Inquiries might have been made, difficulties started, and claims advanced, if there had been any; and these would have been all reasonably and satisfactorily met. And thus a negociation opened with forbearance and carried on with equity would have terminated in a peaceful and amicable settlement. Such is the beginning of God's method for the deliverance of his people from Egypt.

But upon the proud and arrogant mind of Pharoh this temperate dealing has an opposite effect. He breaks out into instant defiance of God, contempt of his ministers, and revenge upon his people. His heart, practised in the arts of tyranny, gains a new degree of obstinacy from its violent recoil against this modest and seemingly feeble whisper of the bond-slave's God. With unaffected simplicity the sacred historian records the disastrous consequences of Pharoh's indignation on the people and their officers, and the sad shock it gave to their infant faith. This was, no doubt, very painful to endure and pitiful to contemplate. But it had its pregnant and salutary lessons, and he who has looked into the after history of this people will be persuaded that this and many subsequent correctives were absolutely necessary to bring them to that depth of piety, strength of principle, and decision of character which conferred a moral dignity on the nation, the traces of which are still to be found in the remnant of Israel.

Even Moses himself is disappointed by the failure of his first attempt, and distressed by the anguish and despondency of the people. Accordingly the Lord, in the beginning of this chapter, opens up to him a new and cheering view of his relation to Pharoh, and sends him again to him with the miraculous authentication of his mission. This second effort of the divine forbearance is also disregarded by the infatuated king. Only on the third appearance of Moses before Pharoh is he authorized to announce and inflict the first plague or stroke of judgment upon the recusant monarch.

1–7. This passage is the expansion of vs. 13 of the previous chapter. A new and encouraging view of his relation to Pharoh is here presented to Moses, inducing him to enter with a willing and intelligent interest into the divine mission with which he has been intrusted. *A god unto Pharoh.* What God was to Moses in point of instruction, that Moses was to be to Aaron (iv. 16); and what God was to him in respect of power, that he was now to be to Pharoh. He was to be the revealer of the divine will to Aaron; the executor of the divine will on Pharoh. God puts his servant in a satisfactory position toward the adversary he has to encounter; and henceforth he proceeds without faltering to carry out the divine intentions. *And Aaron shall be thy prophet.* A prophet is God's spokesman, uttering a message or a prayer by his authority (Gen. xx. 7). Such is Aaron to be to Moses, as explained in the following verse. The plenipotentiary of heaven is now amply furnished for his great undertaking. 3. *And I will harden Pharoh's heart.* We have seen the process already begun. The very patience and moderation which were calculated to subdue a will amenable to reason, only aroused the resistance and vengeance of Pharoh. Every succeeding step in the procedure of God is dictated by a like consideration and forbearance. Though it be true, therefore, that God did harden Pharoh's heart, yet it was by measures that would have disarmed the opposition and commanded the acquiescence of an upright mind. 4. *I will lay my hand upon Mizraim*, because Pharoh is the representative of the Egyptians, because they concur in his sentiments, and because, even when they do not concur, they do not actively dissent from his intentions. Thus nations share the guilt, and therefore the punishment, of their erring sovereigns. Moreover, God will touch the consciences of the nation in this high controversy, and awaken within them that fear of God which ought to regulate and set bounds to the fear of their earthly king (vs. 5). *I will bring forth my hosts.* The hosts of the Lord they were in a literal sense, and a stern work they had to perform in the beginning of their career. Yet they gradually rose to a higher form of warfare, in which they were destined, yet with many auxiliaries, to endure hardness as good soldiers of the Messiah. The term *hosts*, however, is significant even here. It points to the fact that the sons of Israel are to march out of Egypt in battle array, apart from the women, children, cattle, and baggage (xiii. 18). 5. *And Mizraim shall know.* They shall find by experience, whether they take the lesson to heart or not. *That I am the Lord.* That great master-truth of all theology, that the God of the Hebrews is the one true and living God, the founder and mover of heaven and earth. The nations have inherited the vague notion of God, indeed, from their common father; but they have essentially corrupted it, so that their gods are no longer the true God at all, but only a baseless phantom of their imagination. They have lost the historical connection with the God of their remote ancestry. In the one line of Israel, through the providence of God, has the historical revelation of God been preserved pure and entire. This would have been Egypt's day of grace, if the nation had only fully accepted this one lesson, "I am the Lord"; but it became a day of judgment on account of its rejection, and this day continued, until salvation began to go forth from Jerusalem. 6. *And thus did Moses and Aaron.* There is henceforward a prompt and constant obedience to the divine command, with the exception of certain grave inadvertencies into which they are betrayed by the remaining infirmities of the old man. 7. *And Moses was eighty years old.* We are now arrived at the point we had reached in the summary of vi. 13. It is in place to state the ages of the two brothers. As no mention is made of any difficulty in saving Aaron when an infant, it is not improbable that the edict about the execution of the male infants, by casting them into the Nile, was published after his birth, and in fact very shortly before the birth of Moses. Eighty years may seem a ripe age for entering upon an arduous enterprise; but all the ancestors of Moses lived beyond the age of one hundred and thirty years, so that eighty was not more in proportion than forty would be now. This is the proper close of the paragraph beginning with the genealogy (vi. 14), and, therefore, after having expanded vi. 13 in the previous passage, the writer is prepared to go on with the main line of the narrative.

8–13. Moses now understands the position of advantage in which the Lord has put him, and is emboldened to appear the second time before Pharoh. Having armed his servant with miraculous powers so that he is a god to Pharoh, the Lord makes a second overture to the haughty monarch. *Let it become a dragon.* The more general word תַּנִּין is here employed instead of serpent (iv. 3), simply because this is not precisely the same sign that was shown to Moses in the mount of God. The latter was to be exhibited before the people for their conviction (iv. 1–5). The wonders to be done before Pharoh (iv. 21–23) were not the same, though two of them were similar, and seem to have included all the plagues which were afterwards wrought by the hand of Moses. The dragon is here, therefore, a different species of the serpent kind from that which appeared before the Israelites. The kind of animal on each occasion is that which would be most significant to the party concerned. The serpent would recall to Israel the serpent in Eden. The *tannin*, here rendered dragon, after the Septuagint, may have been the asp or basilisk, which was the emblem of royalty, or some other species of serpent equally significant to Pharoh and to Egypt. *The sages and the sorcerers; and the scribes.* The sages and scribes were summoned to Pharoh in the time of Joseph (Gen. xli. 8). It is probable that the scribes, or hieroglyphs, included all the classes of sages, and that the sages included the sorcerers. *They also did so with their enchantments.* It is certain that the charming of serpents has been long practised in Egypt and adjacent countries. The serpent called *hage* by the Arabs, apparently the asp, can be made to appear as dead or rigid as a stick, and of course restored to its natural state again. Now the Scripture does not care to determine whether a given work be done by natural or preternatural means. It grants merely that the thing in question has been done, when it is professed and appears to have been done. It does not concern the sacred writer or his readers how the impression was made on the senses, but only that in fact it was made. *And Aaron's rod swallowed up their rods.* This was a plain and palpable proof that the presence and power of God were with Moses. It may occur to the mind that it would have been as effectual a mode of convincing Pharoh to have restrained his magicians from playing their part before him. And undoubtedly the Almighty could have done so. But it is not his way to interfere by physical force with the free-agency of his responsible creatures (see Gen. iii. 1–7). If it had, he would have restrained Satan from entertaining the intention of resisting his Maker, or at least from afterwards intruding into the garden of Eden; and he would have withheld the woman's hand and desire from the fruit of the forbidden tree, and so actual sin might never have entered into heaven or earth. But where would have been free-agency, or by what means would the existence of creature morality have been known? Let us not imagine, therefore, that even in this small matter we can amend God's mode of procedure. *And Pharoh's heart was hardened.* It is plain that Pharoh had deluded himself by means of his magicians into the fancy that Moses is only a more skilful magician than his own. He attaches no proper weight to the disappearance of their rods, which was the testing miracle. *As the Lord had spoken.* It is the prerogative of the Omniscient to predict the conduct of men. Though we cannot explain this mystery, yet from the known character of a man we can sometimes make a shrewd guess at the way in which he will act in given circumstances.

The interview with the people, the first appearance before Pharoh, the two days after which the officers were beaten, the second interview with the people, and the second with Pharoh, cannot have occupied less than seven days, and therefore bring us to the 20th of January, or thereabout.

14–24. This second appeal having failed to make any impression on the heart of Pharoh, the Lord, as a third and last resort, directs Moses to the infliction of the first of a series of judicial strokes, increasing in intensity of effect, by which the refractory monarch is at length compelled to let the people go. The Jewish Rabbis have not been slow to observe the regular order in which these successive strokes are arranged, and the gradual advance which they make from the external to the internal, and from the mediate to the immediate hand of God. They are in number ten; which is one of the numbers denoting perfection. They are divided first into nine and one; the last one standing clearly apart from all the others, in the awful shriek of woe which it draws forth from every Egyptian home. The nine are arranged in threes. In the first of each three the warning is given to Pharoh in the morning (vii. 15, viii. 20, ix. 13). In the first and second of each three, the plague is announced beforehand (viii. 1; ix. 1, x. 1), in the third not (viii. 16, ix. 8, x. 21). At the third the magicians of Pharoh acknowledge the finger of God (viii. 19), at the sixth they cannot stand before Moses (ix. 11), and at the ninth Pharoh refuses to see the face of Moses any more (x. 28). In the first three Aaron uses the rod; in the second three it is not mentioned; in the third three Moses uses it, though in the last of them only his hand is mentioned. All these marks of order lie on the face of the narrative, and point to a deeper order of nature and reason out of which they spring.

The gradation in the severity of these strokes is no less obvious. In the first three no distinction is made among the inhabitants of the land; in the remaining seven a distinction is made between the Israelites, who are shielded from, and the Egyptians, who are exposed to, the stroke. In these seven which are peculiar to the Egyptians, the order is the reverse of that in the work of creation. Three refer to the animal creation, and three to the vegetable world, the support of animal life. The last of these six is darkness, the opposite of light, the product of the first day; and the seventh is death. The first three affect the health and comfort of man; the next three take away the staff of life; then comes death itself, and the work of destruction is complete.

To understand the deep import of the conflict before us, let us bear in mind that now for the first time since the dispersion of mankind the opposition between the children of God and the children of disobedience is coming out into broad daylight. Egypt, that was the kind fosterer of the chosen family, has now become the persecutor of Israel, and the avowed antagonist of God. The present struggle is therefore no raid for the gathering of booty, nor encounter between two rival nations, nor expedition for the selfish ends of an earthly ambition. It is the controversy between light and darkness, in which the God of heaven and earth manifests his presence and power on behalf of his people and against the defiant nation. This nation is for the time being the representative of all heathendom, which is the kingdom of the prince of darkness; and the battle now fought is the model and type of all future warfare between the seed of the woman and the seed of the serpent. Hence it rises to a transcendent importance in the ways of God with man, and fitly holds a place even in the preface to the ten commandments (xx. 2).

14–18. The announcement of the first plague. *Pharoh's heart is hard*, heavy (כָּבֵד), stupid and insensible to right reason and the real state of things. In the preceding verse it was described as hard, firm (יֶּחֱזַק), obstinate, and inflexible in its own selfish purpose. In the third verse of this chapter we find another word (קָשָׁה), rendered hard, applied to the heart, having the sense of obdurate, steeled against every tender or unselfish feeling. We have only the one equivalent for all these terms. *Go unto Pharoh in the morning.* It appears that Pharoh was wont to be out on the banks of the Nile in the morning, either for an airing, or to bathe in its waters. He could scarcely be supposed to visit the magnificent river without presenting to it some form of adoration. To the Nile Egypt owed its soil and its fertility. The inhabitants esteemed its waters the most delicious beverage, regarded itself as the source of life and prosperity to the nation, and soon began to venerate it as the deity of their land, identical with Osiris and Apis. Royalty would feel itself specially attracted by such a divinity, and bound to take a leading part in its worship. At this river's brink, therefore, was the fit place to meet Pharoh. *The rod which was turned into a serpent*, was the wand of power by which Moses was distinguished as the minister of heaven. *The* LORD. This is the name of present and active power, by which the God of the Hebrews is now to be practically signalized. Pharoh is reminded of the divine message, and of its rejection by him. 17. *In this thou shalt know that I am the Lord.* Pharoh is to know, at least experimentally, if not submissively and penitently, that grand sentence, "I am the LORD." *Behold I smite.* This was to take place immediately, in the very presence of Pharoh. *The water which is in the river*, that very river which was the object of all Egypt's praise and veneration! *And it shall be turned into blood*, blood poured out, and therefore dead, and spreading death instead of diffusing life. Hence the fish shall die, and the river become putrid and loathsome to the smell and the taste. This was sufficient to show, if it was necessary, that the Nile was not a god, but a mere inanimate creature.

19–24. The fulfilment now follows. *Say unto Aaron.* Pharoh is to learn the dignity of Moses, who commands Aaron his prophet to execute this miracle, and thus Moses is a god to Pharoh. *Take thy rod.* This is the rod of Moses (vs. 15) which Aaron bears. *Upon their rivers.* These appear to be the arms or mouths into which the Nile separates itself in the Delta, of which there were anciently seven. They are called "their rivers," that is, those of Egypt, which is here a collective noun denoting the nation. *Their streams* (διώρυγας Sept.) are the canals by which the land was irrigated, *Their ponds* are the marshy lakes, such as Mœris and Mareotis. *And every pool*, every small collection or reservoir for private or special use. *In all the land of Mizraim*, not only in the river and all its connected waters, but in the land, that is, as explained, in all cisterns, whether of wood or stone, for the filtration or preservation of the water. 20. *In the eyes of Pharoh, and of his servants.* A retinue of his courtiers was present on the occasion, including priests and magicians. *And all the water was turned into blood.* The Nile begins to rise about the end of June, and attains its highest point at the end of September. About the commencement of the rise it assumes a greenish hue, is disagreeable to the taste, unwholesome, and often totally unfit for drinking. It soon, however, becomes red and turbid, and continues in this state for three or more weeks. In this condition it is again healthy and fit for use. The miracle now performed was totally different from this annual change. For (1) it occured after the winter, not the summer, solstice; (2) the water was turned into blood, and not merely reddened by an admixture of red clay or animalcula; (3) the fish died, a result which did not follow from the periodical change of color; (4) the river stank, and became offensive, which it ceased to be when the ordinary redness made its appearance; (5) the stroke was arrested at the end of seven days, whereas the natural redness continued for at least three weeks; and (6) the change was brought on instantly at the word of command before the eyes of Pharoh. The calamity was appalling. The sweet waters of the Nile were the common beverage of Egypt. It abounded in all kinds of fish, which formed a principal article of diet for the inhabitants. It was revered as a god by Egypt. But now it was a putrid flood, from which they turned away with loathing. *And the scribes of Mizraim did so with their enchantments.* It has been asked where they got the water. We read (in verse 24) that "all Mizraim digged round about the river for water to drink." We have no doubt the hieroglyphs of Pharoh had wit enough to make the same experiment. The natives of a country in which the only river becomes periodically unfit for drinking would not be unfamiliar with the expedient of digging for water when the ordinary supply failed. These miracle-mongers confine themselves to the safe experiment of imitating on a small scale the work of God's servants. It would have been a clear demonstration of their superiority if they had countermanded the order of Moses, and converted the morbid mass into a limpid stream. This was what Egypt needed. Their trick was but a wretched mockery of help. 23. *Neither did he set his heart even to this.* When the will is strongly bent upon a foregone conclusion, a very small show of proof will beget conviction. The hieroglyphs managed to exhibit the appearance at least of changing a little water into blood. The headstrong monarch is confirmed in his resolve, and returns unmoved by Egypt's misery to his home. 25. *And seven days were fulfilled.* The "smiting" of the river was not a momentary act, but a process that lasted for seven days, and then was remitted. This carries us on to about the 27th of January. We are not informed what length of time was occupied with the other plagues; but it will serve the purpose of order and clearness to suppose that seven days elapsed during the course of each of the seven following.

This miracle was not merely a judicial, but a significant act. It marks the retribution of heaven. Pharoh orders the male infants of the Hebrews to be cast into the river, that they might perish there, and become food for its fish. That very river is changed into a stream of death. It displays also the folly of creature-worship. Pharoh adores the life-sustaining power of nature, as embodied in the majestic river before him. The God of nature transforms the running water into a river of death before his eyes. It demonstrates, in the way that was most striking to the Hebrew and the Egyptian, that the God of Israel was the true and only God of heaven and earth, and that all other objects of worship were but the creatures of God or the works of men's hands.

The next four verses of the Hebrew text, appended in Van der Hooght's edition to this chapter, are here, for the sake of convenience, transferred to the beginning of the next chapter, in accordance with a considerable number of MSS. and some early versions, including the Vulgate. This arrangement of the text is adopted in Walton's-Polyglott and the English Version.

## VI. THE SECOND THREE PLAGUES.—Ex. viii. 20-ix. 12.

### CHAP. VIII.—THE PLAGUES OF (2) FROGS, (3) LICE, AND (4) FLIES.

9. הִתְפָּאֵר. This form elsewhere denotes *to glory or vaunt oneself.* Here, however, the Sept. gives τάξαι, the Vulg. *constitue*, and the Targum of Onkelos, "set thou a time." The former meaning must, in the present passage, be taken in a pregnant sense, and include the latter. The radical signification of the verb, namely, to be *bright, clear*, however, will naturally yield the latter as a secondary meaning.

11

16. כִּנִּם כִּנִּים *lice.* In the Talmud כִּנָּה *a louse.* The Jewish interpreters (including Onkelos and Josephus), the Syriac, the Arabic, and the Talmud, give this meaning, which is supported by Bochart. The Sept. gives σκνῖφες, which Gesenius and others take to mean gnats. But κώνωψ or ἐμπίς is the gnat. The σκνίψ is said to be an ant that preys on figs, or an insect that lives under the bark of trees. Either of these bears more analogy to the louse than to the gnat or mosquito. The louse is also found "on men and beasts," while the gnat flies in the air. The former is also more clearly distinguished from the עָרֹב than the latter.

21. עָרֹב *fly.* The Sept. gives κυνόμυια, *dog-fly;* Aquila πάμμυια, *all kinds of flies.* It seems probable that as the כִּנָּה is a parasitical animal without wings, so the עָרֹב is a fly that has a long proboscis, piercing the skin, sucking the blood, and leaving a painful and highly inflamed wound. It may derive its name from עֶרֶב *the evening,* when it becomes most troublesome, or from עָרַב *to mix,* because the whole class of flies is included. Kalisch is strongly in favor of the beetle (*Blatta Orientalis*); but this does not attack men. In the absence of any very distinct aid from usage, the word being found only in this passage and in Ps. lxxviii. 45, cv. 31, it seems better to adhere to the generic term, fly, which accords best with all the circumstances noted. It fastens on man, enters houses, and infests fields.

VIII. 1. And the LORD said unto Moses, Go in to Pharoh, and say unto him, Thus saith the LORD, Let my people go and serve me. 2. And if thou refuse to let them go, behold, I will smite all thy border with frogs. 3. And the river shall swarm with frogs, and they shall come up, and go in to thy house, and to thy sleeping-room, and upon thy bed, and into the house of thy servants, and on thy people, and into thine ovens, and into thy kneading-troughs. 4. And on thee and on thy people and on all thy servants shall the frogs come up. 5. And the LORD said unto Moses, Say unto Aaron, Stretch forth thy hand, with thy rod, over the rivers and over the streams and over the ponds, and bring up the frogs upon the

land of Mizraim. 6. And Aaron stretched forth his hand over
the waters of Mizraim, and the frogs came up and covered the
land of Mizraim. 7. And the scribes did so with their
enchantments, and brought up frogs upon the land of Miz-
raim.

8. And Pharoh called for Moses and Aaron, entreat the LORD
and let him take away the frogs from me and from my peo-
ple; and I will let the people go and sacrifice unto the LORD.
9. And Moses said unto Pharoh, Prescribe unto me when I
shall entreat for thee and for thy servants and for thy people,
to cut off the frogs from thee and thy houses; only in the
river shall they remain. 10. And he said, To-morrow. And
he said, Be it according to thy word; that thou mayest know
that there is none like unto the LORD our God. 11. And the
frogs shall depart from thee, and from thy houses, and from
thy servants, and from thy people; only in the river shall
they remain. 12. And Moses and Aaron went out from Pha-
roh; and Moses cried unto the LORD on account of the frogs
which he had brought on Pharoh. 13. And the LORD did
according to the word of Moses: and the frogs died out of the
houses, out of the courts, and out of the fields. 14. And they
gathered them together in heaps; and the land stank. 15.
And Pharoh saw that there was respite; and he hardened
his heart and hearkened not unto them, as the Lord had
spoken.

§ 6.

16. And the LORD said unto Moses, Say unto Aaron, Stretch
forth thy rod, and smite the dust of the land, and it shall
become lice in all the land of Mizraim. 17. And they did so:
and Aaron stretched out his hand, with his rod, and smote the
dust of the land, and it became lice on man and on beast: all
the dust of the land became lice in all the land of Mizraim.
18. And the scribes did so with their enchantments to bring

forth the lice, and could not: and the lice were on man and on beast. 19. And the scribes said unto Pharoh, This is the finger of God. And Pharoh's heart was hardened, and he hearkened not unto them, as the Lord had spoken. § 7.

20. And the LORD said unto Moses, Rise up early in the morning, and stand before Pharoh; lo, he cometh forth to the water: and say unto him, Thus saith the LORD, Let my people go and serve me. 21. For if thou wilt not let my people go, behold I send upon thee, and upon thy servants, and upon thy people, and into thy houses, the fly; and the houses of Mizraim shall be full of the fly, and even the ground whereon they are. 22. And I will sever in that day the land of Goshen, on which my people stand, that the fly may not be there; that thou mayest know that I am the LORD in the midst of the land. 23. And I will put a division between my people and thy people: to-morrow shall this sign be. 24. And the LORD did so, and there came a grievous fly into Pharoh's house and the house of his servants; and in all the land of Mizraim the land was destroyed by reason of the fly.

25. And Pharoh called Moses and Aaron, and said, Go ye, sacrifice to your God in the land. 26. And Moses said, It is not meet so to do; for we shall sacrifice the abomination of Mizraim to the Lord our God: lo, we shall sacrifice the abomination of Mizraim before their eyes, and will they not stone us? 27. We will go three days' journey into the wilderness, and sacrifice to the LORD our God, as he shall say unto us. 28. And Pharoh said, I will let you go and sacrifice to the LORD your God in the wilderness; only ye shall not go very far away: entreat for me. 29. And Moses said, Behold, I go out from thee and entreat the Lord, and the fly shall depart from Pharoh, from his servants, and from his people to-morrow: only let not Pharoh deal falsely any more, not to let the

people go to sacrifice to the LORD. 30. And Moses went out
from Pharoh, and entreated the LORD. 31. And the LORD did
according to the word of Moses, and removed the fly from
Pharoh, from his servants, and from his people: not one
remained. 32. And Pharoh hardened his heart at this time
also; neither did he let the people go. ¶ 11.

In this chapter we have the plagues of the frogs, the lice, and the fly grouped together, probably because they all belong to the smaller tribes of animals. In the conception of the author, however, it is evident that the two former, with the change of water into blood, constitute the first triad of judicial visitations, as two of them are announced beforehand and the third not, according to a law which is observed in each triad.

1–15. The plague of frogs. *Go in to Pharoh.* This infliction is to be announced to Pharoh in his palace, as the former was by the river side (vii. 15). The request for leave to depart is repeated, and in case of refusal the plague of frogs is threatened. 3, 4. *The river shall swarm with frogs.* Frogs abound in Egypt. They appear, when the river overflows the country, in all the pools of water. The common frog, the green or edible frog (*rana esculenta*), and the speckled frog (*rana punctata*), are found in Egypt. The number of eggs in the spawn of a single frog varies from one thousand to fifteen hundred. The appearance of these animals in considerable numbers on land is generally preceded and accompanied by heavy storms of rain (Kitto's Cyclopaedia). Such an accompaniment would render the visitation more appalling to the Egyptians.

The phraseology here is similar to that employed in the six days' creation (Gen. i. 20). Miracles are not the less supernatural because their products are natural objects previously well-known, as frogs, or are placed in ordinary circumstances, as frogs in the standing water of a river, or are even arranged in natural succession, as frogs in the Nile after its change of color. The Author of nature does not put himself out of all relation with the laws he has imposed on nature when he introduces a new effect of his power into the sphere of nature. His wondrous deeds come under the law of reason, and therefore fall in with the law of nature. The miracle consists in the event described, (1) happening accordingly; (2) in the circumstances predicted, or at the word of command; (3) without any ordinary causes either existing or having had time to operate; and (4) further, it may be at an unusual season, and in an unusually magnified form. The last condition, however, is not absolutely necessary. The event is described with considerable minuteness in these two verses. It is evidently aggravated beyond the usual form. The frogs venture into the houses, the sleeping apartments, the very beds. They penetrate into the ovens and kneading-troughs. The baking oven was often a round hole, three feet deep, and plastered with mud. This was heated by burning brushwood in it. The dough was then spread with the hand on its sides, and speedily baked (Layard's Nineveh). A pot of earthenware, of nearly the same shape, was also employed for the same purpose, the fire being placed within, and the dough applied without. Into such a vessel or pit, when unemployed, the frogs might easily enter. They even leap upon the person (" on thee "), probably when reclining for repose. The annoyance of such a visitation can hardly be conceived.

5–7. Aaron stretching forth his hand, with the wand of power, is here the sign, equivalent to the word of command. *The rivers*, see vii. 19. *Upon the land.* Their usual place was the river. *Covered the land.* This extraordinary abundance on the land accounts for their intrusion into the apartments and utensils of the people. Here the event takes place, according to the description, at the sign of command, without any ordinary cause. Frogs are not usually spawned, transformed into tadpoles, and then into frogs, and spread over a country in the course of a few minutes. The magicians imitated this miracle, no doubt at the summons of Pharoh, it is needless to inquire how. It would have been more to the purpose if by their enchantments they had cleared the land of them.

8–15. The removal of the frogs. *And Pharoh called for Moses and Aaron.* He is at length moved. Having at his command all the resources of sovereignty, he may have been tolerably supplied with well-water, even when the river flowed with blood. He did not feel much personal inconvenience from the former plague. But he cannot escape the presence and contact of these loathsome creatures. He suffers more from their offensive intrusion than his meanest subjects. He must take all means to escape from this unutterable pest. His hieroglyphs fail him in the hour of need. Else, he would never have had recourse to Moses and Aaron. *Entreat the Lord.* Here is an explicit acknowledgment of the Lord forced from him who said, "Who is the Lord, that I should obey his voice? I know not the Lord" (vs. 2). *Let him take away the frogs.* He only who sent them can take them away. This is Pharoh's present experience. *And I will let the people go.* He now humbly promises, who once and again had said, "I will not let Israel go." His former language is now completely revoked. It remains to be seen whether the will corresponds with the word.

9–11. *Prescribe unto me when I shall entreat for thee.* The original means, either "glory over me, defy me, by setting the time when I am to do this "or determine for me." The former is a challenge to Pharoh to defy him (Moses) to work the miracle at a prescribed time. The latter is simply leaving the time of performance to be determined by Pharoh. This is the easier sense, and is involved in the former. *Only in the river*, the element in which they are usually seen, when they appear at all. When they retire for hibernation they are not open to common observation,

12–15. *And the Lord did according to the word of Moses.* This is the second and decisive part of the miracle. The frogs suddenly die out of the land, are gathered in heaps or measures, and emit a grievous stench. Thus at the word of Moses they come, and at his word they go. There is a power here above nature. The God of nature is with Moses. He accomplishes what the magicians did not attempt. Pharoh, however, thinks not of this demonstration of the divine power and mercy, but only of the "respite." On obtaining relief his obduracy of heart returns. His promise, it now appears, was from the lip, not the heart.

The plague of frogs was fraught with its own lessons to all parties concerned. One of the feeblest and most harmless of living creatures was by its miraculous multiplication made a source of greater distress to Pharoh than even the turning of the Nile into blood; compelling him to confess the impotence of his own gods and their attendants, to acknowledge the omnipotence of Jehovah, to implore the intercession of his ministers, and to promise all that was demanded of him. God has at hand in the weakest things the most abundant means and the most unexpected ways of chastising the transgressor. The frog, moreover, had a certain significance to Egypt. It was the symbol of human life in embryo. In the hieroglyphics it sat on a ring, one of the emblems of life, and from its back rose a palm branch, the symbol of the month or of time. The frog-headed god is a form of Pthah, the creative or formative principle. Whatever mysterious connection the frog had with life in the mind of an Egyptian, it is evident that the reptile lives and dies at the will of the God of Moses. Whatever divinity or divine attribute was ascribed to it, or denoted by it, the frog itself is but an inferior creature of the true God, moving in a sphere immeasurably beneath that of man, and unconsciously fulfilling its humble function in the economy of nature. This base creature is now made to bend the refractory will of proud Pharoh.

16–19. The plague of lice. We are now come to the third plague. No warning is here given to Pharoh. His treacherous dealing had forfeited even this measure of forbearance. *Say unto Aaron.* As in the former two of this triad, the performance is assigned to Aaron. *Smite the dust of the land.* The frogs had their source in the rivers and ponds; the lice in the dust of the land. The latter plague is thus the complement of the former. *And it shall become lice.* The reasons for retaining this version have been already assigned; to which it is only necessary to add that vermin of the kind is one of the common annoyances of Egypt. Herodotus tells us (ii. 37) that the priests shave their whole body every other day, that no lice or other impure thing may adhere to them when they are engaged in the service of the gods. It is manifest that this species of vermin was particularly disgusting to the Egyptians; and it is said that in the space of a year one of these creatures will produce five thousand eggs or nits. *On man and on beast.* This is one of the aggravations of this plague. The stream of blood was a distant object, which could be alleviated by digging for water. The frogs were a loathsome and disgusting nuisance in the houses and on the furniture of the people; but still they did not ordinarily come into contact with their persons, or inflict pain. The lice, on the other hand, inhabited the skin, sucked the blood, caused a disagreeable itching, created a feeling of uncleanness, and threatened to become a disease of the most frightful description. *And could not.* The magicians of Pharoh attempt to imitate this miracle, but fail. This is a second point in which this miracle surpasses the others. Even so minute an animal as this they are unable to produce. *This is the finger of God.* They are obliged to confess that this was the effect of divine power. It is obvious, however, that this was said to cover their defeat; and therefore their meaning is, that this visitation was brought on by the ordinary providence and power of God, and not by any magic art or miraculous power, either of Moses and Aaron, or of themselves. This accounts for the persistence of Pharoh in his obstinacy. Adopting the solution of his counsellors, he regards this event no longer as a sign or wonder wrought by the ministers of Jehovah, but as a mere effect of the general providence of God, and therefore to be borne with patience so long as it should last.

This plague was not without its weighty lessons. A still more minute and contemptible animal was now made a source of extreme annoyance to the Egyptians. It infested all men, priests as well as others, and therefore unfitted them for entering the temples of their gods. It appeared on all beasts, sacred as well as profane, and therefore on all the animals that were regarded as divinities; and it defiled everything it touched. Thus contempt was brought on everything that was vainly imagined to be sacred among the Egyptians. Next, the miracle-mongers of Egypt are confessedly unable to produce as well as to remove this grievous and loathsome infliction; and hence, we may infer they were equally unable to call into or bid out of existence any other conceivable thing. Lastly, their ready insinuation that this was an event coming from the hand of providence, and not a judgment from Jehovah, inflicted through his ministers, is accepted by Pharoh, not because it is well founded, but because it accords with his wish.

viii. 20.–ix. 12. This passage contains the second triad of plagues, in which God acts without the intervention of any sign on the part of his servants. In the third, indeed, Moses sprinkles the ashes towards heaven, but still makes no sign with the rod. Thus it is made plain that the true wonder-worker is not tied to any mode of introducing his wonders. From this time forward, also, a distinction is put between the Israelites and the Egyptians. The former seem to have been partial sufferers in the first three plagues. They needed the chastisement; and their habitual attachment to the land of their birth was gradually abated by the afflictions thus associated with it.

20–32. The plague of flies inflicted. *Rise up early in the morning.* This plague, like the first, is announced to Pharoh in the morning, and by the river's side. Leave to depart is requested for the people of God, as on other occasions. *The fly.* This term serves to denote a kind of insect that alights on the skin or the leaves of plants, by its bite inflicting pain in the one case, and causing destruction in the other. The swarms of flies in Egypt are usually numerous and excessively annoying. They alight on the moist parts of the eyelids and nostrils, and inflict wounds that produce great pain, swelling, and inflammation. They are also ruinous to the plants in which they lay their eggs. Philo (vit. Mos. ii. p. 110) describes the dog-fly or gad-fly as a grievous pest of Egypt. Gnats and mosquitoes are also abundant and virulent. A plague of such creatures would cause immense suffering and desolation. *Even the ground whereon they are.* The whole land in which the Egyptians dwell will be infested with this fly. 22. *And I will sever,* make distinct, and even wonderful, both of which thoughts are implied in the verb. The land of Goshen, in which the Israelites dwell (stand), shall be free from this and the following inflictions. *That thou mayest know.* Everything God does has a lesson for the intelligent observer. *I am the Lord in the midst of the land.* As the stroke falls upon the Egyptians, and not on the Israelites, it is manifest, (1) that it has come from the God of the Hebrews; (2) that this great Being has equal power in Egypt as elsewhere; and (3) that therefore he is Jehovah, the Creator and Upholder of all things, the one only true and living God. *A division* (פְּדוּת), a release, an untying of the connection between them. *To-morrow.* At a fixed point of time shall this plague make its appearance. Time for reflection is thus given to Pharoh. The miraculous nature of the event is also demonstrated. *The sign.* It is appropriately called a sign, as it bears evidence to all the important truths which have been already noticed. *A grievous fly,* grievous on account of its numbers and noxious effects. *The land was destroyed.*

The verdure with which the earth was now covered was seriously damaged by its attacks.

25–32. The removal of the fly on the intercession of Moses and Aaron. *And Pharoh called Moses and Aaron.* His conjurors are now no longer mentioned. He is compelled to appeal again to the servants of Jehovah. *Go ye, sacrifice to your God in the land.* The time for sacrifice is here conceded, but not the place. *It is not meet so to do.* It is not right in a moral point of view. The reason is assigned in the following verse. *The abomination of Mizraim* is either that which Egypt abominates, or that which the Lord abominates in Egypt. In this case, as the Egyptians were idolaters, the two meanings in a great measure coincide. The matter and manner of the Hebrew sacrifice would be an abomination to the Egyptian. The matter, for the cow was sacred to Isis, the goat was worshipped by the Mendesians, the ram by the Thebans, and the bull by the Memphians and others; the manner, because the minute and punctilious ritual of the Egyptians in regard to the cleanness of the victims would not be observed. The sacrificing of animals whom they worshipped, and without the regulations of a superstitious purity, would prompt them to stone the worshippers. On the other hand, the bulls of Memphis, of Heliopolis, and of Hermonthis, the ram of Thebes, the goat of Mendes, and the other animals worshipped by the Egyptians, could not but be an abomination to the holy and living and true God. 27. *As he shall say unto us.* The Lord had not yet prescribed the manner of sacrifice, but only the place. 28–30. Pharoh now gives a reluctant permission, on which Moses promises the removal of the fly by his intercession, and admonishes Pharoh not to be false a second time to his word. 31, 32. The Lord removes the fly at the appointed time (to-morrow) with as much ease as he had brought it. This is the second and most decisive part of the miracle. Pharoh having no moral principle, returns to his obduracy of heart as soon as the pressure is removed.

Even creatures that came under the designation of the fly were connected with the animal worship of the Egyptians. The beetle (*scarabeus*) was one of the most common sacred emblems of Egypt, and represented the sun. The large class of diminutive creatures to which it belongs is here raised up for the chastisement of the nation, and removed again at the intercession of Moses. The relief of the

Israelites from the plague was calculated to detach them still more from the nation and territory of Egypt, and attach them with a more enlightened confidence and veneration to the God of their fathers.

## VII. THIRD THREE PLAGUES.—Ex. ix. 13-x.

### CHAP. IX.—THE PLAGUES OF (5) PESTILENCE, (6) BOILS, (7) HAIL.

3. דֶּבֶר *pestilence;* r. *follow, persecute, destroy.* It applies to men as well as cattle.

8. פִּיחַ *ashes, dust, αἰθάλη* (Sept.); r. *blow away.* כִּבְשָׁן *furnace.* Smelting furnace, or limekiln (Kimchi). תַּנּוּר *baking oven.*

9. אָבָק *fine dust,* or *powder;* r. *turn, whirl.*

10. שְׁחִין *boil, enflamed swelling.* אֲבַעְבֻּעֹת *blains, pustules; φλυκτίδες* (Sept.); r. *burst* or *gush forth.*

IX. 1. Then the LORD said unto Moses, Go in unto Pharoh,
and tell him, Thus saith the LORD, the God of the Hebrews,
Let my people go and serve me. 2. For if thou refuse to let
them go, and wilt hold them still, 3. Behold, the hand of
the LORD is upon thy cattle which is in the field, upon the
horses, upon the asses, upon the camels, upon the oxen, and
upon the sheep, as a very grievous pestilence. 4. And the
LORD shall sever between the cattle of Israel and the cattle of
Mizraim, and nothing shall die of all that belongs to the sons
of Israel. 5. And the LORD appointed a set time, saying, To-
morrow the LORD shall do this thing in the land. 6. And the
LORD did this thing on the morrow; and all the cattle of Miz-
raim died; but of the cattle of the sons of Israel died not one.
7. And Pharoh sent, and, behold, not even one of the cattle of
Israel was dead. And Pharoh's heart was hardened, and he
did not let the people go. ¶ 12.

8. And the LORD said unto Moses and unto Aaron, Take to

you the hands full of ashes of the furnace, and let Moses sprinkle it toward the sky in the sight of Pharoh. 9. And it shall become dust in all the land of Mizraim; and shall be a boil breaking forth with blains upon man and upon beast in all the land of Mizraim. 10. And they took ashes of the furnace and stood before Pharoh, and Moses sprinkled it toward the sky; and it became a boil breaking forth with blains upon man and upon beast. 11. And the scribes could not stand before Moses because of the boil: for the boil was upon the scribes and upon all Mizraim. 12. And the LORD hardened Pharoh's heart, and he hearkened not unto them; as the LORD had spoken unto Moses. § 8.

13. And the LORD said unto Moses, Rise up early in the morning and stand before Pharoh, and say unto him, Thus saith the LORD, the God of the Hebrews, Let my people go and serve me. 14. For at this time I will send all my plagues into thy heart, and on thy servants, and on thy people; that thou mayest know that there is none like me in all the earth. 15. For now I had stretched out my hand and smitten thee and thy people with the pestilence; and thou wouldst have been cut off from the earth. 16. But for this have I raised thee up, to show thee my power, and to declare my name in all the earth. 17. As yet thou exaltest thyself against my people, that thou wilt not let them go. 18. Behold at this time to-morrow I will rain a very grievous hail, such as hath not been in Mizraim from the day of its foundation even until now. 19. Send now, therefore, and bring in thy cattle and all that thou hast in the field: for upon every man or beast which is found in the field, and is not gathered into the house, the hail shall come down, and they shall die. 20. He that feared the word of the LORD among the servants of Pharoh made his servants and his cattle flee into the houses. 21.

And he that set not his heart to the word of the LORD left his servants and his cattle in the field. ¶ 13.

22. And the LORD said unto Moses, Stretch forth thy hand toward heaven, and let there be hail in all the land of Mizraim, upon man and upon beast, and upon every herb of the field in the land of Mizraim. 23. And Moses stretched forth his rod toward heaven; and the LORD sent thunder and hail, and fire fell upon the earth; and the LORD rained hail upon the land of Mizraim. 24. And there was hail, and fire flashing amidst the hail, very grievous, such as was not in all the land of Mizraim since it became a nation. 25. And the hail smote in all the land of Mizraim all that was in the field from man to beast, and the hail smote every herb of the field, and brake every tree of the field. 26. Only in the land of Goshen, where the sons of Israel were, was there no hail.

27. And Pharoh sent and called Moses and Aaron, and said unto them, I have sinned this time: the LORD is righteous, and I and my people are wicked. 28. Entreat the LORD, and let there be no more thunderings of God and hail; and I will let you go, and ye shall stay no longer. 29. And Moses said unto him, When I come out of the city, I will spread abroad my hands unto the LORD: the thunderings shall cease, neither shall there be any more hail, that thou mayest know that the earth is the LORD'S. 30. And as for thee and thy servants, I know that ye do not fear the Lord God. 31. And the flax and the barley were smitten, for the barley was in the ear, and the flax was bolled. 32. And the wheat and the spelt were not smitten, for they are late. 33. And Moses came out of the city from Pharoh, and spread abroad his hands to the LORD; and the thunders and hail ceased, and rain was not poured on the earth. 34. And Pharoh saw that the rain and the hail and the thunders were ceased, and he sinned yet

more, and hardened his heart, he and his servants. 35. And Pharoh's heart was hardened, neither did he let the sons of Israel go; as the LORD had spoken by the hand of Moses.

15. ¶¶¶ 14.

In this chapter we have the plagues of pestilence, boils, and hail. The first two complete the second triad and close the section in which they are contained.

1–7. The plague of pestilence. *Go in unto Pharoh.* As in the second plague of the former triad (viii. 1), *And wilt hold them still.* This is added to mark the pertinacity of Pharoh, notwithstanding the severe chastisements he had already suffered for his obstinacy. 3. *The hand of the Lord.* This will be more manifest, as no waving of the rod or hand precedes the appearance of the miracle. *Upon thy cattle* (מִקְנֶה), a general name for all domestic animals, that constitute a great part of the *property* of a pastoral or agricultural people. *Which is in the field.* This limits the extent of the pestilence to the animals that were in the open air. *Horses.* The first notice of these is in Gen. xlvii. 17. Egypt was celebrated for its horses, which appear on its sculptures. They were employed in the chariot of war or state. The object of worship at Memphis, Heliopolis, and Hermonthis was the *bull*; at Thebes the *ram*, at Mendes the *goat*. The sheep here (צֹאן) are the small cattle, including the goats. *Asses* are mentioned on the monuments of Egypt. They were used for riding or draught. The Bactrian camel has two humps, the Arabian one. The latter was known and employed on the border-land between Egypt and Arabia; but has not been found on the ancient monuments of the former country. Its presence here favors the supposition that the northeast part of Egypt was at the time under a dynasty of the Shepherd kings, who came from Arabia. *A very grievous pestilence.* We follow the original here in using the more general term, pestilence (דֶּבֶר), as we find it also employed in reference to the human species (vs. 15). The miracle consists in its being very grievous, in being sent at an appointed time (vs. 5) and in being limited to the cattle of the Egyptians. A severance takes place here, as in the preceding plague (viii. 22). *To-morrow.* A set time of inflicting the stroke is as significant of the divine intervention as a set time of withdrawing it (viii. 29). 6. *All the cattle of Mizraim.* This is to be limited to the kinds already mentioned, and also to those of them that were *in the field* (vs. 3). Wilkinson (Ancient Egyptians, 2d series, I. p. 96) informs us that some animals were stall-fed among the Egyptians. This explains the limitation, "in the field," and the existence of some cattle among the Egyptians after the pestilence had done its work (vs. 19). 7. *And Pharoh's heart was hardened.* We may suppose that the pestilence among the cattle did not much affect him personally, and that he was irritated to find that the cattle of the Israelites had escaped.

Hitherto the plagues had given great personal annoyance, but had not involved much loss of property. But now the hand of the corrector comes down upon the main branch of the country's wealth. Cattle, besides being a chief means of food and clothing, were employed by the Egyptians in treading the seed into the ground, in treading out the corn, and in conveying the produce of the country to the place of storage. The destruction of cattle was therefore a serious loss to the Egyptian farmer. The hand of the Lord was manifest here in distinguishing the cattle of Israel from that of Mizraim.

8–12. The plague of boils. This third plague of the second triad is not announced to Pharoh. *Ashes of the furnace.* This is taken to be the fine ash or soot of some of the furnaces for the purposes of art that stood in the open air. *Dust,* a fine powder floating in the air, and pregnant with disease. *A boil* (שְׁחִין). This is afterwards mentioned as *the boil of Mizraim,* and seems therefore to be an endemic disease. Various conjectures have been offered as to its nature, but none of them is satisfactory. The description of it bears some resemblance to elephantiasis, a dreadful form of leprosy prevalent in Egypt, so called because it makes the feet swollen and stiff, like the Elephant's feet. But this disease does not attack the brute creation. *The scribes could not stand before Moses.* At the third plague the magicians of Pharoh failed in their enchantments, and acknowledged the finger of God. At this, the second third, they hasten away from Moses covered with shame and humiliation. The punctilious attention of the Egyptians to personal cleanliness is noted by Herodotus. In particular, the priests shave their whole body every other day. Their dress is entirely of linen. They bathe twice every day in cold water, and twice each night (Herodotus, ii. 37). Their confusion and distress therefore must have been great to find themselves now covered with an eruptive disease, that mocked all their precautions, and rendered them unfit for their sacerdotal duties. *And the Lord hardened Pharoh's heart.* Here it is to be observed that the very means that would have brought an unabiassed and unclouded mind to conviction and submission only begat a stolid and infatuated obstinacy in the monarch of Egypt. The course of the divine interposition has been one of uniform mildness and forbearance, only proceeding to judicial chastisements when negotiation would not avail, and advancing gradually to severer measures only when the more gentle were disregarded. His obduracy is now come to such a pitch of stupidity that we cannot catch a shadow of reason for his conduct.

Hitherto the Lord has tried to move the heart of the king by a series of external privations and penalties. The want of water, the presence of a loathsome reptile, the creeping and biting of a nauseous insect, the fierce stinging of the fly swarm, and the loss occasioned by the pestilence among the cattle, have been all in vain. Now the life is menaced. A boil breaking out in blains or open sores has fallen upon man and beast. We may be sure that the sacred animals that were objects of worship would not escape this plague; and we may imagine what consternation this would create throughout all Egypt.

This closes the second section relating to the plagues. Allowing a week for each of the six plagues already recorded, and twenty days for the previous transactions, we are brought to the 3d of March at the end of the sixth plague.

ix. 13 – x. This section contains the record of the next three plagues — the hail, the locusts, and the darkness. These rise in terrific severity above all that precede them.

13–21. The hail threatened. As usual in the first of each triad, Moses is to meet Pharoh at the usual time, and probably in the usual place, to demand the release of the people, and announce the immediate consequence of refusal. *All my plagues.* This expression occurring in the announcement of the first of another three, is an indication of the ternary arrangement. It refers to all the following manifestations of the divine power, at least to those which form the third series of plagues. *Into thy heart.* By the following judgments Pharoh will be at length brought to feel in his heart the folly and guilt of resisting the Almighty. *None like me in all the earth.* The Egyptians, like the other Gentiles, had now wandered away from the true notion concerning God which had come down from their forefathers. The false gods, fashioned after the vain fancies of a disorderly imagination, bore no moral resemblance to the true God. Pharoh is now to learn this great fact in his experience, if not in his understanding and his heart. *I had stretched out my hand.* I might have smitten thee and thy people with the pestilence as easily as I smote thy cattle, and thou wouldest have been annihilated, thyself and all thy opposition to my reasonable demands. The Lord here gives us some insight into the theory of his administration. It is instructive, corrective, and in the last resort punitive; but in no case merely destructive of moral agents He that would sweep into instant annihilation all the opponents of his will has no idea of God's principle of action or mode of dealing with his rational creatures. Not even a particle of irrational matter is bidden out of existence by the great God who called it into being. Still less will his moral and responsible creatures be sent out of existence, or at once forced into submission by the high hand of an irresistible despotism. He will approach them with love, with reason, with justice. Only when such methods fail, will he have recourse to a patient and duly tempered correction. And Pharoh will be an example to all contemporary nations, and, through the books of Moses, to all succeeding generations, of the mercy, patience, forbearance, justice, and holiness of God. *But for this have I raised thee up;* not stricken thee down with the pestilence, but preserved thee from it in my long-suffering patience. *To show thee my power.* To convince thee while thou livest, and there is yet time to repent, if thou wilt be convinced, of my power, my eternal power and Godhead, in contrast with all impotent and imaginary gods in whom thou hast heretofore trusted. *And to declare my name in all the earth,* to make thy history a perpetual lesson for the instruction of all mankind in the knowledge of my name, my real nature, which has come to be so grievously and fatally misapprehended. *As yet thou exaltest thyself.* Thou still persistest in thy haughty refusal.

There is a sublime dignity in the continued moderation which this expostulation displays.

17–21. *At this time to-morrow.* Pharoh might have learned by this time that the Lord is punctual to his time. *A very grievous hail.* Showers of hail in the winter season were not unknown in Egypt, as even the present passage informs us. But this is to be such as had not been since Egypt was founded, that is, since it became a nation (vs. 24). *Send now, therefore, and bring in thy cattle.* The Lord here remembers mercy, and leaves an opening for faith to assert itself. He looks for believers even among the Egyptians; and he did not look in vain. This warning divided them into two classes, the one fearing the Lord, and the other still disregarding him.

22–26. On the morrow the performance comes. *Stretch forth thy hand,* with the wand of power (vs. 23). Moses is described as the agent in these three plagues (x. 12, 21). *Thunder,* voices (קֹלֹת), voices of God, as Pharoh expresses it (vs. 28). The primitive mind regarded the thunder-peal as the sublimest utterance of the God of nature. Philosophy and theology alike bow to the solemn sentiment that the heavens declare the glory of God. The thunder is but one note in the great accord of universal nature in which he speaks to us of himself. *Fire fell upon the earth,* the lightning-flash, of which the thunder-clap was the accompaniment. *Flashing,* darting suddenly, and *seizing* upon its object. *Smote every herb, and brake every tree.* The lightning and hail that killed every man and beast were sufficient to destroy the green leaves and stalks of the herbs, and the branches as well as foliage of the trees. *Only in the land of Goshen.* Here again Israel is exempted from the effects of this judgment, as we have no doubt they were from the preceding one, though it be not mentioned.

27–30. Pharoh is again overwhelmed by this judgment, and for the third time promises submission. *I have sinned this time.* Now, at length, I acknowledge that I have sinned. The loss of his servants and cattle, with the awful lightnings and thunderings, brings a dawning conviction into his mind that God is right and he is wrong. The expression of this in words is needed, after having twice asked and obtained remission, and as often falsified his word. *Let there be no more thunderings of God.* Let it be enough (רַב), and no more of these awful voices. *And ye shall stay no longer.* A promise of immediate dismissal. True to his character of giving heed to the latest and feeblest appeal to his mercy, the Lord is ready to withdraw his heavy hand. *When I come out of the city.* We learn here incidentally that Pharoh dwelt in a city. The probability is in favor of On or Bubastis, from their proximity to the Nile and the situation of the Israelites. *That thou mayest know that the earth is the Lord's.* Another proof of this great fact is to be afforded to Pharoh, if he have only the heart to understand the lesson. 30. *I know that ye do not fear the Lord God.* Moses has learned much since he entered upon the task of delivering the Lord's people. He can now speak with fluency and precision. The Lord has enabled him to judge of the character of Pharoh and his court. Here, for the first time since Gen. ii. 3, have we Jehovah followed by Elohim in the absolute form. This is not without its significance. The grand primeval truth that the God of the Hebrews is the absolute and eternal God (אֱלֹהִים) antecedent to all creation, and therefore the only Creator and Upholder of heaven and earth (יְהוָֹה), has been presented in the most conspicuous manner to the mind of Pharoh. Moses therefore seasonably intimates by the juxtaposition of the two names that Jehovah, the God of the Hebrews, is no local or national God, but the sole and absolute God. He at the same time intimates that the mere acknowledgment of this vital truth in words is not sufficient. It is the acknowledgment of the heart only that will influence the conduct and issue in spontaneous obedience to the will of God,

31–35. The remission effected. The *flax and the barley.* Egypt was celebrated for its linen. Its mummies we find swathed in this fabric. Barley was extensively sown in this country, and was used for feeding cattle, and making bread and a kind of ale. The sowing time was in October and November. The flax and barley were ripe about the end of March, and therefore the one was in the ear and the other bolled about the beginning of that month. *The wheat and the spelt.* Egypt was most prolific in wheat, which was often seven-headed, and yielded a hundredfold. It was in some measure the granary of the ancient world, as well as the great mart for flax or linen. Rye was not a grain cultivated in Egypt, as it belongs to colder countries. The grain here rendered spelt may have been that which is now known as doora. These grains ripened a month later than the barley and flax. This crop was therefore only injured, not destroyed, by the hail. *He sinned yet more.* Pharoh had confessed his sin, but it appears that this confession was extorted from him not by a penitent heart, but by an overpowering terror (vs. 30). *As the Lord had spoken by the hand of Moses.* This announcement of Moses (vs. 30) was calculated to convince Pharoh, if he had been disposed to give heed to it, that he with whom he had to do was the searcher of hearts, and could not be deceived by a hypocritical pretence.

By this act of judgment a moiety of the crop of Egypt was destroyed, while the minds of Pharoh and his courtiers were evidently awe-struck by the thunder-storm. It is manifest that the Lord is step by step advancing to the universal desolation of Egypt. The supernatural character of this storm is demonstrated by its coming at the time predicted, ceasing at the intercession of Moses, and confining itself to the land of the Egyptians.

## CHAP. X.—THE PLAGUES OF (8) LOCUSTS, (9) DARKNESS.

4. אַרְבֶּה *locust.* This is so called from its numbers; r. *be many.* It is supposed to be the *gryllus gregarius*, or passage-locust.

X. 1. And the Lord said unto Moses, Go in unto Pharoh:
for I have hardened his heart and the heart, of his servants,
that I may put these my signs upon him. 2. And that thou
mayest tell in the ears of thy son, and of thy son's son, that
which I wrought in Mizraim, and my signs which I put upon
them; and ye shall know that I am the Lord. 3. And Moses
and Aaron went in unto Pharoh, and said unto him, Thus
saith the Lord, the God of the Hebrews, How long dost thou
refuse to humble thyself before me? Let my people go and
serve me. 4. For if thou refuse to let my people go, behold,
to-morrow will I bring the locust into thy border. 5. And
they shall cover the face of the land, so that one cannot see

the land, and they shall eat the residue of that which is escaped, which remained unto you from the hail, and shall eat every tree which groweth for you out of the field: 6. And they shall fill thy houses, and the houses of all thy servants, and the houses of all Mizraim; which neither thy fathers nor thy father's fathers have seen since the day that they were upon the ground unto this day. And he turned and went out from Pharoh.

7. And Pharoh's servants said unto him, How long shall this man be a snare unto us? Let the men go and serve the LORD their God: knowest thou not yet that Mizraim is destroyed? 8. And Moses and Aaron were brought back unto Pharoh; and he said unto them, Go, serve the LORD your God: Who are they that go? 9. And Moses said, With our young and with our old will we go, with our sons and with our daughters; with our flocks and with our herds will we go, for we hold a feast unto the LORD. 10. And he said unto them, The Lord be so with you, as I will let you and your little ones go: look ye that evil is before you. 11. Not so: go now ye men and serve the LORD; for that ye did desire. And they were driven out from Pharoh's presence. § 9.

12. And the LORD said unto Moses, Stretch out thy hand over the land of Mizraim for the locust, and they shall come up on the land of Mizraim, and eat every herb of the land, all that the hail hath left. 13. And Moses stretched out his hand over the land of Mizraim; and the Lord sent an east wind upon the land all that day and all the night: the morning came, and the east wind brought the locusts. 14. And the locusts came up over all the land of Mizraim, and rested in all the border of Mizraim: very grievous were they, before them were no such locusts as they, neither after them shall be such. 15. And they covered the face of the whole land, and

the land was darkened; and they ate every herb of the land, and all the fruit of the trees which the hail had left: and there remained not any green thing in the trees or in the herbs of the field in all the land of Mizraim.

16. Then Pharoh hastened to call Moses and Aaron: and he said, I have sinned against the LORD your God, and against you. 17. And now forgive, I pray, my sin only this once, and entreat the LORD your God; and let him take away from me this death only. 18. And he came out from Pharoh and entreated the LORD. 19. And the LORD turned a very strong west wind, and took away the locusts, and cast them into the Red Sea: there remained not one locust in all the border of Mizraim. 20. And the Lord hardened Pharoh's heart, and he did not let the sons of Israel go. ¶ 15.

21. And the LORD said unto Moses, Stretch out thy hand toward the sky, and let there be darkness over the land of Mizraim; and let the darkness be felt. 22. And Moses stretched out his hand toward the sky: and there was a thick darkness in all the land of Mizraim three days. 23. They saw not one another, neither rose any one from his place for three days: and all the sons of Israel had light in their dwellings. 24. And Pharoh called Moses and said, Go ye, serve the LORD; only your flocks and your herds shall be stayed: even your little ones may go with you. 25. And Moses said, Thou must also give into our hand sacrifices and burnt-offerings, and we shall sacrifice unto the LORD our God. 26. Our cattle, then, also shall go with us, not a hoof shall be left behind; for thereof must we take to serve the LORD our God: and we know not with what we shall serve the LORD until we go thither. 27. And the LORD hardened Pharoh's heart, and he would not let them go. 28. And Pharoh said unto him, Get thee from me: take heed to thyself; see my face no more,

for in the day thou seest my face thou shalt die. 29. And Moses said, Well hast thou spoken: I will see thy face no more. ¶ 16.

This chapter completes the record of the third group of plagues.

1–20. The plague of locusts. *Go in unto Pharoh*, into his palace in the city, as in the second of each series (viii. 1, ix. 1). *For I have hardened his heart.* A mode of treatment calculated to have a salutary effect on a reasonable mind has produced an opposite effect on a proud and unreasonable temper. *That I may put these my signs upon him.* To put here (שִׁית) is to set before the view of all for their instruction. In him (בְּקִרְבּוֹ) means in his inmost experience, so as to touch his feelings to the quick (ix. 14). *And that thou mayest tell.* These marvels of Egypt are to be a lesson not only for the present, but for all future generations, who may hearken to the recollections of their fathers, or read the books of Moses. *And ye shall know that I am the Lord.* The grand scope of all these signs was to reveal the Creator in his true character to man. This is the lesson of nature, of providence, and of grace, to those who read and understand. 3. *How long dost thou refuse to humble thyself before me?* Eight signs, one of them instructive and seven corrective, had already been given to him. His haughtiness of spirit is not subdued; to humble himself, even before God, he has not yet learned. 4. *The locust.* The descriptions of Joel (i. ii.) and many other eye-witnesses have made us familiar with the locust and its desolating progress. The class to which they belong is described by Moses in Lev. xi. 21, 23, and four species, including the one here mentioned (אַרְבֶּה), are pronounced clean and edible. The native place of the locust is the south of Asia and the parts of Africa south and west of Egypt. These insects are about three or four inches long, have four wings and four feet, the hind legs being adapted for springing. They resemble in form the common grasshopper. The locust, after leaving the egg, exists in three states — the larva, the pupa, and the perfect insect. The larva has no wings the pupa has only the rudiments of them, and they are fully developed only in the perfect insect. Of these three the larva is the most voracious. They breed in October, laying each about three hundred eggs, which they bury in the ground. They make their appearance in March or April, when the verdure is on the ground. Their numbers are immense, and in their flight they are said to cover thousands of square miles, and consume every green thing where they alight. They are used as food, being either cooked whole or ground into meal. *Into thy border.* They came into Egypt generally from the south, but also from the east. 5. *The face of the land.* The eye (עַיִן) of the land is the surface, which looks, as it were, towards us. *That which remaineth unto you from the hail,* the wheat and the spelt, the other moiety of the crop, and whatsoever fruit was left on the trees. 6. *They shall fill thy houses* (Joel ii. 9). They consume everything that comes before them, in the house as well as in the field. *Which neither thy fathers.* The miracle consists in the extraordinary number, size, and destructiveness of these insects, as well as in their coming and going according to the word of Moses.

7–11. The suggestion of Pharoh's servants. *How long shall this man be a snare?* A pitfall of inevitable destruction to us. The magicians and other courtiers of Pharoh understand the state of matters better than himself. *Let the men go.* Let this people depart. They feel that they cannot contend with omnipotence. *Knowest thou not yet?* The sovereign, especially if he be despotic, is often the last to learn the wretchedness of his country; as it may be at the risk of life that his servants venture to hint at so unwelcome tidings. Pharoh seems to have been in a great measure unconscious of the ruin of Egypt. He now condescends to ask who shall go; a question that should have been proposed at the very first. Moses promptly replies that all must go, as it was a feast, a solemn assembly of the whole nation before the Lord. *Look ye that evil is before you.* Pharoh, refusing to let go "the little ones"—a phrase including the young of both sexes, and implying the full-grown women, warns them that "evil is before them." This may mean either that evil is in store for them, or that evil is in their minds. The former is a menace of the effects of his displeasure, if they insisted on all going; the latter a charge of forming a design of leaving the country. The former is more in keeping with the expression, "Look ye." The men alone are allowed to go, and with this concession they are driven out or ignominiously dismissed. Pharoh has become more irritable and violent in his manner.

12–15. The locusts sent. *The Lord raised an east wind.* An east wind, in common phrase, means any wind from the sun-rising, though it may be a good many points north or south. This indicates merely that the present swarm of locusts came not from Ethiopia or Lybia, but from Arabia. *All that day and all the night.* The locust appeared in the morning, and therefore may have come from a considerable distance. "Before them," or "after them," were no such locusts. This statement applies to Egypt, and refers to the extraordinary extent of the present visitation. *The land was darkened.* It is said that the locust swarm, like an opaque cloud, intercepts the light of the sun, and leaves the earth in darkness (Plin. Hist. Nat. ii. 29). *There remained not any green thing.* What the hail had left, the locusts devoured, and the land was *left desolate*, a waste and a void (תֹהוּ וָבֹהוּ), destitute alike of the vegetation which adorns and furnishes it, and of the cattle which form a part of its inhabitants (Gen. i. 2; Jer. iv. 23).

16–20. The locusts removed. And *Pharoh hastened to call.* The awful nature of this devastation strikes terror to the heart of Pharoh. His will also has become more restless and liable to sudden change. *I have sinned.* This is the second confession of sin, and the fourth time he has been led to entreaty. *This death only.* Death only seems now to await the Egyptians, as their crop has been destroyed and their cattle have been greatly diminished. *A very strong west wind.* A moderately blowing east wind carried the locusts in safety over the Red Sea into Egypt. A storm or hurricane sweeps them out of the country and precipitates them into the waters. This is the usual history of these insects. A wind of the sea, that is the Mediterranean, taken as a whole, though due west of Palestine, would be northwest of the Delta, especially the eastern part of it, and therefore exactly fitted to carry the locusts to the Red Sea. *And the Lord hardened Pharoh's heart.* The very long-suffering of the Lord only adds to the infatuation of his ingrate heart.

21–29. The plague of darkness. This is the third of this series and, as usual, no announcement of it is made to Pharoh. *Let the darkness be felt*; a strong figure to describe the intensity of this darkness. Similar is "a thick darkness," literally a darkness of gloom. *Three days.* The only natural phenomenon resembling this darkness is the Simoom or Chamsin, which is a hot wind rising about the vernal equinox, and blowing for about three days. It rises often to a storm, imparts a yellow dimness to the air, and raises such a quantity of dust as to have a stifling effect and produce a sombre gloom. During these days the inhabitants are wont to descend to the lowest rooms of their houses or hide themselves in pits and caverns in order to avoid the inconvenience and danger that attend this tempest. This darkness differs, however, from the Simoom in these essential points: that it is intense in its degree, that it falls upon the land at the will of Moses, and that it does not extend to the region where the Israelites dwelt. After all the disasters that had just befallen the land, we may imagine the dismay and terror that total darkness would produce in the minds of the Egyptians. It was equivalent to a universal blindness, which would unfit the nation for making any effort to attend to the business of life or provide for its continuance. In case of its perpetuation they could only await in despair the slow approach of death by starvation. Pharoh quails before the appalling darkness. He yields another point. The women and children may go with the men, but not the flocks and the herds. Moses, however, cannot go to hold a national festival unto the Lord without sacrifices. Not a hoof of their cattle must be left behind. Pharoh is again exasperated. His proud heart becomes hard as the nether millstone. A reckless madness takes possession of him. He forbids Moses to appear before him again on pain of death. There is something ominous in the reply of Moses. "Well hast thou spoken; I will see thy face no more." He means, as we shall see, more than is here expressed.

There is an awful significance in this plague of darkness. The sun was a leading object of adoration among the Egyptians under the name of Osiris. The very name Pharoh means not only the king, but also the sun, and characterizes the king himself as the representative of the sun, and entitled in some sort to divine honors. But now the very light of the sun has disappeared, and primeval chaos seems to have returned. Thus all the forms of Egyptian will-worship have been covered with shame and confusion in those nine plagues.

Allowing a week for each of the two previous plagues, and four days for this one, we are brought to the 21st of March, and perhaps to the eve of that night on which the paschal lamb was eaten and the first-born of Egypt were slain. The narrative becomes now excited and abrupt as the great crisis approaches.

## VIII. THE TENTH PLAGUE. THE PASSOVER.—Ex. xi., xii.

### CHAP. XI.—DEATH OF THE FIRST-BORN THREATENED.

XI. 1. And the LORD said unto Moses, Yet one plague
will I bring upon Pharoh and upon Mizraim; afterwards he
will let you go hence: when he shall let you go altogether,
he shall actually thrust you out hence. 2. Speak now in the
ears of the people; and let them ask every man of his neighbor, and every woman of her neighbor, jewels of silver and
jewels of gold. 3. And the LORD gave the people favor in the
eyes of Mizraim: moreover the man Moses was very great in
the land of Mizraim in the eyes of Pharoh's servants, and in
the eyes of the people.

4. And Moses said, Thus saith the LORD, About midnight
will I come out into the midst of Mizraim. 5. And all the
first-born in the land of Mizraim shall die, from the first-born
of Pharoh that sitteth upon his throne unto the first-born of
the maid-servant that is behind the mill; and all the first-born
of beasts. 6. And there shall be a great cry in all the land
of Mizraim, the like of which has not been, and the like shall
not again be. 7. And against any of the sons of Israel shall
not a dog move his tongue, from man to beast; that ye may
know that the LORD doth sever between Mizraim and Israel.
8. And all these thy servants shall come down unto me and
bow down to me, saying, Go out, thou and all the people that
follow thee; and after that I will go out. And he went out
from Pharoh in great wrath. § 11.

9. So the LORD said unto Moses, Pharoh shall not hearken

unto you, that my wonders may be multiplied in the land of Mizraim. 10. And Moses and Aaron did all these wonders before Pharoh: and the LORD hardened Pharoh's heart, and he did not let the sons of Israel go out of his land. § 12.

The section now before us recounts the tenth and last stroke inflicted on Pharoh and his people, and, in essential connection therewith, the institution of the Passover. In the eleventh chapter the announcement of the slaying of the first-born is made, as the last words of Moses to Pharoh.

1–3. There was in the words of Moses at the close of the last chapter a foreboding of something not explicitly stated. This is a plain indication that another line of events was going on concurrently with that which the historian was engaged in narrating. While the long train of interviews and transactions with Pharoh has been passing, we are not to suppose that the communication of Moses with his own kindred and people, opened on his return from Midian (iv. 29–31, vi. 1–9), was entirely suspended. On the other hand we are to presume that the whole of the instructions given to Moses (iii. 6–22), together with the signs of his divine authority (iv. 1–9), were in due time, and with full explanations, laid before the people; that when the first barbarities of Pharoh were relaxed, these messages from heaven received a respectful hearing, and that when the hand of the Lord was repeatedly displayed in inflicting chastisements on the Egyptians, from which they themselves were exempted, they began gradually to take courage, to trust in the Lord, and make the necessary preparations for their departure. Indications of this concurrent process and result now begin to appear in the narrative. We have only to call to mind the law of Hebrew narrative, that when one line of events is brought to a suitable resting-place, the author is at liberty to go back and take up another line which is necessary to the full elucidation of his theme. The words of final parting between Moses and Pharoh, though not perhaps the absolute close of the conversation between them, form a striking pause, whether we regard them from a logical or a rhetorical point of view. Accordingly, in the paragraph now before us, we revert to a point of time before the interview with Pharoh just recorded. and after the plague of darkness. This we infer from the intimation in the last words of Moses of something that was in his memory more than what is expressed. This allusion could only be to the communication recorded in the present paragraph; which is therefore now introduced to explain what was hinted at in the words of Moses already given, and in the remaining part of his last address to Pharoh (vs. 4–8).

1. *Yet one plague.* This places the coming judgment in the same class with the nine that had preceded it, though it differs from them in the mode of its infliction, and transcends them all in the wound it gave to the heart of the nation. *Altogether,* men, women, and children, with all their cattle and moveable property, so far as it was convenient or necessary for them to remove it. *Actually thrust you out,* not merely permit, but constrain you to depart. 2. *In the ears of the people.* We are evidently got into a new line of narrative. This is part of the intercourse of Moses with the people. *And let them ask* (iii. 21, 22). It is now plain that asking, not borrowing, is here intended, seeing that this step is to be taken when Pharoh was on the point of driving them out of the country, never to return. There could be no pretence of a return being made in such circumstances. Pharoh indeed repented of this course, and returned, as he was wont, to his old policy. But this does not alter the character of his present procedure. 3. *The Lord gave the people favor.* The people of Egypt saw the past scenes of tyranny, obstinacy, and prevarication on the part of Pharoh, of suffering on the part of the Israelites and themselves, and of forbearance and yet decision in the judicial proceedings of God in a very different light from that in which they were regarded by their sovereign. Many of them would sympathize with the persecuted serfs; many would stand in awe of the reiterated strokes of the divine judgment; and all would feel the calamities that befell the nation far more acutely than Pharoh. Accordingly, when the warning was given to bring in the cattle and servants, lest they should be destroyed by the hail, not a few were found with so much faith in the word of the Lord as to attend to it, and save their property. And on a subsequent occasion the very courtiers ventured to tender the advice to Pharoh that he should save his country from utter destruction by dismissing the chosen people. Thus, in the unsearchable wisdom of God, the same train of events that was hardening the heart of Pharoh, and reviving

the faith and courage of his own people, was inclining the Egyptians to commiserate the suffering people, and help them to make provision for their journey. *Moreover the man Moses.* The modesty of the writer is plain in the unadorned simplicity of the epithet, "the man," not the minister of God, or the leader and deliverer of the nation, but "the man Moses." *Was very great.* After what had occurred, it could not be otherwise. The man who had foiled the magicians of the court, again and again received the submission of the sovereign, and proved himself to be the messenger of heaven by a succession of the most conspicuous miracles, could not but be very great in the eyes of the Egyptians. And the statement of this fact does not derogate from his claim to modesty, but only renders a just tribute of praise to him whose servant he was. We have no doubt also that the moderation, good temper, and unaffected patriotism with which he discharged his duty, commanded the respect and esteem of Pharoh's servants and people. We shall find that the death of the first-born created such alarm for their personal safety that they were ready to sacrifice any amount of personal property to get rid of a people whose detention had brought such unparalleled calamities on their country.

4–8. We are now come up again to the point at which we had arrived at the close of the previous chapter, and the speech of Moses is continued. *About midnight.* This note of time points naturally, though it does not absolutely bind us, to the night following the day on which this was spoken. We conceive, therefore, that in point of fact this was the fourteenth Nisan, or the day before the full moon immediately after the vernal equinox. At all events, there is nothing in the narrative to oppose, and something to favor this view. *Will I come out.* God is said to come out when he proceeds to execute the purposes of his will in any part of his creation, which cannot be regarded as his proper and special residence. *All the first-born.* The first-born is the hope and strength of the house, its representative, and the heir of its privileges. A double portion falls to his lot, and the patriarchal and sacerdotal functions originally belonged to him. To slay the first-born, then, is the deadliest blow the household can receive. *Of Pharoh that sitteth on the throne.* The pride of the haughty monarch will now be brought low. The anguish will even be more acute, if the wailing be not more loud, in the palace of the king than in the cottage of the serf. *The maid-servant that is behind the mill,* the hand-mill, which was invariably wrought by females, and generally by slaves (xii. 29). It consisted of two stones, the nether fixed, and the upper moveable, with a hole in the centre to admit the grain, and an upright wooden handle, by which it was turned. The lower was convex, and the upper concave, so that the meal came out at the edge, and was received on a cloth. *The first-born of beasts.* As the cattle of the Israelites were to have been detained, the cattle also of the Egyptians are to suffer. And if there be any first-born among the animals to which the Egyptians pay divine honors, they also will perish. *A great cry.* Such a wail could have no parallel, unless all the first-born of a nation were to perish again in one night. *A dog move his tongue,* put his tongue in such a form and motion as to snarl, growl, or bark. This is a proverbial expression, to denote security from even the threat of danger. *That ye may know.* This is a lesson to Pharoh and his court, which is now to be repeated for the seventh time. Mizraim represents the world for the time being, and Israel the church. *Come down to me* from the high places of the court and the royal city. *Bow down to me,* humble themselves so far as to do obeisance to me. *And after that I will go out.* When every proud heart will be abased, and all opposition will be broken down, then will I depart. Pharoh had threatened the Lord's servant with death, and now the death of all the first-born of Egypt is announced to its monarch. *In great wrath.* Words of deadly feud had passed between them. Pharoh had threatened Moses with death, simply because he had demanded that the cattle of the Israelites should go with them. With what mingled alarm and indignation would he listen to this last awful menace of heaven's minister. We may infer, therefore, that there was high wrath on both sides at parting.

9, 10. These two verses are a recapitulation of all that has been related after the introductory paragraph in the seventh chapter, especially verse 3. This verse is the prediction; the intervening narrative sets forth the details, and the two verses now before us are the logical conclusion or summing up of the whole. Hence we render the conjunctive particle at the beginning, by the word *so*, as is occasionally done in the English version. This inferential summary could not come in before the speech of Moses, threatening the death of the first-born, as this occurs at the closing interview between him and Pharoh, and presents the latter with the last occasion for rejecting the demands of the Lord. And it could not come in after the death of the first-born, because then Pharoh at length yielded, whereas these verses record his long-continued resistance. They form therefore, the methodical recapitulation of the opposition of Pharoh foretold by the Lord, when that opposition has come to its last efforts. "Pharoh shall not hearken unto you, that my wonders may be multiplied in the land of Mizraim," for the perpetual instruction of mankind in certain sublime and necessary principles of theological truth. And so it has accordingly happened.

### CHAP. XII.—THE PASSOVER. DEATH OF THE FIRST-BORN.

2. חֹדֶשׁ *new moon*, day of the new moon, month; r. *be new.* יֶרַח *month* from יָרֵחַ *moon.*

3. עֵדָה *assembly;* r. *constitute.* A definitely constituted body of men, varying in extent from ten heads of houses to the whole of the men of Israel who are entitled to vote in a regular convention of the people. These were most probably all the males above twenty years of age. Between the full assembly and that of the heads of houses was probably the representative convention, consisting of the princes of tribes, chiefs of families, elders, and officers, each of which had its well-known province and function. It appears, however, that the term "elders," was often employed to denote the whole of these classes (vs. 12). קָהָל *congregation;* r. *gather together.* This denotes the whole community of Israel, including young and old, male and female. It is also used to express any body of people collected together, without reference to definite organization or regular appointment. מֹעֵד *appointed time or place* of meeting, appointed meeting. This is the term constantly used in the phrase אֹהֶל מֹעֵד *tent of meeting*, the tent at the door of which all sacred and civil meetings were appointed to be held in the wilderness.

11. פֶּסַח. Aram. פִּסְחָא πάσχα, *the passover;* r. *pass over.* (1.) The lamb, on account of whose blood, sprinkled on the lintel and the posts, the Lord passed over the Israelites (vs. 13). (2.) The solemnity of

which this lamb was the sacrifice (Lev. xxiii. 5). (3.) The seven days' festival, usually called the feast of unleavened bread, including the proper passover or festival of the preceding evening (Deut. xvi. 1). (4.) The sacrifices belonging to the feast of unleavened bread (Deut. xvi. 2; 2 Chron. xxxv. 1, 7).

24. חֹק *statute, edict, ordinance, rate.* (vs. 14) חֻקָּה; r. *engrave.*

40. אֲשֶׁר יָשְׁבוּ בְּמִצְרָיִם, *who sojourned in Mizraim.* So the Targum of Onkelos may also be rendered. But the Sept. has ἣν παρῴκησαν ἐν γῇ Αἰγύπτῳ, *which they sojourned in Egypt.* Against this rendering are the following considerations. (1.) אֲשֶׁר is usually followed by the personal pronoun after the governing word when it stands for an oblique case, but here it is not. (2.) יָשַׁב is generally intransitive, taking some preposition before the place of abiding, and here it has בְּמִצְרָיִם and therefore does not admit אֲשֶׁר. (3.) When it has a direct object, that object is the place of abode, which it could not be here. (4.) מוֹשָׁב after יָשַׁב signifies a seat (Ezek. xxviii. 2), which it cannot do here. (5.) The cognate objective after יָשַׁב would be שִׁיבָה or שֶׁבֶת rather than מוֹשָׁב. For these reasons we adhere to the former rendering.

49. תּוֹרָה *doctrine, law, principle;* r. *cast,* hiph. *teach.*

XII. 1. And the Lord spake unto Moses and Aaron in the land of Mizraim, saying. 2. This month shall be unto you the chief of months: it shall be first to you of the months of the year. 3. Speak ye unto all the assembly of Israel, saying, In the tenth day of this month they shall take to them every man a lamb, according to father's houses, a lamb for the house. 4. And if the house be too little for the lamb, let him and his neighbor next unto his house take it, according to the number of souls; every man according to his eating ye shall count for the lamb. 5. Your lamb shall be without blemish, a male of the first year; from the sheep or from the goats ye shall take it. 6. And ye shall keep it until the fourteenth day of this month; and the whole congregation of the assembly of Israel shall kill it between the evenings. 7. And they shall take of the blood, and put it on the two posts and on the lintel, upon the houses in which they shall eat it. 8. And they shall eat the flesh on this night; roast with fire and with unleavened bread, on bitter herbs shall ye eat it. 9. Ye shall not eat of it raw, or sodden at all with water; but roast with fire, its head with its legs and its inwards. 10. And ye shall not leave of it until the morning, and that which is left of it until the morning ye shall burn with fire. 11. And thus shall ye eat of it, with your loins girded, your shoes on your feet, and your staff in your hand: and ye shall eat it in haste, it is the LORD's passover.

12. And I will pass through the land of Mizraim this night, and will smite all the first-born in the land of Mizraim, from man to beast, and on all the gods of Mizraim I will execute judgments; I am the LORD. 13. And the blood shall be to you for a token upon the houses where ye are; and I will look upon the blood and pass over you: and there shall be no stroke of destruction on you when I smite the land of Mizraim. 14. And this day shall be unto you for a memorial, and ye shall keep it a feast to the LORD; in your generations ye shall keep it as an ordinance for ever.

15. Seven days shall ye eat unleavened bread; even the first day ye shall put away leaven out of your houses: for whosoever eateth leavened bread, that soul shall be cut off from Israel from the first day until the seventh day. 16. And in the first day shall be a holy convocation, and in the seventh day a holy convocation to you: no work shall be done in them: only that which every soul must eat, that alone may be done of you. 17. And ye shall observe the feast of unleavened bread; for in this self-same day I shall have brought your hosts out of the land of Mizraim: and ye shall observe this day in your generations as an ordinance for ever. 18. In the

first month, on the fourteenth day of the month, at even, ye shall eat unleavened bread, until the one-and-twentieth day of the month at even. 19. Seven days leaven shall not be found in your houses; for whosoever eateth that which is leavened, that soul shall be cut off from the assembly of Israel, whether he be a stranger or born in the land. 20. Nothing leavened shall ye eat; in all your dwellings ye shall eat unleavened bread. ¶ 16.

21. Then Moses called for all the elders of Israel and said unto them, Draw out and take you a lamb according to your families, and kill the passover. 22. And ye shall take a bunch of hyssop and dip in the blood which is in the bason, and strike the lintel and the two posts with the blood that is in the bason: and none of you shall come out from the door of his house until the morning. 23. And the LORD will pass through to smite Mizraim, and shall see the blood upon the lintel, and on the two posts: and the LORD will pass over the door, and will not suffer the destroyer to go into your houses to smite you. 24. And ye shall observe this thing, for an ordinance to thee and to thy sons for ever. 25. And it shall come to pass, when you go into the land which the LORD will give you as he hath spoken, that ye shall keep this service. 26. And it shall come to pass when your sons shall say unto you, What mean ye by this service? 27. Then ye shall say, It is the sacrifice of the LORD'S passover, who passed over the houses of the sons of Israel in Mizraim, when He smote Mizraim and delivered our houses. And the people bent the head and worshipped. 28. And the sons of Israel went and did so; as the LORD commanded Moses and Aaron, so did they. § 13.

29. And it came to pass at midnight that the LORD smote all the first-born in the land of Mizraim, from the first-born of Pharoh that sat on the throne unto the first-born of the captive

that was in the dungeon, and all the first-born of cattle. 30.
And Pharoh rose up in the night, he and all his servants and
all Mizraim; and there was a great cry in Mizraim; for there
was not a house where there was not one dead. 31. And he
called for Moses and Aaron by night and said, Rise up, go
forth from among my people, both ye and the sons of Israel:
and go, serve the Lord, as ye have spoken. 32. Take your
flocks also and your herds, as ye have spoken, and go; and
bless me also. 33. And Mizraim urged the people to send
them out of the land in haste; for they said, We shall be all
dead. 34. And the people took up their dough before it was
leavened, their kneading-troughs being bound up in their gar-
ments upon their shoulders. 35. And the sons of Israel did
according to the word of Moses; and they asked of Mizraim
jewels of silver, and jewels of gold, and garments. 36. And
the Lord gave the people favor in the eyes of Mizraim and
they gave them; and they spoiled Mizraim. ¶ 17.

37. And the sons of Israel journeyed from Rameses to Suk-
koth about six hundred thousand foot, the men apart from the
little ones. 38. And a mixed multitude also went up with
them, and flocks and herds, even very much cattle. 39. And
they baked the dough which they brought out of Mizraim into
unleavened cakes, for it was not leavened: because they were
thrust out of Mizraim and could not tarry, and they had not
made for themselves any provision. 40. And the sojourning
of the sons of Israel, who sojourned in Mizraim, was thirty
and four hundred years. 41. And it was after the end of
thirty and four hundred years, and it was on the self-same day
that all the hosts of the Lord came out from the land of Miz-
raim. 42. It is a night of observance unto the Lord for
bringing them out from the land of Mizraim; such is this
night of the Lord to be observed by all the sons of Israel in
their generations. ¶ 18.

43. And the LORD said unto Moses and Aaron, This is the ordinance of the passover, no alien shall eat thereof. 44. And every man's servant that is bought with money, when thou hast circumcised him, then shall he eat thereof. 45. A sojourner and a hireling shall not eat thereof. 46. In one house shall it be eaten: thou shalt not bring aught of the flesh out of the house abroad, and a bone thereof ye shall not break. 47. All the assembly of Israel shall keep it. 48. And when a stranger sojourneth with thee and will keep the passover to the LORD, let all his males be circumcised, and then let him come near to keep it, and he shall be as one born in the land: and no uncircumcised person shall eat thereof. 49. One law shall be to the home-born and to the stranger that sojourneth among you. 50. Thus did all the sons of Israel: as the LORD commanded Moses and Aaron, so did they. § 14.

51 And it came to pass in the self-same day that the LORD brought the sons of Israel out of the land of Mizraim by their hosts. ¶ 19.

This chapter contains the divine order for the institution of the passover, the directions given by Moses to the people and their compliance with them, the death of the first-born in Egypt, and the dismissal of the enslaved people, the date of their departure, and the determination of the parties who are admissible to the passover.

1–20. The divine ordinance concerning the passover. The parting interview between Moses and Pharoh may have taken place on the 14th Nisan. In the present chapter a new line of events is taken up. It belongs to the intercourse, not of Moses and Pharoh, but of Moses and the people. We therefore go back to the beginning of Nisan, which we have supposed to be about the 8th of March at the earliest. At this time it may be presumed the plague of hail had been removed, and those of the locusts and the darkness had yet to come on.

1. *In the land of Mizraim.* This note of place would have been unnecessary if the writer had not passed from Egypt into the wilder-

ness since the preceding chapter was indited. It is, therefore, an intimation that this portion of the narrative was not committed to writing till after the exodus had taken place. It thus affords an incidental presumption that the narrative was composed by an eye-witness. *This month.* The term here employed denotes the new moon, and hence the day of the new moon, or first day of the month, and lastly the month as defined in its commencement by the new moon. It appears to denote here the beginning of the month. *The chief of months;* the most important among the months on account of the great event which was about to take place in it. *It shall be first.* Israel was henceforth to have a sacred year beginning with this month, which was the seventh of the old civil or common year (see on Gen. ii. 6, vii. 11). From this accordingly the months are henceforth counted, so that the old first month becomes the seventh of the sacred year, though its first day is still distinguished as a festival by the blowing of trumpets and certain special sacrifices (Lev. xxiii. 23–25; Num. xxix. 1–6).

3. *All the assembly.* Three words are with more or less constancy rendered congregation in our English version, עֵדָה, קָהָל, and מֹעֵד. We shall, by way of distinction, translate them respectively by the words assembly, congregation, and meeting, which are already used without exact discrimination in our present version. By assembly or convention we understand a body of men organized for common counsel or action. By congregation or community we understand a more general body or gathering of men, women, and children, having common privileges, civil and sacred, but not all called upon or entitled to vote or act in public affairs. In the former term, regular organization is the prominent characteristic; in the latter the custom of assembling together. The commonwealth of Israel may be designated by either, according to the different way in which it may be viewed. It is obviously regarded in our text as a unity, having its natural centre in Jacob and its spiritual centre in Israel, and in him of whom Israel was the type. By meeting or appointment is to be understood a stated meeting or gathering for a great solemn occasion (xxxix. 42, 43). *In the tenth day of this month.* From the third to the tenth of Nisan the plague of locusts ran its course. The days intervening between the tenth and the fourteenth were probably the days of

darkness. This was perhaps the proximate reason for choosing the lamb on the tenth. At the same time ten is the symbol of completeness; and the tenth day completes the third of the month, as the night of (that is, before) the fifteenth completes the half of the month. The day of atonement was in like manner on the tenth day of the seventh month (Lev. xxiii. 27). *Every man a lamb*, a young animal of the sheep or of the goats (vs. 5 ; 2 Chron. xxxv. 7), though in latter times it came to be invariably the young of a sheep, *According to father's houses*, or smaller families. The family organization was very exact among the Israelites. Under the twelve tribes were the clans or families (מִשְׁפָּחוֹת) ; under these the father's houses (בֵּית אָבוֹת) or smaller families, and under these the several distinct households of which they consisted. *A lamb for the house.* This is the single household, which forms the social unit in the subdivisions of Israel. 4. *And if the house be too little for the lamb.* The Jewish tradition was that a man ate the size of an olive of the paschal lamb, in which case a whole lamb would be sufficient for a very large household. In the Targum Jonathan, ten is given as the least number for a paschal company. Josephus assigns ten as the least number and twenty as not uncommon (Wars of the Jews, vi. 9, 3). The Mishna says, "A paschal sacrifice may not be slaughtered for a single individual only. It may not be slaughtered even for a party of a hundred individuals, if each of them cannot eat thereof the minimum quantity of the size of an olive." This implies that a hundred might partake of the one lamb. At the last supper of our Lord and his disciples, thirteen full-grown men were present. This would give an average of about twenty persons, if women and children were included.

5. *Without blemish.* The lamb is the substitute, at least in type, of the first-born, and is therefore to be perfect of its kind. *A male of the first year.* The male ranks before the female, and is therefore employed to figure a sufficient sacrifice. The phrase "son of a year," means of any age from a month to a full year (Gen. vii. 6, 11).

*Until the fourteenth day.* If, as we presume, the three days of darkness came between the tenth and the fourteenth, though the Israelites had light, as in ordinary days, it was desirable that the lamb should be set apart on the tenth day, that there might be nothing to do on the fourteenth day but prepare it for sacrifice. During those awful days, when darkness, the symbol of chaos, brooded over Egypt, the Israelites had the lamb as the sign and pledge of the divine promise that this darkness would spread no farther, but would at length give way to a new period of light and life and hope. And doubtless they would have occasion, on contemplating this devoted victim, to converse with one another concerning the great deliverance which was before them (see Fagius in Crit. Sac.). But instruction and edification were not limited to those three days. They pervade all time, but especially those great occasions on which God manifests his power in the works of justice and mercy. Hence every event in this great deliverance has its definite lesson to all parties concerned, if they will but learn it. *The whole congregation of the assembly of Israel.* A congregation is any gathering or number of people that may be gathered. The congregation of an assembly is the company of those who belong to an organized or orderly community, having a common head, a representative assembly, and a law of action. The word *Israel* defines the nation, and the word *all* embraces every member of it. Not to partake of the passover on this occasion was to be excommunicated, unless there was some invincible hinderance. The whole congregation are here priests unto God. *Shall kill it,* as a typical substitute for the first-born, a symbol of propitiation by the death of another. *Between the evenings.* The lamb seems to have been slain before sunset and eaten after (see on Gen. i. 4).

7. *Put it on the two posts and on the lintel.* By the door the destroyer enters to slay the first-born. Hence the blood that indicates faith and represents atonement is sprinkled on the fixed boundaries of the doorway, except the threshold, on which the foot treads. It is not sprinkled on the door-leaf itself, which may have been in many cases altogether wanting, and was always less permanent than the lintel and posts in the booths and other slight habitations of a pastoral people (vs. 8, 9). *And they shall eat.* As the sacrificing of the paschal lamb is a symbol of the redemption, by which the death-penalty due by one is paid by another, so the eating of it is a figure of the participation of pardon, acceptance, and full blessedness consequent upon the atonement being made and the law being satisfied. *Roast with fire ;* not raw, that is, unfit for use, and therefore for representing spiritual enjoyment ; nor sodden with water, deprived of any portion

of its savor, and thus not so well adapted to express complete happiness; but roast with fire, submitted to the direct influence of fire, retaining the integrity of its strength and flavor, consequently shadowing forth not only the completeness of the sacrifice, but also the perfection of the salvation thereby obtained. *Unleavened bread.* Bread is the staff of life (Lev. xxvi. 26). Leaven is a mass of sour dough in which decomposition has set in, and is therefore the symbol of corruption (1 Cor. v. 8). Hence unleavened bread is the emblem of purity and life. *On bitter herbs.* These appear to form the basis of the repast, on which the other materials rest. In the Mishna five different kinds of bitter herbs are mentioned, among which are lettuce and endive. The bitter herbs convey no obscure allusion to the bitterness of Egyptian bondage, and of the bondage of sin in general. *Its head, with its legs and its inwards.* It is plain that it was to be roasted whole, without breaking or severing any of the bones. This involved the necessity of its being roasted on a spit before the fire, as the people could not be generally provided with vessels large enough to contain it whole. And it was strikingly expressive of the unity of the sacrifice — of the salvation which it prefigured, and of the people who partook of it (Ps. xxxiv. 20; 1 Cor. v. 7, x. 17).

10. *Ye shall not leave of it until the morning.* It was, if possible to be entirely consumed. But if any portion was left, it was to be burnt with fire. This was the rule for all sacrificial meals, except the vow or voluntary offering (Lev. vii. 15–17). This seems to indicate that they were sacred to the one purpose, and therefore not to be applied to any profane or further use. The atonement and the salvation following are to be all-sufficient, yet not more than sufficient. *And thus shall ye eat it, with your loins girded,* as those who are equipped for expeditious travelling; *your shoes on your feet,* as those who are prepared for rough and untrodden paths; *your staff in your hand,* as a protection and a support on the journey; *in haste,* as those who do not know the moment when they must set out. Here we have a reality which is a true type of the readiness with which the redeemed should wait for other and higher journeys than that which was now before the Israelites. *It is the Lord's passover.* The festival now described is a feast of passing over in sparing mercy, instituted by the Lord himself, and to be observed by all his people in obedience

to his word. As is usual with the first observance of any institution, there are many incidental circumstances that do not occur in the subsequent observance of it. The essential parts of this solemnity are the lamb, the time of sacrificing and eating it, the unleavened bread and bitter herbs, the seven days' feast of unleavened bread. The keeping up from the tenth day was afterwards omitted; the domestic observance by the men, women, and children was succeeded by the celebration at the place which the Lord had chosen (Deut. xvi. 6) by the men only or chiefly; the lamb was slain by the house father or the priest; the blood was sprinkled, not on the lintel and posts of the house, but apparently on the altar (2 Chron. xxx. 16, xxxv. 11); and the attire and attitude of haste and readiness for travelling were afterwards omitted.

(1.) Of the three things essential to the salvation of a fallen creature, two are represented by circumcision and the passover — regeneration and redemption. (2.) Circumcision denotes the new birth, without indicating any of its fruits. The passover, like all sacrificial feasts, points out not only the act, but the effect of redemption. The slaying of the lamb is the act, being the giving up of the life of one for another; the eating of the sacrifice is the effect, being the reception of the rights and enjoyments recovered on its death. (3.) Circumcision, signifying that which is inward, applies to each individual apart, and is therefore a solitary ordinance; the passover, standing for that which is outward, is equally adapted to all who are circumcised, and is therefore a social ordinance, exhibiting the communion of saints. Hence the former began suitably with Abraham, when he was alone, before he became the father of the faithful; the latter appropriately with Israel, after he had become a nation. (4.) In circumcision, which shadows forth the new birth, the recipient is passive; in the passover, which implies the voluntary partaking of the sacrifice, the recipient is active. (5.) Circumcision, symbolizing the new birth, is not to be repeated; the passover, as a sacrifice, represents that sacrifice which is to be offered once for all, but as a feast, it sets forth the constant fare by which the soul is sustained, and is therefore repeated from year to year. (6.) Circumcision, the symbol of the new nature, was not preceded by any other sign of like import. The passover, being a kind of sacrifice, was preceded by the sacrifices of Habel, Noah,

Abraham, and other patriarchs, all prefiguring that great redeeming sacrifice which was to be offered in the fulness of time. (7.) Circumcision was to continue as long as the visible church was limited to the natural or adopted descendants of Israel; the passover was to be observed until the true Lamb of God should come, of which it was only the type. (8.) Regeneration and redemption are necessary to the salvation of man from the date of the fall to that of the resurrection, and therefore belonged to the experience of the saints before these symbols were instituted. We have seen that the symbol of redemption varied according to the varying aspects which its historical progress presented. The passover answers to a new phase of redemption not within the experience of the patriarchs. This leads us to expect that other symbols may be substituted for those of the law of Moses, when the realities for which they stand reach a new stage of development. (9.) The event which gave occasion to the institution of the passover was a temporal redemption, and therefore itself but a type and foretaste of that eternal redemption which transcends all its temporal forms as far as the bondage of inward guilt transcends that of outward force. This brings before us the vast import and grandeur of the present turning-point in the history of God's people, in regard not only to what it is in itself, but to what it prefigures in the history of salvation. (10.) The passover is an advance on all preceding sacrifices; as it signalizes the eating of the sacrifice, and therefore the enjoyment of the benefits of redemption, the rest, the land of rest, the better land; it is a periodical festival, and thereby represents the perpetuity of the heavenly sustenance; and it is commemorative of a great typical deliverance.

12–15. The immediate benefit realized by those who keep this ordinance. *I will pass through.* The Lord himself, without the intervention of Moses and Aaron, is to execute this awful judgment. *This night.* The night after the 14th of Nisan, the previous transactions of which have just been described. *All the first-born, from man to beast.* The first-born is the beginning and the hope of the family (Gen. xlix. 3). To smite the first-born is to begin the annihilation of the race. The cattle came also under this judgment. *All the gods of Mizraim.* The bull, the goat, the ram, and other animals were deified by the Egyptians. The king was also regarded as an impersonation of the sun-god. The extinction of all these creature gods will be menaced, as well as in part executed, by the death of their first-born. *I am the Lord,* the maker, and therefore the absolute disposer, of all things; who speaks, and it is done. The Lord is emphatically the performer, who gives effect to his word, whether of threatening or of promise. *The blood shall be to you for a token,* a token of redemption, of acceptance, and safety. *And pass over you.* Here is the origin of the term passover. I will pass over you, for whom another has, by a type, shed his blood, and who are therefore freed from the penalty of the law. *For a memorial.* At this time every year you will commemorate with thankfulness your present and perpetual deliverance. *Keep it a feast,* a day of rejoicing and thanksgiving for freedom and prosperity, to be celebrated according to the general rules laid down by the Lord. *An ordinance forever,* a perpetual ordinance, lasting in its form as long as Israel is the peculiar people; in its principle as long as the state of redemption which it celebrates, and therefore absolutely for ever.

15–20. The institution of the feast of unleavened bread. *Seven days;* a sacred number of days, in token of entire and perpetual consecration to God. *Eat unleavened bread* (vs. 8). Unleavened bread is the symbol of a holy fare. To eat unleavened bread is the symbol of a holy life, becoming those who have exercised faith in God, the blessed fruit of a new nature. After redemption accepted comes obedience rendered. *Even the first day* of the seven. As this day commenced at the sunset of the 14th of Nisan, the removal of the leaven must have been effected on that day. *Put away leaven out of your houses.* This denotes the avoidance of all contact with sin, and of all temptation to it. *That soul shall be cut off from Israel.* This is excommunication or exclusion from the visible community of God's people. It involved the loss of all the privileges of the chosen people. It was in certain cases accompanied with the penalty of death, but not in others. We cannot suppose that an uncircumcised infant was on that account to be put to death, as the fault was in the parent (Gen. xvii. 14). It is a type of eternal separation from the family of heaven. *From the first day until the seventh day.* This is placed last to intimate that the excommunication is to take place whenever the offence has been once committed during these seven days, and not to be delayed till the expiration of the festival.

16. *In the first day*, the 15th of Nisan. *A holy convocation.* The convocation of holiness (מִקְרָא־קֹדֶשׁ) was an assembly for religious purposes, in which the people of a neighborhood worshipped God by praise and prayer, and it may be, even from an early period, heard portions of the written word read and expounded, and applied to the regulation of life. This convocation was the origin of the synagogue, a term which originally denoted the assembly, and not the place of assembly. They were doubtless at first held in the open air, in the place where it was customary for the people of the district to assemble. This was probably a natural green area set apart for civil and sacred meetings, like the fair green or square of a country town. The days on which holy convocations were held were Sabbaths; *no work shall be done in them* except the works of necessity. *Only that which every soul must eat.* We learn from Lev. xxiii. and Num. xxviii., xxix., that the weekly Sabbaths, the first and seventh days of the feast of unleavened bread, the day of pentecost, the first day of the seventh month, the day of atonement, the first and the eighth days of the feast of tabernacles, were days of holy convocation. Accordingly, there were in the ordinary year of Israel seven days in which no work was done, besides the weekly Sabbaths. Yet the weekly Sabbath and the Sabbath of the day of atonement were distinguished by a cessation of all business from the other six Sabbaths, on which an abstinence from the business of labor only was required. (See chapters quoted.)

17–20. This is to be a perpetual feast. *In this self-same day.* The first day of unleavened bread, for it is the day of their deliverance. *I shall have brought your hosts.* The men above twenty years of age will march in battle array out of the land (xiii. 18). *An ordinance for ever.* See vs. 14, 18–20. The time of eating unleavened bread is here more precisely defined. The prohibition is expressed also with more detail. *A stranger.* The strangers were afterwards distinguished into two classes: proselytes of righteousness (גֵּרֵי הַצֶּדֶק), who were circumcised, and so fully incorporated into the theocratic state, and entitled to all its privileges; and proselytes of the gate (גֵּרֵי הַשַּׁעַר), who were not circumcised, but acknowledged the one true and living God in common with Israel, and confessed themselves bound to observe what were called the seven laws of Noah, that were binding on all men. These prohibited blasphemy, idolatry, murder, incest, plunder, disobedience to the state, and the eating of flesh cut from a living beast. All these, with the exception of the interdiction of incest, and perhaps plunder, may be fairly deduced from Gen. ix. 1–7, in conjunction with the preceding portion of the written word; in other words, from the second Bible of mankind, which terminates with the ninth chapter of Genesis, or with Gen. xi. 9. This is no dark intimation that the Jews, even of a late period (Talmud, from 200 to 500 A.C.), remembered and recognized the Noachic or general covenant with mankind as still co-existing with the Abrahamic or special covenant with Israel. On no other ground can we explain the admission of proselytes of the gate to any standing in the community of Israel, or the remarkable reference to the laws of Noah. These strangers of the gate were so called because they were admitted into the gate of the private or domestic court, though they did not form a part of the proper family, and in the temple were admitted into the court of Gentiles, but not into those that were accessible to the peculiar people. They also enjoyed the privileges of the cities of refuge (Num. xxxv. 15), and certain other advantages incidental to their intermingling with the people of God (Lev. xxv. 35–55); but they were excluded from the passover and the other sealing ordinances of the Abrahamic covenant. *Born in the land.* A descendant of Israel, or of one incorporated into Israel by circumcision, and so a native and an heir of the promised land. *In your dwellings.* The obligation to abstain from leaven is to extend to those who remain at home, as well as to those who resort to the sanctuary for the observance of the passover.

In this passage we have the institution of the feast of unleavened bread, which was the continuation of the passover meal, and was to be celebrated after the departure from Egypt. And we perceive that the sacred writer is more intent on the record of this institution than on the detail of the exodus itself.

21–28. Moses communicates to the people the message he had received from the Lord. The record of this communication is given in brief terms. *Called for the elders of Israel* (Gen. iii. 16). These were the official organs of the people, through whom it was easy for Moses to communicate with the whole of Israel. This message was delivered to them in the beginning of the month, and certainly some days before the tenth. *Draw out.* Separate from the flock, not depart (ἀπελθόντες), as the Sept. freely renders. *A lamb.* The original is "one of the flock" (צאן), which, according to the previous description (vs. 5), here means a lamb or a kid. *And kill the passover.* This is evidently a summary of the directions given by Moses. 22. *A bunch of hyssop.* Here the direction supplies what is wanting in the previous record. The hyssop is apparently a generic term including several species. The species here intended is generally supposed to be, not the *hyssopus officinalis*, but according to Maimonides and others, a plant called *Sahtar* by the Arabs, a kind of organy, an aromatic plant one foot high, growing on stony soil (1 Kings v. 13). A bunch according to tradition consists of three stalks. *And none of you shall come out from the door*, from the blood-besprinkled door, within which is safety. *The destroyer.* The destructive power, agent, or instrument is hereby denoted. The intervention of angels is not necessarily implied. "The destroyer" (ὁ ὀλοθρεύων), of the Epistle to the Hebrews (xi. 28), seems to be the Lord himself, or the Angel of the Lord.

24–27. The perpetual observance of this ordinance, which was enjoined in vs. 14, is here prescribed with great minuteness. *This service.* The ordinance is here designated a service, inasmuch as it was an act of obedience to the Divine Master whose servants they had become. *What mean ye?* This ordinance of God is a reasonable service, and therefore the children have a right to ask, and the parents are bound to give, a reason for its observance. *It is the sacrifice of the Lord's passover.* Here the sacrificial nature of the passover is expressly asserted.

28. The prompt obedience of the people, who were represented by their elders in the presence of Moses, and were informed of their duty through these officials, is here emphatically recorded. This brief statement brings up another thread of the narrative to the point of time when the last plague is to be executed. The selection of the lamb, the keeping of it from the tenth till the fourteenth day, during which interval we have supposed the three days of darkness to have occured, the slaying of the paschal lamb between the evenings, and the partaking of it in the prescribed form, have now been all accomplished.

29–36. We have now the narrative of the death of the first-born and the urgent dismissal of Israel. *At midnight.* This refers to the point when the half of the night is past, and therefore to the darkest period in the whole twenty-four hours. *The Lord smote.* This awful stroke came from the immediate hand of God. Its miraculous nature appears in the prediction of the time and other circumstances of its infliction, in the instantaneous mode of its occurrence, in the selection of the Egyptians alone as its object, and in the further selection of the first-born alone of man and beast. It appears that among men the first-born only that remained unmarried in the house of their parents are here to be understood. The first-born of Pharoh is slain, while he himself is spared, though probably a first-born. It is said that "there was not a house where there was not one dead"; but there might have been grandparents and parents as well as a first-born child deceased in one house, if other than the unmarried first-born had been contemplated in the threatened judgment. *And Pharoh rose up in the night.* The peril was too imminent to admit of delay. The cry of intense anguish arose from every home. The awful feeling that all might in another moment, at all events by another judgment, be struck down, awoke in every breast. *And he called for Moses and Aaron by night.* His indignant resolve to see Moses no more is soon forgotten. The meeting, moreover, could hardly be called an interview, as it was a hurried cry in the dark, imploring them to arise and go forth from among his people, with all the sons of Israel, urging them to take their flocks and herds, and go, and beseeching them to bless him also before they depart. By blessing him he meant releasing him from the menace of any other awful judgment, such as those that had already befallen him through their intervention. It is plain that he makes no condition with them as to returning after a limited time to his service. He is most anxious to propitiate Moses and the God of Moses by granting precisely and fully all that had been demanded. And hence he says, "And serve the Lord, as ye have spoken"; "take your flocks and your herds, as ye have spoken." It is now a case of life and death with him. What need of insisting on a return, if we are to be all dead men? *And Mizraim urged the people.* Their first-born were all dead. The stroke had at length reached their persons, and had laid low the very dearest of every household. No wonder they expected to be all dead men.

34–36. *Took their dough before it was leavened.* Here we see the coincidence of historical fact with the institution of the festival of unleavened bread. This bread was commemorative, as well as symbolical. We are not to infer that it was the design of the people on this occasion to leaven their dough, but that this was the routine that was wont to be pursued on ordinary occasions. *Bound up in their garments.* The garment (שִׂמְלָה) was a square piece of cloth that was thrown over the rest of the dress as a shawl or mantle, and was therefore suitable for wrapping up moveable articles in a journey. 35, 36. *And they spoiled Mizraim.* The transaction here recorded is an act of compliance with a direction given as far back as the commission Moses received at the burning bush (iii. 21, 22), and recalled to mind the day before their departure (xi. 2). The Israelites were now in the ascendant. They held the position of conquerors, and the Egyptians, who had long and grievously wronged them and profited by their unrequited labors, felt themselves to be at their mercy. The demands made and the gifts bestowed in such circumstances were in substance a spoiling of Egypt. The Israelites were now in a position to extort a portion of their just rights, and they used their advantage with great moderation.

37–42. The departure of Israel from the land of bondage. *From Rameses*, not the town, but the tract of country so called Gen. xlvii. 11. It is unwarranted by the text, and inconceivable in itself, that the men, women, and children, with their cattle and moveables, should have assembled at the town in order immediately to depart from it. It is not to be supposed that even the full-grown men started in a formed body from any one town, place it where we will. We have no concern, therefore, with the site of Rameses the town, but only of Rameses the province, and it suffices to know that it was the border land of Egypt towards Arabia. There is much probability in the opinion that it included the wady Tumilat, and so lay east of the Nile, and around the Birket Temsah, or crocodile lake, extending, however, considerably to the north and south of this valley. *To Sukkoth.* This site was probably some point near the western edge of the salt marshes or bitter lakes, that lay between the Birket Temsah, and the Gulf of Suez, and had a lower level than the sea. It is plain that this station was over the border of Rameses, and that it was the first rendezvous of the people. Each family, or party, on receiving gifts which its Egyptian neighbors pressed upon its acceptance, turned its steps, with its flocks and herds and beasts of burden, towards the border. The females, and the males under twenty, attended to the flocks and herds and moveable chattels which they were able to take with them, and never contemplated a junction, even at Sukkoth. They slowly and steadily moved to the east and south along the north end of the bitter lakes, some down the western side, without any fear of the Egyptians, who were engaged in burying their first-born, or at least in paying them the last sad rites. The males over twenty years of age, by previous concert, formed themselves into marching companies at their respective positions, faced toward Sukkoth, and gradually arranged themselves into tribes, and these, it may be, into camps or battalions, by the time they approached Sukkoth. It cannot surprise us that the site of Sukkoth is not to be found. It was possibly only a village, or a convenient place for the halting of a large body of men; and such a temporary resting-place, without entrenchments, left no trace behind.

*About six hundred thousand foot.* This is an avowed round number. It is below, rather than above, the actual number 603,550 (Num. ii. 32, iii. 39). From a calculation of the percentage of deaths up to twenty years of age, it appears that those above that age are to those below it as 12 to 5. Hence the whole number of males would be about 850,000. This would give a sum total of males and females of about 1,700,000. The same result follows from the number of Levites, from a month old and upwards, being 22,000 (Num. iii. 9), while those from 30 to 50 were 8,580 (Num. iv. 48). For the number from 20 to 30 may be taken at half of those from 30 to 50, that is 4290; and the number above 50 may be two-thirds of this, or 2860. Hence those above 20 would be about (8,580 + 4,290 + 2,860) 15,730, and consequently those below would be about (22,000 — 15,730) 6,270. These numbers are nearly in the ratio of 5 to 2. This gives 840,000 for the males, and 1,680,000 for the whole. This sum has to receive a slight augmentation for the exact number and for the Levites, by which it reaches 1,734,540.

The period of sojourn in Egypt was, according to our calculation, 210 years. As the average of seven generations from Arpakshad to Nahor was 31 years, when men lived from 438 to 148 years, we may safely assume 30 years as a generation, and, therefore, seven generations in 210 years (see on Gen. i. 22–26). As Abraham had six sons by Keturah, and Jacob six by Leah, we may also suppose each parent to have four sons on an average, when the divine blessing of fruitfulness was promised (Gen. xxxv. 11), and actually bestowed in Egypt (i. 7). With 68 males for the first term, 8 for the number of terms, and 4 for the common ratio, the last term, or the number of males at the exodus, would be 1,114,112. This is considerably above the actual number, and therefore allows for a smaller number of generations in particular lines, as that of Moses. With a special promise of fruitfulness, and an exceedingly fertile soil this cannot be regarded as either an impossible or improbable increase.

*Apart from the little ones.* The little ones here denote the young of both sexes. The women being not otherwise mentioned, are implied in this term.

38, 39. *A mixed multitude* is literally rendered by the Sept. ἐπίμικτος πολύς, a numerous mixture. It seems to denote a congeries or gathering without order, in contact with the marshalled host of 600,000 men. It is generally supposed to have been a rabble of non-Israelites, consisting of slaves and disaffected Egyptians, who were glad to flee the country, and is usually identified with the gathering (אֲסַפְסֻף) of murmurers or mutineers, who are distinguished from the children of Israel in Num. xi. 4. We do not pretend to deny that such were included. If the shepherd kings were at this time ruling the north of Egypt, we may readily grant that many of the natives would be dissatisfied with their civil condition. But it is possible that the multitude here described comprised the whole of those who did not form a part of the marshalled host, and therefore included the women and youth of the nation, who with the slaves, if there were any such, were employed in looking after the cattle in the various ranges of country where they were feeding. Hence it is added, that *flocks and herds, even very much cattle, went up with them.* At all events, it is plain on the face of the narrative, that the young people and the women were apart from the regular host, and in charge of the cattle. And it is probable that a portion of the full-grown men, those most advanced in years, were also associated with them in their wandering course. *They baked the dough* (see on vs. 34). This was generally the work of women; but we know that the Bedawi in the desert, when on an expedition apart from his household, can cook his own food. We find Abraham directing a young man to dress a calf (Gen. xviii. 7), and Jacob seething pottage for his own use (Gen. xxv. 29). *Unleavened cakes*, round cakes baked on a kind of pan, or even among the cinders, in their present haste. *Any provision.* The word צֵדָה denotes that which is procured by the chase, wild animals of any kind, and here provisions in general, especially for a journey.

40–42. *Who sojourned in Mizraim.* The Sept. in the cod. Vatic. has here ἣν παρῴκησαν ἐν γῇ Αἰγύπτῳ καὶ ἐν γῇ Χαναάν, "which they sojourned in Egypt and in Kenaan." In the cod. Alex. it runs thus: "which they and their fathers sojourned in Egypt and in Kenaan." The Sam. has the verse thus: "and the sojourning of the sons of Israel and of their fathers, who (or which they) sojourned in the land of Kenaan and in the land of Mizraim, etc." These variants serve to prove that the Hebrew text has the correct reading. For ἐν γῇ Χαναaν proves itself to be an addition by coming after ἐν γῇ Αἰγύπτῳ when it ought in point of time to be before it. They also serve to show the meaning attached to the passage by the Sam. copy and the Sept. version. They both reckon the four hundred and thirty years from the call of Abraham. But from a narrow view of the pliancy of language, they concluded that "the sons of Israel" could not be freely used to denote the race from Abraham down, and that the phrase, "who sojourned in Mizraim," did not admit of their having sojourned a previous part of the time in Kenaan. Hence their emendations, or rather explications. But the author evidently used the present name of the race to represent that race, even when the name was not in existence. And he employs the expression, "who (or which they) sojourned in Mizraim," now that he was *sojourning* still, but in another place, naturally enough to describe that sojourning previous to the exodus, of which the residence in Mizraim had been the latest and by far the most significant part. Besides, Abraham had been in Egypt at the very beginning of their sojourning (Gen. xii. 10), and Joseph had been twenty-two years in that country before the arrival of Jacob's family. Other reasons concur to prove that this is the meaning of the author. Abraham is informed that "his seed (1) shall be strangers in a land that is not theirs, and (2) shall serve them, and (3) they shall afflict them four hundred years" (Gen. xv. 13). Now Isaac was born when Abraham was a hundred years old, and therefore thirty years after he was called. The exodus therefore was four hundred years after the birth of Isaac. But Isaac was sixty years old when Jacob was born, and Jacob was one hundred and thirty years old when he came into Egypt (Gen. xxv. 26, xlvii. 9). Hence the sojourn in Egypt lasted 210 [400 — (60 + 130)] years. Again, from Ex. vi. 16–20, we learn that Moses was the grandson of Levi by the mother's side, and the great-grandson by the father's side. As Moses was eighty at the exodus, if Jokebed was born when Levi was one hundred years old, and therefore sixty-six years after the immigration, she must have been sixty-four at the birth of Moses (66 + 64 + 80 = 210). It is manifest that we cannot add two hundred and twenty years to this period without presuming with some expositors that several generations are omitted. The writer, however, plainly gives us all the links of the genealogical chain, and not the slightest hint of any omission. He is precise not only in names, but in relationships and other circumstances. We have no more right to insert new and unknown links here than in the genealogies before and after Noah. And lastly, the Apostle Paul (Gal. iii. 17), affirms that the law was four hundred and thirty years after the covenant with Abraham. Any one of these arguments is sufficient to confirm what we hold to be the fair interpretation of the text. *On the self-same day*, immediately after the close of the four hundred and thirty years. *A night of observance*, to be kept as a commemorative solemnity in honor of the Lord their Deliverer. *For bringing them out.* The occasion of its appointment is here stated. *Such is this night.* The perpetuity of this observance is expressed with solemn emphasis.

43–50. This paragraph determines who are to partake of the passover. This it was necessary to define so soon as the nation became independent, and therefore at liberty to admit and exclude. *No alien*, son of a foreign land, a general term for all non-Israelites. *Every man's servant that is bought with his money.* Such a man belongs to his master, and therefore to his master's nation. It is to be observed here that the legislator finds a kind of bondage in existence, and legislates for it. He determines that the slave is entitled to all the religious privileges of his master. *A sojourner*, an inhabitant who is not incorporated into Israel by circumcision. *A hireling*, a mere day-laborer, who is in the same relation. 46, 47. *In one house.* Where two families are joined in order to form a large enough company for the lamb, they are to assemble in one house. It is not to be separated or part of it carried to another house, and a bone of it shall not be broken. This is to denote the spiritual unity of those who partake of the one unbroken lamb. *All the assembly.* They are to be all one body. As circumcision represents their new birth, the eating of the paschal lamb is to shadow forth the perpetuation of their spiritual life by faith in God. 48, 49. *A stranger*, a foreigner who resides for a longer or shorter time with the Israelites. Having been circumcised, his family is incorporated into Israel, and entitled to all the privileges of the chosen people. Thus the door is opened wide to all Gentiles who wish to partake in the blessings of the Abrahamic covenant, as circumcision would in those days be considered no hardship. 50. This verse closes the account of the celebration of the passover in conformity with all the requirements of the divine command.

51. This verse is properly separated from the preceding paragraph, as it is the closing summary of the narrative of the deliverance of Israel from the land of bondage, which here runs parallel with the record of the institution of the passover.

This chapter completes the account of the ten plagues, by which the king of Egypt is at length constrained to let Israel go out of the land of bondage. He who might have overwhelmed all the might of Egypt by one awful stroke displays his long-suffering forbearance by sending two verbal messages to Pharoh, and only after a second contemptuous refusal, proceeding to inflict a moderate chastisement, to bring him to repentance. The haughty obstinacy of the king requires a tenfold infliction, gradually increasing in severity, before it can be effectually overcome. And it is only finally and for ever subdued by his perishing in the Red Sea.

## SECTION III.—THE EXODUS.

### IX. THE ESCAPE OF ISRAEL.—Ex. xiii.-xv.

#### CHAP. XIII.—SANCTIFICATION OF THE FIRST-BORN.

10. יָמִימָה *to days.* The attachment of ה paragogic to this plural transforms it into an adverb, referring to a stated or natural circle of days. From the other passages in which it is used (Judg. xi. 40, xxi. 19; 1 Sam. i. 3, ii. 19) we are led to conclude that it denotes a year.

12. פֶּטֶר *that which opens* the womb. The first-born; r. *cleave, open.* שֶׁגֶר *the casting,* or young of an animal.

16. טוֹטָפוֹת occurs only in this passage and Deut. vi. 8, xi. 18, where it denotes frontlets bound with a fillet round the head. The root is supposed to mean *to go round.*

18. חֲמֻשִׁים This means *marshalled,* in marching array, or according to some, *having the loins girt.* The root in the former case is the numeral חָמֵשׁ *five,* which is the basis of arrangement; in the latter the noun חֹמֶשׁ rendered *the loin.* The word is here rendered πέμπτῃ γενεᾷ in the Sept., *girded* in the Targ., and *armati* in the Vulgate. It occurs only in four passages, here and in Josh. i. 14, iv. 12; Judg. vii. 11. In Josh. i. 14 it denotes separate from the women and children, and in marching order (Sept. εὔζωνοι). In Josh. iv. 12, 13 it again signifies in marching order, and is distinguished from חֲלוּצֵי הַצָּבָא equipped for the war (Sept. διεσκευασμένοι, and εὔζωνοι εἰς μάχην). In Judg. vii. 11 it refers to soldiers in camp, and therefore points rather to arrangement than armor (Sept. πεντήκοντα). It is evident that the Seventy only conjectured what might be the meaning of the word. From all the contexts in which it occurs the meaning appears to be in marching array, and therefore apart from the women and children, the question of arms being left open.

20. אֵתָם Sept. Ὀθώμ, Etham (*atiom* the border of the sea, Jablonsky). The derivation is uncertain.

XIII. 1. And the LORD spake unto Moses, saying; 2. Sanc-
tify unto me every first-born, that openeth every womb, among
the sons of Israel, of man and of beast: it is mine.

3. And Moses said unto the people, Remember this day, in
which ye came out of Mizraim, out of the house of bondage;
for by strength of hand the LORD brought you out thence: and
nothing leavened shall be eaten. 4. This day come ye out in
the month Abib. 5. And it shall be, when the LORD shall
bring thee into the land of the Kenaanite, and the Hittite,
and the Amorite, and the Hivite, and the Jebusite, which he
sware unto thy fathers to give thee, a land flowing with
milk and honey, that thou shalt keep this service in this
month. 6. Seven days shalt thou eat unleavened bread; and
in the seventh day shall be a feast to the LORD. 7. Unleav-
ened bread shall be eaten the seven days; and nothing leav-
ened shall be seen with thee. neither shall leaven be seen with
thee in all thy border. 8. And thou shalt show thy sons in
that day, saying, It is on account of that which the Lord did
unto me when I came out of Mizraim. 9. And it shall be for
a sign unto thee upon thy hand, and for a memorial between
thine eyes, that the law of the LORD may be in thy mouth:
for with a strong hand hath the LORD brought thee out of Miz-
raim. 10. And thou shalt keep this ordinance in its season
from year to year. ¶ 20.

11. And it shall be when the LORD bringeth thee into the
land of the Kenaanite, as he sware unto thee and to thy
fathers, and hath given it thee, 12. That thou shalt set apart
all that openeth the womb unto the LORD; and every first-
ling that cometh of a beast which thou hast, the males shall
be the LORD'S. 13. And every firstling of an ass thou shalt
redeem with a lamb; and if thou wilt not redeem it, then thou
shalt break its neck: and every first-born of man among thy

sons thou shalt redeem. 14. And it shalt be, when thy son asketh thee in time to come, saying, What is this? that thou shalt say unto him, By strength of hand the LORD brought us out of Mizraim, out of the house of bondage. 15. And it came to pass, when Pharoh would hardly let us go, that the LORD slew all the first-born in the land of Mizraim, from the first-born of man to the first-born of beast: therefore I sacrifice to the LORD all that openeth the womb, being males, and all the first-born of my sons I redeem. 16. And it shall be for a sign upon thy hand, and for frontlets between thine eyes: for by strength of hand the LORD brought us out of Mizraim. 16. § § § 15.

17. And it came to pass, when Pharoh let the people go, that God led them not by the way of the land of the Philistines, though that was near; for God said, Lest the people repent when they see war, and return to Mizraim. 18. And God led the people round by the way of the wilderness of the Red Sea: and the sons of Israel went up marshalled out of the land of Mizraim. 19. And Moses took the bones of Joseph with him: for he had straitly sworn the sons of Israel, saying, God will surely visit you, and ye shall carry up my bones hence with you. 20. And they set out from Sukkoth, and encamped in Etham, on the edge of the wilderness. 21. And the Lord went before them by day in a pillar of cloud to lead them the way, and by night in a pillar of fire to give them light; to go by day and night. 22. The pillar of cloud did not cease by day, nor the pillar of fire by night before the people. ¶ 21.

The record of the first step in the departure out of Egypt is necessarily involved in the narrative of the tenth plague. But though the people have been dismissed, they are not clear out of the country. The grand scene of the exodus yet remains. This is the passage through the Red Sea. And as soon as the people are come to the place where the Lord first appeared to Moses, the exodus may be said to be complete. These events occupy the third six chapters of this book. They contain two subdivisions ; first, the crossing of the Red Sea, in three chapters, and next the journey to Horeb, occupying the remaining three.

The present chapter contains the directions concerning the sanctification of the first-born, and some details concerning the manner of their journey.

1–16. This paragraph relates to the sanctification of the first-born. *And the Lord spake unto Moses.* As the words "in Mizraim" are no longer added, we may presume that this is the first communication given after they reached the border. *Sanctify unto me,* set apart as mine, and therefore holy. *Every first-born* that is a male (vs. 12). *Of man and beast.* As the first-born of man and beast perished among the Egyptians, so are they equally to be given over to the Lord among the Israelites. *That openeth every womb,* the first-born of every mother. *It is mine.* All things belong to God by right of creation. All Israel belonged to him by right of redemption. The first-born belong to him by right of passing over them when Egypt's first-born were destroyed. Hence the consecration of the first-born is clearly connected with the passover, and accordingly is prescribed immediately after the first step of the exodus.

3–10. Hence Moses now proceds to enjoin upon the people the observance of the feast of unleavened bread, which commences with the passover. *Remember this day.* Festivals are commemorative of some great event in the ways of God with man. This day is the first day of unleavened bread, the first day of Israel's emancipation. *Out of the house of bondage,* literally of bondsmen. From a position of freedom and honor they had been unjustly and ungratefully reduced to the condition of serfs. *By strength of hand,* a variation of the phrase "by a strong hand." *Nothing leavened.* The distinguishing mark of this festival is that no leaven shall be used in food. 4. *Abib* is the month of green ears, on the fifteenth day of which was the first full moon after the vernal equinox. 5–7. *Shall bring thee into the land.* This festival is to be a perpetual ordinance in the land of promise. The five tribes here enumerated are all descended from

Kenaan. The Perizzite of Gen. xv. 20 and Ex. iii. 8, is here omitted, perhaps because only Kenaanites are here to be mentioned. *In the seventh day shall be a feast to the Lord,* as well as in the first, which is to be understood from fuller communications. 8–10. *And thou shalt show thy son.* The duty of parental instruction in religious truth is here enjoined. The history of the ways of God with man is a precious trust, to be conveyed faithfully from father to son. A full knowledge of our relation to God is only to be obtained by an acquaintance with the main facts of his past dealing with us. Hence a commemorative ordinance is valuable; but it only rises to its full importance when its origin and significance are clearly explained and well understood. The redemption out of Egypt is the present fulfilment of a great promise, and at the same time an earnest of a still greater fulfilment in the future. The present is always big with the future; and this is nowhere so signally realized as in the promises of God, and the development of man. 9. *A sign unto thee upon thy hand.* The celebration of the passover, being thus expounded and observed from generation to generation, will be for a sign upon the hand, and a frontlet between the eyes. There is a beautiful consecration of personal ornament in this injunction. These ornaments, being embellishments of the person, came often before the eye and the mind as pleasing objects of contemplation. Being gifts, and therefore keepsakes or memorials of pure affection, they became bonds of love and gratitude, attaching the heart to the giver. The armlet or bracelet moreover, clasped the hand, the seat of power, and hinted at the lesson that the actions are to be bound by the law of love. The fillet or frontlet encircles the head, the seat of intelligence, and similarly intimates that the thoughts are to be regulated by the law of truth. The jewel on the forehead, between the eyes, from which this ornament is called the frontlet, being placed on the most conspicuous part of the person, is an emblem of frank confession, or brave glorying in a person or a principle. That the sign on the hand or between the eyes was not a brand, such as was put upon slaves and soldiers, nor a kind of tattooing, such as we still find among savage nations, is manifest from Deut. vi. 8, xi. 18, where they are said to be put on by binding, and from the phylacteries of the Jews, which were bound on the forehead and on the wrist of the left hand. These phylacteries or Tephillin (prayer-bands) were strips of parchment, on which were written, Ex. xiii. 1–10, 11–16; Deut. vi. 4–9, xi. 13–21. These were enclosed in little boxes or cases of leather attached to leather straps, by which they were fastened to the places where they were worn. This custom was not prescribed by the present passage, and can only be regarded as an indication of a feeble and declining piety. Here it is intimated that the observance of the passover, with its accompanying ordinances, is to serve for a sign upon our hands and a memorial between our eyes, and therefore to remind us of the beauty of holiness; to awaken our attachment to the heavenly Friend who gave us this ordinance as the symbol of our redemption to freedom; to bend our actions and our thoughts by true love, the law of reason and of heaven; and to signalize our thankful and open glorifying in the Lord, and in his covenant. The sacraments of the divine appointment, and not the phylacteries of our own invention, are to be the signs upon our hands and the frontlets between our eyes, telling of our faith in God; our reconciliation to him; our entrance into the glorious liberty of the sons of God. They are to be the ornaments of our spiritual beauty, and the speaking instruments of God's everlasting love to us, and of our new-born attachment to him. *That the law of the Lord may be in thy mouth*, as a subject of conversation, and therefore of habitual thought and observance. 10. *In its season*, its appointed time. *From year to year*, literally from days to days. But the word days here is used in a collective sense, to denote a definite and well-known circle of days, that is, a year.

11–16. Moses now communicates to the people the law concerning the consecration of the first-born. *Into the land of the Kenaanite.* This regulation is to come into force when Israel shall reach the land in which he is to dwell. It is here called the land of the Kenaanite, as all the tribes before mentioned were descended from Kenaan. The eventual residence of Israel for forty years in the wilderness was in consequence of the unbelief and disobedience of the outcoming generation, and is, therefore, not here contemplated; but, on the other hand, it is presumed that they are to pass immediately through the wilderness into the promised land. An interval of a year, however, was to be expected in the peninsula of Sinai, and for this period a special provision will be found (Num. iii). *As he sware unto thee.*

He sware unto them when he acknowledged the oath which he sware unto their fathers, in which they were named (Ex. vi. 8; Gen. xxii. 16, xxiv. 7). 12. *Set apart,* cause to pass over unto the Lord as his own. 13. *And every firstling of an ass.* The ass is here specified as an example of what was to be done in the case of unclean animals. It seems probable that the ass was at this time the only, or at all events the chief, beast of burden possessed by the Israelites. It is a much finer animal in the East than in these countries. *Thou shalt redeem with a lamb.* To redeem is to give a quittance for the ass, which is fixed by law to be a lamb, to be offered in sacrifice in its stead. *And if thou wilt not redeem it.* It is the Lord's, from the time that he smote the first-born of every domestic animal among the Egyptians, and not among the Israelites. As it cannot be offered in sacrifice, it is to be put to death. To put a brute animal to death without inflicting unnecessary pain, when occasion requires, cannot be called cruelty. The command of the Creator is at least one occasion on which this may be done, as he who gave life can withdraw it. The alternative of redeeming or destroying the firstling of an unclean animal is a temporary arrangement, until a sacerdotal order has been set up. From that time forward the alternative comes to be to redeem according to the estimate of the priests, and add a fifth part, or surrender it to the priests, by whom it is sold at his estimation (Lev. xxvii. 27). The redemption of the first-born of man admits of no alternative The ransom was five shekels (Num. iii. 47). 14–16. The custom of redeeming the first-born, which naturally flows from the passover, serves, in like manner, for a sign on the hand and a frontlet between the eyes, as explained on vs. 9.

17–22. A single stage, and some general features of the future march of Israel are here stated. *God led them.* One leading feature of their course henceforth is that they are under the guidance of the Most High. Antecedent to this guidance, and irrespective of all covenant with the guided, he is the everlasting Potentate from whom all creation and all providence flow, the King eternal, immortal, invisible. In this character he arranges the first direction given to their course, as far as it depends on the natural relations of things. Two ways were before the people, the one leading northeast, directly towards the land of promise; the other nearly south, towards the Sinaitic peninsula.

Before they started, it was necessary to determine which they were to take, that no time might be lost, and no misunderstanding might arise. *By the way of the land of the Philistines.* This way was familiar to the sons of Israel in former times, when Ephraim asserted a claim and maintained a position in the regions from Shekem to Gath (1 Chron. vii. 21–24), and was well known at all times by the caravans of traders from Damascus and Gilead (Gen. xxxvii. 25). *Lest the people repent when they see war.* This is the determining motive springing from the things of the natural world. It is sufficient to shape their course for the present, and, on the score of economy, no further influence is brought into operation. But other and higher motives, arising in the sphere of the supernatural, lie hid in the counsels of Jehovah, that is, of God as he is, the God of the actual and the spiritual. The natural reason, then, not the supernatural, is here given for directing their course southward. *Round by the way of the wilderness of the Red Sea.* This way was round in reference to Kenaan, the place of their destination. The wilderness of the Red Sea is so called, in contradistinction to that which they would have crossed in the straight road to the land of Kenaan. The former is here called the wilderness of Etham. Both were included under the wider term Shur (Gen. xvi. 7, xxv. 18; Ex. xv. 22). *Marshalled.* From the usage of this word, we infer that the full-grown men formed a body, arranged in columns or battalions, for orderly march, apart from the women and children. The latter were not on this occasion assembled together; but assisted, it may be, by small detachments of men, moved along in separate companies with the flocks and chattels of the nation. Meanwhile, the full-grown men gradually mustered, and now marched in order, arranged on the basis of five, and having probably captains of tens, of hundreds, of thousands, and of greater numbers. We know that ultimately they formed five camps, or battalions, four under the standards of Judah, Reuben, Ephraim, and Dan, and the fifth consisting of the Levites (Num. i., ii.), This body of men was thus enabled to move with precision, and afford an efficient protection to the scattered families that were advancing slowly, encumbered as they were with the cattle and the moveable property that were under their charge.

19. *The bones of Joseph.* What a light this casts upon the living thoughts and cherished recollections of this people. About one hun-

dred and forty years ago Joseph had bound their fathers by an oath to carry his bones with them to the land of promise (Gen. l. 24, 25). This oath, and the hopes inseparably connected with it, were often talked over in the family gatherings of the evening, and the memory of it faithfully handed down from father to son. This little incident warrants us to imagine the frequent and earnest conferences which took place in the homes and social meetings of Israel concerning the promises made to Abraham, Isaac, and Jacob; the land to which they were to return when the iniquity of the Amorite was full; the privileges and blessings that were in store for the seed of Abraham, and in that seed for all the families of the earth; the ancient and universal covenant with Noah, which was yet to be fulfilled by the seed of Abraham, for the salvation of all nations. If the dying request of Joseph was remembered, we cannot suppose that the sublime prospects held out to their own race by the word and oath of the Lord were altogether forgotten. We must presume they were the topics of frequent meditation and fervent prayer.

20–22. *They set out from Sukkoth.* They arrived at this place on the first day of unleavened bread, which was to be kept as a Sabbath. They probably gave it the name Sukkoth, *booths, tabernacles, pavilions* (Gen. xxxiii. 17), because they set up a few booths and spent some portion of the day in holy rest, a thankful rest after liberty achieved. This is the solemn beginning of that dwelling in booths which was afterwards celebrated in the feast of tabernacles in the seventh month (Lev. xxiii. 39–43). *And encamped in Etham.* On the second day they reached this place, which lay probably in the space between the Bitter Lakes and the head of the Gulf of Suez. Niebuhr identifies it with Ajrud. But it was most probably a little farther east. 21, 22. *And the Lord went before them.* Here we enter into the region of the supernatural. God now appears as Jehovah, the Author and Upholder of being, of covenant and promise. *By day in a pillar of cloud.* A visible pillar of cloud or vapor, a conspicuous object that could be seen not only by the marshalled host but by the scattered companies of women and children, as they fed their flocks and followed afar off the marvellous signal of the divine presence. A great host marching through a country without roads or other marks of civilization must be provided with some conspicuous object to serve as a signal to the main body and to all straggling parties connected with it. Hence the round grate full of kindled fuel, elevated on a pole, which was carried before caravans and armies in the East (Curtius v. 2, 7). The ancient Persians carried a sacred fire in silver altars before their armies, and other ancient nations observed a similar custom (Curtius, iii. 3, 9; Diod. Sic., xvi. 66). As the Lord now undertakes the miraculous guidance of the chosen nation, he manifests his presence by a majestic pillar of cloud, reaching from earth to sky. This appears in the day as a dark cloud, contrasted by its shade with the clearness of the sunshine, and in the night as a bright fire to give them light. As the heat of the day was unfavorable for active exertion, it was customary to go by night as well as by day; and hence the pillar was present by night and by day to the journeying people. In it the Lord himself was present as the leader and protector of his people (Ex. xiv. 19, 20; Num. xiv. 14; Ps. cv. 39); and from it he speaks to Moses as the representative and lawgiver of the people (Ex. xix., xxxiii. 9; Num. xii. 5), and on one grand occasion to the assembled people themselves (xx.). He who thus manifests his presence to his people is also called the angel of the God (xiv. 19). The same mode of manifestation is varied merely according to the circumstances in the lambent flame of the burning bush. It appears afterwards also in the cloud over the mercy-seat, between the cherubim, which in the theological language of Israel is called the shekinah (שְׁכִינָה), or dwelling-place of God. The elementary forms of cloud and fire are extremely apposite to the present purpose of guiding the host of the Lord by day and night. They have at the same time a general fitness to indicate the presence of the Lord without awakening any material or carnal misconceptions in the mind of the beholder. They do not belong to the kingdom of nature or art, and therefore do not suggest any debasing views of the Creator, or impute to him any properties of the creature. They are in themselves preternatural, and at the same time do not assume any definite form or resemblance of any creature, and therefore are not in danger of being taken for anything but the surroundings of the present Deity. Fire, in its various forms of flame, light, heat, and electric flash, is a striking emblem of the great Spirit, and the smoke or vapor which accompanies it is a manifest type of the phenomena which surround and conceal the essence, while at the same time they indicate the presence of the Mighty Potentate. The pillar that balances itself in mid-air, unsupported by the earth and unshaken by the winds of heaven, serves well to mark the presence of him who is independent of the laws of nature. And lastly the pillar of fire and cloud (xiv. 24) is manifestly not the Lord, nor a figure of the Lord, but the visible and real sign of his actual presence among his people for their guidance, protection, and comfort. *The pillar of cloud did not cease.* It did not vanish from their view; but was a constant and unerring signal before or in the sight of the people. We have not now the pillar of fire and cloud; but we have the word of God, which is a lamp to our feet and a light to our path. This also is a supernatural revelation of the present Lord and his Messiah by the eternal Spirit, conveyed through the minds and words of holy men. This spiritual flame, kindled from heaven and enshrined in the cloud of human speech, has not been lost or extinguished, but continued from generation to generation, and is in the way of being diffused throughout the whole world, to be the guide of the nations to the land of promise till the days of darkness disappear. It remains a speaking token of the continual presence of the God of all grace — of the Father, the Son, and Holy Ghost — in his church.

## CHAP. XIV.—ESCAPE OF ISRAEL. OVERTHROW OF EGYPT.

2. פִּי הַחִירֹת Pi hachiroth, *the mouth of the caves* (pi-achi-rot, place of reeds or sedge, Jablonski). Hachiroth bears some resemblance to Ajrud.

מִגְדֹּל Migdol, *tower.* The site has not been ascertained, but is supposed by some to be Muktala.

בַּעַל צְפֹן Baal-tsephon, *place of Typhon,* the fiery and mephitic blast, the drought that consumes all vegetable life. But on the other hand it may mean the hiding of Baal, and thus form a local name for the west, or the point where the sun sets.

7. שָׁלִישׁ *third* part; a musical instrument; a third man, τριστάτης, or knight. The last term is here employed in a wide sense, to denote a class of adjutants who were near the king for active and trusty service in peace or war.

XIV. 1. And the LORD spake unto Moses saying. 2. Speak unto the sons of Israel and let them turn and encamp before Pi-hahiroth, between Migdol and the sea; before Baal-zephon, over against it let them encamp by the sea. 3. And Pharoh will say of the sons of Israel, They are entangled in the land; the wilderness hath shut them in. 4. And I will harden Pharoh's heart, and he shall pursue after them; and I will be honored upon Pharoh and upon all his army, and Mizraim shall know that I am the LORD. And they did so. 5. And it was told the king of Mizraim that the people fled: and the heart of Pharoh and of his servants was turned against the people; and they said, What is this we have done, that we have let Israel go from serving us. 6. And he made ready his chariot, and took his people with him. 7. And he took six hundred chosen chariots, and all the chariots of Mizraim, and knights over all of them. 8. And the LORD hardened the heart of Pharoh king of Mizraim, and he pursued after the sons of Israel: and the sons of Israel were coming out with a high hand. 9. And Mizraim pursued after them, and all the chariot horses of Pharoh and his horsemen, and his army overtook them encamping on the sea by Pi-hahiroth before Baal-zephon. 10. And Pharoh drew nigh: and the sons of Israel lifted up their eyes, and behold Mizraim marched after them; and the sons of Israel were sore afraid, and cried unto the Lord. 11. And they said unto Moses, Because there were no graves in Mizraim hast thou taken us away to die in the wilderness? Why hast thou dealt thus with us to bring us out of Mizraim? 12. Is not this the word that we told thee in Mizraim, saying, Let us alone that we may serve Mizraim? For it had been better for us to serve Mizraim than to die in the wilderness. 13. And Moses said unto the people, Fear ye not; stand still, and see the salvation of the LORD, which he will work for you to-day: for whereas ye have seen Mizraim to-day, ye shall see them again no more forever. 14. The LORD shall fight for you, and ye shall hold your peace. ¶ 22.

15. And the Lord said unto Moses, Why criest thou unto me? Speak unto the sons of Israel that they set out. 16. And thou lift up thy rod and stretch out thy hand over the sea and divide it: and the sons of Israel shall go into the midst of the sea on dry ground. 17. And I, behold I will harden the heart of Mizraim, and they shall go in after them; and I will be honored upon Pharoh and upon all his army, upon his chariots and upon his horsemen. 18. And Mizraim shall know that I am the LORD when I am honored upon Pharoh, upon his chariots and upon his horsemen. 19. And the angel of God, that went before the camp of Israel, removed and went behind them: and the pillar of cloud removed from before them and stood behind them. 20. And it came between the camp of Mizraim and the camp of Israel; and the cloud and darkness were *to those*, and it lightened the night *to these:* and the one drew not near the other all the night. 21. And Moses stretched his hand over the sea; and the Lord drove the sea by a strong east wind all that night, and made the sea dry ground; and the waters were divided. 22. And the sons of Israel went in the midst of the sea on the dry ground: and the waters were a wall unto them on their right hand and on their left. 23. And Mizraim pursued, and all Pharoh's horses, his chariots, and his horsemen went after them into the midst of the sea. 24. And it came to pass in the morning watch that the LORD looked into the host of Mizraim in the pillar of fire and cloud, and troubled the host of Mizraim. 25. And he took off their chariot wheels, and made them drive heavily: and Mizraim said, Let me flee from the face of Israel; for the Lord fighteth for them against Mizraim. ¶ 23.

26. And the LORD said unto Moses, Stretch out thy hand
over the sea, and the waters shall return upon Mizraim, upon
his chariots, and upon his horsemen. 27. And Moses stretched
forth his hand over the sea, and the sea returned when the
morning appeared to its force: and Mizraim fled against it;
and the LORD overthrew Mizraim in the midst of the sea.
28. And the waters returned and covered the chariots, and
the horsmen, and all the army of Pharoh that went after them
into the sea: there remained of them not even one. 29. And
the sons of Israel had walked on the dry ground in the midst
of the sea; and the waters were a wall unto them on their
right hand and on their left. 30. And the Lord on that day
saved Israel out of the hand of Mizraim; and Israel saw Miz-
raim dead upon the sea-shore. 31. And Israel saw the great
hand which the LORD put forth on Mizraim, and the people
feared the LORD: and they believed in the LORD, and in Moses
his servant. ¶ 24.

The ten plagues were preceded by a series of miraculous signs by which the Lord attested the commission of his servant. The present chapter records the miraculous escape of Israel through the Red Sea, and the overthrow of Mizraim in attempting the same passage by the return of the waters to their ordinary course. The number ten is expressive of completeness. The twelve interpositions of the Lord on behalf of his people indicate a deliverance according to the covenant of grace which stands between them. The number twelve plays an important part in the series of symbolical numbers; for being composed of the factors three and four, it fits well with the notion of a covenant between God and the world of mankind (see on Gen. ii. 3).

1–14. The Lord's direction to Israel concerning the third day's march. *Let them turn.* The word here employed denotes to return or turn back from the way hitherto pursued. Etham, we have seen, was on the edge of the wilderness to which it gave name (xiii. 20). To go forward, was to pass immediately into the wilderness, whither

Pharoh, on changing his mind, might have pursued without hinderance the embarrassed and imperfectly armed fugitives. If the Lord would not lead them by the direct road into the land of promise, lest they should be discouraged by the appearance of war, much more must he not conduct them straight into the wilderness, where they might be readily overtaken and discomfited by a well disciplined host with all the accoutrements of war. Hence the order to change the line of march. *Encamp before Pi-hahiroth.* The place here mentioned has been by many identified with Ajrud, a fort, with a well of bitter water, on the pilgrim route from Cairo to Mecca, four hour's northwest of Suez. The site is probable enough, and even the name, has a distant resemblance to that in the text. *Between Migdol and the sea.* The place here mentioned is named from its nature, being a tower situated on some eminence or vantage ground, between which and the sea lay a level area of about ten miles extent. In this plain the marshalled bands of Israel are to encamp, having apparently Ajrud, or Hahiroth to the northwest, Migdol to the west, and the sea to the east. *Before Baal-zephon.* In the absence of definite information, and after the local changes of thirty-three centuries, it appears impossible to determine the site thus designated. It seems connected with Baal, or the Sun; and was perhaps a temple erected on a peak, or spur, of Jebel Attaka. Hence it lay, not improbably, on the south of the encamping ground, which was then before Baal-zephon that was over against Pi-hahiroth. Thus the Israelites in their new station would have the mountains on the west and south, and the sea on the east. They were thus brought into the only place where an effectual barrier could be put between them and a pursuing enemy, as the event will show. 3. *And Pharoh will say.* This very position of Israel, which is eventually to relieve them from a harassing and overwhelming foe, seems of all others the most certain to leave them an easy prey to the destroyer. *They are entangled in the land.* They have fallen into a snare, from which it is impossible to escape. It is still in my power to detain them in the land from which their leader has not been able to extricate them. *The wilderness has shut them in.* They have been afraid to face the wilderness, which does not naturally afford the means of supporting so vast a host of men, in addition to the concourse of flocks and herds, for which it might yield a scanty subsistence.

Pharoh will conjecture that the fear of perishing by famine has been the cause of their turning back. 4. *And I will harden Pharoh's heart.* See on iv. 21. *And I will be honored upon Pharoh.* The *Lord* has been already honored in the eleven manifestations of his power before Pharoh. His glory will be still more signally displayed in the twelfth. *Shall know that I am the Lord.* See on vi. 2. *And they did so.* This brief sentence sums up their compliance.

5–9. The pursuit of Pharoh. The third day had now arrived. The panic which had seized the Egyptians had now given way to other feelings. Pride, ambition, and revenge again took possession of the breast of Pharoh. But the narrative reverts to the first or second day after the escape of Israel. *It was told the king of Mizraim that the people fled.* This may have taken place on the second day after their departure. On the first day they must have been too busy with the mournful task of caring for the dead (Num. xxxiii. 4). *The heart of Pharoh and of his servants was turned against the people.* The sight of their own dead, and the thought of those making their escape who had been the occasion of this domestic, as well as national, calamity, aroused the spirit of enmity in their hearts. *What is this we have done?* The fierceness of their disappointment now exceeds the bitterness of their grief. 6, 7. *Made ready his chariot.* Orders for instant preparation were not long in following this exasperation on the part of Pharoh and his servants, and the military part of the nation would be constrained to a prompt acquiescence. On the second or third day, therefore, Pharoh and his people set out in pursuit. *Six hundred chosen chariots,* belonging to the king himself; *all the chariots* belonging to the state. Horses were imported into Egypt from Asia. They are first mentioned on the monuments in the reign of Ames or Amosis, the first of the 18th dynasty, and are supposed to have been introduced by the shepherd kings. Herodotus relates (ii. 108) that Sesostris so intersected the country with canals as to render it unfit for horses or chariots. *And knights over all of them.* The knights here are men-at-arms, who were ready for any service requiring promptitude and fidelity. They cannot now be more exactly defined. 8. *And the sons of Israel were coming out with a high hand.* The people were animated with the triumphant confidence which so great a deliverance by the hand of the Lord had inspired, and their courage had not yet been damped by the sight of the Egyptians pursuing. *Overtook them.* We are now fairly arrived at the third day, on which the Israelites encamped on the sea by Pi-hahiroth before Baal-zephon. The pursuers had probably started on the second day, and the deflection of the Israelites was enjoined in order to place an impassable barrier between them and their implacable enemy.

10. The expostulation of the people with Moses when there seems to be no possibility of escaping from Pharoh. *And Pharoh drew nigh,* so as to come within view. The sons of Israel descry the pursuing enemy, and are sore afraid. They *cried unto the Lord,* doubtless in the extremity of their despair. If they had bethought them of the wonderful interposition that opened their way out of Egypt, or cast their eyes on the pillar of cloud and fire that had begun to accompany them, they might have retained their self-possession, even on the approach of the enemy. But at the sight of their former masters, approaching in all the pomp of war, their courage fails. In a human point of view their case was bad enough. The mountains were on the west and south, the sea on the east, and the war chariots of the well-appointed foe advancing on the north. There was not the slightest prospect of ultimate escape for a fugitive people scantily furnished with the means of defence. 11, 12. In the agony of distress they upbraid their leader with the apparent result of his ill-advised rashness. 13, 14. Moses is still strong in faith. He has had abundant proofs of the power and truth of God, and he has heard him announce that he will now be honored in Pharoh and all his army. He has therefore no doubt of full and timely deliverance. He accordingly exhorts the people to stand still, and see the salvation of the Lord. *Ye shall see them no more for ever.* This implies that he was not unaware of the catastrophe that was approaching. *The Lord shall fight for you.* He only could have delivered a defenceless people from a fully equipped and infuriated enemy; and he has taken his own way of accomplishing the task. He might no doubt have allowed the Israelites to march on into the wilderness, and in some other way arrested the hot pursuit of the vindictive Pharoh. But it is merely impossible for us to shew that any other way would have equally well served all the purposes of salvation to the fugitives,

destruction to the pursuers, and admonition to all the survivors of that memorable night that was drawing nigh.

15–25. The passage of Israel on dry ground through the Red Sea. *Why criest thou unto me?* This is a reply, it may be, to the mere circumstances of the case, that have a voice that reaches the heart of God (Gen. iv. 10), but also no doubt to the earnest supplications of the people, and even of Moses. It seems to intimate that Moses was the representative of the despairing people, or that he was himself either unduly moved by the apparent danger, or in some degree forgetful of what ought to be done at this momentous crisis. *That they set out*, break up their present encampment. It is probable that the marching was done for the most part in the night, or at all events in the evenings and mornings, and that the people had rested some time in their present station. *Lift up thy rod.* It is not recorded that Moses was directcd before this to employ his rod for opening up the way. But the question of the Lord seems to intimate that he might have been prepared for such a command. 17, 18. In these words we have a reiteration of the statement contained in vs. 4, with considerable amplification in the details. *I will harden the heart of Mizraim*, not of Pharoh only. *Upon his horsemen and upon his chariots.* This is a specification of the principal or characteristic parts of Pharoh's host. 19, 20. The issuing of the above command to Moses is the first of a series of steps or movements in the narrative correspondent with the native grandeur of the occasion. These two verses contain the second step. The angel of God, with the pillar of fire and cloud that had hitherto headed the march of Israel's manhood, now moved to the rear, between the camps or hosts of Israel and Mizraim. This awe-inspiring column now assumed a twofold aspect, presenting a dark and cloudy side to Egypt, and a bright and cheering one to Israel, and remaining as a tower of fire between them all the night. 21. The third step is the dividing of the waters. *Drove the sea by a strong east wind.* A strong northeast wind is said to have considerable influence in the present day on the ebb of the tide in the Red Sea, as well as in other places. Such a natural occurrence, however, only drives out the whole body of waters farther from the shore. It does not "divide the waters," and so make them "a wall" on each side of the dry ground, or leave time or space for the passage of a large multitude, or happen precisely at the moment when escape from an advancing foe makes it convenient for the leader of the retreating squadrons to wave over the waters his rod of power. We cannot explain how the sea became dry ground. We only know that the Lord commanded Moses to stretch out his wand, and he did so, and that the resulting change was accompanied with a strong east wind. Whether there was an elevation of the bed of the sea we are not informed, and the letter of the text seems not in favor of it. 22. The next step is the passage of Israel, with a wall of waters on each side. 23–25. Then, in hot haste, the Egyptians rush in between the watery walls. All their host are soon in the midst of the sea. *In the morning watch.* Before the captivity the night was divided by the Israelites into three watches, the first watch (רֹאשׁ אַשְׁמֻרוֹת, Lam. ii. 19), the middle watch (אַשְׁמֹרֶת הַתִּיכוֹנָה, Judg. vii. 19), and the morning watch. It appears that the Israelites had the space of two watches at least, or eight hours, for effecting their passage. *The Lord looked.* An unwonted darting of the lightning flash and rumbling of the awful thunder was the probable accompaniment of this look. *And troubled the host of Mizraim.* Flash after flash shot through the sky; peal after peal broke over their heads; and the midnight darkness prevented them from driving their chariots with safety. *And he took off their chariot wheels.* We are not told whether this was done with or without special means. But we can readily perceive that the boulders, hollows, and other inequalities of a sea-bed, with the mental confusion arising from the thunder, would render the ground, which was passable for footmen with light, very difficult and destructive to the wheels of the Egyptian cars in the dark. The wonders of the few preceding weeks recur to their minds, and the conviction again breaks upon them with irresistible force, that the Lord fights for Israel.

It is of course impossible to determine such details of this extraordinary event as are not expressly laid down in the narrative. And it is but fair to the narrator to abstain from any hypothesis that would not square with its consistency or credibility. We have already seen (xii. 37) that the text does not assert or warrant the assumption that the whole people, with their flocks and herds, ever assembled at one point. The women, children, and servants, accompanied perhaps with a portion of the full-grown men for help and protection, continued in charge of their cattle and moveable property, and we have no doubt, moved with such speed as they might, in small parties, grazing the flocks as they went along towards the wilderness, with which their pastoral life made them perfectly familiar. Intelligence of the general movement would be conveyed to these scattered parties in ways that are habitual to all wandering tribes. The pillar of fire and cloud would also be conspicuous from afar, and would serve to make the ramblers acquainted with the position and progress of the main body of full-grown men. When, therefore, the order was given at Etham to turn back and encamp at "the mouth of the caves," it referred only to the five or six hundred thousand men who were marshalled and encamped, and were the object of attack to Mizraim and the ground of confidence to their own wives and children. Allowing the manhood of Israel to be all present, and assigning a square yard of standing-ground to each, we find they can be placed within the square of half a mile; and, consequently, they have scope enough to deploy and encamp within the plain of ten miles square lying between the hills and the sea. At Suez, which is situated on or by the ruins of the ancient Kolzum or Κλύσμα, about two miles from the most northern point of the shore, the gulf is not more than two thirds of a mile wide. But the position of Suez does not correspond with the description of the place of encampment given in the text. This seems to have been at the base of Jebel Attakah, where the channel is six or seven miles across. If the "dry ground" were a quarter of a mile wide, the Israelites would form a column a quarter of a mile in rank and a mile in file. Such a body might cross a channel of six miles in six hours, and therefore, notwithstanding the roughness of a sea-bottom, might easily decamp, set out, and reach the opposite bank in eight. By the time they had reached the shore, the pursuers, with their chariots of war, would be in the middle of the channel, where the depression of the bottom and the difficulty of progress were the greatest.

26–31. In three more verses the destruction of the Egyptian host is described. *Stretch out thy hand* with the rod of power. *The waters shall return upon Mizraim.* When the power that restrained, for the time, the laws of nature is withdrawn, the waters return to their wonted level. Three or four fathoms would suffice to bury all the host of Egypt in the overwhelming waves. At the appearing of the morning the sea returned to its course. At one fell sweep of the mighty waters all the chivalry of Mizraim is laid for ever low. A mild message, a manifest sign from heaven, only exasperated the pride of Pharoh. Ten awful plagues failed to subdue the obstinacy of his heart. A final judgment, of terrific sublimity, terminates his career of presumption (vs. 29–31). In a style of simple grandeur the Hebrew penman closes his narrative with a brief summary of Israel's deliverance. *And the sons of Israel had walked.* This verse marks the contrast between the march of Mizraim and Israel. *The Lord on that day saved Israel.* The overwhelming sea effectually, and for ever, arrested the pursuit of the Egyptians. The Lord chose this way. If the Israelites had been allowed to advance without deviating from their route into the wilderness, he must have adopted some other way, equally miraculous, of stopping the progress of their foes. *Mizraim dead upon the sea-shore.* The east wind ceasing on the outstretching of Moses's hand, and perhaps even a western breeze springing up, the reaction of the returning sea cast up the greater part of the Egyptian army, with all its chariots and accoutrements, on the eastern shore, at the feet of the Israelites. There is the utmost probability, therefore, in the statement of Josephus (II. xvi. 6), made before recent controversies were mooted, that "on the next day Moses gathered together the weapons of the Egyptians, which were brought to the camp of the Hebrews by the current of the sea, and the force of the winds assisting it; and he conjectured that this also happened by divine providence, that so they might not be destitute of weapons." *The great hand which the Lord put forth.* To make a hand is one of those phrases on which old English and ancient Hebrew coincide. Several salutary consequences of this great wonder which the people had seen, are here enumerated. The fear of the Lord, that reverential and submissive feeling which is the beginning of wisdom, was called forth by the awful grandeur of that scene of judgment and mercy which they witnessed. Trust in the Lord was awakened in their breasts by the discriminating result, in which an awful doom fell upon their adversaries, and a great salvation was accomplished for themselves. That their confidence in Moses should now be established was a necessary consequence of trust in the Lord. There was at the same time a lesson here for all nations that were within hearing to return to the Lord, the God of their being, and submit themselves to his rightful authority and proffered mercy. The intelligent reader will acknowledge that these verses form a meet finale to the preceding narrative.

### CHAP. XV.—THE SONG OF MOSES.

2. יָהּ Jah, *he who has been*, has manifested his being by illustrious acts of divine power. It seems to stand for הָה the perfect of הָיָה as יְלַךְ for הָלַךְ and קָם from קוּם This name occurs for the first time *after* the signs and wonders of the divine presence in the land of Egypt; as the name Ehjeh occurs before these extraordinary events. As the latter denotes him who is about to manifest his being, so the former seems to indicate him who has manifested his being. As Jehovah is the self-existent, the self-manifesting Agent, the constant Causer of all effects; so Ehjeh is the prophetic Jehovah, and Jah the historical Jehovah. This historical shade of meaning is obvious in Isa. xii. 2, where the first clause of verse 2 is quoted with Jah Jehovah, instead of the simple Jah, and in Isa. xxvi. 4, where the same combination occurs. This conjunction of the names also teaches us that they are not synonymous, but have a perceptible difference of meaning, such as we have indicated. In the prayer of Hezekiah (Isa. xxxviii. 11) we cannot mistake the same reference to him who has actually and signally manifested his being in the former history of his chosen people, and will yet still further vindicate his title to this emphatic designation. This name also occurs forty-one times in the Psalms, which are full of historical allusions. In Ps. cxviii. 14, the present clause is again repeated, and the name recurs six times in all. The doxology הַלְלוּ־יָהּ is repeated twenty-four times. The name is natural in such a combination, as praise often turns upon benefits actually conferred.

זִמְרָת old form of זִמְרָה.

אַנְוֵהוּ *I will glorify* or *celebrate*. Others, I will *cause to dwell, make a habitation for*.

20. מִרְיָם Miriam, Μαριάμ, Μαρίᾳ, *exalted, contumacious* or bitter.

תֹּף *timbrel*, the Spanish aduffa or diff; r. *strike*.

23. מָרָה Marah, *bitterness.*
27. אֵילִם Elim, *trees.*

XV. 1. Then sang Moses and the sons of Israel this song unto the Lord, and they spake, saying:

I will sing unto the LORD, for he hath triumphed gloriously:
The horse and his rider hath he thrown into the sea.
2. My strength and song is JAH, and he became my salvation:
He is my God, and I will glorify him;
My father's God, and I will exalt him.
3. The LORD is a man of war, the Lord is his name.
4. Pharoh's chariots and his army hath he cast into the sea:
And the choice of his knights are drowned in the Red Sea.
5. The depths have covered them:
They sank into the pools as a stone.
6. Thy right hand, O LORD, is glorious in power:
Thy right hand, O LORD, crusheth the enemy.
7. And in thy great triumph thou overthrowest thy foes:
Thou sendest forth thy wrath; it consumes them as stubble.
8. And with the blast of thy nostrils, the waters were heaved up:
The floods stood upright as a heap:
The depths were condensed in the heart of the sea.
9. The enemy said, I will pursue, I will overtake,
I will divide the spoil: my lust shall be full of them;
I will draw my sword; my hand shall seize them.
10. Thou blewest with thy blast, the sea covered them:
They sank as lead in the mighty waters.
11. Who is like thee among the gods, O LORD?

Who is like thee, glorious in holiness,
Awful in praises, doing wonders?
12. Thou stretchedst out thy right hand; the earth swallowed them:
13. Thou leddest in thy mercy the people thou hast redeemed:
Thou guidedst them in thy strength to thy holy habitation.
14. The nations have heard, they tremble:
Terror hath seized the inhabitants of Pelasheth.
15. Then were the dukes of Edom confounded;
The chiefs of Moab, trembling took hold of them:
All the inhabitants of Kenaan melted away.
16. Horror and trembling shall fall upon them;
By thy great arm they shall be still as a stone:
Till thy people pass over, O LORD;
Till the people thou hast purchased pass over.
17. Thou shalt bring them and plant them in the hill of thine inheritance;
The place of thy dwelling thou hast made, O LORD:
The sanctuary, O Lord, thy hands have established.
18. The LORD shall reign for ever and ever.

19. For the horse of Pharoh went with his chariot and his
horsemen into the sea; and the LORD brought back upon them
the waters of the sea: and the sons of Israel went on the dry
ground in the midst of the sea. ¶ 25.

20. And Miriam the phrophetess, the sister of Aaron, took
the timbrel in her hand; and all the women came forth after
her with timbrels and with dances. 21. And Miriam answered
them, Sing ye to the LORD, for he hath triumphed gloriously;
the horse and his rider hath he thrown into the sea. § 16.

22. And Moses led Israel from the Red Sea; and they came
out into the wilderness of Shur: and they went three days in
the wilderness, and found no water. 23. And they came to

Marah, and could not drink the water out of Marah, for it was bitter: therefore they called the name of it Marah. 24. And the people murmured against Moses, saying, What shall we drink? 25. And he cried unto the LORD, and the LORD shewed him a tree, and he cast it into the water, and the water was made sweet: there he set them a statute and an ordinance, and there he proved them. 26. And he said, If thou wilt diligently hearken to the voice of the LORD thy God, and do that which is right in his eyes, and give ear to his commandments, and keep all his statutes, no disease which I put upon Mizraim will I put upon thee; for I am the LORD that healeth thee.

§ 17.

27. And they came to Elim, where were twelve springs of water and seventy palm trees; and they encamped there by the water.

A reverential fear and a grateful trust in the Lord were the sentiments that swelled in the breasts of Israel as they beheld the issue of that awful interposition by which they themselves were saved and their enemies destroyed. These emotions find expression in the following song of Moses, the highest merit of which is its fitness for the occasion. It is a triumphal ode, in which the joyful people celebrate the praises of their divine deliverer. They ask not wisely, who demand a long training or a high culture as the needful antecedent of a nation's songs. The nation that is capable of achieving or estimating noble deeds is wont to contain within itself some voice that gives meet utterance to its loftiest emotions in harmonious numbers. The man who was able to describe in fitting symmetry of style the ancient ways of God with man was also competent to express, in the measured flow of winged words, the devout thanksgiving of Israel to the God of his salvation. This ode consists of eighteen verses, arranged in alternate stanzas of three and two verses. It consequently begins and ends with a stanza of three verses. The long stanzas refer to the Lord and his ransomed people, and the short stanzas to their defeated or dismayed opponents. If read according to this arrangement the import of the ode will come out more finely and strikingly. The song, and the circumstances which accompanied its singing, occupy twenty-one verses, and the remaining seven verses of the chapter record the journey to and the encampment at Elim.

1–18. The song of Moses. *Then sang.* On the very occasion when the mind of Moses was strung up to the highest pitch under the influence of the Spirit of the Lord was this ode composed. *Moses and the sons of Israel.* The primitive tribes of mankind seem to have had a singular aptitude for taking up the strain of emotion, and chanting it in concert to some simple measure. The harp and the pipe were among the earliest discoveries of the race, and these presuppose the modulated cadences of the human voice. The untutored ear of the enthusiast arranges the coming words into the artless warblings of immortal verse. The fine melody, laden with the noble sentiment, finds an echo in other breasts, and the sublime harmony of sound and feeling bursts from the assembled multitude. Music is the handmaid of memory and the shadow of reason. It cannot surprise us, then, to find Moses and the sons of Israel on the scene and in the hour of so great a deliverance giving utterance to their common emotions in the triumphal ode. *This song unto the Lord.* There wanted but this addition, "unto the Lord," to give its true character to the solemn anthem which now rose from the many thousands of Israel. Man never rises to the height of his dignity until he realizes his relation to his Creator. The following hymn is a model and a storehouse of materials for all future songs of praise.

1–5. These verses contain the first period of song. Three verses celebrate the praises of the Lord; two dwell on the downfall of his enemies. *I will sing.* Each patriot for himself lifts up the general song of praise. *Unto the Lord,* unto God, whose character it is to give existence to his purpose and promise. *For he hath triumphed gloriously;* he has manifested the grandeur of his power to save the oppressed and destroy the oppressor. *The horse and his rider.* This is a general reference to the scene of the preceding night, in which the promise-performing character of God was conspicuously displayed. 2. *Jah,* He who has manifested his being by signal acts of power. *My strength and song.* He has proved himself able to deliver me, and therefore he is the object of my praise. *Became my salvation.*

By actually saving me from the might of Egypt, he has earned his title to the name Yah. *My God.* I have, in my own person, experienced his goodness, and with appropriating faith I gratefully confess him to be mine. *I will glorify him.* I will proclaim his excellency. *My father's God,* the God of history and of covenant, who chose the head of that peculiar people to which I belong. *I will exalt him,* acknowledge his transcendent majesty. 3. *A man of war.* A mighty potentate, who encounters and vanquishes all the adversaries of good. *The Lord is his name.* It is his essential characteristic to be the Author and sole Fountain of all existence, and the performer of his promise. Never since the beginning of things did this property of God receive a more practical proof than in the rescue of Israel from the bondage of Mizraim. After this triad of praise follow two verses of song on the downfall of Egypt. 4. *Pharoh's chariots and his army.* This verse forms a fine synthetic parallel, in which the second member ascends above the first, and so the two constitute a climax. The next verse is a briefer climax of a similar kind.

6–10. In this second wave of song three verses, again, are dedicated to the Lord, and two to the adversary. In vs. 6 we have a parallel, in which the first member dwells on the cause and the second on the effect. In vs. 7 the parallel is in the sense rather than the form of the words. In vs. 8 three parallel members lend their emphasis to the deed of wonder which they celebrate. The former triplet referred more to the character of God; the present gives more prominence to his procedure. The two verses relating to the adversary are full of compressed energy. In vs. 9 six intents of the enemy are condensed into one short utterance, which may be divided into two parts, of three sentences each, according to the punctuation, or into three members, of two sentences each, according to the printing. In the next verse of two members, the breath of God's mouth is enough, not only to upset all these arrogant purposes, but to sink the proud boasters into the depths of the sea. In the former couplet the outward array of Pharoh's host was depicted, in the present the inward vaunting of their soul is expressed; in both the same disastrous end is poetically recorded.

11–15. This is the third swell of this sacred anthem, and it is a step in advance of the other two. *Among the gods,* among the mighty ones, the imaginary deities whom the nations adore. *Glorious in holiness.* The characteristics of God here set forth are those on which he has been on this occasion distinguished from all conceivable objects of comparison. Holiness, or absolute purity of nature, is one of these attributes of God, in which he transcends all fallen man's imaginary gods. The gods of Greece, Rome, India, and all other heathens, partook of the moral infirmity of their votaries. On the contrary, holiness is the glory, the conspicuous excellence, of the divine essence. *Awful in praises.* Praises are here put for the praiseworthy deeds which come from him whose glory is holiness. In regard to the holiness of these deeds he is truly awful, because he taketh vengeance for transgression with as much exactness as he giveth recompense for obedience. His judgment on the oppressor is as signal as his mercy to the oppressed. *Doing wonders.* His power is equal to his holiness and equity. The proud doer is destined to give way to his will, or perish in the attempt to resist it. Holiness and omnipotence mark the administration of God, and hence he is awful in praises. In these respects he is incomparably above the so-called gods of the heathen. In the two following verses we have the judicial and merciful works proclaimed that entitle him to be described as awful in praises. 13. *Thou hast guided them in thy strength to thy holy habitation.* The habitation of his holiness is most simply understood in a large sense of the land wherein his people are to dwell. He is their God, and will dwell with them, and consecrate the land of their habitation. Into this land they may be fairly said to have entered when they crossed the Red Sea, for its bounds were to be from the Red Sea unto the sea of the Philistines (xxiii. 31). Hence the statement "thou hast guided them," in the perfect tense, is literally true. But, according to the Hebrew idiom, even that which is purposed and determined in the mind and words of the speaker is indicated by the perfect form of the verb (Gen. xxiii. 11), much more that which, in its main substance, has been already effected. Now the chief part of their guidance into the holy land was accomplished when they were brought out of the bondage and territory of Mizraim. The remainder was as sure as if it were already completed in the promise and power of God. This third triplet celebrates the triumph of Jehovah. 14, 15. The Egyptian host is at rest for ever in the silence of death. The poet's eye, therefore, turns to the surviving nations who might throw obstacles in the way of the redeemed people. The nations in general tremble. In particular the Philistines, who bordered on the one entrance into the land of holiness, and the Edomites and Moabites, who lay on the other route by which it might be entered, were filled with alarm. The inhabitants of Kenaan, who were doomed to extirpation because their iniquity was now full, melted away at the reports of Mizraim's overthrow. All this is expressed in the high-strung language of poetic realism, because that is conceived to have a hold on existence which is the inevitable and immediate consequence of things that have already taken place.

16–18. The bard of emancipated Israel now turns to the future. The further doings of the Lord for his people are sketched in a few master touches. First, a sudden and overwhelming trepidation unmans the adversary, and the people of the Lord are unopposed in their progress. This was the natural result of the divine interposition, and would have been the actual and uniform consequence, but for the unbelief and disobedience of the chosen people. 17. *Thou shalt bring them and plant them.* This is a figure taken from a tree planted on a hill. The tree is the holy people (Ps. i. 3); the hill is the land of promise, which was not a river valley, like Egypt, but a high land lying between the Jordan and the Mediterranean. To the hill of Zion there may be a distant allusion. *The place for thy dwelling*, is the fixed abode where he will constantly dwell. *The sanctuary.* In these three parallels we have the climax of country, home, and altar. 18. *The Lord shall reign for ever and ever.* In this closing verse the Lord is announced as perpetual king. The introduction of three dispensations relating to man is clearly marked out in Scripture. First, The creation begins an economy in which man forms a part of the kingdom of God, until the fall begins the kingdom of Satan on the earth. Then the exodus commences a dispensation in which the kingdom of God begins to stand out in visible opposition to that of Satan, in the narrow sphere of the seed of Abraham and the land of Kenaan. The kingdom thus rising into visibility never again disappears from the earth. Lastly, the birth, death, and resurrection of Christ ushers in a dispensation in which the kingdom of God is destined to penetrate more and more into the usurped kingdom of

Satan, until the latter be utterly destroyed, and the former be universally restored on the earth. There is a hopeful emphasis in the closing sentence of this sublime anthem.

19. This verse is a recapitulation of the auspicious occasion on which the above hymn was composed.

20, 21. The refrain of Miriam and the daughters of Israel. It is most probable, as we have already seen, that the women and children were principally with the flocks and herds, and not with the marshalled host that crossed the Red Sea. But a joyful reunion of as many of them as could leave domestic cares would be sure to take place on this joyful occasion. Miriam, and a few of the females of higher rank, may have even accompanied the host. Miriam is here described as the prophetess, as one who was well known to possess the gift of speaking to God for men, or to men for God, in prose or in song (Gen. xx. 7 ; Num. xii. 2). She is called the sister of Aaron, as he and she were older than Moses, and yet at the same time inferior to him in point of official rank. *Took the timbrel*, the well-known instrument for the female and the dancer. It was composed of a hoop or rim covered with skin, like a drum-head. It was sometimes provided with little brass rings or bells fastened round the rim, which added a jingle to its drum-like sound. *And with dances* Miriam led the way with the timbrel in the dance, and all the women followed. The females danced in a separate choir, and the males also by themselves (2 Sam. vi. 14). The dance is here used for the expression of a sacred joy. The song articulates, the dance gesticulates, the emotions of joy and congratulation. *And Miriam answered them.* She led the refrain, as Moses seems to have led the song itself. The song begins thus, "I will sing unto the Lord"; the refrain thus, "Sing ye to the Lord." This may have been chanted after every period of five verses, and at the end of the ode, as a completion of the last period. This is much more probable than the introduction of the refrain at the end of every verse, especially as the verses are of very unequal length.

22–26. The journey from the Red Sea to Elim. *The wilderness of Shur* (Gen. xvi. 7). Part of this wilderness takes its name from Etham which was on its border (xiii. 20; Num. xxxiii. 8). *They went three days.* If they paused at Sukkoth on the first day after the passover night, ecamped at Etham on the second, and at Hahiroth on the third, crossed the Red Sea on the night of that day, and then advanced three days into the wilderness, they would arrive at Marah on the seventh day of the feast of unleavened bread. In the interval of two miles between the shore and Ayun Musa (the wells of Moses), they celebrated their deliverance by chanting the song of Moses. The Ayun Musa are seven in number, according to Robinson, with many lesser springs around. After having refreshed themselves here they may have proceeded some way towards Marah, and so performed their first day's journey. The distance from Ayun Musa to Ain Hawarah, which is usually identified with Marah, is sixteen and one half hours, or about forty miles. The route lies between the Gulf of Suez, and the range of Jebel er Rahah. Ain Hawarah is a fountain of bitter water about three feet deep, contained in a basin of ten feet in diameter, and six feet in depth. The palm and the thorny ghurkud are found around it. It still merits the title of Marah, as its waters are bitter. 24. *And the people murmured against Moses.* We now hear the first murmur arising from the redeemed people. The marshalled host advancing as a regular body felt the want of water much more severely than if they had been scattered over the country like their wives and children. They had been wont to enjoy ample supplies of water in Egypt, and to search not in vain for it even in the wilderness, when divided into families and small parties. For the wilderness was not unfamiliar to them as nomads or roving shepherds, though the present route may not have been trodden by many of them before. The wilderness, it is to be remembered, is land affording a scanty pasture, but not fit for tillage (Gen. xxi. 14). With the exception of the Debbet er Ramleh (plain of sand) and a narrow strip along the Mediterranean, the wilderness of the peninsula is not a sandy but a gravelly soil, producing a sparse vegetation wherever there is any moisture. But the assembled multitude are grievously distressed by the want of water, and do not refrain from expressing their dissatisfaction. Moses however, having travelled this way before, must have been aware that water was near. Accordingly, on the evening of the sixth day, or early on the seventh, they arrived at Marah. A new trial of their patience is presented by the bitterness of the water, which was the more disagreeable to those who had been accustomed to the sweet waters of the Nile. To obviate this inconvenience the Lord pointed out a wood to Moses which sweetened the waters. Burckhardt suggests that the berries of the ghurkud might have produced this effect. But this fruit ripens in June, two months later than the time when the people of Israel arrived at Marah; and this was a tree or species of wood, not a berry. The effect was probably not natural, but miraculous, and the kind of wood is unknown. *There he made them a statute and an ordinance.* If this was on the seventh day of the feast of unleavened bread, and therefore a Sabbath of holy convocation, in which, however, extraordinary works of necessity and mercy had to be done, we can see how opportune was the time for making a statute and an ordinance. The slaying of the passover was a solemn entering into covenant with the Lord, and the last day of the feast was the completion of this act. They had now also gone three days into the wilderness, and therefore arrived at the place and time for performing the proposed sacrifice unto the Lord their God, as he should command them (viii. 27). A statute (חֹק) is a form of words engraven on a hard substance, such as stone, and therefore a fixed edict or decree, binding the people to follow the Lord. An ordinance (מִשְׁפָּט) is a judicial sentence or authoritative injunction, affirming the duty of the people, and accompanied with an intimation of the good and evil consequences of obedience and disobedience. The solemn consent of the people to this ordinance was given on this appropriate occasion. A similar transaction is recorded when Joshua renewed the covenant with the people (Josh. xxiv. 25). The substance of the statute and the ordinance is evidently contained in the following verse. The general obligation only to obey the Lord in all things is here tendered and accepted. The special terms of the divine law are to be communicated on a future occasion. *And there he proved them.* The want of water for three days, and the bitterness of the water when at length found, were the touchstone to test their hearts, to discover what qualities or dispositions were within, to try whether they had the beginning of faith and patience. 26. *If thou wilt diligently hearken.* Here the condition of perfect obedience to the occasional, as well as to the stated, commands of God, is explicitly laid down. *No disease.* The reward of obedience is expressly announced, and the consequence of disobedience not obscurely intimated. The very blessings of the Egyptians were turned into curses on account of their disobedience.

The sweet waters of the Nile were changed into blood. On the other hand the disadvantages the Israelites might meet with on the way would be converted into blessings if they were obedient to the voice of the Lord. The bitter waters of Marah are made sweet. This single instance indicated the rule of all God's future dealings, and so furnished the test by which their character was to be proved. *I am the Lord that healeth thee.* He had preserved them from the diseases of Egypt, the death of the first-born, and the destruction which overtook the Egyptians. So would he be their deliverer in every trouble which should befall them. Thus Marah, with its bitter waters, sweetened even the commencement of that testing process which this people had to undergo in the wilderness.

27. *Elim.* This is identified with Wady Ghurundel, which is two hours or a few miles from Marah. The twelve springs and seventy palms made it a most delightful halting-place for the thirsting host. "Wady Ghurundel is fringed with trees and shrubs, forming a charming oasis. Here are the stunted palms, with their hairy trunks and dishevelled branches; here, too, are the feathery tamarisks, with gnarled boughs; and here is the accaia, with its gray foliage and bright blossoms, tangled by its desert growth into a thicket" (Porter, in Murray's Hand-book of Syria and Palestine). This refreshing valley is but a step from Marah, and may be regarded as the first resting-place of the sons of Israel after their departure from Egypt. Here, accordingly, they remained for the space of three weeks (xvi. 1), during which they had leisure to accommodate themselves in some measure to desert life, to the habits of freedom and independence, and, above all, to the solemnities of a people reconciled to God and resolved to walk in newness of life. At this point, therefore, the chapter appropriately closes.

## X. JOURNEY FROM ELIM TO SINAI.—Ex. xvi.-xviii.

### CHAP. XVI.—QUAILS AND MANNA.

1. סִין I. Sin, *clay* (Ges.). Pelusium or Tine (mud-town?). II. Sin, *bush, thorn.* The wilderness described in the present passage.

סִינַי, Sinai, *thorny, scraggy* (Meyer), the mountain on which the law was proclaimed. This name is apparently connected with the preceding. It is probable that both belong to the same root with סְנֶה a species of thorn (iii. 2).

13. שְׂלָו *quail*, ὀρτυγομήτρα (Sept.), mother of quails, rail or quail king. Not locusts, as Patrick supposes, since they are nowhere else called by this name; nor the *Kata* of the Arabians, a kind of partridge which abounds in Arabia and Syria.

14. חָסַף *peel* (Ges.), *run, cast, freeze* (Meyer).

15. מָן *manna*; r. מן *divide, separate.* Hence it means the secretion, or sweet gum exuding in shining drops on the twigs and branches of the turfa or tamarisk when punctured, it is supposed, by the *coccus manniparus.* This is now called *man assama*, the gift of heaven, by the Arabs, according to the common habit of ascribing a later and more familiar meaning to the word than that which it originally possessed. It falls on the leaves, twigs, or stones beneath, and has to be gathered before it is melted by the sun. It is then cleansed, boiled, strained, and put into leathern bottles, and keeps for a long time. This manna is not peculiar to Arabia nor to the tamarisk; is produced in small quantities in wet seasons, and nearly disappears in dry ones; is gathered in the month of June, and is used only as a condiment with the unleavened bread or pottage of the country.

23. שַׁבָּתוֹן *rest, cessation from labor.* The word is found only in Exodus and Leviticus, and shows no change of vowel. Here only is it before שַׁבָּת. It is also without the article, simply because it is either the predicate or in the construct state. Hence there is no ground for the supposition that its indefinite form marks the introduction of the Sabbath as a new thing hitherto unknown.

31. גַּד, κόριον (Sept.), *coriander.* Αἰγύπτιοι ὄχιον, Ἀφροὶ γοίδ, quotes Celsius from the annotator of Dioscorides, when speaking of this plant. Γοίδ is evidently the Heb. גַּד. *Coriandrum sativum* is an umbelliferous plant, the leaves of which are used in soups and salads. Its seeds are globular, about the size of a pepper-corn, and of a greyish color. They form an agreeable spice, employed by confectioners, druggists, and distillers. This plant is common in Egypt and other parts of Africa, Arabia, Persia, India, and the south of Europe, and is cultivated in some parts of England.

36. עֹמֶר *sheaf of corn.* In the present chapter alone, *omer*, a dish or other vessel containing probably the grain obtained from the sheaf, and therefore always nearly of the same size, and so fitted to be a rough measure. It is to be distinguished from the homer (חֹמֶר) which contained ten ephahs, and therefore one hundred omers.

XVI. 1. And all the assembly of the sons of Israel set out from Elim, and came unto the wilderness of Sin, which is between Elim and Sinai, on the fifteenth day of the second month of their departure out of the land of Mizraim. 2. And all the assembly of the sons of Israel murmured against Moses and Aaron in the wilderness. 3. And the sons of Israel said unto them, Would that we had died by the hand of the Lord in the land of Mizraim, when we sat by the flesh-pot, when we ate bread to the full! For ye have brought us forth into this wilderness to slay all this congregation with hunger. § 18.

4. Then said the Lord unto Moses, Behold, I will rain for you bread from heaven, and the people shall go out and gather a certain rate every day, that I may prove them whether they will walk in my law or not. 5. And it shall be on the sixth day that they shall prepare that which they bring in, and it shall be twice as much as they gather daily. 6. And Moses and Aaron said unto all the sons of Israel, At even, then shall ye know that the Lord hath brought you out of the land of Mizraim. 7. And in the morning, then ye shall see the glory of the Lord, since he heareth your murmurings against the Lord: and what are we that ye murmur against us? 8. And Moses said, When the Lord giveth you in the evening flesh to eat, and bread in the morning to the full, since the Lord heareth your murmurings which ye murmur against him, what then are we? Your murmurings are not against us, but against the Lord. 9. And Moses said unto Aaron, Say unto all the assembly of the sons of Israel, Draw near before

the Lord, for he hath heard your murmurings. 10. And it
came to pass, when Aaron spake unto all the assembly of the
sons of Israel, that they turned toward the wilderness; and
behold the glory of the Lord appeared in the cloud. ¶ 26.

11. And the Lord spake unto Moses, saying, 12. I have
heard the murmurings of the sons of Israel: speak unto them,
saying, Between the evenings ye shall eat flesh, and in the
morning ye shall be filled with bread; and ye shall know that
I am the Lord your God.

13. And it came to pass at even that quails came up, and
covered the camp; and in the morning the dew lay round
about the camp. 14. And the dew that lay went up; and
behold upon the face of the wilderness something fine and
crisp, fine as the rime on the ground. 15. And the sons of
Israel saw it, and said one to another, It is manna. For they
wist not what it was. And Moses said unto them, it is the
bread which the Lord hath given you to eat. 16. This the
thing which the Lord hath commanded; Gather of it every
man according to his eating, an omer to the poll for the num-
ber of your persons; take ye every man for them that are in his
tent. 17. And the sons of Israel did so, and they gathered,
some more, some less. 18. And they meted it with the omer;
and he that gathered much had nothing over, and he that
gathered little had no lack: they gathered every man accord-
ing to his eating. 19. And Moses said unto them, Let no man
leave of it till the morning. 20. And they hearkened not
unto Moses; and some left of it till the morning, and it bred
worms and stank: and Moses was wrath with them. 21.
And they gathered it every morning, every man according to
his eating: and when the sun waxed hot it melted.

22. And it came to pass on the sixth day that they gathered
twice as much bread, two omers for each one, and all the

rulers of the assembly came and told Moses. 23. And he said unto them, This is that which the LORD hath spoken. To-morrow is the rest of the holy Sabbath unto the LORD: bake that which ye will bake, and seethe that which ye will seethe, and all that remaineth over lay up for you to be kept until the morning. 24. And they laid it up till the morning, as Moses bade; and it did not stink, neither was there any worm therein. 25. And Moses said, Eat it to-day, for to-day is the Sabbath unto the LORD: to-day ye shall not find it in the field. 26. Six days ye shall gather it; and on the seventh day, the Sabbath, on it there shall be none. 27. And it came to pass on the seventh day, that some of the people went out to gather, and they found none. § 19.

28. And the LORD said unto Moses, How long refuse ye to keep my commandments and my laws? 29. See ye that the LORD hath given you the Sabbath; therefore he giveth you on the sixth day the bread of two days: abide ye every man in his place; let no man come out of his place on the seventh day. 30. And the people rested on the seventh day. 31. And the house of Israel called the name thereof manna: and it was like coriander seed, white; and the taste of it was like a cake made with honey.

32. And Moses said, This is the thing which the LORD hath commanded, Fill an omer of it to be kept for your generations, that they may see the bread wherewith I fed you in the wilderness, when I brought you forth from the land of Mizraim. 33. And Moses said unto Aaron, Take a pot, and put therein an omer full of manna, and lay it up before the LORD to be kept for your generations. 34. As the Lord commanded Moses, so Aaron laid it up before the testimony to be kept. 35. And the sons of Israel ate manna forty years, until they came to a land inhabited: they ate manna until they came to the

border of the land of Kenaan. 36. And the omer was the tenth part of the ephah.

The subsection containing this chapter and the following two records the important particulars of the journey from Elim to Sinai. In Numbers xxxiii. 10–15 are enumerated five stations between these points, of which only the second, the Wilderness of Sin, and the last, Rephidim, are mentiond here. The present object of the historian is to notice the provision, protection, and government of the people in their wanderings. They were provided with quails, manna, and water from the rock; they were protected from the enemy in the victory they gained over Amalek; and they were governed by Moses, with the advice of Jethro, his father-in-law. The mixture of evil with good which is displayed in the conduct of the people, is what might be expected from a tribe of fallen men, long corrupted by the habits of bondage, under a nation ignorant of the God, or the law of truth, when they are but recently brought under the influence of the Spirit of truth, freedom, and holiness.

1–3. The second ground of complaint among the multitude is want of food. Any supplies they may have brought from Egypt were now exhausted. *All the assembly of the sons of Israel.* The difficulties of procuring water and food were enormously increased to a collected host. The wives and children who were scattered over the country, as the Bedawin or wanderers of the desert, were able to make some shift for themselves, from the smallness of their parties and their acquaintance with a desert life. But the marshalled multitude in a desert, without a well-arranged commissariat, could only subsist by supernatural means. *And came into the wilderness of Sin.* From Num. xxx. 10 it appears that when they left Elim their first encampment was by the Red Sea. Proceeding at present from Wady Ghurundel, in two and a quarter hours, we come upon Wady Useit, or Waseit, in which are a few brackish springs, with groves of palms and tamarisks. In four hours more we arrive at the point where Wady Shubeikeh and Wady Humr unite to form Wady Taiyibeh. Thence to the plain on the shore of the Red Sea is a distance of two hours. This is probably the place of encampment by the Red Sea, where the people might have a supply of water, and obtain a last view of the land of Egypt, and at the same time catch a glimpse of the mountain peaks towards which they were journeying. Over the headland of Zelima, two hours farther, lies the plain Murkhah, where there is also a fountain. We may suppose the main body of the six hundred thousand sons of Israelites spreading themselves over all the interval between Taiyibeh and Murkhah by the Red Sea. *And went unto the wilderness of Sin.* The next station mentioned in Num. xxxiii. 11 is in the Wilderness of Sin. This region is said to be between Elim and Sinai. It is more narrowly limited by the station at the sea and Rephidim (xvii. 1). And though the station at the entrance into this wilderness is the only one mentioned here, yet we know from Num. xxxiii. 12–14 that two other stations, Dophkah and Alush, were occupied in it. Among the three stations in this extensive range of desert at least a week seems to have been spent. The tradition that they arrived here on a Sabbath coincides well with the details of the narrative. Yet the site of the present station is by no means determined. From the Red Sea at Taiyibeh three routes to Sinai are possible: one southern, by the barren plain el-Kaa, lying along the Gulf of Suez, and up the Wady Hibran; another intermediate, by the Wadys Shellal, Mukatteb, Feiran, and Sheikh; and a third north of both, by the Wady Humr, the Debbet er-Ramleh, and the Wady Sheikh. The intervening stations are the wilderness of Sin, Dophkah, Alush, and Rephidim, all of which being unknown fail to give us any aid in determining the route actually pursued. The first route, however, extending to nearly one hundred miles, while the others are about eighty miles, may be rejected as too long for five days' march. If the Wilderness of Sin be the Plain of el-Kaa, the route must have been through the Wadys Mukatteb and Feiran, as this alone of the remaining two touched on that plain. If it be the Debbet er-Ramleh, the route must have been the most northern of the three. Wady esh-Sheikh forms the closing part of both these routes. The northern one seems the most open for a large body of men. The intermediate one is that preferred by most scholars. It merely touches upon el-Kaa at Ain el-Murkhah. Its main attractions lie in the Wady Mukatteb and Wady Feiran. The former, the written valley, is remarkable for the number of its rude sculptures, consisting of inscriptions in the Nabathaean, Greek, and Latin characters, and figures of men, animals, and some other objects, on the flat surfaces of the freestone rocks of which the valley is composed. But these, though noticed by Cosmas as early as 535 A.C., are not yet proved to have any connection with the Israelites, and moreover are not confined to the Wady Mukatteb. Wady Feiran contains the ruins of Feiran, the Faran of early Christian times, the resort of pilgrims, and the see of a bishop as early as the fourth century. Hence many have been disposed to find here the Paran of Scripture, and thus establish at least one identification of names in this region. But (1) the narrative contains no mention of Paran; (2) the people did not reach the wilderness of Paran till they had travelled at least five days' journey in a northerly direction from Sinai (Num. x. 12, 33, xi. 3, 35, xii. 16); and (3) the two occurrences of Mount Paran (Deut. xxxiii. 2; Hab. iii. 3) connect it with Sinai not more closely than Seir and Teman, and therefore afford a very precarious ground for identification. These two passages, however, may have led to a patristic identification of Mount Paran with Serbal, the lofty five-peaked mountain south of Wady Feiran. But even if this be Paran, the omission of so remarkable a name in the narrative, both here and in Num. xxx., is strongly against the hypothesis that Israel travelled by this route. As there is nothing in the text demanding this middle route, so there are some considerations that seem not unfavorable to the one more to the north. (1.) There is but one station on the Red Sea. If the line of march had lain in el-Kaa, there would have been more than one on the shore. (2.) The Wilderness of Sin is said to be between Elim and Sinai; which agrees very well with Debbet er-Ramleh, but can only be applied in a very loose sense to el-Kaa. (3.) The marching host would be kept as near the wandering families and flocks as possible. This is favorable to the line farthest north, and decidedly against that by el-Kaa. For the wanderers would go as little toward the south as possible, seeing they were eventually to turn to the north. They would linger about the wadys, where water and fodder were accessible. We can imagine some of them in the Wadys Mukatteb and Feiran, and still more in the Wady Wutah, and along the slopes of Jebel et-Tih, north of the Debbet er-Ramleh. It would be very desirable that the collective body that formed the centre of the horde should be somewhere between the wandering parties of women and young people, and therefore in the south border of Debbet er-Ramleh. (4.) The Wilderness of Sin would then be the Debbet er-Ramleh, or "Sandy Plain," the first part of which, the Debbet en-Nusb, would be reached in one day's march from Wady Taiyibeh, and might be left in another march by penetrating into the system of wadys that lie on its south side. (5.) The stations Dophkah and Alush, which possibly correspond with Wadys Mureikhy and Akhdar, present no notable feature or incident, and are therefore omitted in the present narrative, a circumstance not so likely in Wadys Mukatteb and Feiran. (6.) The route by Debbet er-Ramleh is the more open and easy for a large body of men. There are some very difficult passes in the other route, which render it passable only for small companies at a time, and, therefore, insuperable for six hundred thousand men in five days march. For all these reasons we must reject the route by el-Kaa, unless we are prepared to take Jebel Um-Shaumer, the most southern peak of the mountain group, for Sinai. And for some of them, chiefly (2) and (5), we are strongly inclined to prefer the northern route, as the most probable. We are the more contented to rest in this conclusion when we imagine the Wadys Mukatteb and Feiran, and all others lying either south or north of Debbet er-Ramleh, abundantly peopled with the women and young people under twenty years of age, who are disannexed from the central host. It is extremely desirable that these, who are nearly double the number of the full-grown men, should have as much scope as possible in the environs of the main body, for the sustenance of themselves, and their flocks and herds. We do not feel at liberty to confine them even to the south of Jebel et-Tih, the great cretaceous range, running in an east-southeastern direction, and separating et-Tih, or the wilderness of Paran, from the mountainous region of the south. For these roaming companies could only in a very limited degree partake of the miraculous supplies, especially of water, afforded to the congregated host, and must therefore have an ample range for the water and herbage that will meet the most pressing wants of their numerous cattle.

Assuming, then, that Debbet er-Ramleh is the wilderness of Sin, we ascend Wady Humr, which, according to Robinson, is broad, and opens out into a large plain, with another broad wady coming into it from the east. The plain is contracted by Sarbut el-Jemel into a wady, where the limestone gives place to the sandstone. A broad belt of sandstone runs between the limestone of Jebel et-Tih, and the granite of the Jebel et-Tur, to which Sinai belongs. After passing this wady, which contains some specimens of the rock sculptures, the road again emerges on a broad plain sprinkled with herbage. Somewhere about the entrance of Wady en-Nusb, in which is a fine spring not far from the route, we may suppose the host to have encamped in the Wilderness of Sin. *On the fifteenth day of the second month of their departure*, that is, of the year of their departure. A full month, therefore, after they left Rameses, they reached the Wilderness of Sin, with resources completely exhausted.

2, 3. *All the assembly.* This refers we conceive to the six hundred thousand men of the marshalled host. *Murmured against Moses and Aaron.* The want of food now began to be sharply felt. They saw nothing but starvation before them, and they regarded Moses and Aaron as the authors of their present strait.

4–10. He that destroyed the harvest of Egypt by the hail and the locust now engages to rain bread for them from heaven. *Gather a certain rate every day.* This was to be daily bread. *That I may prove them.* As the abundance of Egypt vanished away before the indignation of the Lord, so the very barrenness of the wilderness gave way to the bountiful hand of the Lord, supplying their daily wants. In all this he was continuing the process of their probation. Their patience, faith, dependence, and thankfulness of spirit were constantly put to the test in their present experience. 5. *On the sixth day* double allowance shall be gathered. This is one element in the miraculous nature of the present supply. *They shall prepare*, measure, pound, or grind the whole quantity gathered (Num. xi. 8). It may also extend to the cooking (v. 23). 6, 7. Moses and Aaron now communicate the benignant design of the Lord to the people. *Then shall ye know.* By experience of his wonder-working power they would have a new proof that he had brought them out of Egypt. They seemed to forget his wonders in Egypt, when they ascribed their present position to Moses and Aaron. *Then ye shall see the glory of the Lord.* This is the parallel of the preceding sentence. The glory of the Lord is seen when his hand is put forth for the protection of his people by the discomfiture of their enemies, and for their preservation by the preternatural bestowment of the means of life. *Since he heareth your murmurings.* In his long-suffering mercy he will give another proof of his presence and love, that his people may at length lay aside their impatience and unbelief, and feel that their murmuring is really against the Lord, and not against the mere executors of his will. 8. Moses alone now explains to the people what the Lord is about to do. 9. He then directs Aaron to summon the people before the Lord, that is, to draw near to the place where the pillar of cloud and fire was. 10. The people at the word of Aaron turned toward the wilderness. *The glory of the Lord appeared in the cloud.* Such a dazzling brightness burst through the cloud as manifested the immediate presence of the Lord.

11, 12. The Lord, having now manifested his glorious presence in the cloud to the beholding people, charges Moses with a message to the people, promising relief to their hunger. *Between the evenings*, from the beginning of the evening before sunset to the end of twilight (see on Gen. i. 4). *Ye shall know that I am Jehovah your God.* The instruction of his people is a primary object with God. He has gifted them with reason, and he expects to be served with the understanding and the will. This can be done only so far as they know him to be God, the Eternal and Almighty, to be Jehovah, the Creator and Upholder of all things, and to be their God, to whom they are reconciled through his pardoning, redeeming, and quickening mercy. It is manifest that every event in his gracious dealings with them is a step in the process of their spiritual training. This alone will explain the various preparatory steps in this miraculous interposition. He first allows the people to feel their need (i. 3); then he intimates his intention to Moses; then Moses and Aaron admonish the people; then Moses announces the promise of food; then Moses directs Aaron to call the people before the Lord; then the Lord, manifesting his presence, recapitulates his message to Moses, and lastly performs his promise.

13–21. The performance of the promise is now recorded. *Quails*, literally "the quail" in a collective sense, a well-known species of migrating bird, that passes the winter in inner Africa and the summer in the northern regions. These are brought in great numbers to the camp of Israel, when, being wearied with their long flight, they are easily taken and killed. The miracle consisted in bringing the quails at the stated time to the required place, and in sufficient numbers for the supply of a large host, and in announcing beforehand their arrival.

*Came up.* Came up on the wing, and therefore made their appearance from a lower ground in the air. *And filled the camp*, alighted on the area occupied by the wide-spread host. *The dew lay.* Literally, there was a lying or layer of dew, a deposit on the surface from the surrounding atmosphere. We say a fall of dew. The former is the more exact figure.

14, 15. *The dew that lay went up.* A natural figure for the evaporation of the dew that had fallen during the night. *Something fine and crisp, fine as the rime on the ground.* This indicates a small grain, scaled or hardened after the drying up of the moisture. The smallness or fineness of the grain is compared with that of the rime or hoar-frost on the ground. We shall have other qualities of the manna as we proceed (vs. 31). *It is manna.* The original words, מָן הוּא are generally rendered as in the margin of our authorized version, "What is this?" But the former rendering appears to be demanded by the following reasons: (1.) "What is this" is expressed by a different phrase, מַה־הוּא, in the next sentence. The Masoretes favor this distinction, by pointing מָן הוּא, not מַן־הוּא, as in Dan. iii. 15. (2.) The explanatory sentence, "for they wist not what it was," is superfluous, if the latter meaning of מָן אוּא be taken. For the question, "What is this?" implies that they knew not what it was. The presence of this sentence, therefore, suggests another meaning for the previous words. (3.) The former meaning gives a significance to the explanatory clause. The people say one to another, in an inquiring way, "It is manna." By a common law of analogy or conversational generalization they give it the name of a comparatively scanty product of nature, to which it bears a considerable resemblance in locality, color, form, and perhaps taste, though it differs in origin, season, quantity, and other properties. They do this in the ignorance of the moment. This is what is expressed by the explanatory clause, "for they wist not what it was." They had no name for a new product, and they take the common method of calling it by the name of that which most nearly resembled it. Moses does not reject the name; but proceeds to explain the nature and origin of that which they had so named provisionally. *It is the bread.* Such is its nature. *Which the Lord hath given you.* Such it its origin.

The natural manna is gathered early in June, a month later than the present time, and in small quantity, not sufficient for the chief support of life. The supernatural manna was gathered every day, Sabbaths excepted, throughout the whole year, and in quantities sufficient for the main sustenance of a nation of at least one million six hundred thousand souls during a period of forty years.

16–21. The manner of gathering the manna is here prescribed. *Every man according to his eating*, according to the number of his family. This is explained by the following words. *An omer* (see vs. 36) *to the poll for the number of your persons.* This was the rate at which each gatherer was to aim. *For them that are in his tent.* The tent (Gen. iv. 20) is an awning or outside covering of any kind over the wooden poles or framework which formed the principal feature of the booth. The tent was older than the deluge, and the phrase, "them that are in his tent," indicates a man's family or company, whatever might be the covert under which they took shelter in the desert. It does not therefore determine that all or any were actually possessed of fully-equipped tents of hair-canvas, but that in general each had a family or company with which he tabernacled as best he could in this temporary mode of life. 17, 18. *And they gathered some more, some less.* Every man endeavored to gather at least as much as would serve his need, but some were more successful than others in the unmeasured result. *And he that gathered much had nothing over.* If the grasping hand of covetousness or a more favorable ground occasioned a greater gathering by some than by others, yet was the omer filled for each, and neither more nor less. A potent argument to teach them, if they would learn, that all men are equal in the sight of our Heavenly Father. There was a miracle here, take it how we will; and it would be the height of absurdity to meddle with the natural meaning of the words in order to give a simpler form to the miraculous act. He that distributed his bounty here could equalize each single gathering as easily as the collected whole with the ration allotted to each. 19–21. *Let no man leave of it till the morning.* Another mighty leveller for all the selfishness of pride. No store is to be accumulated. It was in vain that any one disobeyed this command. That which was reserved till the second day became putrid. This in itself was miraculous, as the natural manna kept for a considerable time. *And when the sun waxed hot, it melted.* The portion that was ungathered in this manner disappeared.

22–27. Not only the supply, but the manner of it, is miraculous. On five days a quantity sufficient for one day, on the sixth enough for two days, and on the seventh none whatever is found. *All the rulers of the assembly,* These are the heads of tribes, and of fathers' houses (Num. iii. 24, 30, 35). *Came and told Moses.* Moses had not communicated the intimation that on the sixth day they would receive a double supply. The arrangement was a deviation from the law of nature, which knows nothing of a seventh day's rest. The phenomenon, therefore, demanded an explanation. *To-morrow is the rest of the holy Sabbath to the Lord.* The word "rest" is here put first, because the thing to be noted is the cessation of labor on the morrow as a reason for the double supply on the sixth day. It does not appear that the rulers were unacquainted with the Sabbath. But they had no experience hitherto of a special provision on the Lord's part for its convenient observance. In the annual return of the ordinary harvest a store was laid up for the year from which they could supply themselves for the Sabbath. But now they were nourished from day to day. Hence the necessity of a double ration on the sixth day, if the Sabbath was to be duly kept. It is possible that the Sabbath was imperfectly observed, or altogether neglected, during the bondage of Israel in Egypt, though there is no positive indication of this in the text. That it should have been forgotten, however, is contrary to the traditionary customs of many other nations besides the Jews. Traces of the septenary division of time have been found among the Egyptians, Hindoos, Chinese, and Peruvians. From the first of these it is said (Dion Cassius) to have passed to the Greeks, Romans, and the Teutonic nations. If it has left its mark on these scattered Gentiles, much more must it have been remembered among the chosen people, who were so near the origin of mankind, and seem to have possessed a continued thread of well-authenticated tradition. *All that remaineth over,* after partaking for the day, of the two omers which had been prepared for food in whatever manner they pleased. *Lay up for you,* ready for eating on the following day. Hence Moses says on the Sabbath (vs. 25), not "bake or seethe," but "eat it." 24. *It did not stink.* That it should have become putrid the day after being cooked is no new difficulty, when we are in the region of the miraculous. 25, 26. Directions are now explicitly given regarding the days on which the manna was to be gathered. 27. *Some of the people*, from inadvertence or ignorance of the directions given, make the experiment, and find the prophet's word good.

28–31. The transgressors are now rebuked through Moses for their heedless disobedience. *My commandments and my laws* (see on Gen. xxvi. 5). The former probably refer to the special regulations concerning the manna; the latter to the standing institution of the Sabbath. 29. *The Lord hath given you the Sabbath.* There is in the previous passage no express giving of the Sabbath, but rather a tacit assumption that it has been already given. This is in accordance with its institution at the creation of man recorded in Gen. ii. 1–3. It is here to be noted that the Sabbath is a gift to man, who is doomed to labor in his fallen state (Gen. iii. 17–19). A periodical recurrence of relief from labor and leisure for fellowship with God and with one another is a precious boon of heaven to the toil-worn in body or mind. *Abide ye every man in his place.* Come not out for any business, such as gathering manna. They were at liberty to go abroad for any purpose accordant with the Sabbath, such as attendance on the holy convocation (Lev. xxiii. 3; Acts xv. 21). Even works of necessity or mercy, that cannot be put off till the next day, are not regarded as a real breach of the Sabbath (Matt. xii. 1–13; Mark ii. 23–28). There seems to have been no limit to the distance to be walked on the Sabbath beyond that of convenience, leisure from business, and release from toil. The Rabbinical rule of later times, however, was that a Sabbath day's journey should consist of two thousand cubits, about five or six furlongs. This was imagined to be the distance of the remotest part of the camp from the tabernacle. It was the distance of the Mount of Olives from Jerusalem (Acts i. 12). 30. *Rested*, וַיִּשְׁבְּתוּ, kept the Sabbath, or day of rest.

31. We have already seen that the manna from heaven (Ps. lxxviii. 24, cv. 40) was like a fine grain, as small as the hoar-frost. We are now informed that it was like coriander seed in form, of a whitish color, and of the taste of a cake made with honey. It could be also baked or seethed; and this is in accordance with the statement in Num. xi. 7, 8: "And the manna was like coriander seed, and the

color thereof as the color of bdellium. And the people went about and gathered, and ground it in the mill, or beat it in the mortar, and baked it in the pan, and made cakes of it; and the taste of it was as the taste of oil cates." From the description given above, it will be apparent that the miraculous manna bore such a resemblance to the natural product so called, as to lead to the employment of a name common to both. But the natural manna differed from the supernatural in its chemical ingredients; the former being of a gummy or resinous nature, and the latter containing a farinaceous element. Hence the latter could be ground and baked into bread or boiled into pottage, for which the former was only a condiment. The natural manna also could be kept for years; the supernatural became putrid in a night. Other differences have been noted on verses 14, 15. The taste of the "cake made with honey" was probably much the same as that of the "oil cates." But the one may refer, as some think, to the taste of the raw and the other to that of the baked manna. The color of bdellium when fresh and pure was probably whitish.

32-36. This great gift of bread from heaven to the chosen people during forty years in the wilderness was worthy to be had in perpetual remembrance. It was in itself a marvellous boon; it taught the grand lesson of entire dependence upon the Almighty Father of all; and it was a striking type of the bread of God, which cometh down from heaven, and giveth life unto the world. Hence the command to lay up an omer-full of the manna to be kept for the generations to come. 33. *A pot.* The word in the original occurs only here, and probably denotes a more permanent vessel than a mere basket. In the Sept. we find *στάμνον χρυσοῦν*, a golden jar, a rendering which is adopted in the Epistle to the Hebrews (ix. 4). *Before the Lord.* This is explained in the next verse by the phrase, "before the testimony." This testimony of God to the great principles of morality was the law, written on the tables of stone, and deposited in the ark (xxv. 16), thence called the ark of the testimony. "Before the testimony," therefore, means in the ark of the testimony (Heb. ix. 4), whence, however, it had disappeared in the time of Solomon (1 Kings viii. 9). 34. *So Aaron laid it up.* This act of Aaron must have been performed after the ark was made and the tables of stone were deposited in it. The record of it, though not written till after these events, is appended here to complete all that is necessary to be told concerning the manna. 35. *Ate manna forty years.* We are told in Josh. v. 12 that the manna ceased on the morrow after they had eaten of the new corn of the land, which was on the morrow after the passover. As the manna commenced on or after the fifteenth day of the second month, and therefore a month after the passover in Egypt, the people ate of the manna forty years, wanting a month. *Until they came to a land inhabited.* In contrast with the wilderness, in which were only wanderers, and not settled inhabitants. This verse determines, in a general way, the place as well as the time of the ceasing of the manna, more widely in the phrase quoted, and more strictly in the words "until they went to the border of the land of Kenaan." There can be no doubt that the people had in most places, and especially when they had made the conquest of Persia, some ordinary supplies of food. But those who needed would still go out to gather, until the supply of the new corn of the land satisfied the demands of all. This verse was no doubt added when Moses was revising and completing his materials for Exodus, in the plains of Moab, by Jordan, near Jericho (Num. xxxvi. 13), or in the valley over against Beth-peor (Deut. iii. 29). The sentence is evidently such as might be written by a prophet who was aware that the forty years of wilderness life were drawing to a close, and perceived the supply of manna waning to its end, according as the natural products of the land were approaching to a full satisfaction of the people's wants.

36. *The omer.* This name of a measure seems to have gone out of use in the space of forty years. Moses, therefore, in the revising of the book of Exodus at the end of that period, takes occasion to add that the omer was the tenth part of an ephah. Josephus (Antiq. viii. 2. 11) assumes the bath or ephah to be equal to 72 xestai. Now, it was estimated by Bertheau that a bath or

| | | | | | |
|---|---|---|---|---|---|
| metretes | = | 12 choes | = | 8.6696 | gallons. |
| chous | = | 6 xestai | = | .7225 | " |
| sextary or xestes | = | 2 cotylae | = | .1204 | " |
| | | cotyla | = | .0602 | " |

The omer would thus be .8669 gal., or about 7 pints. According to the Rabbins, however, a log was equal to the contents of six eggs; and therefore a bath, or ephah, containing 72 logs, held, according to the estimate of Thenius, 4.4286 gal., and consequently the omer .4428 gal., or above $3\frac{1}{2}$ pints. Now, 3 pints of meal is sufficient, on an average, for the daily support of each member of a family. As the manna, then, would be pure nutriment, without any considerable loss in the preparation, we must regard the Rabbinical estimate as a close approximation to the truth, and that of Josephus as an exaggeration. This author is not precise in his identifications ; as he makes the fourth part of a cab = xestes = .1204 gallons.

| | | | | |
|---|---|---|---|---|
| ∴ | | cab | = .4816 | " |
| 6 cabs | = | seah | = 2.8896 | " |
| 3 seahs | = | bath | = 8.2688 | " |

His value is thus only approximate. But in Antiq. iii. 6. 6, the omer is made = 7 cotylae = .4214 gal., and therefore the bath = 4.214. This, we perceive, deviates much from his other estimates, and approaches very nearly to that of the Rabbins. We subjoin a table of Hebrew measures of capacity :

| | | | gal. | qt. | pint. |
|---|---|---|---|---|---|
| Homer | = 10 ephahs or baths | = | 44 | 1 | 0.0 |
| Ephah | = 3 seahs = 10 omers | = | 4 | 1 | 1.4 |
| Seah | = 6 cabs | = | 1 | 1 | 1.8 |
| Omer | | = | 0 | 1 | 1.54 |
| Bath | = 6 hins | = | 4 | 1 | 1.4 |
| Hin | = 12 logs | = | 0 | 2 | 1.9 |
| Log | = 6 eggs | = | 0 | 0 | 0.5 |

CHAP. XVII.—WATER FROM THE ROCK. AMALEK SMITTEN.

1. רְפִידִים Rephidim ; r. *spread out, rest upon.* Piel. *support.*

2. תְּנוּ *give ye*, referring to Moses and Aaron. Some MSS., the Sam., Sept., Targ., and Vulg. have תְּנָה, agreeing with Moses alone. It is an easier reading.

6. חֹרֵב Horeb. *Drought, waste.*

7. מַסָּה Massah, *πειρασμός, temptation.* מְרִיבָה Meribah, *λοιδόρησις, chiding, strife.*

9. יְהוֹשֻׁעַ Jehoshua, *Jehovah saves.* See Num. xiii. 16.

11. יָדוֹ. יָדָיו in both cases is the reading of the Sam., Sept., Targ., Syr., and Vulg. This also is an easier reading.

12. חוּר Chur, *noble.* אֱמוּנָה either *firmness*, the substantive for the adjective, or *firm*, the singular, not the plural, because Moses held up only one hand at a time.

13. כְּתֹב *write.* שֹׁטֵר has occured in Ex. v. 6, denoting a scribe or accountant.

15. יְהוָה נִסִּי Jehovah-nissi, *the* LORD *my banner.*

16. כֵּס יָהּ *throne of Jah.* כֵּס is here supposed to be for כִּסֵּא, which is indeed the reading of the Sam. for these four letters. This meaning of the word is found in the Targ., Arab., Pers., and Vulg. The Sept. has ἐν χειρὶ κρυφαίᾳ, evidently reading כְּסֻיָה. One MS. is said to have נֵס, which is a favorite reading with many expositors. It is however without support, and besides affords no better sense than the common reading.

XVII. 1. And all the assembly of the sons of Israel set out from the wilderness of Sin, after their journeys, according to the mouth of the LORD; and they pitched in Rephidim; and there was no water for the people to drink. 2. And the people chid with Moses, and said, Give us water to drink. And Moses said unto them, Why chide ye with me? Why tempt ye the Lord? 3. And the people thirsted there for water, and the people murmured against Moses; and they said, Wherefore is this that thou hast brought us out of Mizraim to kill me and my sons, and my cattle with thirst? 4. And Moses cried unto the LORD, saying, What shall I do unto this people? They are almost ready to stone me. 5. And the LORD said unto Moses, Pass before the people, and take with thee of the elders of Israel; and thy rod wherewith thou smotest the river take in thy hand, and go. 6. Behold, I stand before thee there upon the rock in Horeb; and thou shalt smite the rock, and water shall come out of it, and the people shall drink. And Moses did so in the eyes of the elders of Israel. 7. And he called the name of the place Massah and Meribah, because of the chiding of the sons of Israel, and of their tempting the LORD, saying, Is the LORD in the midst of us or not? ¶ 28.

8. Then came Amalek and fought with Israel in Rephidim.
9. And Moses said unto Joshua, Choose us out men and go out, fight with Amalek: to-morrow I will stand on the top of the hill, and the rod of God in my hand. 10. And Joshua did as Moses said to him, and fought with Amalek: and Moses, Aaron, and Hur went up to the top of the hill. 11. And it came to pass, when Moses held up his hand that Israel prevailed; and when he let down his hand Amalek prevailed.
12. And the hands of Moses were heavy, and they took a stone and put it under him, and he sat upon it: and Aaron and Hur stayed up his hands, the one on this side and the other on that side; and his hands were steady until the going down of the sun. 13. And Joshua discomfited Amalek and his people with the edge of the sword. ¶ 29.

14. And the Lord said unto Moses, Write this for a memorial in the book, and rehearse it in the ears of Joshua: for I will utterly blot out the remembrance of Amalek from under heaven. 15. And Moses built an altar, and called its name Jehovah-nissi. 16. And he said, Because a hand was upon the throne of JAH, the LORD will have war with Amalek from generation to generation. 17. ¶¶¶ 30.

1–7. The striking of the rock in Horeb. *All the assembly.* The attention of the reader is still kept to the marshalled host. *Set out.* They had passed two Sabbaths, and the intervening week at the stations in the Wilderness of Sin. *After their journeys.* There may be here a passing allusion to the two stations, Dophkah and Alush, which, as they were included in the Wilderness of Sin, and were not the scenes of any new event of importance, are therefore omitted from the present narrative. *According to the mouth of the Lord,* who by the pillar of cloud and fire undertook their guidance (xiii. 21, 22). *Pitched in Rephidim.* This is to be sought in the Wady Sheikh, which runs in the form of an arc around the north of that cluster of mountains to which the general name of Horeb appears to have been given. It was certainly arid and waste, as its name implies. Rephidim was a wide-spreading plain at the base of the mountain, fit for encampment, but destitute of water. It is placed with some probability on the northeast of the mountainous block. 2. *The people chid with Moses.* They had probably endured the almost intolerable thirst for some time in silence, expecting that Moses would find means to extricate them out of this new difficulty, at length, impatient of delay, they break out into unmerited reproaches, as if he were trifling with their sufferings. *Give us water.* They evidently recognize the divine commission of Moses, and expect him to have interfered on their behalf before now, *Why tempt ye the Lord?* He reminds them that he was but an agent, and that the Lord alone was to determine the time and way of their deliverance. Against him therefore they were really murmuring. 3. *And the people thirsted.* Their distress became every moment more insufferable. *To kill me.* Each in his impatience begins to speak for himself, as he pines after the refreshing draught for himself, his household, and his flocks. 4. *And Moses cried unto the Lord.* The occasion for importunate supplication is come. Moses was in perplexity and danger. "It is only to wait a little and they will stone me." 5. The Lord is not slow to answer. *Pass before the people.* Go on in advance of them. *Take with thee of the elders of Israel,* as concurrents and witnesses of thy acts; that no one may say that the Lord did not work by him, but that fountains were there from of old, (Rashi). *And thy rod, wherewith thou smotest the river,* wherewith he was now about to smite the rock for water. 6. *Behold, I stand before thee there.* The Lord was to be there, probably in the pillar of cloud to manifest his power. *Upon the rock in Horeb.* The mountain was towering on the right of the people. Toward this Moses was to approach till he reached "the rock," the projecting cliff which he was to strike. Rephidim was a day's march from Mount Sinai (xix. 1). This is sufficient to prove that the rock in Horeb was not the large boulder in the valley below Mount Sinai which tradition points out to the traveller. *And Moses did so in the sight of the elders.* And the

Lord was there to give forth the reviving streams, even from the hard rock. It was there demonstrated that the Lord was indeed in the midst of them to make their bread and their water sure, and to re-affirm the heavenly mission of his servant. At this now blessed spot they abode for the remaining days of the week.

8–13. Amalek smitten. *Then came.* The country of these nomades lay south of the Philistines (Gen. xiv. 7). They went therefore out of their own territory to assail the Israelites. As their pasture-grounds penetrated far into the land of Kenaan (Judg. v. 14, xii. 15), they would regard with a hostile feeling a people who were on the way to take possession of that country. With them, accordingly, first after the political independence of Israel was established, began the Gentile antagonism to the people of God (Num. xxiv. 20) to make its appearance. *And fought with Israel.* It appears from Deut. xxv. 17, 18, that this was an attack upon the rear of Israel when they were faint and weary. *In Rephidim,* a part of the great plain er-Ramleh, where there was space for a military encounter. 9. *Joshua* is here mentioned for the first time. His original name was Hoshea (Num. xiii. 8, 16), but Moses changed it to Joshua, partly, we may suppose, in allusion to the event now about to be recorded. He is the ninth in descent from Joseph, and of course the eighth from Ephraim (1 Chron. vii. 20–27). He is thus the representative of one of the most important tribes of Israel. *Choose us out men.* Israel was now to gird on his sword and contend for his national independence. This was evidently no flying raid of the Amalekites, but a war of conquest. *To-morrow,* the enemy awaits them in battle array. *I will stand on the top of the hill.* Moses, with the rod of wonder-working power, takes his station on the neighboring eminence (not הָהָר but הַגִּבְעָה), there to take his appropriate part in the approaching conflict. 10. *Hur* was the fourth in descent from Judah, and the grandfather of Bezaleel (xxxi. 2; 1 Chron. ii. 9–20). As he was the grandfather of a full-grown man, and a member of the distinguished tribe of Judah, he was the meet companion of Aaron in attendance upon Moses. 11, 12. Israel or Amalek prevails according as the hand of Moses is held up or let down. Accordingly Aaron and Hur stayed up his hands alternately, so that they were steady till sunset. The rod is not mentioned here. This is not a miraculous interposition, but an ordinary exercise of faith in God accompanying the use of means. The lifting up of the hand or hands is, among other things, a gesture in prayer (Lev. ix. 22; Ps. xxviii. 2, lxiii. 4; 1 Tim. ii. 8). It is here, therefore, a figure for prayer. The continual holding up of the hands denotes perseverance in prayer. Aaron and Hur joining in the upholding of Moses's hands present a striking emblem of common prayer. 13. There is power in this prayer of Moses. Joshua conquers. *Amalek and his people.* The one field suffices to vanquish Amalek's army and his nation; as they had put forth their whole might in this first effort. The next effort was not offensive, but defensive, and in alliance with the Kenaanites (Num. xiv. 45).

14–16. The importance of the victory over Amalek is set forth. *Write.* Here for the first time this singularly interesting word occurs. It is implied, indeed, in the noun "book" (סֵפֶר), which appears in Gen. v. 1, as well as here. It indicates that writing was now become so common that the word for it was used in no other sense. *This* refers to the assault of Amalek, the victory over him, the manner in which it was obtained, and the purpose expressed in the close of the verse. This was the first encounter with the heathen; and every particular here enumerated was only a type and an earnest of what should take place in every future conflict between the children of repentance and the children of disobedience. *For a memorial.* Writing is a necessary help to recollection when life is short and memory feeble. *In the book.* The article before this word indicates either that the book in question was well known, or that a book was then a well-known object. *In the ears of Joshua,* who was to be the leader of the people, and the conqueror of their enemies. There was special admonition and encouragement for him in the mode and issue of this battle. *Blot out the remembrance of Amalek.* The fate of Amalek may be read in Deut. xxv. 19; 1 Sam. xv. 30; 2 Sam. i. 1, viii. 12, from which we learn that they were subdued partly by Saul and wholly by David, after which they are no more mentioned. Such will be the end of all God's adversaries. 15. *An altar.* This is the first altar the erection of which is on record, since the time of Jacob. It marks a new aspect in the affairs of the people of God. They have now asserted their independence, and, through the grace of God, gained the first victory over their enemies. This is an omen for all time to come. The erection of an altar is always in Scripture a confession of the personal unworthiness of fallen man, of the assured hope of an atonement, and of humble and grateful reliance on the grace of God. Hence the grace of God in giving the victory, and the gratitude of the people in receiving it, here appropriately meet. *Jehovah-nissi.* The name of the altar is expressive of thanks for the past and trust for the future (Ps. xx. 5–7). 16. We have given a literal version of this obscure verse. The meaning turns upon the person to whom the word hand is referred. If it refer to God, the sentence is an oath, as in the Targ., Onk., and the Auth. Ver. But the form of oath is unusual, and the connection with the context is far from being obvious. If it refer to Moses (Bush) or to Israel (Keil) the meaning is, "because the hand of faith and prayer is toward the throne of God," etc. This has the advantage of reference to the context; but the meaning here given to the preposition עַל is unusual, and the first clause does not afford a good reason for the second. If the hand refer to Amalek (Kalisch), the sentence runs thus, "because his (Amalek's) hand was against the throne of Yah (the kingdom of God, which includes his people), etc." The meaning is here simple and easy; the connection with what goes before is sufficiently plain; and the reason assigned for perpetual war until Amalek be extirpated is intelligible and suitable.

CHAP. XVIII. — JETHRO.

2. שִׁלּוּחִים *dismissal.*

4. אֱלִיעֶזֶר Eliezer, *God-help.*

6. אֲנִי. The Sam., Sept., and Syr. have הִנֵּה. The sentence then runs, "And *one* said unto Moses, Behold," etc.

18. עֲשׂהוּ an old form equal to עֲשׂוֹ.

26. יִשְׁפּוּטוּ an unusual form and pointing for יִשְׁפְּטוּ. It seems to arise from the proximity of a pause falling on a very short word.

XVIII. 1. And Jethro, the priest of Midian, Moses's father-in-law, heard all that God had done for Moses, and for Israel his people; for the LORD had brought Israel out of Mizraim.

2. And Jethro, Moses's father-in-law, took Zipporah, Moses's wife, after he had sent her back: 3. And her two sons, of whom the name of the one was Gershom; for he said, I have become a stranger in a foreign land; 4. And the name of the other Eliezer; for the God of my father was my help, and delivered me from the sword of Pharoh. 5. And Jethro, Moses's father-in-law, and his sons and his wife came unto Moses into the wilderness where he encamped at the Mount of God. 6. And he said unto Moses, I, thy father-in-law Jethro, come unto thee, and thy wife, and her two sons with her. 7. And Moses came out to meet his father-in-law, and bowed himself, and kissed him, and they asked each other of their welfare; and they went into the tent. 8. And Moses told his father-in-law all that the LORD had done unto Pharoh and to Mizraim for the sake of Israel, all the travail that had come upon them by the way, and how the Lord delivered them. 9. And Jethro rejoiced over all the good which the LORD had done to Israel, whom he had delivered out of the hand of Mizraim. 10. And Jethro said, Blessed be the Lord who hath delivered you out of the hand of Mizraim, and out of the hand of Pharoh; who hath delivered the people from under the hand of Mizraim. 11. Now I know that the Lord is greater than all the gods, for he has prevailed in the thing wherein they dealt proudly with them. 12. And Jethro, Moses's father-in-law, took a burnt-offering and sacrifices for God; and Aaron went, and all the elders of Israel, to eat bread with Moses's father-in-law before God.

13. And it came to pass on the morrow, that Moses sat to judge the people; and the people stood by Moses from the morning unto the evening. 14. And Moses's father-in-law saw all that he did to the people, and he said, What is this thing that thou doest to the people? Why sittest thou thyself alone,

and all the people stand by thee from morning unto evening?
15. And Moses said unto his father-in-law, Because the people
come unto me to inquire of God. 16. When they have a matter
they come unto me, and I judge between one and another, and
I make known the statutes of God and his laws. 17. And
Moses's father-in-law said unto him, The thing that thou
doest is not good. 18. Thou wilt surely wear away, thou and
this people that is with thee: for this thing is too heavy for
thee; thou canst not do it thyself alone. 19. Now hearken to
my voice, I will advise thee, and God shall be with thee; be
thou for the people before God, and bring thou the causes
unto God. 20. And thou shalt teach them the statutes and
the laws, and show them the way wherein they must walk,
and the work that they must do. 21. And thou shalt provide
out of all the people, able men, fearing God, men of truth,
hating coveteousness, and place over them rulers of thousands,
rulers of hundreds, rulers of fifties, and rulers of tens. 22.
And they shall judge the people at all times; and it shall be
that every great matter they shall bring to thee, and every
small matter they shall judge themselves: and thou shalt
relieve thyself, and they shall bear with thee. 23. If thou do
this thing and God command thee, then thou shalt be able to
endure, and also all this people shall go to their place in peace.
24. And Moses hearkened to the voice of his father-in-law, and
did all that he had said. 25. And Moses chose able men out
of all Israel, and made them heads over the people, rulers of
thousands, rulers of hundreds, rulers of fifties, and rulers of
tens. 26. And they were to judge the people at all times;
the hard cause they were to bring to Moses, and every small
matter to judge themselves. 27. And Moses let his father-in-law depart; and he went his way unto his own place. ¶ 31.

Moses had formerly led the flock of Jethro as far as "the mount of God in Horeb." As soon as he arrives at this point, therefore, he is in the neighborhood of Jethro, who accordingly pays him a visit, accompanied by Zipporah and her two sons. The chapter contains the reception of Jethro, and the advice he tenders to his son-in-law concerning the government of the people. It is probable, as we shall see (vs. 5), that this visit took place after the assembly had encamped before the mount. The record of this collateral occurrence is placed here, at a convenient pause, that it may not interfere with the main current of the narrative, (see on וַיֹּאמֶר Gen. i. 3).

1–12. The arrival of Jethro. *Heard all.* The spread of intelligence is much more rapid among nomadic tribes than in a settled population. 2. *Took Zipporah.* He received her when she retured from Moses; but now he takes her to bring her back to him. *After he had sent her back,* שִׁלּוּחֶיהָ. This word occurs twice elsewhere (1 Kings ix. 16; Micah i. 14). In the former passage it denotes a present to a daughter sent away in marriage; in the latter it denotes a figurative dismissal. It is here applied to the dismissal of his wife and children, most probably when the youngest child was circumcised on the way to Egypt, and was therefore unable to proceed (see on iv. 26). 3, 4. *Gershom,* (see on ii. 22). *Eliezer.* This is the second son indicated in iv. 20, 24. בְּעֶזְרִי in or for my help. Moses had a grateful remembrance of his deliverance from the sword of Pharoh. 5, 6. *Encamped at the mount of God.* "The mount of God" is that mount in Horeb on which the law was delivered. This we take to be an indication that Moses had left Rephidim, and was now encamping (חֹנֶה) within sight of Sinai. Hence the visit of Jethro takes place after the arrival of the people at the Wilderness of Sinai, (see on xix. 1). *And he said unto Moses,* by a messenger in advance. This is a frequent expansion of the meaning attached to this phrase (xii. 3, 21).

7–12. The reception of Jethro. *Moses came out to meet.* He pays all honor to Jethro as his father-in-law, and as the priest of Midian. He naturally rehearses to him the wonders of the short period during which they had been separated. 9–11. Jethro gives expression to the joy he felt in the deliverance of Israel. *Blessed be the Lord.* Jethro here explicitly acknowledges Jehovah as God. He was no doubt acquainted by the tradition of his Hebrew fathers with the being and the mercy of God, and he might have learned the significant name Jehovah from Moses, if not before. *The Lord is greater than all the gods.* A man in Jethro's position could not be ignorant of the polytheism that had now resulted from the division of human interests and opinions. Yet his spontaneous confession may convey simply the conviction of the infinite pre-eminence of Jehovah. *For he has prevailed,* or showed himself greater, in the very thing in which the Egyptians dealt proudly with the Israelites. The authorized version gives precisely the same sense, though with a different application, of the word עֲלֵיהֶם. 12. Jethro gives a practical exhibition of his acknowledgment of the Lord by offering sacrifice. The burnt-offering is the completest symbol of the atonement for sin (Gen. viii. 20). The sacrifice being eaten partly by the worshipper expresses communion with God as the result of atonement. The common participation *before God* of the sacrifice is the emblem of the communion of the worshippers in the blessings of the divine favor.

13–27. The counsel of Jethro concerning the administration of justice. *On the morrow.* The day after the sacrifice, which was offered on the day of or the day after Jethro's arrival. *Moses sat.* Sitting is the posture of the judge, standing that of those who come to receive judgment. *From the morning unto the evening.* During the whole of that part of the day assigned to public business. 14–16. Moses explains to Jethro the necessity of this constant sitting. *To inquire of God,* is to come to his minister or representative to obtain an answer to any inquiry which is beyond human solution. In the present case the object of the inquiry is a judicial decision in a dispute between man and man. In a theocracy this proceeds from God through his ministers. Hence to appeal to them is virtually to appeal to God (xxi. 6). *And I make known.* This was a process of instruction especially necessary for a new nation for which a code of jurisprudence had not yet been provided. At the same time it was not possible for one person to instil the principles of law into the hearts of all the people, much less to administer justice to a community of at least one million six hundred thousand individuals. *The statutes of God and his laws* (xii. 24, 49), his occasional decisions and edicts, and his general laws and principles of rectitude.

17–23. The plan suggested by Jethro. He disapproves of the

present practice of Moses, as too laborious and tedious. *Thou wilt surely wear away.* The causes that will arise among the people will occupy all thy time to the exclusion of needful leisure for recreation and for other duties. *And the people that is with thee.* They will be wearied in waiting for the decision of their litigations, which will be delayed in consequence of thy inability to determine them as fast as they arise. And this delay may tempt them to take the law into their own hands, and so anarchy and outrage may pave the way for their gradual annihilation. *Thou canst not do it thyself alone.* Hence a division of the labor is necessary, that it may be done promptly and efficiently. 19, 20. *And God shall be with thee,* approving of thy course, and aiding thee in its execution. Jethro means that he should not proceed without the divine concurrence. Be thou for the people before God, between God and the people, to represent him to them, and their causes to him. *Thou shalt teach them,* expound the regulations and principles of civil and religious law. *The way,* the moral principle of their conduct. *The work,* the conduct which they are to pursue in the way which the law directs. Moses is thus to be, under God, the great teacher of the people, the promulgator of law, and the director of its administration. 21, 22. *Provide out of,* look out among you. This was done by the people themselves proposing men to be approved and appointed by Moses, as he himself explains (Deut. i. 13, 15), "*Give ye* wise men, and understanding, and known among your tribes, and *I will make them rulers over you.*" "And I took," accepted at the hand of the people. *Able men,* having the requisite abilities for the office. This is the first qualification. *Fearing God,* men of piety. *Men of truth,* whose word may be trusted. *Hating covetousness,* that will not therefore be bribed to pronounce unjust decisions. An admirable choice and order of qualifications. *Rulers of thousands.* It has been calculated by the Talmudists, and even by Grotius, that according to this arrangement seventy-eight thousand six hundred judges would be required for six hundred thousand men. But we cannot suppose that the patriarchal rule, which is a law of nature, was to be superseded by this regulation. A father was still to be acknowledged as the governing head of his descendants during his life, especially when they dwelt with him in the same house or tent. And he is the unit intended in the thousands, hundreds, fifties, and tens here mentioned. Thus in Josh. vii. 16–24 we find Israel divided into tribes, the tribe of Judah into clans (מִשְׁפָּחוֹת), the clan of Zarhi into *men* (גְּבָרִים), individuals or units, of whom Achan was one. But Achan has sons and daughters and a tent, and is therefore the father of a house. Such a house, including children, might contain from five to fifty individuals. We may take twenty as a reasonable average of a grandfather's family. Ten such families would in that case amount to two hundred individuals, and ten such heads are the smallest number allowed by the Talmudists to constitute a synagogue. In a people of at least one million six hundred thousand there would thus be eight thousand rulers of tens, sixteen hundred rulers of fifties, eight hundred rulers of hundreds, and eighty rulers of thousands, and therefore ten thousand four hundred and eighty rulers in all. The number of appeals from rulers of tens would be proportionately greater than from the higher judges, because they were not much in rank above the fathers of houses; and hence the rulers of fifties seem to be introduced to distribute the burden which would otherwise fall on the rulers of hundreds. *Every great matter* would come up to Moses either by appeal, where the parties were dissatisfied with the judgment of the inferior courts, or by reference, when these courts were deterred from judging by the difficulty of the cause. The latter is the mode expressly recognized in the text, and was probably, in the custom of the people, inclusive of the former. *And God command thee.* Jethro submits his proposal to the decision of God. *Go to their place in peace.* Prompt and impartial administration of justice will allay quarrels and beget that mutual confidence and good feeling which tends to peace. Jethro presents his modest proposal as a temporary expedient, until the people should arrive in a country where they might have settled institutions.

24–26. *And Moses hearkened to the voice of his father-in-law.* This sentence throws light on the ways of Providence and on the character of Moses. The practical mind of Jethro, on the first glance at a great evil, is prompted to suggest an immediate remedy. Moses, on the other hand, being a man of a more educated mind and more deferential spirit, and aware that this evil has only lasted for a month or two, and will very soon be removed by the promulgation of a complete code of laws, waits in reverential patience, as is his wont, for the intimation of heaven to initiate the needed change. But the suggestion of Jethro he receives with that respectful attention which was then paid to age, acknowledges to be agreeable to the dictates of his own reason, and accepts as the mode presented in the dispensation of Providence for the removal of the present difficulty. The method of the providence of God, is evidently out of the given emergency to elicit the required measure, either by an immediate communication from heaven, or by a suggestion of human reason adequate to the occasion, and approved by God. Neither the disposition nor the past training of Moses inclined him to step before the Almighty in devising a remedy for ordinary difficulties; and even this meekness was no small qualification for his high office. 25. *And Moses chose.* By a common figure he is said to do that which he caused to be done. The people chose at Moses's direction.

27. *And Moses let his father-in-law depart.* The sacred writer, as usual, brings one line of events to a close before passing to another. We are not bound, therefore, to conclude that Moses completed the introduction of his new measures for the administration of justice, and parted with his father-in-law before the series of events recorded in the following chapters had commenced. So far as the form of the narrative goes, we are at liberty to suppose that the interview with Jethro took place any time during the encampment at the "mount of God." The parallel passage (Deut. i. 9–18) referring to the institution of civil magistrates, dates this measure with precisely the same latitude. On the other hand, we are not constrained to suppose these proceedings unfinished, if the time suffice for their accomplishment. Now the assembled host arrived at the Wilderness of Sin on the fifteenth of the second month. If this was the first day of the week, and the whole of this week was spent at the three stations in this wilderness, eight days would remain for the journey to Rephidim, the smiting of the rock in Horeb, and the battle with Amalek. It appears from the following chapter that the journey to the Wilderness of Sinai took place on the first of the third month. It is possible that the interview with Jethro, and the tendering of his counsel, may have taken place on the second and third, and the carrying of this proposal into effect on the fourth and fifth. And it seems reasonable that Moses should be at once relieved of the burden of personally hearing and

deciding upon every case of litigation that might arise among the people. Jethro, however, may have taken leave for a time on the third day. It is most probable that, during the eleven months and twenty days of the sojourn of Israel in the Wilderness of Sinai, there were frequent interviews between Moses and his relatives by marriage, as they were in the immediate neighborhood. The passage in Num. x. 29–32, however, refers to the farewell and final parting between them, when the marshalled host set out for the Wilderness of Paran on their way to the promised land.

## SECTION IV.—THE LAWGIVING.

### XI. THE MORAL LAW.—Ex. xix.-xx.

#### CHAP. XIX.—PREPARATION FOR LAWGIVING.

13. יֹבֵל *the blower*, horn, cornet; r. *flow*, *blow*, *go*. It is equal to קֶרֶן הַיֹּבֵל, the horn of blowing or sounding, and שׁוֹפָר, cornet. It differs from חֲצֹצְרָה, the straight trumpet. It is probable that it was originally a ram's horn. The Rabbins and others affirm that יֹבֵל signifies a ram. In Phoenician inscriptions it is said to have this meaning.

XIX. 1. In the third month of the departure of the sons of Israel from the land of Mizraim, on this day were they come to the wilderness of Sinai. 2. And they set out from Rephidim and went to the wilderness of Sinai, and pitched in the wilderness; and there Israel pitched before the mountain.

3. And Moses went up unto God, and the Lord called unto him out of the mountain, saying, Thus shalt thou say to the house of Jacob, and tell the sons of Israel. 4. Ye have seen what I did unto Mizraim, and how I bare you on eagle's wings, and brought you unto me. 5. And now if ye will obey my voice indeed, and keep my covenant, then ye shall be a peculiar treasure unto me above all the peoples: for all the earth is mine. 6. And ye shall be unto me a kingdom of priests, and a holy nation. These are the words which thou shalt speak unto the sons of Israel. 7. And Moses went and called for the elders of the people, and laid before them all these words which the LORD commanded him. 8. And all the people answered together and said, All that the LORD hath spoken

we will do. And Moses returned the words of the people unto the LORD. 9. And the LORD said unto Moses, Lo, I come unto thee in the thick cloud, that the people may hear when I speak with thee, and so believe thee forever. And Moses told the words of the people unto the LORD. 10. And the LORD said unto Moses, Go unto the people, and sanctify them to-day and to-morrow, and let them wash their clothes. 11. And be ready for the third day: for on the third day the Lord will come down in the sight of all the people upon mount Sinai. 12. And thou shalt set bounds to the people round about, saying, Beware ye of going up to the mount, or touching the border of it: whosoever toucheth the mount shall be surely put to death. 13. There shall not a hand touch him, but he shall be surely stoned or shot through; whether beast or man, it shall not live: when the trumpet soundeth long, they shall go up to the mount. 14. And Moses went down from the mount unto the people: and he sanctified the people, and they washed their clothes. 15. And he said unto the people, Be ye ready for the third day: come not at your wives.

16. And it came to pass on the third day, in the morning, that there were thunders and lightning, and a thick cloud upon the mount, and the sound of the trumpet very loud; and all the people that were in the camp trembled. 17. And Moses brought forth the people from the camp to meet with God; and they stood at the nether part of the mount. 18. And Mount Sinai was all asmoke, because the LORD came down upon it in fire: and the smoke thereof went up as the smoke of a furnace, and the whole mount trembled greatly. 19. And when the sound of the trumpet waxed louder and louder, Moses spake, and God answered him by a voice. 20. And the LORD came down upon Mount Sinai, on the top of the mount; and the Lord called Moses to the top of the mount, and Moses

went up. 21. And the LORD said unto Moses, Go down, charge the people, lest they break through unto the Lord to gaze, and many of them perish. 22. And let the priests also, who come near to the LORD, sanctify themselves, lest the LORD break forth upon them. 23. And Moses said unto the LORD, The people cannot come up to Mount Sinai; for thou hast charged us, saying, Set bounds about the mount, and sanctify it. 24. And the LORD said unto him, Go, get thee down, and thou shalt come up, thou and Aaron with thee; but let not the priests or the people break through to come up unto the LORD, lest he break forth upon them. 25. And Moses went down unto the people, and spake unto them. § 20.

The exodus from Egypt is now past. That great event includes two concurring elements in the moral history of the people — redemption and renovation. They are redeemed from the bondage of Egypt; they are renovated in their feeling of allegiance to Jehovah, the God of heaven and earth. Their redemption appears in their deliverance from the plagues of Egypt, from the power of Egypt in the passage of the Red Sea, and from drought and famine in the miraculous supplies of manna, quails, and water with which they have been favored in the wilderness. Their renovation of conscience and will is discovered in their faith in Moses as the attested minister of Heaven, their unanimous observance of the significant solemnity of the passover, and in their ready and thankful departure from Egypt at the instance of the Lord, who had guaranteed their deliverance. After the new birth comes new obedience to Heaven's eternal law. The co-existence, however, of the old nature with the new principle of spiritual life in the heart of the nation renders the promulgation of law necessary as well as seasonable. It is seasonable precisely when power to comply with it has been engendered in the soul. And it is necessary because the infant will and the awakened conscience need to be enlightened and guided by a code of laws in checking and rooting out the old habits of sin which have blinded the eyes, warped the original bent, and marred the moral beauty of the soul. Hence the legislation comes in the train of the redemption and spiritual renewal of the nation. Hence the law is a doctrine (תּוֹרָה) for the information of the conscience and the training of the will. Hence it consists mainly of prohibitions for the repression of those habitual tendencies which linger in the renovated soul from the evil bias of the past.

The lawgiving is accordingly a step in advance of the exodus. It is an end to which the exodus is the means. It stands forth, therefore, as the second prominent theme in the book before us. Like the exodus, it occupies six chapters, of which the first is a preface and the last a conclusion. In the preparatory chapter we have the arrival of the people at Mount Sinai, the directions for the purifying of the people, and the description of Mount Sinai when the Lord descended upon it.

1, 2. The arrival at the place where the law was to be given. *In the third month.* As the term here employed denotes the new month, and a precise day, "on this day," is indicated, we may safely conclude that the first day of the month is intended. It is therefore now a month and a half since they left Egypt. *Were they come to.* This expression indicates that the events of the preceding chapter reached to a point of time beyond that which is now taken up as the main narrative (see on Gen. pp. 23, 34, 39). It is intended at the same time to date emphatically the day of their arrival. In the next verse the consecutive order of the narrative proceeds.

*Sinai.* From the usage of Scripture, and especially of these chapters, it is plain that Sinai denotes a particular mountain, while Horeb denotes a block or range of mountains, with their intervening wadys, coinciding in a great measure with Jebel et-Tur. This granite mass includes the Wadys es-Sheikh, er-Rahah, and es-Sebayeh, with all their lesser outlets. The Wilderness of Sinai seems to be the plains and wadys in its immediate neighborhood, where cattle might browse or men encamp. We take Sinai to be that detached mass of which Jebel Musa is the highest point, and Ras Sufsafeh is the peak that rises almost perpendicularly over the Wady er-Rahah, for the following among other reasons: (1.) Josephus (Antiq. iii. 5, 1) says it is the highest of all the mountains in that country. Now Serbal, which Lepsius takes to be the scene of the lawgiving, is only six thousand seven hundred and sixty feet high (Stanley, Map of Elevations in Sinai and

Palestine), while the cluster to which Sinai belongs is about nine thousand feet high. Jebel Musa, in particular, rises to seven thousand five hundred and sixty feet. (2.) There are the Wadys er-Rahah, es-Sheikh, and, according to Laborde (Comment, p. 108) and F. A. Strauss (Sinai, p. 134), es-Sebayeh, in the vicinity of Jebel Musa, which are amply sufficient for the encampment of a large host. Robinson (Biblical Researches, i. p. 140) measured across the water-shed of er-Rahah, and found it to be nine hundred yards, while the distance from the foot of the mountain was two thousand three hundred and thirty three yards. The northern slope of the plain he judged to be somewhat less than a mile in length, by one third of a mile in breadth. The whole plain he estimates at two miles long, and from a third to two thirds of a mile broad. "This space is nearly doubled by the recess to the west and the Wady es-Sheikh." Here, then, is an open space of about two square miles. Of the Plain es-Sebayeh Strauss reports that the side on which the Wady es-Sebayeh enters the plain is fourteen hundred feet in breadth, and at the southwestern foot of the mountain eighteen hundred feet; that the latter is the breadth at its central part, and its length from east to west is twelve thousand feet; and that towards the south it rises very gradually, and even the mountains which bound it on the south have a gentle slope. This plain is therefore about a square mile in area. It is acknowledged that there are no such open spaces in the vicinity of Serbal. (3.) The way to Jebel Musa is much more open for a large host than that to or from Serbal. (4.) The stations before and after the former can be more readily accounted for than before and after the latter. On this point we can only refer to Robinson. (5.) The tradition is in favor of Jebel Musa. This is unquestioned up to the time of Justinian, who founded a church on one of the wadys of Sinai in 527 B.C., according to Procopius. Before this period, however, it is contended by Lepsius and others that the tradition was in favor of Mount Serbal, on the supposed authority of Eusebius, Jerome, and Cosmas Indicopleustes. But Eusebius, according to the rendering of Jerome (De situ et nom. Heb.) thus describes Horeb — Choreb mons Dei in regione Madian juxta montem Sina super Arabiam in deserto (Cui jungitur mons et desertum Saracenorum, quod vocatur Paran. Mihi autem videtur, quod duplici nomine idem mons nunc Sinai nunc Choreb vocetur). From this passage it is evident that Eusebius places Horeb in Midian, while Serbal belonged to Amalek, or at least not to Midian. And Jerome regards Paran, the mountain of the Saracens, or, as he explains, the Ishmaelites, as adjoining the desert in which Horeb was situated. Now mount Paran is in Jerome's estimation either Serbal, or it is not. If it be, then Sinai and Horeb are different from it. If it be not, then Eusebius and Jerome say nothing whatever of Serbal. These authors (on Faran) also report that the children of Israel marched through Paran *when they left Sinai*, and that Pharan is three days' journey from Ailah or Elath. Serbal, therefore, if it were Paran, could not be identical with Sinai. But it cannot be the same with Paran, as it is about seventy-five miles from Ailah, which would be at least four days' journey. They also record (*Raphidim*) that Rephidim is beside Horeb, and near Paran; a statement which, after the preceding notices, implies only that it lay between the two, and by no means that the two are identical. Cosmas (Topogr. Christ. lib. v.) writes, Εἶτα πάλιν παρενέβαλον εἰς Ῥαφιδὶν, εἰς τὴν νῦν λεγομένην Φαράν. This merely intimates that Rephidim was in the region then called Pharan. Hence, he says, Moses proceeds to Mount Horeb, which is in the Sinaic (range) about six miles from Pharan (εἰς Χωρὴβ τὸ ὄρος, τουτέστιν, ἐν τῷ Σιναίῳ ἐγγὺς ὄντι τῆς Φαρὰν ὡς ἀπὸ μιλίων ἕξ). The present ruins of the *town* Feiran are about sixteen miles from Jebel Musa, and about six miles from the nearest point of the granitic block to which it belongs, while it cannot properly be said to be any distance from Serbal, at the foot of which it lies. Cosmas regards Horeb as a part of the Sinaic cluster of hills, and hence he speaks loosely of the inscriptions, which he says are found *in all the stations of the Israelites*, as existing in the desert of the Sinaic range (ἐν ἐκείνῃ τῇ ἐρήμῳ τοῦ Σιναΐου ὄρους ἐν πάσαις καταπαύσεσι). We may here observe, indeed, that these inscriptions are found to be due, not to the Israelites or the Christians, but to the inhabitants, or the pilgrims of a heathen superstition, and therefore afford no ground for determining the mount of the law. (See Beer, Inscr. Vet.; Credner, Heidelb. Jahrb. 1841, p. 980; Fr. Tuch, Versucheiner Erklärung von 21 Sin. Inschr.; Kurtz on the Covenant, v. iii. p. 61). The fact then seems to be that these three authors have been misunderstood, and are really in harmony with the general tradition, indicated even in the name Jebel Musa, the mount of Moses.

2. *And they set out from Rephidim.* As the previous verse looks back to the events of the foregoing chapter, so this verse looks forward to the continuance of the narrative from chap. xvii. Then we were at Rephidim, and now we depart from it. *The Wilderness of Sinai* is a phrase comprehensive of the mount of the lawgiving, and the surrounding desert. It seems to be co-extensive with Horeb, the central granitic block of mountain and glen now called Jebel et-Tur. *Before the mountain.* This expression signifies over against, or within sight of it, but not necessarily close by or contiguous to the mountain. We may imagine the main body of the encampment to be in the Wady es-Sheikh, and its wings or straggling outskirts in the adjacent glens, partly it may be in the Plain es-Sebayeh, and generally within view of some part of Sinai.

3–15. The directions for the preparation of the people. *And Moses went up unto God.* The pillar of cloud now rested on Mount Sinai, and was conspicuous before the eyes of all the people. The going up of Moses unto God means, not that he ascended the mountain, which is not here asserted, but that he drew nigh to God in the customary way. And as the Lord now manifested himself on a mountain-top, the approach of Moses was an ascent, even though he only reached the base. This interpretation of the words is manifest from the following sentence: "And the Lord called unto him *out of the mountain.*" This implies that Moses was not on the mountain, but at such a distance from the Divine presence as to warrant the word "called" instead of "spake."

3–6. The words of the Lord here contain a tendering again of his covenant to the people, for formal and final acceptance. They indicate, *first*, the party who are to enter into covenant with God. The "house of Jacob" is the parallel of the "sons of Israel," the former, however, pointing to their natural, the latter to their spiritual relations, (see Gen. xxxii. 23–33). *Secondly*, the keeping of the covenant on God's part is put forward in a short and striking appeal to the people. *Ye have seen.* This was a matter of personal experience with them. *What I did in Mizraim.* The eleven manifestations of his power on their behalf in that country. *And how I bare you on eagle's wings.* In the twelfth miracle, at the Red Sea, he delivered them from the perils of the surrounding waters and the pursuing Egyptians, with as much care as the eagle takes in teaching its nestlings to make the first essay in flight among the beetling heights where it has its abode (Deut. xxxii. 11). The parent bird, it is said, sweeps gently past the young ones perched on a ledge of rock, and when one, venturing to follow, begins to sink with drooping wing, glides underneath, and bears it aloft again (Duns, Biblical Natural Science, ii. 46). This beautiful figure strikingly illustrates the patient tenderness with which the Lord labored to train his people for the escape from Egypt, and guarded them from the hazards of the way. *And brought you unto me*, brought you home to adoption and inheritance with your God and Father. *Thirdly*, the acceptance of the covenant is lovingly proposed to the people. *If ye will obey, obey my voice.* The repetition is emphatic, "if ye obey me promptly and heartily." *And keep my covenant*, the parallel of the previous clause; "be faithful to me, as I have been to you"; a touching appeal that wins a ready assent from a true heart. *Lastly*, comes the promise in new and expressive terms. It contains the three elements of salvation, appropriation, propitiation, and sanctification. Here for the first time occur three remarkable phrases, which become household words in the church. They throw a new light on the privilege and responsibility of the believer. (1.) *A peculiar treasure unto me.* To belong to God is an inestimable blessing. How much more to be his in a special sense above all others, λαὸς περιούσιος, a peculiar people! *For all the earth is mine.* This is to explain the phrase "above all peoples." All the inhabitants of the earth belong to God by right of creation and general benefaction; but ye belong to him, over and above all this, by special grace and covenant; and out of his free grace flows to you all that is comprised in remission, redemption, and regeneration. This part of the promise is therefore a comprehensive summary of all the blessings of salvation. (2.) *A kingdom of priests.* This is a pregnant sentence. It presupposes the people to be themselves the objects of priestly intercession and royal protection. It expressly elevates them into the dignity and authority of performing priestly functions, and dispensing royal favors to others. "A kingdom of priests" the Septuagint renders by βασίλειον ἱεράτευμα, a priesthood of kings. This is sufficient to show that a kingdom was here understood to be a community of persons invested with the powers of sovereignty, such as commanding, judging, defending, punishing, and rewarding, and bound to exercise them, under God, for the good of mankind. The benignity of their sway is indicated by the facts that they are to be priests as well as kings. They find mankind under the ban of disobedience, the doom of death. Their office calls them to make atonement for the sins of the world, intercede for the returning penitent, and reconcile him to God. This function of sublime beneficence involves questions of the deepest import in the salvation of mankind, which do not meet their full solution until we approach the end of the volume of inspiration. Who can independently mediate between God and man? What can be an all-sufficient propitiation for sin? We abstain from anticipating the answer to these questions, which does not belong to the interpreter, and is familiar to every reader of the New Testament. Meanwhile, we contemplate with profound admiration the nation that has a mission to discharge these benign functions, and a history pregnant with a great king, priest, and sacrifice that will be able to accomplish the salvation of the soul. 3. *A holy nation.* Along with a free pardon and an all-prevalent intercession, the third requisite for salvation is a sanctified nature. But this is introduced here not merely as an element of their own salvation, but as a qualification for that high function of reigning and reconciling which they are to exercise for the salvation of the world. There is a beautiful unity given to this ideal when we regard Israel as the son, the first-born of God (Ex. iv. 22). This son is the king and priest, the holy one of the present passage. This collective or national Israel contains within its bosom the individual and actual Son of God, of which it is the type in its regal and sacerdotal dignity, as it is the emblem of the church in its peace and purity. Thus God sets before his chosen people a new ideal, which is to be represented for their instruction in the typical institutions of the ceremonial law. It is to have a twofold realization; on the one hand in the grateful reception of salvation from age to age by a growing number, until at length the whole of mankind are gathered into this kingdom; and on the other hand in the gracious dispensing of this salvation until the Messiah have come once to make atonement for sin, and again to bring in the new heavens and the new earth, wherein dwelleth righteousness. *These are the words which thou shalt speak unto the sons of Israel.* These pregnant words are to take root in the hearts of the people, and bear fruit in all future ages.

7, 8. The consent of the people to the covenant is warm and prompt. *Moses went and called for the elders of the people.* Here we have the usual order of communication with the people. The elders are the representatives of the people, who convey to them the message of the Lord by Moses, and act as their spokesmen in replying to it (xii. 21). *And all the people answered together.* They gave a unanimous response. *All that the Lord hath spoken we will do.* They freely close with the gracious terms of the covenant. Moses reports their favorable answer to the Lord.

9–13. The directions to the people to sanctify themselves, and keep at a distance from the mountain. *Lo I come unto thee.* This is the usual phrase for an intended action. *In the thick cloud,* in which my presence is usually manifested. *That the people may hear when I speak with thee.* The Lord does not demand confidence in his messenger and minister without giving abundant evidence of his commission. He had before given the signs of the rod turned into a serpent, and the hand changed from soundness to leprosy, and again to soundness; but these were exhibited before the elders as the representatives of the people (Ex. iv. 29–31). He had also wrought the miracles of the deliverance from Egypt by the hand or the word of Moses; but many of these were not under the eye of the people. But now he will answer Moses in the audience of all the people, that they may *believe* him *forever.* The Lord knew the inconstancy of the people, and therefore condescends to give them a universal and personal attestation to the authority of his prophet and delegate. *Forever,* without interruption. *The words of the people.* This was the proper plan for introducing the formal and unanimous assent of the people to the covenant of the Lord. 10. *Sanctify them to-day and to-morrow.* These days were supposed to be, according to tradition, the fourth and fifth of the third month. It is probable that the fifth was the Sabbath, or closing day of the seven weeks after the passover. This rests on the twofold assumption that the 15th of Nisan coincided with the weekly Sabbath, and that the first month contained twenty-nine, and the second thirty days. The "sanctifying" consisted in washing their clothes and abstaining from conjugal intercourse (v. 15; Lev. xv. 18). These serve for the outward form of sanctification in the absence of any ceremonial enactment. 11. *And be ready for the third day.* According to the supposition already mentioned, the sixth of the third month would be the fiftieth day after the Sabbath in the seven days of the feast of unleavened bread. We know that this fiftieth day was afterward one of the three great annual festivals of Israel; and as the other two had special reference to momentous events in the history of the people, the feast of weeks may have had reference to the giving of the law. This affords an additional argument in favor of the fiftieth day being that of the lawgiving. 12. *Set bounds to the people.* These bounds were at some distance from the base of the mountain. *Beware ye of going up to the mount.* This forbids not merely ascending the side, but going up to the foot of the mount. *Or touching the border.* They were not to pass the bounds marked out by Moses, or approach the border or skirt of the mount. *There shall not a hand touch him,* who transgresses the bounds and touches the mount. No one shall cross the bounds prescribed in order to drag him back or punish his presumption. He shall only from a distance be stoned or shot through. *Whether man or beast.* The owner is punished for his carelessness by the loss of his beast. But, even apart from this consideration, the awful sanctity of the divine presence is not to be violated by any unseemly intrusion. *When the trumpet soundeth long.* When the cornet gives a long and swelling note, *they shall go up to the mount.* As we are said to go up to the capital of a country, so here they go up to the mount, when they draw nigh to it without either ascending it or touching its skirts. "They" (הֵמָּה) is emphatic in the original, and refers to the people in contrast with Moses, who was authorized to come into contact with the mountain. At the sounding of the trumpet they are to approach to the boundaries that have been marked out; but they are on no account and at no time to proceed farther. 14, 15. *And Moses went down from the mount.* He had drawn nigh, but not necessarily ascended to the summit, to hold converse with God. *Sanctified the people,* gave the necessary orders for their sanctification. *Come not at your wives.* See vs. 10 and Lev. xv. 18.

16–25. The descent of the Lord on Mount Sinai. *A thick cloud.* A heavy, dark mass of clouds. *In the camp,* in view of, but at a considerable distance from, the mountain. We do not deem it necessary to determine further than the text warrants, even with all the light that modern travellers have cast upon the locality, the precise spot in which the people were encamped. 17. *And Moses brought forth the people.* On the given signal (vs. 13), namely, the long and swelling blast of the trumpet, Moses leads forward the trembling people to hear the giving of the law. We must here bear in mind that Moses issued his commands, as the general of a great army, by means of the elders or acknowledged leaders of the people (vs. 17). *They stood at the nether part*, or foot of the mountain, outside of the barrier which Moses had erected to prevent intrusion. A scene of ineffable grandeur now presented itself before them. 18. *All asmoke.* The disengaged and partly unconsumed matter arises, and envelopes, as usual, the fire in which the Lord descends. *The whole mountain trembled greatly* with the reverberations of the thunder. 19. The trumpet sound waxed louder and louder, as the people were gathering into their appointed station before the mount. The origin of this sound we leave, as the text does, undetermined. On the sudden silence which followed this awful trumpet blast, *Moses spake, and God answered him by a voice*, by an audible and articulate form of words. This is the fulfilment of the promise made in vs. 9. What were the words uttered on this sublime occasion we cannot venture to determine. The statement may refer to, or at least include, the whole of the following communications so far as they were audible to the people. This is favored by the discernible pause which the narrative here makes. The recognition of this pause gives point and emphasis to the present statement, and imparts a solemn stateliness to the progress of the narrative.

20–25. *And the Lord came down.* This sublime event has been as yet only incidentally indicated to account for (מִפְּנֵי אֲשֶׁר v. 18) the smoking of Mount Sinai. It now comes forward in a direct statement with the precise intimation that the Lord descended on the top of the mount. He now called to Moses (לְמֹשֶׁה) to go up to the top of the mount. Here for the first time we conceive Moses proceeded farther than the foot of the mountain, and advanced some distance on its slopes, without however reaching, or even approaching, the actual summit. It is only asserted that *Moses went up*, without adding how far. 21. *Go down, charge the people.* We may conceive that the people from the camp were pressing forward under the direction of their leaders, and that there was some danger that the front ranks of this multitudinous host should be urged over the barriers that had been set to the people. Without for a moment imagining that the women and children were all within the valleys immediately around the mount, we can easily understand that the vast mass of deeply-agitated men would need the reiterated directions of their supreme commander to prevent any involuntary intrusion from the pressure in the rear. In these circumstances the Lord mercifully sends down Moses to charge the people, lest they break through the boundaries, gaze upon that which no eye is to behold, and many of them perish. 22. *The priests also.* We know that Abraham, Isaac, and Jacob erected altars and offered sacrifices to the Lord, and that Moses informed Pharoh that Israel was commanded to go three days' journey into the wilderness to sacrifice unto the Lord. The presumption is, that there were some among them who were appointed to act as priests. Every head of a family killed the first paschal lamb for his own household, thereby practically evincing that the people were all kings and priests unto God. And we read (xxiv. 5) before the appointment of Aaron and his sons, that "Moses sent young men of the sons of Israel who offered burnt-offerings." Here we perceive that the nation was not without sacred officers who discharged the functions and were entitled to the name of priests. Who they were we do not learn from the narrative, probably because their service at the altar was merely temporary, until Aaron should be called to the priesthood. *Who come near to the Lord* to intercede for the people. *Sanctify themselves*, keep themselves apart outside of the boundary, observing the same rules as the people. These occasional priests have no privileges beyond the rest of Israel, who are all priests unto God. 23. Moses here intimates that the people cannot touch the mountain on account of the bounds by which it is separated and sanctified. 24. But the Lord directs him to go down, and prevent the people and the priests, who had not yet got any special charge, from breaking through the barrier. It is intimated that Moses and Aaron are to come up to the mount. But this seems not to have taken place until a second intimation of the proper time is given (xxiv. 1). 25. Moses accordingly goes down, and reiterates the charge to the people and the priests.

### CHAP. XX.—THE MORAL LAW, AND THE ALTAR.

2–17. The reader of the original will observe that these verses are provided with a double accentuation, the one referring to the verses, the other to the commandments, and called the lower and upper accent. Where only one accent stands, the two coincide. Where a principal pause of the one concurs with a minor pause of the other, a double vocalization may occur, the short vowel being lengthened by the one accent and not by the other. For the same cause a letter of double power at the beginning of a word is read as a semi-vowel with the one accentuation, and as a mute with the other. In some copies, vs. 13, 14, 15, are included in one. פ is found at the end of the seventh verse, indicating the primary division of the Decalogue. ס is found at the end of vs. 6, 11, 12, 13, 14, 15, 16, and after the first clause of vs. 17, marking the subdivisions. This is plainly the primary form of the Decalogue. The deviations of the copy in Deut. v. will be best considered there. In some copies of the Sept. vs. 13, 14, 15, stand in the order 14, 15, 13.

9. מְלָאכָה *work, business, ministry*; r. un. *employ.* It is more comprehensive than עֲבֹדָה *labor, service, bond-service*; r. *to labor, till the ground, serve.*

12. After *μητέρα σου*, the Sept. has *ἵνα εὖ σοι γένηται, καὶ*, corresponding with a similar clause in Deut. v. 16.

17. At the end of this verse the Sam. Pent. has a long passage agreeing mostly with Deut. xxvii. 2–7. It is not found in Onk. or the Sept.

19. The Sam. Pent. here omits דַּבֵּר אַתָּה עִמָּנוּ וְנִשְׁמָעָה and inserts a passage contained in Deut. v. 21–24. It is not followed, however, by Onk. or the Sept.

XX. 1. And God spake all these words, saying, § 21.

2. I am the LORD thy God, who have brought thee out of the land of Mizraim, out of the house of bondage.

3. Thou shalt have no other gods before me.

4. Thou shalt not make unto thee any graven image, or any likeness of anything that is in the heaven above, or that is in

the earth beneath, or that is in the water under the earth. 5. Thou shalt not bow down to them, nor serve them: for I the LORD thy God am a jealous God, visiting the iniquity of the fathers upon the sons, upon the third and upon the fourth generation of them that hate me; 6. And showing mercy unto thousands of them that love me and keep my commandments. § 22.

7. Thou shalt not take the name of the LORD thy God in vain; for the Lord will not acquit him that taketh his name in vain. ¶ 32.

8. Remember the Sabbath-day to hallow it. 9. Six days shalt thou labor, and do all thy work. But the seventh day is a Sabbath to the LORD thy God: in it thou shalt not do any work, thou, nor thy son, nor thy daughter, thy man-servant, nor thy maid-servant, nor thy cattle, nor thy stranger that is within thy gates: 11. For in six days the LORD made the heaven and the earth, the sea and all that in them is, and rested the seventh day: wherefore the LORD blessed the Sabbath-day, and hallowed it. § 23.

12. Honor thy father and thy mother; that thy days may be long upon the land which the LORD thy God giveth thee. § 24.

13. Thou shalt not kill. § 25.

14. Thou shalt not commit adultery. § 26.

15. Thou shalt not steal. § 27.

16. Thou shalt not bear false witness against thy neighbor. § 28.

17. Thou shalt not covet thy neighbor's house; § 29. Thou shalt not covet thy neighbor's wife, nor his man-servant, nor his maid-servant, nor his ox, nor his ass, nor anything that is thy neighbor's § 30.

18. And all the people saw the thunderings, and the light-

nings, and the sound of the trumpet, and the mountain
smoking: and when the people saw it, they drew back and
stood afar off. 19. And they said unto Moses, Speak thou
with us, and we will hear; but let not God speak with us, lest
we die. 20. And Moses said unto the people, Fear not; for
God is come to prove you; and that his fear may be before
you, that ye sin not. 21. And the people stood afar off: and
Moses drew near to the thick darkness where God was. § 31.

22. And the LORD said unto Moses, Thus shalt thou say
unto the sons of Israel, Ye have seen that I have spoken with
you from heaven. 23. Ye shall not make with me any idol;
gods of silver or gods of gold shall ye not make unto you.
24. An altar of earth thou shalt make unto me, and thou
shalt sacrifice thereon thy burnt-offerings, and thy peace-offerings, thy sheep and thine oxen: in every place where I record
my name I will come unto thee and bless thee. 25. And if
thou make me an altar of stones, thou shalt not build them
with hewing; for if thou lift up thy tool upon it, thou dost
pollute it. 26. And thou shalt not go up by steps unto mine
altar, that thy nakedness be not discovered thereon.

18. ¶ ¶ ¶ 33.

The chapters xx.–xxiii. contain that code of laws which is called the book of the covenant (xxiv. 7) It is clearly distinguishable into two parts — the general principles of morality common to all mankind, and the special enactments pertaining to the people of God. The former are called "the words of the Lord," which he spake with an audible voice, and wrote upon the two tables of stone (xxiv. 3, xx. 1, xxiv. 12). In reference to their number, they are called the ten words or commandments (xxxiv. 28). The latter are described as the "judgments," or determinations of right between man and man. These are communicated to Moses, by whom they are delivered to the people by word of mouth, and also in writing for their permanent guidance. The ten commandments, with certain arrangements preliminary to the special legislation, are contained in the present chapter.

1–17. The Decalogue. The Masoretic mark for an open section at the end of the seventh verse, indicates the primary division of this grand compend of law in the estimation of these venerable annotators. If the principle of division be the essence of the Deity, this distribution is undoubtedly correct. The previous paragraph, referring to the unity, spirituality, and deity of God, which belong to the essence of his nature, is of universal and eternal moment, and is thus fundamentally distinguished from the following one regarding the Sabbath and the relative duties of men, which are incidental to that effect of his creative action to which man belongs. The former of these paragraphs the authors of the Massorah subdivide into two close sections, and the latter into eight. The first commandment thus apparently includes verses 2–6, on the principle that polytheism and idolatry are identical, or two modes of apostasy from the one true God. But in fact, these two are not less distinct from one another than each of them is from that mode of degrading God which is noted in the seventh verse. The true principle is, that there are three ways of dishonoring God, or robbing him of his glory — the first referring to his unity, the second to his spirituality, and the third to his deity. Hence vs. 2, 3 must be regarded as the first commandment; vs. 4–6 as the second; and vs. 7 as the third. The Talmud, the Targum of Johnathan, several Jewish Rabbis, Peter Martyr, and others, hold vs. 2 to be the first commandment. But the second and third verses are plainly distinguished as the positive and negative sides of the one commandment. The propriety of this threefold subdivision is further demonstrated, by its obviating the necessity of subdividing the seventeenth verse into two commandments, in order to make up the number ten. If these two errors of subdivision be corrected, "the ten words" are divided into three and seven on a tenable and intelligible principle,— the three referring to the immutable essence of God, the seven originally to man, the intelligent part of the six days' creation, and ultimately to the people whom God has taken for his peculiar treasure. It is well known that three has also a typical or mystical reference to God, and seven to the church. If the two tables of stone were to contain, as nearly as possible, the same quantity of matter without breaking up a commandment, the Masoretic division makes the nearest approach to this arrangement, the numbers of letters in each portion being respectively (errors excepted) two hundred and seventy-seven and three hundred and forty-three; whereas, if the commandment concerning the Sabbath, containing two hundred and three letters, were transferred to the former side, the numbers would be four hundred and eighty and one hundred and forty.

The Masoretic division, however, though it have a basis in the structure of the text, is founded on the idea of God, and not on the nature of law. It has a deep metaphysical import; but it regards the document before us rather as a chapter of philosophy than a compend of law. Considered as a summary of law, this document bears on it only one obvious principle of primary division, namely that of the party to whom the duty is owed, In this, its natural aspect, it contains two great divisions — the duty of man to God, in four commandments, and the duty of man to man, in the remaining six. It is strange that Augustine, having adopted this primary division, yet retained the two glaring faults of subdivision to which we have already adverted. In this way, though making his primary division at the end of the eleventh verse, he still conceives that there are three in the first table and seven in the second. In this he has been followed by the Latin and Lutheran Churches. He generally makes the prohibition to covet another man's wife the ninth commandment, according to the arrangement of Deut. v. 21; in which he is not followed by these churches. Other Jewish and Christian interpreters, including Philo, Josephus, Irenaeus, Origen, Jerome, the Eastern and Reformed Churches, agree in correcting the errors of subdivision which are exhibited in the Masoretic text. The primary division here under consideration was adopted not only by Augustine, but by Origen, and subsequently by Calvin and his followers, and hence appears not only in the Latin and Lutheran, but also in the British Churches and the documents of the Westminster Assembly of Divines.

A third ground of primary division is the relation of equality or inequality between the parties to whom the duties refer. In this respect the Decalogue is divided into duties to superiors and duties to equals. Here the father and mother are associated with God as superiors, and all men including parents are classed together as equals. The point of division is carried forward to the end of the twelfth verse, and each table contains five of the "ten words." This is the primary division of Philo, Josephus, and the modern Jews, of the Eastern and some Reformed Churches. It has the advantage of giving a numerically equal partition of the ten commandments, and of bringing out into prominence the dignity of parents as the natural representatives of God to their children. Nevertheless it appears to be a more superficial ground of distribution than either of the others. Between God and man the line of demarcation is much more trenchant than between superiors and inferiors when men are found on both sides.

The mere numerical equality of the two tables is a consideration of no moment; and the dignity of parents is sufficiently indicated by the position of the fifth commandment in the Decalogue. For these reasons we adhere to the second of the fundamental divisions described, as the most logical and suitable for common use. Which of them was exhibited on the two tables of stone we need not speculate. But it is obvious that the second corresponds with that grand classification of all law which our Lord brings out into conspicuous prominence from the Old Testament, "the first and great commandment," to "love the Lord thy God" with all thy powers, and the second like unto it, to "love thy neighbor as thyself" (Matt. xxii. 35–40).

1. *And God.* The use of this name of God here (the Everlasting, Eternal, Almighty) intimates that the fundamental principles of law have their standing in the abstract relations of theoretic truth antecedent to the actual creation of a universe of things. *Spake.* Whatever media, whether elementary or angelic, God was pleased to employ on this occasion, it is manifest that the speech was his own, not merely as to the words spoken, but as to the articulate sounds actually perceived by the ear. We are aware that vibrations of the air are the usual medium for affecting the sense of hearing, and we have no reason to doubt that these were employed on the present occasion. We are informed that Moses stood between the Lord and the people "to show them the word of the Lord"; yet it is expresssly said that it was the Lord that talked with them face to face in the mount (Deut. v. 4, 5). It appears from the Old and New Testament (Deut. xxxiii. 2, 3; Ps. lxviii. 18; Acts vii. 53; Gal. iii. 19; Heb. ii. 2) that angels were present and active at the promulgation of the law. The passages in the Old Testament merely intimate their presence. Those in the New

point to some kind of agency. The phrase of Stephen (ἐλάβετε τὸν νόμον εἰς διαταγὰς ἀγγέλων) "received the law by the arrangements" or ministry "of angels," may be regarded as equivalent to that of Paul (διαταγεὶς δι' ἀγγέλων) "arranged" or ministered "through angels." Attention is to be paid to the preposition διά, "through," which is used in the New Testament to denote the medium or intermediate agent, while the ultimate or proper agent is introduced by ὑπό, "by" (Matt. i. 22, ii. 15, xxii. 31; Acts ii., xvi., xxviii. 25; Rom. i. 2). This serves to elucidate the historical description of the law in Heb. ii. 2. (ὁ δι' ἀγγέλων λαληθεὶς λόγος) "the word spoken through angels." It is plain from the narrative now before us, that God was the actual speaker, in accordance with which the angels are here described as intermediate agents in the accomplishment of the act. We recognize the instrumentality of the atmospheric vibrations in the formation of articulate sounds. And as we notice the agency of the lightning flash in exciting those reverberations which produce the inarticulate sound of thunder, we may be prepared to hear of the agency of angels who are spirits and ministers who are a flaming fire (Ps. civ. 4), in awakening or regulating those discrete pulsations which constitute the articulate utterance of speech. How this was effected, what was the arranging or dispensing part of the angels in this great drama, as it is not revealed, we do not pretend to say. But as the performer is the source of the music, notwithstanding the concurrence of the bellows-blower, the organ pipes, and the ambient air, so we can understand that God was the real speaker of the ten words, notwithstanding the intervention of the dispensing angels and the vocal atmosphere. *All these words.* This oral communication consists of ten words or axioms of moral truth, that form a complete and orderly whole, and afford a broad basis for a system of ethical science. It is composed in the scriptural method of stating not a bare abstract principle, but a circumstantial concrete example, embodying the principle, ruling all like cases, and making a deeper and stronger impression on the mind. It presents the law, also, in the aspect of righteousness rather than goodness (Rom. v. 7), because it is designed to restrain those who have already fallen into disobedience. And hence it generally takes a negative form, and deals in prohibitions rather than requirements. It must be understood, however, that the prohibition involves the requirement, and we find that the requirement itself is given when it admits of equal or greater brevity of expression than the prohibition.

### THE FIRST COMMANDMENT.

3, 4. The more closely we examine these two verses, the more surely will we come to the conclusion of the Jewish Rabbis, that the former is an essential part of the first commandment. It states a positive fact in the conviction and for the acknowledgment of the people, to which the latter verse merely adds the negative precept that gives strict precision and exclusiveness to the previous statement. The latter verse presupposes the former, and is incomplete without it. The consequent "thou shalt have no other gods" needs the antecedent "thou hast me." Yet in the admirable economy of this address, the former of these verses serves at the same time for the preface to the whole. It has therefore a twofold bearing on what follows — it is an integral part of the first commandment, and it is an introduction to the whole Decalogue.

As an introduction to the whole law this verse identifies the parties to the covenant in the present instance. These are Jehovah and his people. It also lays down the only solid foundation of all obligation to keep this law. This is threefold: (1.) He who commands is the Lord, Jehovah, the Self-existent, the Creator, the absolute Author, and therefore Governor, of all persons and things. This is the primary rock on which all authority on his part and all obligation on ours rest. It is, moreover, not limited in its range, but co-extensive with the universe of responsible being. It is therefore the fitting term to stand at the head of a code of law. (2.) He is *thy God.* Here "thy" is the characteristic word. "God" (אֱלֹהִים) the Everlasting, Almighty, antecedent to all creation, is presupposed as common to the whole definition of the great Being. The possessive word "thy" points to the covenant between God and his people. When taken in the utmost depth of its meaning it involves two things; *first,* That God has chosen them to be his people; and *second,* That he has sent his Spirit into their hearts, in consequence of which they have taken him to be their God. He that is born of the Spirit is become capable of spiritual acts. This is the sole ground of human ability to keep the commandments. To have God in this full sense for our God is, therefore, the meet preparation for doing his will. He is the Regenerator. He gives ability. Ability begets obligation. Will tenders obedience. (3.) He is the *Redeemer*. He has brought his people *out of the land of Mizraim, out of the house of bondage*. This in the manner of Scripture and of Providence is the earnest and the guarantee of their deliverance from all other and greater kinds of bondage. The present is the type of a grander future. We must descend the stream of revelation to the New Testament before we fathom the depths of this great deliverance. But the redemption from Egypt is the immediate benefit before the minds of this people. It obviously binds them to gratitude and devotedness. Thus the appeal of God touches the inmost springs of their moral nature, and draws them by the threefold tie of creation, sanctification, and redemption, to reverence, obedience, and affection.

The attentive observer will note the unity of the party addressed, indicated by the singular pronoun "thy, thee." God's people are one in a very profound sense, as they have one Creator, Regenerator, and Redeemer (Gen. xvii. 7; Ex. iv. 22; Gal. iii. 16; Eph. iv. 2–16). But this pointed form of address at the same time brings home the obligation of the law of heaven to the indvidual as well as the community. It is another instance of the happy choice of words in this piece.

As the affirmative part of the first commandment this verse admonishes the people that Jehovah, the Creator, who has singled them out as his own, and has redeemed them from bondage, is their God. This is itself the root of all obligation, and this obligation is expressed in the word "thy," which asserts the connection between creature and Creator. This brings out the relation of right. God had the right of creation to man, and he has the right of regeneration and redemption to his people. Man has, inherently, no right to anything. These two propositions are the basis of all eternal law. God made a grant to man on his creation with a necessary reserve (see on Gen. ii. 15–17). Man infringed on this reserve under temptation, and so forfeited the divine grant. Yet God bears with man, proclaims his mercy, and accepts the returning penitent who trusts in his word. It is obvious that such come under new obligations to the Almighty, re-enforcing the great principles of moral truth.

3. The first commandment in its negative form refers to the unity of God. It enjoins the owning of this unity. It is therefore against polytheism. This precept is of universal obligation. The idea of God, the Everlasting and Almighty Jehovah, the Creator and Upholder, involves in its very nature the idea of unity; and so this negative verse is implied in the affirmative one that precedes. But the nations had lost the consciousness of their own unity as a race, and with this the consciousness of the unity of their common Creator. Each principality, each town, and at length each family, began to regard the god of its erring fancy as different in individuality from that of others. The step was easy to the recognition of gods many and lords many. Hence it became necessary to add the definite exclusion of all other imaginable objects of worship to the express acknowledgment of the Lord God. The original form of the expression is here worthy of attention. "There shall not be to thee other gods upon my face." Here it is demanded that the non-existence of other gods be recognized. This presupposes the affirmative of such non-existence. Such gods are אֱלִילִים nonentities. לֹא יִהְיֶה "there shall not be," is directly opposed to אֶהְיֶה "I Am," and to יְהוָֹה the Author of existence (iii. 14, vi. 3), the exclusive names of the God of creation and of covenant. *Before me* is literally "upon my face." It supposes those other gods to be set up before the true God as antagonists in the eye of God, and as casting a shade over his eternal being and incommunicable glory in the eye of the worshipper.

### THE SECOND COMMANDMENT.

4–6. The second commandment refers to the worship of God. It guards the immateriality or spirituality of his nature. It opposes idolatry, that is, the worship of an idol or image of God, or of God through an idol. We are not to make, *worship*, or *serve* an idol. *Any graven image.* This is a carved image of stone or wood. *Any likeness.* The word תְּמוּנָה denotes any form presented to the eye (Num. xii. 8; Job iv. 16), and therefore includes all sorts of pictures as well as images. It is probable that the Israelites were acquainted with the pictorial representations of idols in Egypt. At all events, the specific instance involves the general rule, that every kind of visible similitude is to be avoided in the worship of the invisible God. *In heaven above.* The Egyptians had images of celestial, terrestrial, and aquatic objects of worship (Wilkinson). *The water under the earth.* It is important to notice that "under" here means "lower in level," lest the Scriptures be accused of propounding the theory, that the interior of our sphere is filled with water. 5. *For.* The reason here assigned applies equally to the first and second commandments, and warrants the Masoretes in placing the verses (2–6) containing them in close contiguity. *A jealous God.* The passions of a moral being have their right as well as their wrong use. Hence anger, jealousy, hatred, and revenge are ascribed to God, not as passions, but as the feelings of a holy being in regard to that which is evil (Deut. xxxii. 21, 22, 35). As the Judge of the universe, God has the supreme right not only to entertain these feelings, but also to carry out their holy behests in the administration of his everlasting dominion. This is the first distant allusion to the semblance of the covenant between God and his people to a marriage contract. *Visiting the iniquity*, pursuing and overtaking the offender with condign punishment. There is significance in the phrase "visiting the *iniquity*," as it shows that the sons are not involved in the penalty if they are not found in the iniquity of their fathers. The iniquity here spoken of is that of polytheism or idolatry, of having or making any other God. For the idol, or the being it represents, is not the true God, but another god, after the fashion of a vain imagination (Rom. i. 21–25). He that makes and worships an idol has lost the knowledge of the true God. This iniquity is called the iniquity *of the fathers*, inasmuch as it originates with them, and is only perpetuated in the sons who adhere to it. The history of the world shows that the ungodliness of the fathers is, as a rule of fallen nature, followed by the sons. Only grace interrupts the succession of sin. *Upon the sons, upon the third and upon the fourth generation.* This is a timely guard against a common error to which men have been prone in all ages, namely, that the opinions and customs of their forefathers, even though they be wrong, are an excuse or justification for the sons walking in the same errors of judgment and conduct. The fathers will have to account for their own iniquity, not only as men, but as fathers setting a bad example to their household. But the sons who, on arriving at the exercise of a natural judgment, walk in the same iniquity will be treated as responsible beings, and visited for the iniquity which they have made their own. Many evil consequences, indeed, such as poverty, disease, and infamy, befall the children of ungodly and vicious parents. But a profounder truth is taught in this passage, and the example of it was patent before the eyes of the audience assembled in Horeb. The forefathers of the Egyptians had departed from the living God, and devised for themselves the eight gods of the first order, the twelve of the second, and the seven of the third, besides their countless modifications and subdivisions of the divine essence. Their sons of the existing generation not only followed, but outstript, their fathers in the abominations of superstition and deification; they contemptuously ignored the true God, whom their fathers acknowledged (Gen. xli.), and trampled upon his people. In this instance the Lord had signally visited the iniquity of the fathers upon the sons in the ten plagues, and in the overwhelming of their hosts in the Red Sea. Upon all the gods of Egypt he had executed judgment, and caused the Egyptians to know and acknowledge that he was the Lord (vii. 5, viii. 8, ix. 27, xii. 12).

With these tremendous judgments of the past few months still fresh upon their memories, the awe-struck hearers would have a vivid conception of what was meant by the jealous God visiting the iniquity of the fathers upon the children unto the third and fourth generation. The despotic and barbarous measures of the new king that knew not Joseph had been commenced in the time of Moses's father, and therefore about four generations from the time then present. Each generation had only been advancing in the severity with which they oppressed the chosen people of the Lord, until their cry ascended to heaven, and the Lord interposed for their vindication. Overwhelming was the visitation for their aggravated and infatuated hostility to God and his people. God admonishes the world by terrible examples of his righteous indignation; and then pauses to leave men the full exercise of their free-agency. *Of them that hate me.* To have or to make another god is to hate the true God. Here let it be observed that in the estimate of God there is no difference between forsaking him for another and hating him. The negative state of indifference to him or inclination to another necessarily involves the positive state of hatred to the true God. Nothing can be more base or blameable than to forsake the very Author of our being and all our blessings for the mere phantom of a delusive imagination. It is the special temptation of descendants, whether in the nation or the family, to follow their ancestors in apostasy from God or the truth which he has revealed concerning himself and his ways. Hence at the birth of this nation whom he has chosen for himself he lifts up a monitory voice, reminding them of the judgment of Egypt, and warning them to beware of incurring a like visitation. To allow free scope for that voluntary return to confession and obedience which can alone be pleasing to God, he may in long-suffering withhold the full force of his correcting hand even to the fourth generation. But a nation or a family that neglects opportunities of knowing God and his mercy need not expect to be long without the dread experience of his power and justice.

6. *And showing mercy.* Mercy is that form of the divine goodness which reason dare not affirm and revelation alone can proclaim. And to show mercy or do kindness, not to requite merit or reward righteousness, is the most favorable language that can be employed concerning any portion of a fallen race. It forms the contrast here to "visiting iniquity." *Unto thousands.* Here is a cheering prospect and a sweet assurance to godly parents. "Thousands" may be fairly understood to mean the thousandth generation, and therefore to intimate the possibility, if not the probability, of piety becoming hereditary, or being perpetuated in the given line to the end of time. And the comforting promise is, that God will never fail to show mercy to all successive generations that humbly and thankfully own him for their God. We observe how mercy rejoices over judgment: God visits iniquity unto the fourth generation; he shows mercy unto the thousandth. *Of them that love me and keep my commandments.* The objects of the divine mercy are those who have the Lord for their God, and worship him in spirit and in truth. They meet his mercy with an earnest, confiding gratitude; and this feeling displays itself in "loving him and keeping his commandments." There is an intense interest connected with the expression "them that love me." It plainly intimates that those who have no other God before the true God, and make no other God beside him, are those who at the same time love him. It proves that the negative quality of not forsaking the true God is understood to imply the positive quality of being

faithful to him and loving him. This gives a new character to the whole Decalogue. It now becomes not a mere negative law of righteousness, but a positive law of love. This principle applying to the first two precepts will extend to the whole. Besides, if we love him that begat, we shall love those who are begotten; and therefore love to God will naturally result in love to all his creatures. This closing sentence would sink deep into the hearts of those reverential auditors in Horeb's glens. It forms the bright counterpart to the dark menace conveyed in the preceding one. As the former has its dread exemplification in the judgments executed on Egypt, so the latter finds its hopeful illustration in the chosen race. Those who then stood before the mount of God were about the tenth generation from Abraham, the father of the faithful. The faith of their great forefather was still the profession, of all and the inward experience of a goodly number, in that vast multitude. And God had been unchangeably faithful in "showing mercy" to them during all that interval, and especially to the tenth generation who had been brought out of the land of bondage and were on their way to a land of blessing. Here, then, was the warning against apostasy on the one hand and the encouragement to fidelity on the other, presented in the most striking examples to this new-born nation.

It is interesting to find the glad tidings of the mercy of God presupposed and incidentally proclaimed in this address from the mount of God. It is important also to note the place where the two alternatives of judgment and mercy are inserted in this legislative address. They come after the two precepts enjoining the exclusive and direct owning and worshipping of the true God. This indicates that to have the Lord for our God, and to have and to make no other god, is the basis of all religion, and the substance of the covenant between God and his people. All that follows after is the mere carrying out of this fundamental and fully expressed principle. This deep and important thought fully bears out the Masorah in throwing verses 2–6 into one paragraph.

### THE THIRD COMMANDMENT.

7. After the acknowledgment of the One Great Spirit as our God comes the manner in which we ought to treat him. *The name* of God

is that "by which he makes himself known." In the realistic style of Scripture, where names are significant, the name indicates the nature of God. It is expressive, therefore, of his godhead or deity. It especially intimates that great attribute which is the sum and substance of the divine nature. Power belongeth unto God (Ps. lxii. 11; Rom. i. 20) as the essence of his being; for power implies freedom, and freedom will, and will intelligence; power, will, and intellect are the three essentials of a spirit. To *take the name of God in vain* is to violate his essence, power, truth. This commandment is therefore directed against blasphemy, perjury, and all other modes of dishonoring the name of God. In its form it serves to illustrate that feature in the style of Scripture according to which a plain and familiar case is set forth to embody a general principle. And hence in a profounder sense it is opposed to pantheism, naturalism, creaturism, or the applying of the name of God to the creation or any part of it, or dealing with it as if it belonged to a creature.

The sin here forbidden has been as prevalent as polytheism or idolatry. It has assumed all forms, from the deification of a fetish to that of the sun, moon, and stars, or of the universe. It has appeared not only as a superstition, but as a philosophy, falsely so called. It consists in the ascription either of divine attributes to a creature, or of creature attributes to God. The latter is the form chiefly contemplated in the command, as it is addressed to those whose God is the Lord. It tends to atheism.

*Will not acquit him.* There is here an allusion to the "visiting of iniquity" mentioned in the previous passage. The iniquity of taking the name of God in vain is akin to that of having another god, or making an idol before the living and true God. It is a form of apostasy and ungodliness, and therefore involves the same guilt, doom, and penalty. This raises the third commandment to the same gravity of character with the former two. The investigation of the nature of that crime which it prohibits has led us to the same conclusion regarding its primary importance.

The first commandment, then, guards the unity of God; the second, his spirituality; the third, his deity, or essence. In the first we are forbidden to make God one of many, when he is the only One; in the second, to liken him to a corruptible image, when he is the incorruptible Spirit; in the third, to identify him in any way with the creature, when he is the Creator. The three combine to form the fundamental law of monotheism; but at the same time they present an adumbration of the Father, the Son, and the Spirit. The Father is God, the invisible one; the Son is the express image of the Father (Heb. i. 2); and the Spirit is the inward power or essence of God.

It is manifest that the ontological division of this solemn proclamation from Sinai takes place at this point. All that goes before refers to the essence of God; all that follows relates, not to his essence, but to his work. This division rests on the theological aspect of the "ten words."

## THE FOURTH COMMANDMENT.

8–11. This grand compend of law now descends from the personal rights of God to the day of his rest. The former precepts are purely moral; the fourth is partly moral and partly positive. The principle that man's time should be divided between labor under the eye of God and leisure for the solemnities of his worship is moral. The apportionment according to the example of God is positive. The first three precepts are of universal obligation whenever and wherever there is a rational creature. The fourth is specially binding on man, being founded on the six days' work and the seventh days' rest in that creation of which he formed the crowning part. It is therefore to him of perpetual significance and obligation. Referring to a day of rest for appearing before God, it inculcates religion and prohibits secularity. It has a twofold form: affirmative — "Remember the Sabbath day to hallow it;" negative — "In it thou shalt not do any work."

8. *Remember.* Pointing to an event of the past it is the precept of memory. It deals with the commemorative principle. This is in keeping with the constitution of man. Memory is the faculty of history; and the remembrance of events that have a momentous influence on the interests of man is congenial with all the tendencies of his nature. *The day.* It is not without significance that the law contains a commandment concerning time, and none concerning space. Human action occupies a certain time, while it has no definite relation to

space. It also implies forethought, deliberation, purpose, volition. It involves an agent and a patient, a cause and an effect. As a course of conduct runs through a certain length of time, action and duration come to be measures of each other. Hence history and chronology are inseparably associated. Spirit may be said to be to time as matter is to space. The one fills time with the successive acts of its free powers; as the other occupies space with the wide-spread field of its constant forces. The day is the natural unit of time, and affords the measure for the division of time in the fourth commandment. It extends from sunset to sunset (Lev. xxiii. 32). *Sabbath*, a rest, not that of sleep or death, but vacation from business, leisure for converse with God. *To hallow it*, set it apart from the rest of time for sacred rest.

9. *Six days shalt thou labor.* There is here an injunction to labor in so far as it is necessary for the support of life. There is at the same time a permission to employ six successive days in labor. Experience proves that this is more than sufficient for raising from the ground the sustenance needful for man. *And do all thy work.* Work or business is a more extensive term than labor. The latter refers to out-door work or manual labor, requiring effort and entailing toil; the former includes, moreover, the routine of domestic operations, the management of affairs, the transactions of buying and selling, and all that is usually meant by the term "business."

10. *But the seventh day.* While six days are allowed for business, the seventh is assigned to leisure. The number seven has acquired a typical sacredness from its application to the Sabbath. The rest of God after six days of creative activity, in which a habitation was prepared, and man, the intended inhabitant, created, is the historical foundation for the Sabbath. But the proportion of time for labor and for rest is not only derived from the history but adapted to the nature of man. The operations of the corporeal frame consist of three parts: first, that which is involuntary and without intermission, as the action of the heart and other internal functionaries of the vital organism; second, that which is instinctive, as the travail of the animal powers in search of food, shelter, and other natural requirements; and third, that which is rational, as the effort to attain a certain end beyond the merely animal wants. The first part of the movement is kept in

constant vigor by the regular supply of food. The second has its recompense in the natural repose of sleep. The third remains over, to be relieved by a recurring period of rest to be determined by reason. As on the whole about a third part of the exertion of our powers may be due to this last source, and that for the half of the natural day, it follows that a sixth part of each natural day needs its compensating repose. After six days, therefore, a seventh day of rest seems needful to repair the waste and weariness accruing from voluntary rational effort. At all events the special activity of the rational powers evidently stands in need of being recruited by a third provision, not of the animal, but of the rational nature, and that is plainly the Sabbath.

*A Sabbath to the Lord thy God.* Rest and dedication to God are the properties here assigned to the Sabbath. The observance of the Sabbath connects man with the origin of his race, with the six days' creation, and with the Creator himself. The connection is manifestly a historical one. He that observes the Sabbath aright holds the history of that which it celebrates to be authentic, and therefore believes in the creation of the first man, in the creation of a fair abode for man in the space of six days, in the primeval and absolute creation of the heavens and the earth, and, as a necessary antecedent to all this, in the Creator, who at the close of his latest creative effort rested on the seventh day. The Sabbath thus becomes a sign by which the believers in a historical revelation are distinguished from those who have allowed these great facts to fade from their remembrance (xxxi. 13). The leisure of the Sabbath-day, moreover, affords the opportunity for the holy convocation, and for the public and private exercises of praise, prayer, reading, expounding, and applying the word of God. The observance of the Sabbath, then, becomes the characteristic of those who cherish the recollections of the origin of their race, and who worship God not merely as Elohim, the Everlasting Almighty, but as Jehovah, the historical God, the Creator, who has revealed himself to man from the dawn of his existence as the God of love, and afterwards of mercy and grace, of promise and performance.

*Thou shalt not do any work.* Both labor and business (עֲבֹדָה and מְלָאכָה, the latter including the former) are excluded on the weekly Sabbath. *Thou, nor thy son, nor thy daughter.* These are the free.

The remainder, commencing without the copulative conjunction, are the bond. It is remarkable that this enumeration intimates the duties of superiors to their inferiors. It points to the right and duty of parents, masters, and hosts to restrain those under them from sin and train them to holiness. It makes the mother, the wife, the mistress, not subject in this respect, but equal to the husband. It marks the accountability of owners also. In like manner it affirms the right of children, servants, and strangers to the observance of the Sabbath, and, by parity of reason, to the free exercise of all other religious duties. It inculcates the kind treatment of the lower animals. Especially it claims the seventh-day rest for the domestic animals that labor for and with man in the pursuit of his rational ends. *Thy stranger that is within thy gates* (see on xii. 19). They were sojourners, not yet incorporated by circumcision into the community of Israel.

11. *For.* A reason is assigned for the observance of this precept, as there was for all that preceded it. God requires a rational service. The reason is historical. It refers to the original division of time into six days of work and a seventh day of rest on the occasion of the creation of man. Then God not only rested after the six days of creation, but blessed the Sabbath day and hallowed it. He thus instituted a seventh-day Sabbath of perpetual obligation, and therefore now enforces its constant remembrance and observance (see on Gen. ii. 1–3). Reminding him of his exalted origin and bringing him into contact with his Maker, it awakens in his breast all those feelings of joy and thankfulness which the possession of conscious being naturally evokes.

From the essence of God we naturally pass to his action. As the former three precepts indicate his intrinsic essence, so the fourth reveals the foundation of his authority over the creature. The act of creation is the origin of all title to the creature and to the obedience of the intelligent creation. The creation of man is commemorated in the fourth commandment. Hence it contains the fountain-head of all authority in God and all duty in man. The former three are negative. This is affirmative. The former regard eternity. This refers to time, and deals with man's conduct towards God, dividing it into innocent business and recreation on six days, and holy leisure for converse with God on the seventh. The absolute authority of God is no less important to us than his necessary being. The former three commands relate exclusively to God. The fourth introduces man on the stage of existence. It forms, therefore, the natural transition from the rights of God to those of man.

Regarding the ten words as a law, we are now come to the point of main division. A law determines what is due to each class of persons; and therefore may be divided according to the various rights due, or the various parties to whom they are due. In a primary division these two principles come ultimately to the same thing, inasmuch as the nature of the right depends entirely on the nature of the person to whom it is due. The present summary of law is divided on the latter principle into the duties of man to God, and of man to man. The subdivisions that flow from such a primary classification are merely the analysis of the sum of right due to each class of individuals.

### THE FIFTH COMMANDMENT.

12–17. We are now come to that series of commandments which contain our duty to man. This is divided into our duty to superiors, contained in one, and our duty to equals, contained in the remaining five.

12. This commandment prescribing our duty to superiors is properly arranged after the four that determine our duty to the great Supreme. It is also the meet companion of the fourth, inasmuch as they are both founded on the history and nature of man: the former pointing to the origin of the race; the latter to that of the individual. *Honor thy father and thy mother.* We have here a beautiful instance of the scriptural method of laying down a principle by enunciating its most striking and important example. The parents are the only natural superiors, for they are, under God, the authors of the existence of those children for whose maintenance and training they labor with all the assiduity of natural affection. This sublime scheme of general jurisprudence does not condescend to notice the ephemeral arrangements of artificial society, but selects the primeval distinction of parent and child as the theme of legislation concerning superiors and inferiors. The parent stands to the child in the relations of progenitor, benefactor, teacher, and ruler. As progenitor he is, under God, the author of the child's existence; and this gives him a rightful authority over

the child second only to that supreme authority which creation gives to God over both parent and child. Parental affection moves the father, and especially the mother, to those unwearied efforts of tender, loving, fostering care that are demanded by the helplessness of infancy and childhood, and forms the type and shadow of that disinterested beneficence which comes out in other circumstances in the priestly office. The wisdom and experience of age qualify him to cultivate the intellectual, active, and moral powers of his child; in the discharge of which duties he foreshadows the functions of the prophet, the teacher, and the preacher. His authority as parent entitles him, and his affection and experience befit him, to exercise a benignant sway over his child, and therein to adumbrate the affairs of the elder or ruler in the politcal and ecclesiastical worlds.

The "father" and "mother" are distinctly specified to indicate that they are equal in authority, and therefore equally entitled to that "honor" which the mother will attract by her love and the father will enforce by his power. This honor naturally resolves itself into reverence for the authors of our being, gratitude for the nameless blessings of a home, docility to the patient and persevering educators of our infant minds, and obedience to the commands of our natural superiors. The patriarch was father, priest, prophet, and king in his household or clan. In the more complex arrangements of nations and empires the magistrate and the priest came out into prominence and influence as distinct orders, and even the teacher sometimes asserted a standing and a rank for himself in the social scale. But all these subdivisions of authority find their origin and standard in the parental relation and the fifth commandment. This commandment enforces all lawful authority, and is opposed to all the levelling and deranging fancies of anarchy and democracy.

*That thy days may be long in the land.* This is the first commandment with promise. To comprehend all the meaning of this we must remember that the personal pronoun "thou, thy," is to be taken both in a collective and individual sense. In the collective sense it refers to the whole people, and conveys the assurance that compliance with this command will prolong or perpetuate their possession of the promised land. In the previous commandment parents were required to impress upon their children the observance of the Sabbath and the maintenance of that reverence for God, remembrance of his creative power and authority, and devotion to his worship which are inseparably associated with the day. The dutiful attention of children to these instructions will serve to perpetuate fidelity to God among the people from generation to generation, and therewith to perpetuate the inheritance of the land of their forefathers. On the other hand, the neglect of the parents to enforce, or of the children to maintain, the observance of the Sabbath, and all its associations with the origin of their race and with the Creator and Preserver of their being, will inevitably tend to apostasy from the true God, and consequent expulsion from the land of all their natural and religious affections. The subsequent history of this people to the present day forms a striking comment on the sentence now before us. The great economic law, however, that filial obedience is the main foundation of national stability and prosperity, is not peculiar to the Jews. The domestic virtues have in all nations been the prolific source of social greatness and progress.

The personal application, however, of this promise is no less just and important. Length of days or of inheritance is a law running through the moral government of God, counteracted, no doubt, and modified by the interference of other laws that contribute no less to the ultimate, if not immediate, good of the individual. For if life be shortened to a child of God, he only enters the sooner upon a better and higher life; and if the inheritance be shorter than the life, yet he cannot be deprived of that precious and present inheritance that all things, even affliction, work together for his good.

*Which the Lord thy God giveth thee*, is going to give thee, is in the purpose and process of giving thee, as the imperfect or current participle denotes. The mention of this circumstance concerning the land favors the wider interpretation of this promise, as it was to the whole people the Lord was about to give the land. It does not however preclude its reference to individuals. It is to be noted that if we regard the second verse as an integral part of the first commandment, the phrase "the Lord thy God" occurs in each of the first five commandments.

This is the third and last point at which the main division of the Decalogue may be placed; the ground of distinction being the rank of the parties to whom the rights are assigned. The first five refer to the rights of superiors, and the second five to those of equals. But the second point of division is much more marked than this. The contradistinction between God and man is incomparably more important than that between superiors and equals, when among the superiors God and man are classed together, and opposed to men as equals. It is obvious that the fourth and fifth commandments form the easy and gradual transition from the higher to the lower sphere of legislation. They stand together in many respects. They have a positive form. The one introduces us to the family of heaven; the other to the family of earth. The former touches incidentally on the duties of parents and masters; the latter relates to the duties of children and servants. The one respects the "honor" due to the Great Father of all; the other that which is due to his natural representative and type among men.

13–17. These verses contain the five precepts regarding equals. Three of these refer to deeds, one to words, and one to thoughts. They guard the life, the chastity, the property, and the character of our neighbor, not only from the outward act, but from the inward thought of violence. It is, indeed, in all cases, the intent that gives moral character to the act.

### THE SIXTH COMMANDMENT.

13. This commandment protects life, and is against all endeavors that endanger the life of our neighbor. As there is no object expressed, it prohibits suicide as well as homicide. It also forbids violence, passion, lust, intemperance in eating or drinking, or anything that tends to shorten life. The peculiar sacredness of human life lies in this, that man is a responsible being, liable to be rewarded or punished according to his deeds. Life is the reward of obedience, and death is the penalty of disobedience. The circumstance that this life is to the sinner the season of invitation to return to God, who will have mercy on him, deepens immeasurably the crime of cutting short his life in the midst of his impenitence. All these considerations are wrapped up in the paramount reflection that man was created in the image of God. Life is also used in a pregnant sense in Scripture. It rises from the mere natural life to the spiritual life, which is rekindled in the dead soul by the Spirit of life through the word of life. This widens immensely the

scope of this commandment. And if we now advance from the mere negation of refraining from evil to the position of abounding in good, we behold opening before us a boundless prospect of well-doing for the children of God.

### THE SEVENTH COMMANDMENT.

14. This commandment sanctions marriage and prohibits fornication, adultery, and all unchaste acts. Among mankind, who are naturally gifted with reason and conscience, the cohabiting of the sexes ought to be after the solemn compact of lawful wedlock by mutual consent. Marriage ought to be between one man and one woman who are not within the forbidden degrees of consanguinity. Nothing dissolves its bonds but adultery. Married life is not sinful or defiling. On the other hand it calls forth some of the tenderest, fairest, finest feelings of humanity; and gives scope for as high and holy duties as any relation in life. This commandment guards the home from the external intruder on its chastity, as the fifth does from the internal disturber of its peace.

The formation of the woman out of the man indicates in a striking and beautiful manner the unity of the married pair. The fourth and fifth commandments concur with this in presupposing a parity of right between the husband and wife. The law of Moses and the law of Christ agree in vindicating the natural right of woman against the arbitrary might of man. And Judaism and Christianity have been honorably distinguished among the nations for respecting the rights of the weaker sex. This is the more remarkable, as they both originated in the East, where the harem prevails.

Marriage has been peculiarly ennobled by being employed to typify the union between God and his people; while apostasy has been odiously branded as fornication and adultery.

### THE EIGHTH COMMANDMENT.

15. This precept guards property, and is directed against taking that which does not belong to us, whether by violence or fraud. The most heinous breach of this commandment is the stealing of man. If property be taken in a large sense, this precept includes the two preceding,

as the life and the body are strictly property. If it embrace what belongs to another as a debt or a right, then this commandment covers the whole field of relative duty. The Maker is the only ultimate proprietor. Not a tree of the garden belongs to Adam till the Creator makes the definite grant. All men are equal in point of natural right. The only natural superiority is that of the parent. All other authority of man over man is by covenant or tacit consent. This, then, is the most comprehensive of all the commandments. And it occupies the central place among the laws between equals.

The three preceding commandments refer to action, and in this we see a warrant for grouping them in one verse, as is done in some manuscripts. They also bear a certain analogy to the first two or three commandments. To have another god is a practical annihilation of the true God. Idolatry is a spiritual adultery. Stealing, in a large sense, will include taking the name of God in vain. It is in one sense the only thing of which we can rob God.

### THE NINTH COMMANDMENT.

16. This commandment refers to speech, enjoins truth, and is directed against falsehood. It covers the same ground as the preceding three; as falsehood may imperil life, chastity, or property. It assumes its darkest form when the falsehood is uttered avowedly in the presence of God, who searches the heart, and will bring every word into judgment. In this aspect it bears the same relation to the third commandment which the three preceding do to the first two or three. Besides the common applications of this law, its importance is enhanced by the circumstances that most of our information concerning the present or the past comes to us in the form of language, and that our knowledge of God, of his work, and of his grace is conveyed to us in his word. The eternal, then, as well as the temporal, interests of man are linked with spoken and written words. How awful, then, the responsibility of those who are endowed with the faculty of speech.

### THE TENTH COMMANDMENT.

17. This commandment refers to the thoughts, inculcates disinterestedness, and prohibits indulging a desire after that which belongs to

another. The first clause is followed by a closed space indicating a snbordinate separation from the following clauses. The verb is also repeated at the beginning of the second clause, intimating a marked distinction, and warranting a certain pause, though not a subdivision of the Decalogue. The transposal of the first two clauses in Deut. v. 21 is sufficient to show that in the estimate of the transcriber the two were included in one of the ten words. This precept, also, is co-extensive with the three precepts referring to the outward acts. A man cannot covet his neighbor's life; but he may desire his death, if it would make way for his acquiring possession of any coveted thing that belonged to him. In the arrangement of the present book, "the house" is placed first. This is generally understood of the material building in which a man dwells. We prefer regarding the prominent thought implied in it here to be the family, including the parents, and especially the sons and daughters of all living generations; inasmuch as, (1) the other objects specified are living creatures, and "anything that is thy neighbor's" includes the goods and lands; (2) the children are not otherwise mentioned, though of more importance than servants or cattle; (3) a due subordination is thus introduced into the details, the house coming first, as including the parents and children, the wife next, as the separable part of the neighbor, and then the servants, cattle, and inanimate objects. In Deuteronomy the prominent thought in "house" seems to be the material building; and hence the wife, who is also the mother, and includes the children, is placed first, the house and the field are associated together in the next place, the service by which these are rendered comfortable and profitable has the third rank, and the products of their labor hold the last. The arrangement in Exodus corresponds closely with the three precepts concerning the outward acts; as the sixth commandment bears upon the family in its widest sense, the seventh especially on the wife, and the eighth in some sense upon the servants, the cattle, and the goods.

The improper desire is the root of all evil. It can seldom be reached by human legislation. But it is open to the Searcher of hearts. The intent is that which, in the last resort, determines the moral character of the act. This last "word" is, therefore, the interpreting clause of the whole Decalogue (Rom. vii. 7). It raises the code immeasurably above every code of man, who looketh on the outward appearance of conduct, and at once renders it worthy of the Lord who looketh on the heart. Covetousness here includes envy, malice, and every other selfish or unholy state of the feelings. Its prohibition involves the inculcation not merely of disinterestedness, but of all the forms of unselfish benevolence. This commandment is, therefore, virtually the law of love, and in this positive sense gives that loftier aspect to the Decalogue, the traces of which have been already noticed.

As the ninth commandment is related to the third, so the tenth has several points of relation with the fourth: (1.) It enjoins disinterestedness, and the observance of a seventh day's rest is a most powerful and practical demand for the same state of the affections. (2.) It contains an enumeration of the inmates and surroundings of the home; and the fourth commandment does the same, and with much of the same intent. (3.) It strikes at the root of all inhumanity in the words and acts of men; and the law of the Sabbath strikes at the root of all ungodliness in a world that is prone to secularity. There is no command of the Decalogue by which the public sense of religious obligation has been so deeply tried and found wanting as the fourth; and the obvious and almost avowed spring of all worldly opposition and natural antipathy to it is the selfish, grasping, avaricious spirit which is condemned in the tenth.

This brings out a curious proof of the internal coherence of these ten words. If we connect together the first and second commandment, and likewise form the sixth, seventh, and eighth, that relate to the outward conduct, into one group, we bring to view a remarkable analogy between the former and the latter; and the same analogy appears between the third and ninth, and between the fourth and tenth. Thus the law is found to fall naturally into a sevenfold division, three members of which relating to God are before the fifth commandment, and three relating to man after this central precept relating to parents. The number ten points to the perfection of this code, and this internal septenary arrangement to its holiness. There is, therefore, a wonderful display of unity and comprehensiveness in this moral discourse. While adopting the concrete form that comes home to the common mind, it embodies at the same time in its familiar examples all the great abstract principles of moral truth. The mild voice of a paternal authority is heard in it, inasmuch as while it warns the decided or defiant apostate of certain retribution, it whispers mercy to every returning penitent. It is addressed, no doubt, to the sons of Israel, and alludes to their recent deliverance from bondage; but it purports to be the utterance of the Almighty, the Creator of heaven and earth. It does not suffer any limitation by being proclaimed to that portion of the human race which remained in professed communion with God, since it forewarns the apostate nations of approaching visitation, and clothes its precepts in the garb of denunciations against their most glaring sins. Many of its precepts are of universal and eternal obligation, and none of them is narrower than the whole compass and duration of the human race on earth. To the heirs of immortality, when they have become the spirits of just men made perfect, when they neither marry nor are given in marriage, and have more things common than air and water, the principles contained in the sixth, seventh, and eighth commandments, if they require to be republished, will assume a new form adapted to their new condition. But the principles themselves, and even the form in which they are now presented, can never cease to be self-evident and self-binding.

18–21. The effect of the spectacle which Mount Sinai presented upon the people is here described. We may suppose that the awful silence which prevailed during the delivery of the law was followed by a return of the thunderings and the lightnings, and the clang of the trumpet. *All the people saw.* The verb is here used in a pregnant sense. They saw the scene which was accompanied by the dread crashing of the elements and the thrilling notes of that unearthly cornet. *They drew back and stood afar off.* The solemnities of the divine presence beget the feeling of reverential awe, under the influence of which they retire to a respectful distance. They have no more any doubt of the divine commission of Moses; and they entreat, by their elders, that God would speak to them through Moses, and not directly and personally, lest they die. Human consciousness in its fallen state shrinks from immediate contact with God (vs. 20). Moses pronounces the encouraging word, *Fear not*, a word long remembered afterward (Hag. ii. 5). *To prove you.* The test of their fidelity to the Lord their God was the law which was now promulgated from Sinai with all the advantages of the immediate presence and audible voice of God. Faith in God is a dead form, if it do not bring forth the fruit of penitence and obedience. Hence he sets before them in the most conspicuous light the standard of a perfect morality that he may prove them, *that his fear may be before them that they sin not.* The signal demonstrations of his presence and power will leave them without the excuse of any obscurity in the oracles they have received, and awaken a salutary sense of the infinite majesty and sanctity of the Supreme (vs. 21). *And Moses drew near to the thick darkness where God was.* We learn from the supplementary narrative of Deuteronomy that Moses communicated the petition of the people to the Lord, who was pleased therewith, and gave them leave to retire to their tents (Deut. v. 28).

22–26. The altar. The paragraph now before us is the close after the ten words and the preface to the legislation of the three following chapters. It is in the form of a message to Israel. It reminds them of the palpable fact that he had spoken to them from heaven. 23. *Ye shall not make with me* any idol. The construction here is remarkable. The first "make" has no object expressed. It is designed to make emphatic the accompanying "with me" by which the exclusive unity of the Godhead is intimated. The object is then supplied and the verb repeated.

24. *An altar.* This prohibition to make any image of God is designed to introduce the permission or injunction to make an altar to him. The only outward thing in the salvation of the soul is the atonement. The necessity of propitiation is accordingly symbolized in the altar. The mercy of God needs no type, and has its place in the proclamation on Siani. The propitiation which makes way for his mercy to the penitent sinner by satisfying his justice, has its type in the altar and the sacrifice thereon. This special provision for the salvation of sinners, though it would be out of place in the ten words, yet forms the main substance of all that is shadowed forth in the whole ceremonial law. It therefore comes in here as the necessary antecedent of all acceptable approaching to God and walking with him. The word altar connects Moses and the people of Israel with Noah and his rescued family (Gen. viii. 20). *Of earth.* Earth was the scene of man's sin; it is also to be the scene of the sacrifice for sin. The altar of earth is merely the definite spot of this earth set apart

for sacrifice, and elevated to raise the offering towards God, who is in heaven. *Thy burnt offerings.* The two great classes of offerings are the expiatory and the eucharistic. The former is here represented by the עֹלָה or burnt-offering (Gen. viii. 20), which implies on the part of the offerer the confession of guilt and of the need of an atonement. *And thy peace-offering.* This is that species of offering which was designed to express the thanksgiving of the offerer for peace with God or any of its attendant benefits. It was also expressive of devotedness to him. *Thy sheep and thine oxen.* The ordinary kinds of animals employed in sacrifice. Goats were included along with the sheep. *In every place where I record my name,* where I cause my name to be remembered and invoked. This intimates some change of the place where the altar was to be erected. The patriarchs were wont to build an altar wherever God appeared to them. *I will come unto thee and bless thee.* The presence and the bounty of God are here promised.

25, 26. The altar may be of stones, if unhewn. It is thus entirely a work of God, and so in keeping with that propitiation which comes entirely from God. *If thou lift up thy tool upon it, thou dost pollute it.* This teaches, by a figure, that the sinner only defiles, and therefore cannot have any part in atoning. The altar of rude stone was common among the ancient nations. Motives of decency dictated that the altar was not to be approached by steps.

The prescription here concerning the altar appears in the most general form. The details of legislation on this subject will appear in their proper place.

## XII. THE CIVIL LAW.—Ex. xxi.-xxiv.

### CHAP. XXI.—LAWS OF SERVITUDE AND PERSONAL SAFETY.

XXI. 1. And these are the judgments which thou shalt set before them. 2. When thou gettest a Hebrew servant, six years shall he serve; and in the seventh he shall go out free for nothing. 3. If he come in by himself, he shall go out by himself; if he be married, then his wife shall go out with him.

4. If his master give him a wife, and she have borne him sons
or daughters, the wife and her children shall be her masters,
and he shall go out by himself. 5. And if the servant shall
plainly say, I love my master, my wife, and my children; I will
not go out free: 6. Then his master shall bring him unto
God: and shall bring him to the door or to the door-post;
and his master shall bore his ear through with an awl; and he
shall serve forever. § 32.

7. And when a man sells his daughter to be a maid-servant,
she shall not go out as the men-servants do. 8. If she please
not her master, who hath not betrothed her, then he shall let
her be redeemed: to sell her to a strange people he shall have
no power, when he hath deceived her. 9. And if he betroth
her to his son, he shall deal with her after the manner of
daughters. 10. If he take him another wife, her food, her rai-
ment, and her duty of marriage shall he not diminish. 11.
And if he do not these three unto her, then shall she go out
free without money. § 33.

12. He that smiteth a man, so that he die, shall be surely
put to death. 13. And if a man lie not in wait, but God
deliver him into his hand, then I will appoint thee a place
whither he shall flee. § 34.

14. But if a man come presumptuously on his neighbor to
slay him with guile, thou shalt take him from mine altar to
put him to death. § 35.

15. And he that smiteth his father or his mother shall surely
be put to death. § 36.

16. And he that stealeth a man and selleth him, or in whose
hand he is found, shall surely be put to death. § 37.

17. He that curseth his father or his mother shall surely be
put to death. § 38.

18. And if men quarrel, and one smite another with a stone

or with his fist, and he die not, but is laid on his bed: 19. If he rise and walk abroad on his staff, then shall he that smote him be quit; only he shall pay for his loss of time, and cause him to be thoroughly healed. § 39.

20. And if a man smite his servant or his maid with a rod, and he die under his hand, he shall surely be punished. 21. But if he continue a day or two, he shall not be punished; for he is his money. § 40.

22. And if men strive, and hurt a woman with child, so that her fruit depart from her, and no mischief follow, he shall be surely fined, according as the woman's husband will lay upon him, and he shall give as the judges determine. 23. And if mischief follow, then thou shalt give life for life; 24. Eye for eye, tooth for tooth, hand for hand, foot for foot; 25. Burning for burning, wound for wound, stripe for stripe. § 41.

26. And if a man smite the eye of his servant, or the eye of his maid, that it perish, he shall let him go free for his eye's sake. 27. And if he knock out the tooth of his servant, or the tooth of his maid, he shall let him go free for his tooth's sake. ¶ 34.

28. And if an ox gore a man or a woman, and he die, the ox shall be surely stoned, and his flesh shall not be eaten; but the owner of the ox shall be quit. 29. But if the ox were wont to gore in time past, and it hath been testified to his owner, and he hath not kept him in, and he hath killed a man or a woman, the ox shall be stoned, and his owner also shall be put to death. 30. If a price be laid on him, then he shall give for the ransom of his life whatsoever is laid upon him. 31. Whether he gore a son or gore a daughter, according to this judgment shall it be done unto him. 32. If the ox gore a servant or a maid, he shall give unto his master thirty shekels of silver, and the ox shall be stoned. § 42.

33. And if a man shall open a pit, or if a man dig a pit and cover it not, and an ox or an ass fall therein, 34. The owner of the pit shall make it good: the money he shall return to its owner, and the dead beast shall be his. § 43.

35. And if one man's ox gore another's, and it die, then they shall sell the live ox and divide the money of it; and the dead ox also they shall divide. 36. Or if it be known that the ox was wont to gore in time past, and his owner did not keep him in, he shall surely pay ox for ox, and the dead shall be his. § 44.

1. *And these are the judgments which thou shalt set before them.* This is the heading of the four chapters which contain the civil polity of the Jewish theocracy. It will aid very much the intelligent perusal of these chapters if we mark the orderly arrangement of the topics of which they treat. The main features of this arrangement have been grasped by the Hebrew and Christian expositors. With some variance from the usual division, and some endeavor after a more extensive elucidation, it is exhibited in the following scheme:

| | | | |
|---|---|---|---|
| I. | Of Servitude, | xxi. 1–11, | 5th Commandment. |
| II. | Of Personal Safety, | xxi. 12–32, | 6th " |
| III. | Of Property, | xxi. 33 – xxii. 14, | 8th " |
| IV. | Of Conjugal Fidelity, | xxii. 15–30, | 7th " |
| V. | Of Veracity, | xxiii. 1–9, | 9th " |
| VI. | Of Set Times, | xxiii. 10–19, | 4th " |
| VII. | Of Piety, | xxiii. 20–33, | 10th " |

The first of these sections refers to the duties of masters and servants, and is therefore a natural expansion of the fifth commandment, which relates to parents and children. The second treats of injuries destroying or endangering life, and hence comes under the sixth commandment. The third, relating to property, is an expansion of the eighth. The fourth is of a somewhat diversified character; but its various precepts bear upon the marriage vow, either between husband and wife, or between God and his people. The injunctions concerning the stranger, the widow and orphan, and the poor will naturally come under the latter head, if we remember that God avouches himself the guardian of all such. This section is thus analogous to the seventh commandment. The fifth section, on truthfulness and integrity in witness-bearing and judging, developes the ninth commandment. The sixth, on the observance of set times, finds its germ in the fourth word of the Decalogue. The seventh, on the acknowledging, worshipping, and serving of Jehovah alone, who searches the hearts and estimates the motives, is closely allied with the tenth commandment.

It follows that the civil code is capable of being divided into seven sections, corresponding with the last seven precepts of the Decalogue, though exhibiting a different order. The order depends in each case on the material to be arranged and the end to be attained. There the matter was the moral relation between the Creator and a race of intelligent creatures, and the end a compend of universal law. Here the matter is the moral relation between the Sovereign and his subjects, and the end a code of civil jurisprudence. Here the subject of law is regarded, (1) as a master; (2) as a neighbor; (3) as an owner; (4) as a consort; (5) as a speaker; (6) as a disposer of time; and (7) as a child of God. The basis of this arrangement appears to be a gradation in the rights and responsibilities of man. It is manifest that the first section touches upon his lowest stage and the last upon his highest. The serf is one who is denuded of some part of his natural rights. The neighbor is in possession of that great original right of one creature against every other, namely, the inviolability of his person. The owner is invested with certain additional rights, acquired originally by the grant of the Creator, which is the only just title to property. The consort indicates a still higher degree of responsibility, as the social compact which it involves brings into view reason and will, and fidelity and trust. The speaker is endowed with the organ of that sociality which is implied in the consort. The occupant of time has within his power the set time of meeting, private or public, which affords the possibility of social conference. The child of God rises to the highest privileges of social happiness in the great family of heaven and earth. A piece of composition that admits of such analysis must have an internal harmony and unity.

Bertheau, and after him Baumgarten, maintain that as the "ten words" constitute the great Decalogue, so each of these sections forms a minor decalogue. There is, we conceive, some tenable ground for this subdivision. This brings out in a striking light the wonderful system lying in the structure of this seemingly unconnected collection of injunctions. Seven groups of ten precepts each form the fundamental polity of the commonwealth of Israel.

*The judgments.* These are decisions on points of law that may arise between man and man. They are therefore authoritative sentences or precepts for the regulation of civil society.

### I. LAWS OF SERVITUDE.

2–11. Here are ten verses containing the first decade of laws. They relate to serfdom, or the degraded state of man in which he is stripped of some of his natural rights. The only natural rights are rights of person, such as liberty, life, and inviolability of person. Offenders against the law are in all states deprived of some or most of these rights as the penalty of their offence. Even insolvency in some states has involved the loss of liberty and life. Captives in war have been often treated as offenders against the state, and consigned to bondage for life. It must be admitted that the withdrawal of freedom, or the imposition of labor for a term of years or for life, according to the degree of the offence, is a legitimate mode of state punishment. Hence serfdom and forced labor are warrantable in the case of crime. Even the apprenticeship of six years for the acquisition of handicraft, or any other craft, such as domestic service, with proper restrictions, might be an improvement on our social system. And in ancient times, when servitude merely meant the performance of service with the understood condition of receiving food and raiment in return, many were glad to accept the terms without stipulating for a personal freedom which was to them of no practical value. The present decade of laws does not institute servitude, or commit itself to the approbation of every kind of bondage. It merely implies that some form of it, such as that of criminals under correction, or the dependant who voluntarily enters into it, is admissible. It recognizes the fact of its existence, without entering into the origin of this degraded condition. The decade of precepts is divided into two fives, each beginning with *when* (כִּי, vs. 2, 7), followed by four *ifs* (אִם). The former five relate to the man-servant, the latter to the maid-servant.

2. *If thou get*, acquire in any way, it may be by the voluntary offer of the individual, who sometimes sold himself into servitude, such as is here contemplated, as a means of improving his temporal condition (Lev. xxv. 39; Deut. xv. 12). *A Hebrew servant.* A servant is merely a laborer. The term does not of itself indicate the loss of freedom. We see no reason why the term Hebrew should not be taken here in its full extent of meaning as a descendant of Heber, at least as far as this relationship still lived in the memories of men, and no disturbing event interfered with its application. We have no doubt that in process of time the term was gradually narrowed in application, until it came to be of the same extent, though not precisely of the same meaning, with Israelite or Jew. This first decision limits the period of servitude for a Hebrew to six years. As, however, all the Hebrew servants became free in the jubilee, or fiftieth year (Lev. xxv. 10, 40), this period would be shortened if it commenced within the six years immediately before the jubilee. It is plain from this statute that the involuntary servitude of a Hebrew could not be prolonged beyond six years. He then goes out free *for nothing*, or without any redemption. Nay, it is further enjoined in Deut. xv. 12, 18, that he shall be furnished with a stock to enable him to enter upon a life of self-dependence.

3. This verse contains two enactments, that are the complements of one whole. He that comes in *by himself*, with his body only, shall go out by himself. But if he come in married, his wife also shall go out with him at the end of the six years. This includes, no doubt, the family, if any, as they go with the mother.

4. The fourth decides that in case his master give him a wife, she and her children shall remain with the master when the husband goes free. The wife belonged to the master. The children go with her who can tend them in their infant years, and sustain them out of her master's abundance. The difference in condition between the husband and his wife does not however necessarily dissolve the tie of wedlock between them. The husband's "going out by himself," simply means that his wife does not share his freedom with him. It does not of itself dissolve the marriage bond. They may continue to live as husband and wife, though it is possible that, in the loose manners of the times, the connection would be sometimes entirely broken off. The liberation

of the husband may have made it inconvenient, difficult, or sometimes impossible for them to live together. Such a case is provided for in the following enactment.

5, 6. The fifth clause of this section presents a very agreeable aspect of servitude as existing in Israel. *Shall plainly say*, declare in all the earnestness and warmth of his heart. *I love*, I have learned to love my master. *I will not go out free.* Here is a case of voluntary servitude, and that not for a limited term of years. 6. *Shall bring him unto God.* Here is the first mention of the magistrate in the commonwealth of Israel. The supreme ruler in this singular community is God himself. His ministers, governors, and judges, therefore, speak with an authority paramount to all other. The Sept. aptly renders πρὸς τὸ κριτήριον τοῦ Θεοῦ, to the court of God. The freed man is to make his solemn declaration "I will not go free" before the authorities of the land, who will see to it that the act is of his own free will. *To the door or to the post,* whichever is the more suitable. The latter is always available, but the door-leaf may sometimes be wanting. *His master* shall do the act, as the chief party concerned. *Bore his ear through with an awl.* The awl through the ear is to be driven into the door or the post (Deut. xv. 17), to signify the permanent attachment of the bondsman to the family of his master. *And he shall serve for ever.* Josephus and the Rabbins explain this to be a service till the next jubilee. This seems natural, as the phrase "for ever" is to be explained according to the nature of that to which it it is applied. It could not in this case extend longer than the natural life of the servant.

7–11. These five verses contain the law of the maid-servant. To *sell his daughter to be a maid-servant* was partly the resource of poverty and partly the custom of the country. It is plain that the maid-servant so bought was to have the place of a wife or a concubine, either to her purchaser or his son. In either case she is not to *go out as the men-servants do.* If she please her master, she has an acknowledged position of right in his house, which the marriage bond secures to her.

8. *If she please* him not, and accordingly he do not *betroth* her or give her this rightful place, *he shall let her be redeemed* by some of her kindred. He is not at liberty to sell her to a foreigner, *when he has*

*deceived her* by refusing her the rights of marriage. This last clause is only a circumstance necessitating her release. The illegality of selling her to a foreigner rests on the fact of her Israelitish descent.

9. *If he betroth her to his son*, she shall be treated as a daughter and not as a bondsmaid. She is to have all the privileges of a wife.

10. *If he take him another wife.* This may refer either to the father or the son. The latter seems preferable. A second wife is not to exclude the former from the rights of food, raiment, and conjugal intercourse. Here again we find the law not instituting either polygamy or concubinage, but guarding the rights of the wife.

11. If these three rights be withheld, the bondsmaid is to go free without any redemption. A servitude in which the bondsmaid might become the honored wife of the master or of his son, or in case of neglect be released from her bondage, was thus secured for the poor daughter of Israel.

### II. LAWS OF PERSONAL SAFETY.

12–32. From man divested of the natural right of freedom we advance to man invested with the natural right of personal inviolability. This is the most fundamental right that belongs to intelligent creatures. As they come from the hand of the Creator, one individual has no right to harm another, and each has a right to be left unharmed by every other. The Creator has the authority and the obligation to enforce this law upon the intelligent portion of his creatures; and in a fallen state civil government is instituted on the ultimate basis of the patriarchal authority to check its infringment and guard personal safety. The special form of personal violence prohibited in this set of judgments is injury to life or limb. It is therefore an expansion of the sixth commandment. The injury may come directly from our neighbor (vs. 12–27), or indirectly from his ox (vs. 28–32).

12–14. Intentional killing, or murder, is placed first. The general rule is first laid down. The murderer shall surely be put to death. No satisfaction or pecuniary fine was to be taken for the life of a murderer. The rich and the poor were to stand here on a footing of perfect equality (Num. xxxv. 31). Then the two cases of premeditated and unpremeditated manslaying are distinguished. *If a man lie not in wait.* If the intention be not harbored in his mind; if a plot be not laid. *But God deliver him into his hand.* Here the particular providence of God is recognized in the most emphatic manner. This clause is merely the complement of that which precedes, If the slayer had no hand in bringing about the meeting, then it falls under the general head of the divine administration. It is only the meeting of the parties that is here referred to this head. The broader question of the occurrence of all events, moral and physical, in subordination to divine providence is not here mooted. *A place whither he shall flee.* This contains a reference to the avenger of blood (גֹּאֵל דָּם גֹּאֵל, Num. xxxv. 9–32), the nearest of kin, who was by primeval custom antecedent to all statute law entitled and bound to maintain the cause of the deceased in general, and in the case of death by violence to pursue the slayer, and, if he overtook him, to put him to death. The life of man is infinitely precious, both because he has been created in the image of God, and because he is responsible hereafter for what is done here. Hence even unintentional homicide is regarded as an awful deed, which is not to be passed over without check or censure. But though the avenger of blood is recognized as the minister of a prompt and natural justice, yet a way of escape is opened for the unintentional manslayer by the institution of six cities of refuge (Josh. xx. 7, 8), so situated that the fugitive had not more than twenty-five or thirty English miles at most to flee. And as in most cases he would have a start of from one to twenty-four hours, he would generally be beyond the reach of his pursuer in the course of a day. The cities of refuge were all Levitical, and therefore in a peculiar sense belonging to God, who shields the unintentional manslayer. The elders or council (עֵדָה) of the city of refuge shall receive him, and not surrender him to the avenger of blood (Josh. xx. 4, 5). They shall hand him over to the council (עֵדָה) or elders of his own city (Num. xxxv. 24, 25; Deut. x. 12), who shall decide whether he be guilty of manslaughter or murder, and in the former case "restore him to the city of his refuge," and in the latter "deliver him into the hand of the avenger of blood, that he may die." 14. The murderer, as he acts from malice prepense, with presumptuous daring, or unmanly guile, is here, by way of contrast with the milder sentence of the unpremeditating manslayer, emphatically condemned to death, from which not even the altar of God, much less the city of refuge, shall shelter him. This indicates both the fact that the altar was already regarded as a sacred and almost inviolable asylum for the defenceless, on account of its intimate connection with the Supreme Being, and the reason why Levitical cities, which belonged specially to God, were selected as cities of refuge.

15. In this second enactment we pass from the murderous stroke to the blow of violence inflicted on a father or a mother. To strike a parent, even though the blow be not fatal, is to lift the hand of violence against the author of our being. It is akin to rebellion against God himself, the great Father of all. It is here regarded with such abhorrence as to be visited with the penalty of death. We learn from this and other passages (vs. 17; Deut. xxi. 18–21) that wilful and obstinate disrespect to parents was a crime that came under the cognizance of the civil judge.

16. The third judgment condemns the manstealer to death. From the violent blow we proceed to the violent seizure. To steal a man and make merchandise of him is by its present connection regarded as aiming a blow at his life. It is, at all events, doing violence to his person, and therefore comes naturally under the sixth commandment. It differs entirely from the treatment of one who has come into legitimate bondage, to which the previous section is devoted. This enactment leads to the remarkable conclusion that the stealing or selling of a free man without his fault, or against his will, was in the polity of Israel a crime of the deepest dye; and accordingly that lawful servitude could only arise from the consent or the crime of the serf (see on vs. 2–11). This form of the law differs from the corresponding one in Deut. xxiv. 7 in the universality of its application.

17. The preceding enactments refer to the hand of meditated violence; the fourth to the tongue. Some copies of the Sept., regarding the parents as the point of connection, transpose the sixteenth and seventeenth verses. But the Hebrew arrangement rests on the more fundamental gradation from the hand to the tongue. Cursing father or mother is a crime cognate with the breach of the third commandment. The legislator evidently takes a comprehensive view of the principle involved in the sixth commandment, similar to that of our Lord in the sermon on the Mount (Matt. v. 21–26). Hence "cursing," wishing evil to a parent, is treated as a most flagrant breach of this

commandment. It violates the majesty of God, of whom the parent is the natural representative.

18, 19. In this fifth "judgment" from malice prepense, we proceed to sudden outbursts of violence arising from strife or passion. The present case refers to strife or angry debate between equals. From words they come to blows. A bruise is inflicted with a stone or the fist, which does not cause death, and yet confines the sufferer to his couch. Here both parties may be culpable; and if the disabled man so far recover as to walk about on his staff, the striker is only to pay for the loss of time and the costs of the remedy. If, however, death ensue, either in the strife or before he leave his bed, the case is provided for by the first enactment of this section (vs. 12–14). It will come under the head of manslaughter, unless malice prepense can be proved.

20, 21. The sixth law refers to sudden violence on the part of a master. The chastisement of a servant, or even a child, with a rod was in perfect harmony with the allowed custom of the times. If, therefore, death under his hand should follow, it was to be presumed that the master did not intend to kill his servant. *He shall surely be punished.* If he had without intention slain a free man, he would have fled to the city of refuge, and remained there till the death of the high priest. In the case of a bondsman, then, we cannot suppose, with the Talmud, that the penalty was death by the sword. In the absence of an avenger of blood we presume the elders of his city would examine whether the act was murder or manslaughter, and deal with him according to the spirit of the first enactment (vs. 12–14). This would involve at least banishment to the nearest city of refuge for the usual time. But it is possible that death resulting from the excess of a legitimate mode of chastisement was punished by a fine of thirty shekels or upwards, the average value of a slave, along with the cost of burial and the maintenance of the surviving family. This is favored by the decision that if the slave survive a few days it is to be presumed that he did not intend to compass his death, and the loss of the slave is to be counted as a fine for the abuse of power.

22–25. This seventh decision passes to bodily injuries that fall short of the loss of life. In the case of strife or bodily conflict it is not unnatural for the softer sex to interfere by their intreaties or personal efforts to restore peace or protect the party in whom they are interested.

A woman with child may thus be injured, and abortion take place without any further mischief resulting. The offender is in this case to be fined according to the damages laid on by the husband and regulated and enforced by the judges. The rendering of the Sept. μετὰ ἀξιώματος is free, but according to the sense. Some understand "her fruit departing from her" of premature birth, and refer the "mischief" to the loss of either the mother's or the child's life. 23. If mischief follow, the decision is, "thou shalt give life for life." The *lex talionis*, or law of retaliation, is here laid down as the great principle by which the magistrate is to be guided in the administration of justice. A great deal of unreasonable obloquy has been heaped upon this law, as if it inculcated or implied the right of private revenge. A little reflection will show that it is the simple and only principle of all retributive justice. If two men were the only intelligent beings in existence. neither would have any right to hurt or apply any force to the other. On the other hand the law of self-love would suggest the obligation to love the other as himself. If the one did injure the other, the latter would not thereby acquire any right to injure the former to the same or to any amount, or to quench or abate the feeling of benevolence already entertained towards him. But he would have the right of laying his cause before the ultimate fountain of all authority. And it is clear as day that the Creator is the supreme judge of all his creatures, and is bound by the simple law of equity to indemnify the sufferer and to impose an adequate penalty on the offender. This, and this alone, is the true import of the *lex talionis*. It is merely the law of equity expressed thus: as is the offence, such is to be the penalty. But its adminstrator is not the private individual, but the duly authorized magistrate. The error of many Jews in our Lord's time (Matt. v. 38–48), and of the carnal mind in all times, is to assume the right and indulge the spirit of private revenge, to the extinction of that spirit of love which ought to actuate the breast of one intelligent being towards another. But this does not touch the abstract principle of equity, or the authority and obligation of the civil magistrate to maintain it between man and man. 24. The arrangement of the members here is obvious. 25. The fire, the sword or other sharp instrument, and the fist or some blunt instrument inflict these injuries. It is expressly stated (Num. xxxv. 31, 32) that no satisfaction (כֹּפֶר, expiation, redemption) is to be taken for the penalties of murder and manslaughter. This implies that satisfaction or commutation of punishment was known and practised, and that it was admissible in other cases.

26, 27. The eighth enactment provides for the case of a slave being mutilated by his master. The loss of an eye or a tooth by violence is to be compensated by the emancipation of the slave. This is a clear case of commutation. These verses in the Hebrew close an open parasha, or greater section, obviously because the legislator now passes from injuries done *by* men to injuries inflicted by cattle. But we conceive that injuries done *to* men and injuries to property form the fundamental basis of division.

28–31. The ninth judgment refers to the goring of a free man by an ox. If death ensue, the ox is to be stoned, and his flesh is not to be eaten. The loss of the ox is to stand for the penalty of the owner, if he be otherwise blameless. The law is remarkably earnest in the protection of human life. 29. If the ox be dangerous, and the owner have been advised of it and have not kept him in, then the ox is to be stoned, and the owner also put to death. 30. But a commutation of punishment is expressly allowed in this case. 31. The child is to be equally protected with the full-grown man.

32. The tenth, and last of this group of laws applies to the case of a slave being gored by an ox. The redemption price is in this case fixed at thirty shekels of silver. Estimating the shekel at two hundred and twenty grains of silver, or about 2s. 3d., we find thirty shekels equal to £3 7s. 6d. If the relative value of silver was formerly greater than now, the estimated value of a slave must be proprotionately increased. Some suppose it was, in the time of Moses, ten or twenty times its present value. A freeman above twenty and under sixty years of age was estimated at fifty shekels of silver, a woman at thirty. For other ages, the estimates varied according to a fixed rule (Lev. xxvii. 1–8). A close section, or minor paragraph of the Hebrew text, here terminates, because the laws relative to the ox are not yet completed. The laws referring to the defence of life, however, are at this point separated from those treating of the protection of property. This is, therefore, the second break in this civil code.

It is here to be noted that the distinction of intentional or unintentional, which is signalized in the first of these enactments, runs through the whole, and modifies the degree of guilt and the amount of the penalty.

### III. LAWS OF PROPERTY.

xxi. 33–xxii. 14 (15). From man invested with the bare rights of nature we now rise to man endowed with the acquired rights of property. Adam, as soon as he came from his Maker's hand, had the right of personal inviolability. As soon as his Maker made him a formal grant of all the trees of the garden that were suitable for him he had received the right of property, which assumed an endless variety of forms in the progressive development of the race.

33, 34. The first "judgment" refers to the case of a man opening a pit already made and covered, or digging a pit, and in either case leaving it uncovered. If an ox or an ass fall therein and be killed, the owner of the pit shall make it good. The money value he shall give to the owner of the animal, and himself retain the dead. This is a good instance of the *lex talionis*, varied by commutation, and exhibited as in principle the return of an equivalent.

35, 36. In the second enactment it is provided that where an ox gores another to death the owners shall divide equally the value of the living and the dead animals. But if the live ox was addicted to goring his owner shall pay ox for ox, and the dead shall be his. It is obvious that to pay ox for ox is to give either an ox of equal value or the fair price of the ox killed.

In the English version this chapter ends here. This division corresponds with a minor section of the Masoretic text, and with the sense. But a more appropriate ending for the chapter would have been at vs. 34, where the legislator passes from the subject of personal safety to that of property.

## CHAP. XXII.—LAWS OF PROPERTY AND CONJUGAL FIDELITY.

18. מְכַשֵּׁף *enchanter* or sorcerer (vii. 11). יִדְּעֹנִי *wizard*, one wise in black arts. אוֹב the ghost of the departed conjured up to give answers concerning the future. These two terms generally occur together, and refer to the necromancer.

20. חָרַם *to prohibit from common use*, to devote to God without possibility of redemption (Lev. xxvii. 28, 29), and hence utterly to destroy and exterminate.

29. מְלֵאָה *the fulness* of the corn harvest; the first-fruits of this fulness offered to God in grateful acknowledgment. דֶּמַע *the tear*, the trickling juice of the fruit-tree harvest, of which the first-fruits were also to be presented to the Lord.

XXII. 1. If a man steal an ox or a sheep, and kill it or sell it, he shall restore five oxen for an ox and four sheep for a sheep.

2. If the thief be found breaking in, and be smitten that he
die, there shall be no blood for him. 3. If the sun be risen
upon him, there shall be blood for him; he shall make full
restitution; if he have nothing, then he shall be sold for his
theft. 4. If the theft be certainly found in his hand alive, be
it ox, or ass, or sheep, he shall restore double. § 45.

5. If a man graze on a field or vineyard, and put in his beast and graze on another's field, of the best of his field and of the best of his vineyard shall he restore. § 46.

6. If a fire break out and catch on thorns, and a stack of corn, or the standing corn, or the field be consumed, he that kindleth the fire shall surely make restitution. § 47.

7. If a man shall deliver unto his neighbor money or stuff
to keep, and it be stolen out of the man's house; if the thief
be found, he shall restore double. 8. If the thief be not found,
then the master of the house shall be brought unto God, to
swear that he hath not put his hand unto his neighbor's goods.

9. For all manner of trespass, for ox, for ass, for sheep, for raiment, for anything lost, if one say that that is it, the cause of both parties shall come unto God; and whom God shall condemn, he shall restore double to his neighbor. § 48.

10. If a man deliver unto his neighbor an ass, or an ox, or

a sheep, or any beast to keep, and it die or be hurt or taken away, no man seeing; 11. An oath of the Lord shall be between them both, that he hath not put his hand to his neighbor's goods; and the owner of it shall accept this; and he shall not make it good. 12. And if it be stolen from him, he shall make it good to the owner thereof. 13. If it be torn in pieces, he shall bring it for witness: he shall not make good that which was torn. ¶ 35.

14. And if a man borrow aught of his neighbor, and it be hurt or die; if the owner thereof be not with it, he shall surely make it good. 15. If the owner thereof be with it, he shall not make it good; if it be hired, it went for its hire. § 49.

16. And if a man entice a maid that is not betrothed and lie with her, he shall surely endow her to be his wife. 17. If her father utterly refuse to give her unto him, he shall pay money according to the dowry of virgins. § 50.

18. Thou shalt not suffer a witch to live.

19. Whosoever lieth with a beast shall surely be put to death. § 51.

20. He that sacrificeth to any God, save unto the LORD only, shall be devoted to death.

21. And thou shalt not vex a stranger or oppress him; for ye were strangers in the land of Mizraim. 22. Ye shall not afflict any widow or fatherless child. 23. If thou afflict them in any wise, and they cry at all unto me, I will surely hear their cry. 24. And my wrath shall wax hot, and I will slay you with the sword: and your wives shall be widows and your children fatherless. ¶ 36.

25. If thou lend money to any of my people that is poor by thee, thou shalt not be to him as a usurer: thou shalt not lay upon him usury.

26. If thou at all take thy neighbor's raiment to pledge,

thou shalt restore it to him at the going down of the sun. 27.
For that is his only covering; that is his raiment for his skin:
wherein shall he sleep? and it will come to pass that he shall
cry unto me and I will hear; for I am merciful. § 52.

28. Thou shalt not revile God nor curse a prince among
thy people.

29. Thou shalt not delay the first-fruits of thy corn and of
thy wine: the first-born of thy sons shalt thou give unto me.
30. So shalt thou do with thine ox, and thy sheep: seven days
shall it be with its dam; on the eighth day shalt thou give
it me.

31. And ye shall be holy men unto me; neither shall ye
eat flesh that is torn of beasts in the fields; ye shall cast it
to the dog. § 53

1. In this third law we proceed from injuries to property arising from inadvertence or negligence to those which are intentional. The case of the thief having got off with his booty and killed or sold it is placed first. The fivefold and fourfold restitution is intended to cover the time, trouble, and cost which the theft may in this case have occasioned over and above the mere loss of the animal stolen. The theft of an ox involves in this respect a somewhat greater accompanying loss than that of a sheep, and this is allowed for in the fivefold restitution.

This verse is attached to the preceding chapter in the original, seemingly because, like the previous verses, it treats of oxen. But as it treats of theft it is preferable, with the English version, to connect it with the following verses, which refer to the same subject.

2–4. The fourth enactment treats of a thief caught in the act. This gives rise to three cases: (1.) He loses his life by night. In this case no blood is to be shed for him. By his nightly intrusion he endangers life directly or indirectly. His life is the forfeit of his intended crime. (2.) If he be smitten by day, the slayer shall suffer; because there is no necessity for his death. He has been seen, and if he get off he can be overtaken by justice, and compelled to make restitution as already prescribed. *If he have nothing*, and therefore cannot make the required restitution, *he is to be sold for his theft.* This is a clear case of servitude being the judicial penalty of crime. (3.) If the thing stolen be found alive in his hand, and therefore without the trouble and cost of a tedious search, he shall restore double.

5. The fifth decision regards the introduction by fraud or negligence of cattle into the field, especially the grain-field or vineyard, of a neighbor. It is presumed that the damage occurs by carelessness. At all events compensation to the full amount is to be made from the best of the trespasser's field or vineyard.

6. The sixth refers to the breaking out of fire in a stack, or standing corn, or a field. It is customary in pastoral districts to kindle fires in the fields at all seasons; and it is not unusual to set fire to the herbage for the purpose of promoting the fertility of the soil. If the wind and the lie of the field are not attentively considered, there is much danger of the fire spreading either to the standing or to the garnered grain. The careless kindler of the fire is to make restitution for the damage done. This is analogous to the preceding case. The other cases also in this section go together to a certain extent in pairs.

7, 8. The following determinations refer to the entrusting of property, either as a deposit or a loan. In the present case, money or articles of any kind are entrusted to another. If the thing entrusted be stolen, and the thief be caught, he shall restore double. If not, the trustee is called upon to make oath before God that he has not put his hand to his neighbor's goods. If he can do so, he is acquitted.

9. But if he do not clear himself in this way, he comes under the present regulation. This applies to any kind of thing missing, or said to be missing, that is found with a man who denies it, while it is challenged by another as that very thing which he has lost. This is evidently a case of some complication and difficulty. It is to come before the delegates of the Most High for adjudication, and he with whom the article missing is adjudged to be found, though denied, is to restore double.

10–13. This regulation refers to animals committed to the keeping of another. The Rabbins make a distinction between paid and unpaid trustees; the latter being entrusted merely with money or articles that require only house-room, the former with cattle that require sustenance.

It is obvious that in this case the caretaker must be remunerated at least for the cost of the animal's keep. If the animal die, or be maimed, or carried off secretly, and the guardian make oath that he is innocent of the loss, he shall not make it good. 13. If it be torn by a wild beast, and he bring the remains of it as a proof, he is to be acquitted.

This verse terminates a major section of the Masoretic text, because the next refers not to trusteeship, but to lending. But the two following verses relate to property as well as the preceding; while the subsequent verses relate to conjugal fidelity. The major division should in this view be placed after the fifteenth verse of the English version, or the fourteenth of the Hebrew text.

14, 15. The tenth regulation of this law section refers to borrowing any article or animal from a neighbor. If it be injured or killed in the absence of the owner it is to be made good. But if the owner be present the thing borrowed is not to be made good; and if hired, it is to go for its hire.

### IV. LAWS ON CONJUGAL FIDELITY.

16–31. The regulations under this head are somewhat miscellaneous. To give a unity to them we must suppose the relation between God and his people to be symbolized by that between husband and wife; and we must regard God as the avowed guardian and representative of the stranger, the widow, and the orphan. The covenant between God and his people (Gen. ix. 9–17, xv. 18, xvii. 1–24; Ex. vi. 4, 5, xix. 5, 6), in which he engages to be their God, and takes them to be his people, warrants the former symbol, which becomes frequent in the later scriptures. The stranger (Gen. xv. 13; Ex. xx. 10), the widow and the fatherless are special classes of the unprotected, whom God will hear if they be oppressed and cry unto him (Ex. ii. 23, 24, iii. 9).

16–17. The first precept affords protection to the unbetrothed female who is enticed or beguiled into unchastity. The enticer shall *endow her to be his wife*. The dowry was a portion given by the bridegroom for his bride to her parents (Gen. xxix. 18–20, xxxiv. 12; 1 Sam. xviii. 25). The present passage favors the supposition that it was originally intended for the use of the bride. If the father refuse to give her, *he shall pay money according to the dowry of virgins.* To pay money is here to weigh silver which was not yet coined. The sum afterwards fixed by law was fifty shekels of silver (Deut. xxii. 29).

18. The second judgment. A wizard (יִדְּעֹנִי) is one who endeavors to accomplish a selfish end by the powers of darkness. The masculine form of the term here employed (מְכַשֵּׁפָה) denotes a sorcerer or enchanter, who employs the charm or muttered chant to bring a preternatural power to his aid (Ex. v. 11). The practiser of such arts, or the pretender to them, is by the very fact an apostate from God, a breaker of that solemn and gracious covenant which he has made with his people, and a traitor to the theocracy under which he lives. And his example at least would tempt the people to all these crimes. Such a one is, accordingly, not to be suffered to live. The penalty for witchcraft is stoning (Lev. xx. 27), and this, no doubt, extended to all its forms. The phrase לֹא תְחַיֶּה is employed to denote the immediate and extreme necessity of exterminating this lurking form of enmity against God and man. The male and female are no doubt included in this judgment; but the wizard seems to have been less common than the witch.

19. The third rule condemns an unnatural crime of the kind that rendered Sodom infamous. Such a crime implies a being dead to all fear of God as much as to the very instincts of nature.

20. The fourth law declares the man who sacrifices to any being but the true God to be accursed, and therefore given over to extermination.

21–24. This fifth provision, as well as the two following, has reference to the unprotected classes — the stranger, the widow, the fatherless, and the poor. *Thou shalt not vex.* This word signifies to harass by unworthy treatment, and is followed by another implying a greater degree of violence and injustice. *A stranger.* While the Lord is constrained by the ungodliness of the world to select for himself a people whom he may teach and bless, the stranger is to be peculiarly welcome among this people, and every facility afforded for their admission into all the rights and privileges of the theocracy. Whatever, therefore, may have been the conduct of Israel in different periods of her history, it is clear that the God of Israel and his ministers are to be completely exonerated from the charge of exclusiveness. The stranger is not to be discouraged or oppressed, but welcomed to sojourn and even to be incorporated in the commonwealth of Israel. *For ye were strangers.* An affecting appeal is here made to the bondage which seven weeks could not have effaced from their memories. A provision was made, as we have already seen, for the stranger being admitted to the ordinance of the Passover (xii. 48), and allowed and required to observe the Sabbath (xx. 10). We shall meet with other tokens of consideration for the stranger as we proceed (Lev. xix. 9, xxiii. 22; Deut. xiv. 28, 29, xvi. 11–14, xxiv. 17–22, xxvi. 11–13). 22. *Ye shall not afflict*, tread down or oppress. *Any widow or fatherless child.* There is a touching nicety and correctness in the use of fatherless child for orphan in the English version; inasmuch as the decease of the father leaves both the widow and the child without their natural protector and sustainer, whereas the motherless child has still the father as its stay. 23, 24. God threatens to be the avenger of the widow and the fatherless by bringing the sword of war on the ruthless oppressors.

25. The sixth ordinance requires that no usury or interest be taken upon money lent to the poor. The poor may be regarded as a fourth class of the dependent, who were exposed to base and cruel wrong in ancient times. The Lord declares himself the affectionate and resolute guardian of the poor, and inculcates upon his people a regard for the feelings of humanity, which had been almost extinguished in the heathen world. The lending of money for a percentage to the wealthy for commercial operations is not contemplated in this precept.

26, 27. The seventh is the law of pledges, which was much restricted in consideration of the poor. The receiver was not at liberty to enter the house, but must wait at the door for the pledge (Deut. xxiv. 10–13). He must also restore it at sunset. The garment referred to was a large shawl or plaid, now called haik, which was worn by day, and was the covering of the poor man, who threw himself on his couch with his clothes on, by night. The "merciful" God will hear the cry of the wretched poor.

28. The eighth precept condemns the blasphemer. God is here contemplated as the author of that providence which dispenses the affairs of men. He is virtually a breaker of covenant with God who rails at his providential dealings. The selfish heart is prone to murmur against

the Almighty, whether he be regarded as the withholder of prosperity or the restrainer of crime. But the afflicted poor and the disappointed oppressor are alike warned against the temptation to blaspheme the name of God. The prince is conjoined with God as the minister of his law and the magistrate of his people in a theocratic state. The responsibility to rule for God belongs to all sovereigns, and the obligation to honor the ruler rests upon all subjects.

29, 30. The ninth is the general law of first-fruits and firstlings. *Thou shalt not delay*, keep back or withhold. *The first-fruits of thy corn and of thy wine*, the fulness of the harvest and the trickling juice of the vintage were to come in the first-fruits to God, who gave them. This is more fully ordered afterwards (Lev. xxiii. 10–21 ; Deut. xviii. 4). *The first-born of thy sons.* This has been already arranged (xiii. 2). *On the eighth day.* After seven days the offspring has a hold of life and individuality (Gen. xvii. 12). It is then fit to be presented to God.

The offering of the first of everything is the acknowledgment that all is due to God, and the token of a soul in covenant with him. This precept, therefore, comports with the general principle of faithfulness to covenant engagements.

31. The tenth ordinance inculcates sanctity. Sanctity of the outward person is symbolic of that purity of heart that ought to characterize those who are in communion with God. That which was torn was imperfectly separated from the blood, which is the life, and was otherwise unclean. The dog was the emblem of the unbeliever.

## CHAP. XXIII. — LAWS OF VERACITY, OF SET TIMES, AND OF PIETY.

6. אֶבְיוֹן *the needy*, who feels the pinchings of want; r. *desire, want.* דַּל *the dependent ;* r. *hang, swing.*

11. שָׁמַט *to remit* or release from cultivation. Hence שְׁמִטָּה *release*, cessation from agricultural labor.

XXIII. 1. Thou shalt not bear a false report: put not thy hand with the wicked to be a wrongful witness. 2. Thou shalt not follow a multitude to evil. Neither shalt thou answer in a cause to lean after a multitude to wrong. 3. Neither shalt thou countenance a poor man in his cause. § 54.

4. If thou meet thine enemy's ox or his ass going astray, thou shalt surely bring it back to him again. § 55.

5. If thou see the ass of him that hateth thee lying under his burden, then thou shalt forbear to leave him, thou shalt surely leave with him. § 56.

6. Thou shalt not wrest the judgment of thy needy in his cause. 7. Thou shalt be far from a false matter: and the innocent and righteous slay thou not; for I will not justify the wicked. 8. And thou shalt not take a gift; for the gift blindeth the open-eyed, and perverteth the word of the righteous. 9. And thou shalt not oppress a stranger: and ye know the heart of a stranger; for ye were strangers in the land of Mizraim.

10. And six years shalt thou sow thy land and gather in the fruit thereof. 11. But the seventh year thou shalt let it rest and lie; and the needy of thy people shall eat, and what they leave the beast of the field shall eat. So shalt thou do to thy vineyard and thy olive.

12. Six days shalt thou do thy work, and on the seventh day thou shalt rest; that thine ox and thine ass may rest, and the son of thy handmaid and the stranger may be refreshed. 13. And in all that I have said to you be circumspect; and mention not the name of other gods, nor let it be heard out of thy mouth.

14. Three times shalt thou keep a feast unto me in the year. 15. Thou shalt keep the feast of unleavened bread: seven days shalt thou eat unleavened bread, as I commanded thee, in the set time of the month Abib; for in it thou camest out from Mizraim: and none shall appear before me empty: 16. And the feast of harvest, the first-fruits of thy labors, which

thou sowest in the field: and the feast of in-gathering in the end of the year, when thou gatherest in thy labors out of the field. 17. Three times in the year all thy males shall appear before the Lord JEHOVAH.

18. Thou shalt not offer the blood of my sacrifice with leavened bread; neither shall the fat of my feast remain until the morning. 19. The first of the first-fruits of thy ground thou shalt bring into the house of the LORD thy God. Thou shalt not seethe a kid in its mother's milk. ¶ 36.

20. Behold I send an angel before thee: to keep thee in the way, and to bring thee into the place which I have prepared. 21. Beware of him, and hear his voice; provoke him not: for he will not pardon your transgressions; for my name is in him. 22. For if thou indeed hear his voice, and do all that I speak, then will I be an enemy unto thine enemies and an adversary to thine adversaries. 23. For mine angel shall go before thee, and bring thee to the Amorite and the Hittite, and the Perizzite and the Kenaanite, the Hivite and the Jebusite; and I will cut them off. 24. Thou shalt not bow down to their gods nor serve them, nor do after their works; but thou shalt utterly overthrow them and quite break down their pillars. 25. And ye shall serve the LORD your God: and he shall bless thy bread and thy water; and take away sickness from the midst of thee. § 57. 26. None shall miscarry or be barren in thy land: the number of thy days I will fulfil. 27. I will send my fear before thee, and confound all the people to whom thou comest; and make all thine enemies turn their back unto thee. 28. And I will send the hornet before thee; and it shall drive out the Hivite, the Kenaanite, and the Hittite from before thee. 29. I will not drive him out from before thee in one year, lest the land become desolate, and the beast of the field multiply against thee. 30. By little and little I will drive him

out from before thee, until thou be fruitful and inherit the land. 31. And I will set thy border from the Red Sea even to the sea of the Philistines, and from the wilderness unto the river: for I will deliver into your hand the inhabitants of the land; and thou shalt drive them out before thee. 32. Thou shalt make no covenant with them nor with their gods. 33. They shall not dwell in thy land, lest they make thee sin against me: for thou wilt serve their gods; for it will be a snare to thee. ¶ 38.

### V. LAWS OF VERACITY.

1–9. This group of precepts relates chiefly to sincerity in speech and integrity in judgment. By a natural expansion, however, it includes two precepts which refer to honesty and kindliness of purpose, and are therefore quite in harmony with truthfulness of language.

1. The first precept refers to witness-bearing, with an intent either to deceive or to wrong. To *bear a false report* is either to raise or to carry it, but especially the latter. *A wrongful witness* is one who testifies falsely so as to inflict a wrong upon another.

2. This verse contains two precepts, which are connected by the common reference to a multitude. The former is general, prohibiting the following of a multitude in anything that is evil. The latter is special, prohibiting a similar compliance in bearing witness so as to wrong the righteous in his cause.

3. To countenance or honor the poor man in his cause is to convive at his criminality from a mistaken compassion for his poverty. This rule is extended to the rich as well as the poor in Lev. xix. 15.

4. The fifth injunction transcends the obligation to speak the truth. He that meets his enemy's beast going astray is not only not to be silent on the subject, but not to refrain from interfering. He is to beat down the exasperated feeling of his heart, and bring back the straying animal to his enemy, as if he were a friendly brother. This would be a happy means of softening many asperities.

5. The sixth precept comes in here on the principle of association. *Then thou shalt forbear to leave him.* This seems to be the simplest

mode of rendering this somewhat obscure phrase. It enables us to give the usual meaning of עָזַב (*leave*) consistently throughout. *Thou shalt surely leave with him.* Leave the place with the owner and his ass relieved. These two precepts breathe the spirit of forgiveness and brotherly kindness. In this, as in every other respect, the Old Testament is in harmony with the New (Matt. v. 44).

6. In the seventh precept of this series we again return to truthfulness of speech. The needy and dependent are exposed to oppression and injustice in a selfish world. But the man of God is not to wrest the judgment of the needy. *Thy needy*, thy brother who is needy. This touches the feelings of a common humanity.

7. The eighth inculcates the avoidance of all connection with a false matter, particularly in lawsuits, where it may involve the judicial slaying of the innocent and the righteous. *I will not justify*, I will most assuredly condemn, *the wicked.*

8. The ninth refers to bribery. The acceptance of a gift is forbidden on the ground that it blinds the eyes and perverts the tongue.

9. In regard to judicial truth, the stranger is entitled to the same equitable treatment as the home-born. On this subject the appeal is made to their own past experience. It is evident that this series of precepts finely enforces truth of purpose and honesty of heart, and forms a noble commentary on the ninth commandment.

### VI. LAWS REGARDING SET TIMES.

10–19. The set times of the Lord are here treated in their bearing on civil affairs. This series of ordinances forms a brief but comprehensive development of the commandment that introduces the element of sacredness into the disposal of our time.

10, 11. The first precept regards the Sabbatical year. "Six years" of sowing and reaping are to be followed by a seventh year, in which men are to rest from sowing, and leave off gathering in that which grows of itself. The spontaneous growth is to be for the needy and for the beast of the field. The same rule is to apply to the vineyard and the oliveyard. This is one of the most distinctive institutions of a theocratic state. No merely human legislator could venture to enact a law suspending the cultivation of the soil for a year, because he has not the power to secure the subject from the famine that might thereby ensue. It is otherwise, however, with the Author of all things, who can command an extraordinary fertility in the previous year, that will sustain his people for two years (Lev. xxv. 20–22). The scriptural use of the number seven in sacred things is to be deduced not from the division of the natural month into four periods of seven days, which is not exact in itself, nor from the seven planets, from which some nations have derived distinctive names for the days of the week, but from the six days of creative work and the seventh day of rest with which the present order of things was introduced. This historical fact the Scripture records, and makes the base of a weekly commemoration. The other fancies of a later age it does not recognize, and must not be forced to accept. In that great event God came into immediate and manifest contact with the heavens and the earth, reconstituted the system of physical things, clothed the dry land with vegetation, and peopled it with animated nature. On this occasion, for the first time, a rational inhabitant was placed upon the earth. The cycle of seven days during which this creative process was completed and celebrated imparted an association of sacredness to the number seven.

The Sabbatical year, which is here mentioned for the first time, is also called the year of release. In this year, (1.) the land was to be left uncultivated, and its spontaneous growth made common to the servile, the poor, the stranger, and the wild animals. Several remarkable effects would follow from the honest carrying out of this arrangement. The spirit of avarice would be kept in constant and effectual check. The opposite feelings of compassion, charity, benevolence, and brotherly kindness would be brought into play. The original equality of all men in point of birth and right would rise to the surface of human observation. The habits of prudence and economy would be cherished, as the produce of six years must be so husbanded as to serve for seven years. A profound and practical sense of dependence upon the Lord of providence would be awakened in the breast (Lev. xxv. 2–8; Joseph. Antiq. iii. 12, 3). This institution thus harmonizes with the Sabbath in breaking down the narrow selfishness of the fallen nature, and fostering the disinterested kindliness that springs up in the new heart. (2.) A debt owed by a poor man who had nothing to pay was to be remitted, or at all events not exacted. This is a natural consequence of the intermission of cultivation during the seventh year. He that receives no fruits from the soil is not in a condition to pay debt. This carries the liberality of the affluent brother to its ultimate extent. The poor man is not to be allowed to perish, though he have nothing to pay (Deut. xv. 1, 2). (3.) On this year, during the feast of tabernacles, the law was to be read aloud in the audience of all the people. On this Sabbath-year it was appropriate that the great principles of morality should be solemnly presented to the minds of the people. The septennial Sabbath thus bore a complete analogy to the hebdomadal, which was to be celebrated by a holy leisure for the offices of public worship.

12, 13. The seventh-day Sabbath is here introduced in its relation to civic rights. The cattle, the servile, and the stranger are to be partakers in this rest. 13. *And in all that I have said to you be circumspect.* This admonition appears to refer to the precept concerning the Sabbath. *And mention not the name of other gods.* The import of this injunction is to be ascertained from the nature of the enactment to which it refers. The fourth commandment belongs to that table which contains our duty to God. It prescribes, moreover, the day on which religious exercises are to be statedly observed. It is the only precept in the Decalogue which involves the ordinances of a perpetual worship, and keeps alive in the breasts of the people the remembrance of God, of his will, and of his grace. Hence it is natural that the people should be guarded against devoting themselves or any of their thoughts on this day to any false god. This is, therefore, not a separate precept, but an incidental warning in regard to the special solemnities of the Sabbath.

Some have regarded this verse as a concluding formula of admonition, referring to the preceding part of the chapter and marking it off from that which follows. But it is remarkable that the Masoretes have no division whatever at this point of the text. This plainly indicates that they regarded this verse merely as the completion of the precept concerning the Sabbath, and not an independent rule or closing exhortation.

14–17. The next five precepts refer to the annual festivals. The first determines that there shall be three such festivals in the year. 15. The second enjoins the feast of unleavened bread. *As I commanded thee.* The passover or feast of unleavened bread has been already instituted (xii). *And none shall appear before me empty.* This applies to all the three festivals, and refers to the obligation of all, without exception, to provide the things requisite for the celebration of each. Freewill offerings might be presented on such occasions; but they are not implied in these words. 16. The third relates to the second festival (Lev. xxiii. 15–22; Num. xxviii. 26–31; Deut. xvi. 9–12). It was called *the feast of harvest*, because the grain harvest was drawing to a close at the time of its celebration; *the day of first-fruits*, because then the two loaves made of the new corn were presented (Num. xxviii. 26; and *the feast of weeks*, or Pentecost, because it was kept on the morrow after the seventh Sabbath from the Sabbath of the feast of unleavened bread (Deut. xvi. 10). The fourth refers to the third festival (Lev. xxiii. 33–43; Num. xxix. 12–39; Deut. xvi. 13–15). This is called *the feast of in-gathering*, because the fruit harvest was then completed and the whole produce of the ground gathered in; and *the feast of tabernacles*, because the tabernacling of the people in the wilderness was then commemorated. These three festivals correspond in the main with the three elements of salvation: the passover with the atonement; the pentecost with the new birth; and the feast of in-gathering with pardon and its accompanying plenitude of blessings. The pentecost is regarded as the completion of the passover; and so sanctification invariably accompanies justification. Mercy flows forth in pardon, as the end of which the atonement and the new birth are the means. So the feast of in-gathering in the beginning of the ancient year is mediate by the feasts of the passover and of weeks in the beginning of the new year. 17. The fifth precept affirms the obligation of all males to appear at each of the three festivals.

18. The two directions in this verse are united into the eighth regulation by their common reference to the passover. *The blood of my sacrifice*, of the passover lamb, which was peculiarly God's sacrifice and pre-eminently the type of the Messiah (Jno. i. 29). *Leavened bread.* Leaven is that which dissolves and corrupts. It is therefore a fit emblem of sin, which is to be excluded from the service or the offerings of God (xii. 10). *The fat of my feast.* The paschal lamb was to be wholly consumed in the evening, and no part left till the morning. This is the rule, whether we understand "the fat of my feast" to be the best of sacrifices, that is, the passover, or, what is more likely, the fat of the paschal lamb, which was to be offered to the Lord, while the flesh was eaten by the worshippers.

19. This verse contains two regulations. That concerning the first-fruits refers to the feast of weeks, when the two wave-loaves, which may be called the first of the first-fruits of the ground, were offered unto the Lord (Lev. xxiii. 17). And next the Eastern custom of occasionally seething in milk here comes into view, and has survived to this day. The prohibition to seethe a kid in the mother's milk has reference to all the festivals or set times of the Lord. It appears from the regulations concerning these (Num. xxviii. 29) that one kid of the goats for a sin-offering was to be offered in the beginnings of the months, on each of the seven days of the feast of unleavened bread, on the day of the first-fruits, on the first and the tenth days of the seventh month, and on each of the eight days of the feast of tabernacles. The flesh of this kid was to be dressed and eaten by the priests in the holy place (Lev. vi. 26). Hence the general precept comes in here that a kid is not to be seethed in its mother's milk. The dam is the natural mother and nurse of the kid, and the milk is the natural aliment by which life is sustained. To employ the milk of the very dam to aid in cooking the kid for food is a rude violation of the order of nature, and to prohibit such a custom is to cultivate those feelings of consideration and tenderness in the daily routine of our thoughts which sin tends to quench, and moral training is intended to rekindle. This minute regulation on behalf of right feeling involves the great principle that the course of human feeling and conduct ought, in its finest as well as its broadest lines, to be brought into harmony with the law of universal benevolence.

### VII. THE LAWS OF PIETY.

20–33. It is manifest that the law of moral thought cannot be spread out into the same distinguishable branches as that of external action. Accordingly, this passage, which is marked off in the Masorah, both at the beginning and the end, as a major section, is not very obviously divisible into ten rules or judgments. It bears also a temporary aspect, inasmuch as it treats of matters that come to a termination when the people are settled in the land of promise. And it consists very largely of promises, which scarcely enter into the other sections of this code of civil jurisprudence. Nevertheless, it evidently forms an integral part of the common law of Israel. It is appropriate and essential that promises should have a direct or indirect part in "the book of the covenant." Accordingly, in this conclusion of the civil code, promises are intermingled with injunctions; and though some of them are terminable, yet they prefigure blessings of a higher order, and of perpetual duration. And a decade of commands seems to be here intermingled with a decade of promises.

20–23. This portion contains three commands and three promises. 20. *Behold.* This word is frequently used to introduce an important intimation concerning the future. *I send an angel before thee.* The angel here promised is very closely allied with the speaker and sender. He has power to "pardon transgressions." The reason assigned for this high prerogative is, "for my name is in his inmost"; my nature is in his essence. This intimates a substantial identity. We conclude that the angel here is God manifest in angelic offices to his people. They are to "beware of him, to hear his voice, and provoke him not." To "hear his voice" and to "do all that I speak" appear to be of the same import. All these phrases corroborate the conclusion that the angel is God. He is sent before the people for the important purposes of keeping them in the way, and bringing them to the place prepared for them. This is the great promise of the passage. It is in continuance, and at the same time in advance, of former assurances (iii. 8, xiii. 21, 22). It intimates, at the same time, a certain distance in point of moral condition between God and his people, which is bridged over by means of his angel (Gen. xvi. 7).

21. This verse contains three injunctions regarding this angel. *Beware of him.* Give reverent heed to him, as the Supreme God is in him. *Hear his voice.* Understand and obey him, as the Lord revealing himself by his word. *Provoke him not.* Let not your will come into conflict with his will, as he is the Great Spirit, who is to be worshipped in spirit and in truth.

22. The central command is recapitulated and elucidated in the condition "If thou indeed hear his voice, and do all that I speak." This verse presents a second promise, consequent upon the former. *Then will I be an enemy unto thine enemies.* This phrase refers to the inward feeling, as the following one does to the outward display of hostility. It is here intimated, in general terms, that the Lord and

his people, while they were one in feeling and interest, have common enemies in this world.

23. A fuller specification of the end of their journey is here followed by a third promise. *The Amorite, and the Hittite, and the Kenaanite, the Hivite and the Jebusite,* are among the twelve tribes to which Kenaan gave rise, eleven being named after his descendants and one after himself (see Gen. xv. 19). The Perizzite makes his appearance along with the Kenaanite in the history of Abraham (Gen. xiii. 7). These six tribes were the prominent inhabitants of Kenaan in the time of Moses (iii. 8). The Amorite is now placed first, as the most prominent in transgression, and the first with whom the Israelites are to come into contact. *And I will cut them off.* This promise is in accordance with a purpose long since announced. Four hundred years before, the Lord had informed Abraham that "the iniquity of the Amorites was not yet full" (Gen. xv. 16). This is no arbitrary procedure on the part of the Most High Possessor of heaven and earth. It is an act of retributive justice. What was the original offence of the Kenaanite, whether it was an early apostasy from the living God, the ruthless invasion of a preoccupied country, and the barbarous oppression of the Shemite inhabitants, among whom the knowledge of the true God still lingered, we are not informed. But we perceive that the original crime had been aggravated by a course of transgression which made the nation ripe for a penal extirpation.

24–26. These three verses contain four injunctions and four promises. 24. *Thou shalt not bow down to their gods nor serve them.* These nations are manifestly idolaters, apostates from the living and true God, and therefore ranking among those that hate him (xx. 5). Their idols will come under the notice of Israel when they enter the land. The idea of local or national gods had become familiar to them in Egypt. And a superstitious dread of entering into possession without propitiating the supposed gods of the land might still lurk in their breasts. Hence the reasonableness of this precept, reiterating the prohibition of the second commandment. *Nor do after their works.* These are the works of the people of the land; and chief among these, the making and worshipping of idols, and the licentious vices which accompany the service of their national deities. It is only necessary to reflect, that the principal objects of their worship were a male deity, Baal, the sun-god, coinciding in attributes with the Apollo and Jupiter of the Greeks and Romans; and a female, Beltis, Ashtoreth, the moon-goddess, resembling in her character and worship the Aphrodite or Venus of these nations, in order to understand the revolting nature of the bloody and lascivious rites and customs by which the very name of religion was profaned. Human sacrifice and prostitution in the national worship were sufficient to bury all moral feeling in the grave of carnality. *Thou shalt utterly overthrow them.* The people and their gods seem to be here associated as one great system of evil, to be overwhelmed with destruction. "Their pillars" are the monumental stones, connected in a rude, uncivilized age with the worship of these fallen gods.

25. *And ye shall serve the Lord your God.* This is the fourth of this group of injunctions, forming the counterpart of the three that went before. It is followed by the four promises of this passage. *He shall bless thy bread and thy water.* Bread and water, the main elements of subsistence, stand for all the rest. The divine blessing gives these all their value to a rational creature. *And take away sickness from the midst of thee.* Next to the means of life, is health to enjoy them. Without the latter the former are of no avail. 26. *None shall miscarry or be barren in thy land.* This secures the perpetuation of the race. *The number of thy days will I fulfil.* Length of life in peace and prosperity is here ensured to the faithful nation. The sum of all earthly prosperity here described, is at the same time an earnest and type of still greater blessings in an advanced stage of existence. God begins with the present, and will never fail his confiding people through an endless future.

27–33. This passage adds the remaining triad of promises and commands. *I will send my fear before thee.* The fame of the mighty deeds by which Egypt was humbled in the dust, and Israel delivered and kept in safety through the wilderness, would awaken a sense of alarm in the nations who were living in rebellion against the living God. Discouraged and troubled in mind, they would make only a feeble effort at resistance, and ultimately turn their backs to the victorious invader.

28–30. *And I will send the hornet before thee.* The hornet is here used collectively for a plague of hornets infesting the land. This plague is again mentioned (Deut. vii. 20), and a passing allusion made to its fulfilment (Josh. xxiv. 12). Some suppose this to be a figurative description of certain otherwise unknown calamities that befel these nations in the war of extermination. But Bochart (Hieroz. iii. p. 409) has shown that frogs, mice, and other small animals have been the means of annoying and banishing whole tribes from their settlements. And the rapid conquest of two such powerful kingdoms as those of Sihon and Og, and the immediate occupation of their cities (Num. xxi. 21–35) by the invaders, are explained by the fact that they had been enfeebled and diminished by a plague such as that here described. There is no reason whatever, therefore, to retire from the ground of plain matter of fact, historically recorded, into the region of a dark, figurative unknown, which cannot be filled up even by the imagination. The Hivite, the Kenaanite, and the Hittite are to be the chief sufferers from the plague of hornets. But the Amorites also were exhausted by their inroads (Josh. xxiv. 12). 29, 30. A gradual removal of the former inhabitants is here intimated, on the ground that the land without occupants would be infested by wild beasts, as was the case at the time of the exile of the ten tribes (2 Kings xvii. 25). If the former nations had been instantly exterminated, a people consisting of one million six hundred thousand could not have at once occupied the whole land. Besides, the territory here promised was much more extensive than the land of Kenaan.

31. The boundaries of the promised land are here indicated. The "Wilderness" is that of Etham and Shur. The "river" is the Phrat. The extent of territory within these bounds cannot be less than four hundred and ninety miles by one hundred, and therefore four or five times the area of Palestine proper. It is to be remembered that these promises are here made conditional on obedience; and therefore their fulfilment was in some degree modified by the subsequent conduct of the people. *And thou shalt drive them out before thee.* This is the injunction laid on Israel as the executioner of the judgment of God.

32. The second injunction is to make no covenant with the people or their idols.

33. The idolatrous people are to be banished from the land, that they may not be a temptation to the children of Israel. The order of thought is, their dwelling in the land will be a snare to thee, and thou wilt serve their gods, when thou hast tolerated themselves and their idolatrous ways.

This completes the book of the covenant, in four chapters, containing the ten commandments for the moral government of man, and seventy judgments for the regulation of civil life.

### CHAP. XXIV.—THE LAW ACCEPTED.

XXIV. 1. And to Moses he said, Come up unto the LORD,
thou and Aaron, Nadab and Abihu, and seventy of the elders
of Israel; and worship ye afar off. 2. And Moses alone shall
come near the LORD, but they shall not come near; and the
people shall not come up with him. 3. And Moses went and
told the people all the words of the LORD and all the judgments: and all the people answered with one voice, and said,
All the words which the LORD hath spoken will we do. 4.
And Moses wrote all the words of the LORD, and rose up early
in the morning, and built an altar under the mount, and twelve
pillars for the twelve tribes of Israel. 5. And he sent young
men of the sons of Israel, and they offered burnt-offerings, and
sacrificed peace-offerings of oxen to the LORD. 6. And Moses
took half of the blood and put in basins; and half of the blood
he sprinkled on the altar. 7. And he took the book of the
covenant, and read in the ears of the people; and they said,
All that the Lord hath spoken will we do and obey. 8. And
Moses took the blood and sprinkled on all the people; and
said, Behold the blood of the covenant, which the LORD hath
made with you according to all these words

9. Then went up Moses and Aaron, Nadab and Abihu, and
seventy of the elders of Israel. 10. And they saw the God of
Israel: and under his feet as a paved work of sapphire and as
the substance of heaven for purity. 11. And upon the nobles
of the sons of Israel he laid not his hand: and they beheld
God, and ate and drank. § 58.

12. And the Lord said unto Moses, Come up to me into the
mount, and be there: and I will give thee tables of stone and
the law and the commandment which I have written to teach
them. 13. And Moses rose up and Joshua his minister; and
Moses went up to the mount of God. 14. And to the elders
he said, Sit ye here for us, until we come back unto you: and
behold Aaron and Hur are with you; whosoever hath any
matter, let him draw near unto them. 15. And Moses went
up into the mount, and the cloud covered the mount. 16.
And the glory of the Lord abode upon Mount Sinai, and the
cloud covered it six days; and he called unto Moses the
seventh day out of the midst of the cloud. 17. And the sight
of the glory of the Lord was like devouring fire on the top of
the mount in the eyes of the sons of Israel. 18. And Moses
went into the midst of the cloud, and went up into the mount;
and Moses was in the mount forty days and forty nights.

19. ¶ ¶ ¶ 39.

The formal ratification of the covenant between God and his people is the appropriate close of the legislative section which forms the kernel of the Book of Exodus. The admission of Moses and the other representatives of the people into the presence of God is the natural result of the sealing of the covenant. These are, accordingly, the two topics of this concluding chapter.

1–8. The closing of the covenant. *And to Moses he said.* The words "and to Moses," being placed first in the original, are emphatic. This places the following words addressed to Moses in contrast with the communication begun in xx. 22, and addressed to the people. *Come up.* This indicates an approach to the mountain in general. In the present case it includes an ascent of some part of the mountain side. Moses and Aaron ascend as the prophet and priest of God; Nadab and Abihu, as the elder sons of Aaron, henceforth to be associated with him in the priesthood; the seventy elders as the representative heads of the people. The number seventy, which we might expect to be a round number for seventy-two, or six out of every tribe, has most probably a historical reference to the number of souls that constituted the whole family of Jacob when he came down into Egypt (see on Gen. xlvi. 27). *And worship ye afar off.* This shows that they were not to ascend to the summit of the mountain. Moses shall come near; and only the representatives prescribed shall come at all.

3. *And Moses went.* The call to come up to the mount is subsequent both in its utterance and in the time of its execution to the directions given in xx. 22, 26, which imply all that Moses now proceeds to do. *And told the people.* The acceptance of the covenant is to be an intelligent service. *All the words of the Lord.* This may refer to all the words contained in the preceding four chapters, or in the twentieth chapter only. The ten "words," pre-eminently so called, Moses may have now rehearsed to the people. *And all the judgments,* the seven decades of regulations contained in the previous three chapters. *Will we do.* The unanimous assent of the people is the virtual acceptance of the covenant.

4–8. This passage contains the solemn ratification of the covenant. *And Moses wrote.* All the words of the Lord now written constitute the Book of the Covenant afterwards mentioned. *Built an altar.* This is the first altar erected in compliance with the precept in xx. 24. The altar indicates the presence of God in covenant with his people. *The twelve pillars,* placed probably in a circle round the altar, indicate the presence of the twelve tribes in this great solemnization of the covenant. They do not seem to have had a monumental character, as we hear no more of them.

5. *And he sent young men of the sons of Israel.* These youths are not to be further defined as first-born or Levites, but as fit persons selected by Moses himself, who is the principal agent in mediating the covenant, out of a people who are all a "kingdom of priests and a holy nation" (xix. 6). They are merely the ministers of Moses, and not the representatives of the people, who are the seventy elders, and occupy a different position in this great transaction. *Burnt-offerings and peace-offerings,* types of atonement and thanksgiving (xx. 24).

6. *And Moses took half of the blood.* The blood is that which

makes atonement, and thereby lays the foundation for a covenant of peace. Hence it ratifies the covenant. For this purpose it is divided into two equal parts. The one is reserved in basins; the other is sprinkled on the altar. There it makes a propitiation, and in the present instance signifies concurrence in the covenant.

7. *The book of the covenant,* which he had just written, contains the "words" and "judgments" of the previous four chapters. *And read.* Before, he told or reported; now, he solemnly recites. The former assent of the people authorized the step of solemnizing the covenant. This unanimous consent, after a second deliberate hearing, is the formal acceptance of the covenant.

8. *The blood.* This is the part reserved in basins. The blood has here two functions to fulfil — first to make reconciliation, and then by its application to determine the parties reconciled. Its offering on the altar conditionates the covenant; its application to the people makes them parties to the covenant. It is the one blood that accomplishes the pacification. Hence Moses sprinkles the reserved portion of the atoning blood on the people, saying, "Behold the blood of the covenant, which the Lord hath made." *According to all these words.* The book of the covenant which Moses had read contained the terms of the covenant to which they had now consented.

9–11. The ascent to a certain point in the mountain side, to which reference was made in the first verse, is now accomplished. To what point they ascended would be a very unprofitable inquiry. It is incomparably more important to mark the fact that now, when the covenant has received its solemn and final sanction, the people have access to God. Hence by their representations they enter into the presence of God. 10. *And they saw the God of Israel.* We take these words in their simple sense. Whatever were the sensible circumstances of the divine presence, they were permitted to see with the eye of sense. Whatever aspect of God himself with face averted from them was presented to them, they discerned, we may venture to presume, with the eye of the spirit. Hence they do not say a word of the "similitude of any figure" of the Divine Being, because they had not seen any such (xxxiii. 20–23; Deut. iv. 15–19). *The God of Israel.* As he was the God of Abraham when alone, the God of Jacob when the head of a family, so now he is the God of Israel as a people in covenant with him. *A paved work of sapphire.* But the spectators of that heavenly vision can only describe the outwardly visible glory that came before them. This phrase is otherwise rendered "a work of the whiteness or transparency of sapphire." It is not of great importance which rendering is adopted, as what they saw is only compared with this, and therefore only distantly illustrated by it. But we prefer the former rendering, with Aben Ezra, because the sapphire is of various colors, blue, red, yellow, and white, and the word "work" (מַעֲשֵׂה) is generally connected, not with color, but with the material, the art, or the artificer. A paved work of sapphire is descriptive of a scene of matchless splendor, having the qualities of adamantine solidity, transparence, and brilliancy. *The substance of heaven for purity.* The substance of heaven is a phrase for the very heaven itself. Nothing less than the spotless purity and lustre of the skies above is fit to be compared with the inexpressible beauty and grandeur of that which was beneath the feet of the God of Israel. With this short sentence ends the description. A fancy sketch would have been more copious. 11. *Upon the nobles of the sons of Israel he laid not his hand.* He did not consume them with the fire of his holiness, because they had now with the whole consent of their minds entered into a covenant of peace with him through the blood of atonement. They were therefore favored with the vision of the Almighty. *They beheld God.* This is the verb generally employed to denote the vision of the prophet. It denotes attentive and absorbed contemplation. *And ate and drank.* Notwithstanding the contemplation of the infinitely holy One, they continued to discharge the functions of an earthly life. This is supposed to refer to their partaking of the peace-offerings on their descent; but it seems to be merely a proverbial phrase to denote the continuance of life.

12–18. This passage describes the ascent of Moses to the actual summit of the mount. *Come up.* This may be understood to imply that Moses and the others had descended to partake of the sacrificial feast. At all events, they were still within reach of any of the people who might have business with them. But Moses was now to ascend farther. *And be there.* Abide there for a considerable time. *Tables of stone*, slabs or tablets on which the law was written. *The law*, or doctrine concerning God and his rights. *The commandment*, the authoritative rule for the conduct of man. The reasonable nature of the ten words inscribed on the tables of stone appears from the fact that they first reveal a doctrine, and then impose an obligation founded on that doctrine. *Which I have written.* These words were not only spoken by the voice, but written by the finger, of God, who herein displays a wondrous care of his chosen people. *To teach them.* In the original we have here the same root that is contained in the word rendered "law." God's law is a doctrine, a philosophy, a theology.

13. *And Moses rose up*, from a state of rest and contemplation. *And Joshua his minister.* Joshua has already come before us as captain of the host against Amalek (xvii. 9). He is described here as the minister, attendant, or adjutant of Moses. His presence has not been noticed among those who went up to the mountain. He must have been in attendance upon Moses. Some suppose he was one of the seventy elders, but his youth militates against this view. 14. Before leaving them, Moses commanded the elders to await his return where they were, and pointed out Aaron and Hur as his representatives to the people. 15. He now at length ascends into the mount, accompanied by Joshua alone to the very verge of the cloud which covered the mount. 16. Six days he waits in the precincts of the cloud, and on the seventh day he is summoned into the presence of the Majesty on high. If the giving of the law fell on the sixth of the third month, and a day be allowed for the ratification of the covenant, the seventh day after, on which Moses at length ascends into the mount, will be the fourteenth of the third month, 17. The sons of Israel contemplated with solemn awe the glory of the Lord displayed on Mount Sinai, which appeared to them as a vast flame of devouring fire. 18. Into this flaming mount Moses, at the call of God, ascended, and abode in that wondrous scene forty days and forty nights. The stately march of the narrative throughout this passage corresponds with the unparalleled grandeur of the occasion.

## SECTION V.—THE TABERNACLE.

### XIII. PLAN OF THE TABERNACLE.—Ex. xxv.-xxxi.

#### CHAP. XXV.—THE ARK, TABLE, AND CANDLESTICK.

2. תְּרוּמָה gift, ἀπαρχή, that which is lifted up or heaved, and hence denoting specially the heave-offering, which got its name from the manner in which it was heaved up when presented.

4. תְּכֵלֶת ὑάκινθος, *violet or blue*, a dark blue obtained from the murex, a shell-fish of the coasts of Phœnicia, Laconia, and North Africa. The dye is originally white, then green, and lastly a blue purple.

אַרְגָּמָן πορφύρα, red, *purple*, obtained from the purpura, a fish of Syrian and Peloponnesian shores.

תּוֹלַעַת *worm.* שָׁנִי *crimson*, from a root signifying *to shine.* The two words denote the Kermes worm, or the dye obtained from it. This worm or insect is found on the ilex or holm oak in Palestine and the south of Europe.

שֵׁשׁ βύσσος, *flax*, the shenti of old Egyptian, which was fine flax, not cotton.

5. תַּחַשׁ is variously conjectured to be the badger, the seal, the dolpin, and the tacasse, a species of antelope found in Africa; r. חָשָׁה *be silent*, it is said from its hibernation.

6. בֶּשֶׂם or בֹּשֶׂם *sweet smell, spice.* בָּשָׂם the *balsam*, by the insertion of *l* in the Arabic form of the word. This plant is common in Palestine. סַמִּים *spices, perfumes*, from the sweet smell.

16. עֵדוּת *testimony.* עוּד *to be fast, firm, sure.* הֵעִיד *assure, attest.* עֵד *witness.* יָעַד *fix, appoint.* עֵדָה *appointed meeting, regularly constituted assembly.*

17. כַּפֹּרֶת ἱλαστήριον, ἐπίθεμα, propitiatorium, *mercy-seat*; r. in Kal, *lay on* (pitch); in Piel, *expiate.*

29. קְעָרָה τρύβλιον, a large dish or plate for bread. Those presented by the princes of Israel weighed each one hundred and thirty shekels, or about five pounds troy weight (Num. vii. 13).

כַּף *palm, sole.* In pl. *θυίσκαι, bowls* or smaller plates for holding frankincense, which were placed upon the bread. Each of those presented by the princes weighed ten shekels, or about four and a half ounces.

קְשָׂוֹת σπονδεῖα, bowls or flagons holding wine for libations.

מְנַקִּיּוֹת κύαθοι, cups used in drink-offerings.

XXV. 1. And the LORD spake unto Moses, saying: 2. Speak
unto the sons of Israel, that they take for me an offering: of
every man whose heart is willing ye shall take my offering.
3. And this is the offering which ye shall take of them; gold
and silver and brass. 4. And blue and purple and crimson;
and fine linen and goats' hair; 5. And rams' skins dyed red,
and badgers' skins; and shittah wood; 6. Oil for the light;
spices for the anointing oil and for the incense of perfumes;
7. Onyx stones, and stones for the ephod and for the breast-
plate. 8. And they shall make me a sanctuary, that I may
dwell among them. 9. According to all that I show thee,
after the pattern of the tabernacle and the pattern of all its
instruments, even so shall ye make it. § 59.

10. And they shall make an ark of shittah wood: two cubits
and a half shall be its length, a cubit and a half its breadth,
and a cubit and a half its height. 11. And thou shalt overlay
it with pure gold, within and without shalt thou overlay it:
and thou shalt make upon it a crown of gold round about.
12. And thou shalt cast for it four rings of gold, and put them
on its four feet: and two rings shall be on the one side of it,
and two rings on the other side of it. 13. And thou shalt
make staves of shittah wood, and overlay them with gold. 14.
And thou shalt put the staves in the rings on the sides of the
ark, to bear the ark with them. 15. The staves shall be in the
rings of the ark; they shall not depart from it. 16. And thou
shalt put into the ark the testimony which I shall give thee.

17. And thou shalt make a mercy-seat of pure gold: two cubits and a half shall be its length and a cubit and a half its breadth. 18. And thou shalt make two cherubim of gold; of beaten work shalt thou make them, on the two ends of the mercy-seat. 19. And make one cherub on the one end and the other cherub on the other end; out of the mercy-seat shall ye make the cherubim on its two ends. 20. And the cherubim shall spread out two wings above, covering the mercy-seat with their wings, and their faces each to the other; toward the mercy-seat shall the faces of the cherubim be. 21. And thou shalt put the mercy-seat on the ark from above: and in the ark shalt thou put the testimony that I shall give thee. 22. And I will meet with thee there, and speak with thee from above the mercy-seat, from between the two cherubim which are upon the ark of the testimony, of all that I command thee concerning the sons of Israel. ¶ 40.

23. And thou shalt make a table of shittah wood: two cubits shall be its length, and a cubit its breadth, and a cubit and a half its height. 24. And thou shalt overlay it with pure gold, and make for it a crown of gold round about. 25. And thou shalt make for it a border of a handbreadth round about, and make a crown of gold for the border thereof round about. 26. And thou shalt make for it four rings of gold; and put the rings on the four corners of its four feet. 27. Over against the border shall be the rings for places for the staves to bear the table. 28. And thou shalt make the staves of shittah wood, and overlay them with gold; and the table shall be borne with them. 29. And thou shalt make its dishes, and its bowls, and its flagons, and its cups, to pour out withal: of pure gold shalt thou make them. 30. And thou shalt set on the table shew-bread before me alway. ¶ 41.

31. And thou shalt make a candlestick of pure gold: of

beaten work shall the candlestick be made ; its block and its shaft, its cups, its knops, and its flowers, shall be of the same.
32. And six branches shall come out of the sides of it ; three branches of the candlestick out of the one side, and three branches of the candlestick out of the other side.
33. Three almond-shaped cups in one branch, a knop and a flower ; and three almond-shaped cups in another branch, a knop and a flower : so for the six branches coming out of the candlestick.
34. And in the candlestick shall be four almond-shaped cups, its knops and its flowers.
35. And there shall be a knop under two branches of the same, and a knop under two branches of the same, and a knop under two branches of the same ; for the six branches coming out of the candlestick.
36. Their knops and their branches shall be of the same ; all of it shall be one beaten piece of pure gold.
37. And thou shalt make the seven lamps thereof ; and he shall set up the lamps thereof and give light over against it.
38. And its snuffers and its snuff-dishes shall be of pure gold.
39. Of a talent of pure gold shall he make it with all these vessels.
40. And see that thou make them after their pattern, which thou wast shown in the mount. § 60.

The substance of the covenant made in the previous section may be conveyed in the formula: "I will take you to me for a people, and I will be to you a God" (vi. 7, xix. 5, 6, xx. 2). The natural consequence of this is that he will take up his abode among them, and enter into all the intercourse of sacred fellowship with them. For this purpose an abode is to be prepared for God, and provided with the needful furniture. But inasmuch as the people belong to a fallen race, upon whom the curse of disobedience has descended, a type at least of propitiation and intercession must form a part of the ceremonial intercourse between God and his people, until the reality of these priestly functions has at length arrived.

The tabernacle is the home of God among his ransomed people. It is in general an adumbration of the great primeval dwelling-place of God, where he holds converse with the manifold ranks and estates of his rational and righteous creatures. We are wont to imagine this to be some central place whither the myriads of the intelligent universe may convene for the business of heaven, and for the recreations of hospitable and friendly intercourse in the heaven of heavens. But we are not to bind the Omnipresent to this habitual conception of our minds. For aught we can know there may be as many centres of home for the Supreme as there are spheres of spiritual beings susceptible of the unutterable joys of the divine home and presence and converse. Hence there may be a broad basis of truth in all the varying interpretations which the prolific imaginations of thoughtful men have put upon this profoundly interesting portion of scripture. But with a due regard to the occasion on which the tabernacle was instituted, the stage at which human knowledge had then arrived, and the life and freshness of the truth which it shadows forth, it is best to adhere to the simple idea of a home, where God dwells on terms of affectionate and familiar intimacy with his redeemed and reconciled people. This is the generic conception of the tabernacle. Yet we should come far short of a correct apprehension of its nature, if we did not bring out into conspicuous prominence its specific difference. It is to be remembered as a fact of essential moment that the people among whom God is here to dwell are undergoing a process of sanctification, which is begun in each individual by accepting a pardon freely bestowed and a propitiation typically made on his behalf. Hence the paternal house or heaven, which the tabernacle represents, is not merely the general home of the intelligent universe, but the heaven of the redeemed, where the Lamb will be a conspicuous figure, and the psalm of praise will be the new song of redemption, transcending in its revelation of the divine nature the older song of creation. Hence the whole service of the sanctuary is typical of the higher blessings of salvation, of the true High Priest, of the really atoning sacrifice, of the heaven of redemption, and of that spiritual fellowship which the saints will have with the Lord in glory. It is the flower of the whole economy of grace, giving fair promise of the fruit in due season. Hence we can understand the place and space given to the tabernacle in this book of the exodus. The tabernacle expands and completes what was represented in brief by the lamb of the passover. It sets forth the blessings which flow from reconciliation. It is the glorious end to which all the preliminary steps of the deliverance and the covenant lead. It occupies a proportionate amplitude of space in the records of God's dealings with his people. Seven chapters are devoted to the specifications of the tabernacle, and six to its construction and erection, between which are three chapters giving an account of a lamentable act of unbelief and apostasy on the part of the chosen people.

Of the seven chapters of specification three are assigned to the tabernacle itself, three to the priest of the tabernacle, and one to the arrangements for having the whole carried into effect in an efficient and irreproachable manner.

The present chapter contains directions concerning the contribution of the materials, and the construction of the ark, the table, and the candlestick.

1–9. The order for the contribution of materials to construct the tabernacle. *An offering* is here a gift called by the name of the heave-offering (xxix. 27). *Of every man whose heart is willing.* A forced service is only a bodily service. A free-will offering is alone acceptable to the Searcher of hearts. 3–7. The materials of the offering and of the tabernacle are all definitely prescribed. There are three metals; three colors of animal origin; two textile fabrics, the one vegetable, the other animal; two sorts of skins; one species of wood; oil from the olive; spices; onyx stones, and other precious stones, twelve in number, for setting. Reckoning spices as one class, and precious stones as another, we have here twice seven kinds of material, of which four are from the mineral kingdom, four from the vegetable, and six from the animal. *Blue* is a purple color from the *murex; purple* is the red purple obtained from the *purpura;* and *crimson* the red extracted from the coccus or kermes, supposed by some of the ancients to be a berry, but in reality an insect adhering to the holm oak. *Fine linen,* a product for which Egypt was celebrated. *Rams' skins dyed red.* This cannot be naturally rendered skins of red rams. *Badgers' skins.* The badger is a native of Europe. It is probable that the animal here intended is different; but whether it be the seal, dolphin, tacasse, or some other animal is a matter of conjecture. The familiar word badger may be retained with the understanding that it is used for an unknown animal easily obtained in the peninsula of Sinai. *Shittah wood.* This is the Egyptian and Arabic *shant,* or acacia, which must have been large and abundant in the time of Moses. It is now employed by the Arabs for making charcoal, and is therfore seldom allowed to attain to a great age. *Oil* is obtained from the olive tree, a native of Asia, and abounding in the south of Europe. *Spices.* Arabia is celebrated for its spices, which are here comprehended under a generic term. The precious *stones* are afterwards enumerated (xxviii. 16), and the ephod and breastplate described (xxviii. 6, 15).

8, 9. *A sanctuary.* A holy place, where God might dwell among his people. Its chief distinction was its holiness, as it was to be among the children of the fall, who were morally impure. *According to all that I show thee.* I am about to show thee the pattern of the tabernacle, and of all things connected with it. The tabernacle itself was a type of the dwelling-place of the Most High in the heaven of heavens. But the pattern of it was the ideal form or plan according to which it was to be constructed for earthly use. The divine origin of this plan proves the profound significance of the tabernacle and all its appurtenances.

It is obvious that there is an analogy between the tabernacle service and the ritual of the Egyptians and other Gentiles. But it is equally obvious that the resemblance between them is not the result of servile imitation or simple adoption on the part of Moses. It is founded on deeper and more recondite principles. In the first place, the constitution of the human race involves a fundamental similitude in the modes of human worship. This race was in its head created after the image of God in reason, will, and power, and then by an act of disobedience plunged into the abyss of guilt and sin. The common reason, though stunned by this fall, will arrive at certain common principles of religious truth, mingled and distorted, no doubt, by dark and fatal misconceptions. In the next place, tradition has left indelible traces of primeval facts and thoughts upon the mind of man, which have entered into combination with the thousand strange and grotesque vagaries of a wanton imagination. And lastly, Moses was, in the providence of God, learned in all the wisdom of the Egyptians of that day, and equally familiarized with all the experience of the Midianites in the wilds of Arabia. Through a mind so trained for twice forty years the Lord was pleased to convey to his people the written revelation of his will, the funda mental principles of his law, and the minute specifications of his worship. These facts are sufficient to account for the originality and independence of the Mosaic economy, and for the resemblances and differences which may be traced between it and the religious institutions of surrounding nations. It is to be expected, not that the early customs of the Egyptians and Midianites will throw much light on those of the Israelites, but rather that the latter in their plainly-written form will contribute to the elucidation of the former. And accordingly this expectation has already been in a very signal manner realized. The antiquities of Eastern nations, from Egypt to Assyria and Babylonia, are constantly receiving illustration from the Bible.

10–16. *The ark of the testimony.* The ark, like the tabernacle itself, derives its whole importance from that which it contains. It is a box or chest of *shittah wood.* The shant of Egypt and Arabia grew to the height of twenty or twenty-five feet. Its wood was light, durable, and capable of taking a polish and of resisting damp. The *cubit* is the length from the elbow to the tip of the middle finger, and is variously estimated at a foot and a half and upwards to a foot and three quarters. It contains two spans, and each span three palms or handbreadths, The Babylonian cubit, which consisted of seven palms, seems to have been sometimes employed (2 Chron. iii. 3; Ezek. xl. 5), but only after the captivity. 11. *And thou shalt overlay it* This was not a mere gilding, but a covering of the surface with thin plates of gold, as we infer from 1 Kings vi. 16, and 2 Chron. iii. 6. The Talmud goes so far as to conclude that three chests were made, an outer one of gold plate, a middle one of shittah timber, and an inner one of gold plate. *Upon it a crown of gold.* This was a border or cornice of pure gold round the upper edge of the ark, adorning, and at the same time strengthening it for the support of the mercy-seat. 12. *Four rings* or staples of gold are to be fastened on the two sides or ends of the ark. They are to be attached to *the feet* or supports by which the ark was raised above the level of the floor. 13–15. The staves or poles were of acacia wood overlaid with gold. They passed through the rings at the ends of the ark, and as these were attached to the feet the ark was elevated above the bearers (1 Kings viii. 8). 16. *Thou shalt put into the ark the testimony.* This testimony is the ten commandments engraven on the two tables of stone (xxxi. 18). These ten words are the testimony of the Lord to the people concerning the relation subsisting between them, and the duties consequent thereon. The contents of this cabinet distinguish it from all heathen chests of a similar kind in which were deposited certain symbols of the powers of nature which man regarded with a superstitious veneration. Here are placed the two tables, on which are traced in plain and literal characters the great principles of eternal rectitude, not as an object of worship, but as the basis of all moral dealing in the intercourse between God and man. There is a significance in the very order in which the portions of this symbolical structure are specified. The moral law is the very centre of the whole system of moral things; and accordingly this is first defined and located. The ark in which it is to be deposited is the first article provided for the house of God.

17–22. *The mercy-seat.* The ark is but a part of a greater whole; and hence there is rightly no break here in the Hebrew text. The mercy-seat is not the mere covering of the ark, which had most probably a lid forming a constituent part of itself. It is a separate piece, composing, with the ark, a unity, not so much in outward form as in inward design. It is of pure gold, to denote that expiation maintains the unalterable sanctity of the moral law; as everything must be absolutely perfect which proceeds from or comes into contact with God. Its length and breadth correspond with those of the ark which contains the testimony, as the propitiation must satisfy the law in all its length and breadth. *Two cherubim.* For a description of the cherubim, see on Gen. iii. 22–24. The cherubim here are symbolic figurations of those celestial attendants on the divine majesty. They are to be *of gold*, as representative of pure and perfect beings. *Of beaten work.* They are to be formed by the hammer of malleable gold. 19. *Out of the mercy-seat shall ye make the cherubim on its two ends.* It appears from this that the cherubim on the two ends and the mercy-seat formed one piece of workmanship, either by being beaten out of one mass, or by being permanently fastened together into one whole. The former seems the more natural sense of the words. 20. These figures have wings, spread out so as to overshadow the mercy-seat; and their faces are towards one another, and towards the mercy-seat. These cherubic figures had two wings and only one face. They had the attitude of observant attention, and guarded with their wings the place of the divine manifestation, as became the intelligent and potential ministers of the divine presence. These figures, then, are the symbolic indication of the Shekinah, or dwelling of God among men; an abstraction which is often applied in Rabbinical style to the present Deity.

21, 22. *The mercy-seat on the ark from above.* The mercy-seat, with the attentive overshadowing cherubs, is placed above the ark which contains the testimony. This arrangement is significant of the intercourse of God with fallen man, being founded on the basis of immutable rectitude, through a propitiation which meets all the demands of the violated law. *And I will meet thee there*, appoint a meeting, and meet thee by appointment. Hence the tabernacle is called the tent of meeting by appointment. *And speak with thee ..... of all that I command thee concerning the sons of Israel.* This is to be the place of revelation. A definite place is necessary for man, especially in his infantile state, though not for God, who is omnipresent. The cherubim, however, are no part of Deity, and their figures no semblance of God. They merely indicate and mark the boundaries of the place where God manifests his presence.

Hence we perceive, that the ark, mercy-seat, and cherubim form one piece of emblematic workmanship, symbolizing not God, but the atonement; the holiness of God expressed by the law, and his mercy indicated by his manifested presence between the cherubim, being mediated or brought into harmony by the propitiation figured by the mercy-seat. The great fundamental principle of reconciliation is mooted here, to be afterwards developed and illustrated in the other parts of the tabernacle. From this centre of communication with God we proceed in this remarkable specification of the parts of the tabernacle toward the circumference where the communicating people assemble.

23–30. *The table.* The table is of acacia, two cubits long, a cubit broad, and a cubit and a half high. It is overlaid with pure gold. A border rises a handbreadth from the leaf. This seems to be an addition to the table, and not the upper part of the trestle on which the leaf rests. The edge of this table, and that of the border upon it, are adorned with crowns or wreaths of gold, the one of which, therefore, appears at the top and the other at the base of the border. Four rings are attached to the legs *over against the border*, and therefore beneath the leaf, as keepers for the staves or poles on which it is to be borne. These staves, like the table, are to be overlaid with gold.

29. *Its dishes* were bread-plates, of which two were placed on the table, containing six cakes each (Lev. xxiv. 5, 6). These cakes cannot have been ten handbreadths by five, according to Jewish tradition, as one dish holding such a cake would have occupied the whole table, which was only twelve handbreadths by six. *Its bowls* were smaller vessels for holding pure frankincense (Lev. xxiv. 7), which were placed upon the two piles of cakes. *Its flagons* were large cans or decanters, in which a supply of wine was kept for pouring into the cups or smaller vessels used for making libations or drink-offerings. The drink-offering varied from the fourth part to the half of a hin of wine, that is, from a pint and a half to three pints, according to the value of the victim (Num. xv. 1–12). The dishes, flagons, and cups must have been of such a size that two of each could stand conveniently on the table. The bread-trays might have been five by two and a half or three handbreadths.

30. *Shew-bread.* The shew-bread was to consist of twelve cakes, each made of two tenth deals, about three and a half quarts, of fine flour (Lev. xxiv. 5, 6). This is called shew-bread, or bread of the face, because it was on the table in the Lord's house, and brought God and man face to face on terms of reconciliation and communion. The table is the place of paternal and hospitable entertainment. The twelve cakes correspond in number with the twelve tribes of Israel. They may be called in one respect the united meat-offering of all the people; but they have a higher significance when they are actually partaken of by the priests in the holy place (Lev. xxiv. 8, 9). In this respect they represent the abounding and all-sufficing blessings of eternal life, dispensed by God, as he manifests himself, and dwells among his people. The priest partaking of the bread represents the family of God bountifully and constantly regaled by him at his paternal board. The tabernacle swells to its true significance as the type of the heavenly home when God is surrounded by his intelligent creatures enjoying, each according to the measure of its capacity, the precious sweets of a susceptible moral existence. This home, however, is here presented in that aspect which alone is real, and at the same time

comfortable to the ransomed sons of a fallen race, the salvation of whom, through the superabounding grace of God, gives a touching character to, and sheds a mild lustre on, the heaven of man. It has its table spread with heavenly fare. The dishes are constantly replenished with bread, and the flagons and cups are not there without being filled with wine, which was the drink-offering accompanying every sacrifice. Bread and wine are the bloodless feast after the sacrifice, and are emblematical of all the blessings of those who are pardoned and accepted as righteous through the atoning sacrifice on the altar of propitiation (see on Gen. xiv. 18–20).

31–40. *The candlestick.* This was to be made of pure gold, beaten with the hammer *Its block*, or pedestal; *its shaft*, or stalk; *its cups, its knops, and its flowers*, ornaments on its branching stalks, shall be all of one piece. 32. *Six branches* come off, two and two, from the main shaft, at three separate points, in the same plane, and curved in the form of a quadrant, so that the lamps, resting on their extremities, are all in the same horizontal line with that on the central stalk. 33. Three cups, in the form of an almond nut, were on each branch. These appear to have been surmounted by a knop or ball, like the apple of the pomegranate, and a flower which is not specifically described. 34–36. *And in the candlestick*, that is, the main shaft, shall be four cups, knops, and flowers. Under each pair of branches, and under the central lamp, a cup, knop, and flower; and all these beaten out of the one mass of gold. 37. The seven lamps rest on the flowers at the extremities of all the stems. He who sets on the lamps shall place the candlestick with its lamps parallel to the south side of the tabernacle, so as to throw its whole radiance on the opposite side, where the table is situated. 38. The snuff-tongs and snuff-dishes explain themselves. 39. The whole is to be made of a talent, about one hundred and twenty pounds of gold. Jewish tradition fixes the height of the candlestick at three cubits, or twice the height of the table. This fits it for throwing light over the table, and is therefore more probable than the conjecture of Bähr, that its height was a cubit and a half, or equal to that of the table. The same tradition estimates the breadth at two cubits, the same as that of the table. The candlestick was placed on the south side of the holy place, probably at the middle, opposite the table of shew-bread.

As a piece of furniture, the candlestick evidently serves to give light to those who are in the tabernacle or home of God. It is an emblem of spiritual light. The sevenfold light is the sanctifying efficacy of the Spirit, as seven is the number of holiness. The three pieces of furniture already described are evidently regarded by the divine revealer as forming one whole, since at the close of their specification Moses is solemnly admonished in these words; "and see that thou make them after their pattern, which thou wast shown in the mount." This ideal unity rests in the salvation of the sinner that returns to God, which consists of peace with God, represented by the mercy-seat; propitiation, the benefits of which are set forth in the table, with its bread and wine; and purification, which is symbolized by the candlestick. The number three appears not only in the mercy-seat, with the tables of the law beneath, and the cherubim of the divine presence above; but also in the ark, the table, and the candlestick. It points to a trinity of persons in the unity of the Godhead.

## CHAP. XXVI.—THE TABERNACLE.

1. מִשְׁכָּן *dwelling, abode, habitation, mansion.* This consists of the inner curtains or set of curtains, the tabernacle proper or booth סֻכָּה, and the tent אֹהֶל the outer set of curtains or awning of goats' hair. The two additional coverings of rams' skins and badgers' or seals' skins are designed to protect the inner fabric from the weather.

חֹשֵׁב a weaver who raises figures in the web. אֹרֵג a plaiter or weaver in general. רֹקֵם an embroiderer who works figures with the needle.

XXVI. 1. And the tabernacle thou shalt make with ten curtains of fine linen twined, and blue, and purple, and crimson; with cherubim of cunning work shalt thou make them. 2. The length of one curtain shall be eight and twenty cubits, and the breadth of one curtain four cubits: all the curtains shall have one measure. 3. Five curtains shall be coupled one to another; and five curtains coupled one to another. 4. And thou shalt make loops of blue on the selvedge of the first curtain at the end of the coupling: and so shalt thou make on the selvedge of the last curtain in the second coupling. 5. Fifty loops shalt thou make in the first curtain, and fifty loops shalt thou make in the edge of the curtain that is in the second coupling: the loops matching one another. 6. And thou shalt make fifty taches of gold, and couple the curtains one to another with the taches; and the tabernacle shall be one.

7. And thou shalt make curtains of goats' hair for a tent over the tabernacle; eleven curtains shalt thou make. 8. The length of one curtain shall be thirty cubits, and the breadth of one curtain four cubits: the eleven curtains shall have one measure. 9. And thou shalt couple five curtains by themselves, and six curtains by themselves; and thou shalt double the sixth curtain in the fore-front of the tent. 10. And thou shalt make fifty loops on the selvedge of the one curtain that is last in the coupling, and fifty loops on the selvedge of the curtain in the second coupling. 11. And thou shalt make fifty taches of brass, and put the taches into the loops, and join the tent, and it shall be one. 12. And the remnant that is over of the curtains of the tent, the half curtain that is over shall hang over the back of the tabernacle. 13. And the cubit on this side, and the cubit on that side, that are over in the length of the curtains of the tent shall hang over the sides of the tabernacle on this side and on that to cover it. 14. And thou shalt make a covering for the tent of rams' skins dyed red, and a covering of badgers' skins from above. ¶ 42.

15. And thou shalt make boards for the tabernacle of shittah wood standing up. 16. Ten cubits shall be the length of a board, and a cubit and a half the breadth of one board. 17. Two tenons shall be to one board, set alike one to another: thus shalt thou make for all the boards of the tabernacle. 18.

And thou shalt make the boards for the tabernacle, twenty
boards on the south side southwards. 19. And thou shalt make
forty sockets of silver under the twenty boards; two sockets
under one board for its two tenons, and two sockets under
another board for its two tenons. 20. And for the second
side of the tabernacle northwards there shall be twenty boards;
21. And their forty sockets of silver; two sockets under one
board, and two sockets under another board. 22. And for the
rear of the tabernacle westward thou shalt make six boards.
23. And two boards shalt thou make for the corners of the
tabernacle in the rear. 24. And they shall be doubled beneath,
and together they shall be complete at the top for the one
ring: thus shall it be for the two of them; they shall be for
the two corners. 25. And they shall be eight boards, and
their sockets of silver sixteen sockets; two sockets under one
board, and two sockets under another board. 26. And thou
shalt make bars of shittah wood, five for the boards of the one
side of the tabernacle; 27. And five bars for the boards of
the other side of the tabernacle, and five bars for the boards of
the side of the tabernacle to the rear westward. 28. And the
middle bar in the middle of the boards shall reach from end to
end. 29. And thou shalt overlay the boards with gold, and
make their rings of gold to be places for the bars; and thou
shalt overlay the bars with gold. 30. And thou shalt set up
the tabernacle according to the fashion thereof which thou
wast shown in the mount. § 61.

31. And thou shalt make a vail of blue, and purple, and
crimson, and fine linen twined, of cunning work shalt thou
make it, with cherubim. 32. And thou shalt hang it upon
four pillars of shittah, overlaid with gold, with their hooks of
gold, upon four sockets of silver. 33. And thou shalt hang up
the vail under the taches, and shalt bring in thither within the

vail the ark of the testimony; and the vail shall divide unto
you between the holy place and the most holy. 34. And thou
shalt put the mercy-seat upon the ark of the testimony in the
most holy place. 35. And thou shalt set the table without the
vail, and the candlestick over against the table on the side of
the tabernacle southward; and thou shalt put the table on the
side of the north. 36. And thou shalt make a covering for
the door of the tent of blue, and purple, and crimson, and fine
linen twined, wrought with needlework. 37. And thou shalt
make for the covering five pillars of shittah, and thou shalt
overlay them with gold, with their hooks of gold; and thou
shalt cast for them five sockets of brass. § 62.

After laying down the plan of those pieces of domestic furniture which shadow forth the ultimate form and loftiest stage of salvation for man, we descend to the habitation in which these are to be placed. The tabernacle proper occupies the middle of the three chapters devoted to the material things. It comes after the things contained as the accessory after the principal.

1–17. *The mansion.* The word tabernacle applies chiefly to the wooden structure (סֻכָּה) originally covered with boughs and leaves of trees. The *mansion* is a more general term, referring to its use as an abode. It has been replaced in our version by the word tabernacle, which is hallowed in our early associations, and serves the purpose of a free rendering sufficiently well. The mansion or abode consists internally of a pavilion or set of ten curtains of fine linen thread, interwoven with threads of blue, purple, and crimson. The spinning of the yarn was generally, but not exclusively, the work of women, while the weaving was more frequently done by men. These arts were well known among the Egyptians, as we learn from their numerous and interesting monuments. Figures of cherubim were raised on the curtains. These were the stated attendants on the Divine Majesty, and were therefore appropriate in his symbolic abode. 2. The ten curtains covered a surface of twenty-eight by forty cubits. 3. Ten is the number of completeness. For convenience five of these were coupled or stitched together into one piece, and the remaining five into another. 4. For the purpose of connecting these two halves the outer edges of the two middle curtains are provided with loops. 5. Of these loops there were fifty, and therefore forty-nine intervals in twenty-eight cubits, or seven intervals in four cubits. The distance between the loops was about ten or twelve inches. 6. These loops were conjoined by fifty taches of gold, and the ten curtains were thus formed into one *mishkan* or mansion. This constitutes the inner curtain, which corresponds to the tapestry of later times, or to the plastering and papering of our modern dwellings. It covered the tops, the sides, and the western end of the tabernacle. The cherubic figures, we may suppose, were so placed on the cloth that they were upright on the end wall of the tabernacle, so that they would appear upright above and on the sides to an eye placed above the mercy-seat.

7–15. The tent and its coverings are next described. Curtains of goats' hair form the usual tent in the East. The tent (אֹהֶל) is here distinguished from the mishkan. The one is cast or spread over the other (xl. 19). Eleven curtains composed the tent. 8. They are of the same breadth as the former curtains, but longer by two cubits. 9. One part is formed by sewing five curtains, the other by sewing six curtains together. Half the breadth of the sixth curtain in this part of the tent is to be doubled, that is, to hang over the front of the tabernacle. In this way the seam of the upper curtains would always be over the middle of the lower curtains. 10, 11. The two parts are connected in the same way as before. 12. The tent covers the top, sides, and end of the tabernacle, and as there is an additional length of four cubits, the one half of it hangs over in front and the other remains over in the rear. 13. The single curtain is longer by two cubits than that of the mishkan, and therefore allows a cubit to hang over on each side. The difference is needful, because the one curtain is within and the other without the boards of the tabernacle. 14. The coverings of red rams' skins and of badgers' skins afford protection from the rain.

15–30. The wooden framework, or tabernacle proper. After the pliant materials we come to the firm part of the structure. The shittah, shant, or acacia tree, grows to a considerable height. The use of the plural number, however, admits of one of these boards being composed of more than one trunk. 16. Each board is ten cubits long and a cubit and a half broad, that is, at least fifteen feet by two and a quarter. As the tabernacle was ten cubits wide, and six boards, or a breadth of nine cubits, seem to complete the end (vs. 22), it is probable that the boards were half a cubit thick at the bottom. It is most likely, however, that, for the sake of lightness, they tapered on the outside to a thickness at the top of an eighth of a cubit. In this way the inside would be vertical, the outside slightly sloping, the boards would have a more stable position and be sufficiently strong, and some difficulties in the conception of the structure would be removed. 17. The tenons seem to form part of the length or height of the boards. They are "set alike," or symmetrically situated on the ends of the boards. If they were half a cubit deep, the curtains of the mishkan, being twenty-eight cubits long, would exactly cover the top, of nine cubits, and the sides, being nine and a half cubits each above the socket or mortise. 18. Twenty boards, each a cubit and a half broad, will form a side wall thirty cubits long. 19. The forty sockets of silver either rested on the ground or were attached to a solid sleeper of wood laid on the ground. The latter method would give the greater stability to the structure. 20, 21. The north side corresponds to the south. 22–25. The six boards seem to close in the west end, which they will do if the side boards be half a cubit thick at bottom and the measurement be from outside to outside. The corner boards are different from the others. If the end wall be placed at right angles to the side wall so that their vertical boundary lines coincide, their ends will leave a right angle to be occupied by the corner boards. Let the base of the corner board be a square cubit, wanting a square half-cubit on the outer corner, and let it taper on all its outer sides to a top that shall be a square eighth of a cubit. It is obvious that this board will be "doubled" or twinned beneath, as it will have two projecting parts at right angles to each other. Its base will be half a cubit thick, and so correspond with the thickness of the others. Its breadth will be a cubit every way, and so it will fill up the void square at the corner, and project half a cubit in the direction of the side and the end. Being reduced at the top of the mishkan to a square of an eighth of a cubit, it will exactly fill the square at the top, and so be "complete." One ring or clamp of metal will serve to make it fast to the adjacent boards of the sides and end. As its breadth, omitting the part that is counted a second time, is a cubit and a half, it has two tenons like the other boards. This seems to be an intelligible explanation of this somewhat obscure description.

26–28. As the middle bar in the middle of the boards reached from end to end, it is probable that the other bars were half its length, and hence that three rows of rings or keepers ran along the sides—one in the middle for the full length bars, and the other two between this and the extremities. As the lower ends of the boards were fastened by the sockets, it is not improbable that the upper ends were in some way secured. 29. It is generally supposed that the bars were on the outside, and therefore the boards were overlaid on the outside as well as the inside with gold, as Josephus asserts. But it is possible that the bars were on the inside, and the boards only overlaid with gold on the inner side. This would give greater lightness to the boards, and would afford the greater reason for making the keepers of gold and overlaying the bars. But the point in question is of little importance. 30. A visible form of the tabernacle was presented to the mind of Moses on the mount, according to which it was to be constructed.

31–37. The vails and their pillars are now described. The first vail was to be of the same material, color, and pattern as the interior curtains of the mansion. 32. The pillars would probably be half a cubit in diameter at the base. If one were placed in contact with each wall, the three equal spaces would measure two and a third cubits, or about three and a half feet. 33. The vail is to be suspended under the taches of gold connecting the two halves of the internal covering. Hence it separates the tabernacle into two parts—the most holy place of ten cubits, and the holy place of twenty. If the pillars were outside the vail, the interior of the most holy place would be curtained on every side. 34, 35. The tabernacle being now divided into its compartments, the position of the articles of furniture already made is determined. The ark of the testimony is to stand at the middle of the western wall in the most holy place. It is probable that the table occupied the middle of the north side, and the candlestick that of the south side. We have already seen that these three articles form a unity of symbolic meaning in themselves, apart from the articles yet to be described (xxv. 40).

36, 37. The covering or outer vail is of the same material and colors as the inner, but it differs in other respects. The figuration is wrought not by the loom, but by the needle; and the cherubim are not mentioned. It is possible, however, that they were raised on the inner, but not on the outer, side of the hanging; as the latter was exposed to rain, and outside of the tabernacle or presence-hall of God. As the pillars had sockets of a less costly metal, it is probable that they were regarded as external to the tabernacle, and were, therefore, outside the hanging. If the two extreme pillars stood at the ends of the sides, the other three divided the east end of the tabernacle into four openings of fifteen eights of a cubits, or about thirty-four inches each. These pillars were adorned with chapiters, and provided with connecting poles or rods on which the covering was supported by hooks (xxxvi. 38). We are not informed whether the capitals were surmounted by a beam or architrave, giving compactness to the whole front of the tabernacle.

## CHAP. XXVII.—THE ALTAR AND THE COURT.

XXVII. 1. And thou shalt make the altar of shittah wood;
five cubits long and five cubits broad; square shall the altar
be; and the height thereof shall be three cubits. 2. And thou
shalt make the horns of it upon the four corners thereof: its
horns shall be of the same; and thou shalt overlay it with
brass. 3. And thou shalt make its boxes to remove its ashes,
and its shovels, and its basins, and its flesh-hooks, and its fire-
pans: all its vessels thou shalt make of brass. 4. And thou
shalt make for it a grate, a network of brass; and thou shalt
make on the net four brazen rings on its four corners. 5.
And thou shalt put it under the border of the altar beneath,
and the net shall be unto the half of the altar. 6. And thou
shalt make staves for the altar, staves of shittah wood, and
overlay them with brass. 7. And its staves shall be put into
the rings, and the staves shall be upon the two sides of the

altar to bear it. Hollow, of boards, shalt thou make it; as it was shown thee in the mount so shall they make it. § 63.

9. And thou shalt make the court of the tabernacle: for the south side southward shall be hangings for the court of twined fine linen, a hundred cubits long for the one side. 10. And its pillars twenty, and their sockets twenty, of brass; the hooks of the pillars and their rods of silver. 11. And likewise for the north side in length shall be hangings a hundred cubits long: and its pillars twenty, and their sockets twenty, of brass; the hooks of the pillars and their rods of silver. 12. And for the breadth of the court on the west side shall be hangings of fifty cubits. 13. And the breadth of the court on the east side eastward shall be fifty cubits. 14. Fifteen cubits shall be the hangings for the one wing: their pillars three and their sockets three. 15. And for the other wing the hangings shall be fifteen cubits; their pillars three and their sockets three. 16. And for the gate of the court shall be a covering of twenty cubits of blue, and purple, and crimson, and twined fine linen, wrought with the needle; and their pillars four and their sockets four. 17. All the pillars of the court round about shall be joined with rods of silver; their hooks shall be of silver and their sockets of brass. 18. The length of the court shall be a hundred cubits, and the breadth fifty everywhere; and the height five cubits of twined fine linen, and their sockets of brass. 19. All the vessels of the tabernacle in all the service thereof, and all its pins and the pins of the court shall be of brass. 20. § § § 64.

20. And thou shalt command the children of Israel, and they shall bring thee pure olive oil beaten for the light, to set up a continual lamp. 21. In the tent of meeting without the vail, which is before the testimony, Aaron and his sons shall order it from evening to morning before the LORD: a statute for ever to their generations from the sons of Israel. § 65.

We now pass into the court of the tabernacle. The chief object here is the great altar. In the holy of holies we have the ark of testimony, an adumbration of mercy and truth met together. In the holy place we find the table and the candlestick, the emblems of justification and sanctification. In the court we come upon the altar, the symbol of propitiation, standing alone in all its solemn impressiveness. This is the order of things in the history of redemption. The purpose of mercy is formed in the divine breast. The blessings of spiritual renovation and heavenly inheritance forthwith begin to be dispensed, The atonement, through which these legally come, is made in the fulness of time. Hence we perceive that the plan of the tabernacle first leads us down by sensible stages from God to man.

1–8. *The altar.* All former appearances of the altar were occasional: now at length it comes before us as a permanent institution. Its framework is composed of the shant, the only timber employed about the tabernacle. Its horizontal surface is a square of five cubits, or seven and a half feet, and its height three cubits, or four and a half feet. 2. *Its horns shall be of the same.* We conceive that the angle posts of this primitive wilderness altar were three cubits high. The horns were the parts of these posts that projected above the upper surface of the altar. If they were half a cubit in height, the table or upper plane of the altar would be three and three quarters feet from the ground. At this height the priest could perform all his functions with convenience standing on the ground. The wooden frame is wholly overlaid with plates of brass, which would preserve it from the weather and the fire. 3. The boxes for removing the ashes, the shovels for transferring them to the boxes, the basins for sprinkling or pouring the blood, the flesh-hooks, and the fire-pans, were to be made of brass. 4, 5. The brazen grate of network has been variously interpreted. Many, including Kurtz and Keil, understand by the border (כַּרְכֹּב) a ledge half a cubit or a cubit broad going round the altar at half its height, on which the priest might stand when officiating, and by the grate a network descending from its outer edge to the ground. But it is obvious that the whole structure, being thus eight or nine feet square, with a large quantity of metal, would be too heavy and cumbrous to be portable. Moreover, the rings for the bearing poles, being attached to the grate, would be at the extreme edges of this square, and therefore placed in the most inconvenient situation either for carrying or preventing a strain on the article to be carried. Kalisch supposes the border to be at the top of the altar, and the grate to reach down to the half height of the altar. But if the grate "reached down from the border to the middle of the altar," we do not see how it could "receive whatever might fall from the altar," or what other purpose it could serve. And it does not seem to have been merely an ornament. By "the half of the altar" we understand not half its height, but half its horizontal area. The grate would in that case be a square of nearly five and a quarter feet in the middle of the area, surrounded by a margin two and a quarter feet broad. This margin, covered at least with a thick layer of brass, would be the border (כַּרְכֹּב) beneath the inner edge of which the brazen grate would be fixed to contain the fire beneath the sacrifice. The fine ashes would fall through the meshes of the network on the ground, to be removed when convenient. This explanation is so far favored by the Sept. that both the border and the grate are rendered by the ἐσχάρα, a hearth. It is to the same extent supported by Josephus (Antiq. iii. 7, 8). The grate also thus comes out to be an essential part of the altar, and a compactness is given to the whole structure. The four rings seem to be the keepers for the staves by which the altar was to be carried. 6, 7. The staves are to be put into the rings, and are said to be on the two sides of the altar. The word for side here (צֵלָע) means not the mere surface, but the lateral portion of a thing, and therefore the staves passing through rings attached to the outer edges of the grate may be fairly said to be on the sides of the altar. An article so weighty would have to be borne on the shoulders of four or eight men. 8. The boarding may not have extended beyond two cubits, leaving half a cubit of the corner posts above for horns, and half a cubit beneath for feet. This simple structure would afford the lightest, and therefore fittest, form for a portable altar of the given dimensions. The grate may have been a cubit deep.

9–19. *The court.* The altar is the principal thing, secondary to which is the court in which it stands. 9–12. The court is a hundred cubits long from east to west and fifty cubits broad. The hanging seems to have been a web of fine linen five cubits broad. This was suspended on silver rods, supported by twenty pillars on each side and ten on the west end. 13–16. On the east side are two wings or shoulders (כָּתֵף) of fifteen cubits, and a gate of twenty. The pillars are reckoned by Philo at fifty-six, the corner ones being twice counted. But in this way the distance between the pillars at the side would be different from that between those at the end, and the account of the east end would be unintelligible without counting the extreme pillars of the gate twice, and so having eight pillars instead of ten, and two other unequal intervals. All is plain, however, when we accept the sixty pillars. Beginning at the east end of the north side we attach the hanging to the corner pillar, but do not count it. After that we count twenty pillars for the twenty equal lengths of five cubits in the one hundred. Beginning again at the north end of the west side, we do not count the corner one, as it was counted already, and ten equal lengths bring us to the fifty cubits of that end with its ten pillars. So we proceed with the south side. And the south shoulder has three pillars beside the corner one counted before. The gate has four beside the extreme one south counted before. And the north shoulder has three pillars including the corner one not counted at first. 17. The pillars are provided with hooks, on which the rods that connect them and support the enclosing canvas rest. The hooks and rods are of silver. We are informed also that the pillars have chapiters overlaid with silver (xxviii. 17). The sockets in which they are inserted are of brass. The pillars themselves are usually supposed to be of wood, though the material is not mentioned in the text. The overlaying of the chapiters with silver favors this view. 19. All the vessels of the tabernacle, with the exceptions already made, were to be of brass. The pins were for fastening the tent and its coverings, and probably the pillars of the courts.

The place of the tabernacle we hold to be, not exactly in the middle of the court, as Josephus may be construed to mean, but, as Philo explains, twenty cubits from the west, north, and south sides of the court. For in this way a perfect square of fifty cubits is left in front, to be occupied by the great altar and the laver, with the company of officials and worshippers, as we shall see hereafter.

The altar is representative of the earth, on which sin has been committed and propitiation has to be made. Its four sides also correspond with the four quarters of the world. Its elevation intimates the lifting up of the sacrifice to the Holy Governor by whom it must be exacted. The horns are emblems of power, and denote the virtue of sacrifice in procuring remission of sin and all its concomitant blessings. The breadth of the altar is five cubits; that of the court is five tens of cubits, the half of its length, and the height of the pillars of the court is five cubits. These are contrasted with ten, three, and one, the numerical factors in the tabernacle. They adumbrate in their own way the pre-eminence of the tabernacle, which is the type of heaven (Heb. ix. 24), over the court, which is the figurative semblance of the earth. And the manifold connections between them, as well as the presence of the altar in the court, indicate the design that the earth should eventually become a constituent part of the kingdom of heaven. We have seen that the ark of the covenant forms a triad in itself, that the ark, the candlestick, and the table form another; and now we notice that the most holy, the holy place, and the court form a third.

20, 21. The oil for the lamps. *Olive oil.* This is uniformly employed for lights in the sanctuary and for anointing. It is a vegetable oil, and fit for the purpose of signifying illumination and sanctification. The fat of beasts was employed to represent propitiation. *Pure,* taken from the olive alone. *Beaten,* obtained from olives not pressed in a press, but pounded in a mortar. The latter is said to be a sweeter, finer oil, and of a whiter color. *To set up a continual lamp,* a lamp that shall burn without interruption, that is, every night, in the sanctuary. Some suppose, however, that at least one of the seven lamps on the candlestick was allowed to burn all day, so that a perpetual flame was kept up in the tabernacle. *In the tent of meeting* or appointment. The tabernacle is here called the tent, because it is viewed from the exterior, where it was a tent, not from the interior, where it was a mishkan or pavilion. It is designated the tent of meeting, because at its door or at the gate of its court was the place for the appointed times of the Lord's meeting with his people. The gate, in the East, was the customary place of meeting and transacting business between prince and people. Hence to this day we have the Ottoman Porte. *Without the vail* in the holy place stood the candlestick. Aaron and his sons were to set the lamps on the candlestick and light them in the evening, and in the morning clean them and supply them with fresh oil (xxx. 7, 8; Lev. xxiii. 3, 4). *A statute for ever,* an institution to be observed as long as the whole ceremonial economy should remain in force. *From the sons of Israel,* to be supplied by them for this sacred use.

A new synagogue lesson begins with these two verses, whereby their connection with that which follows is signalized. They form indeed a transition from the tabernacle to the priest of the tabernacle. The oil for the lamps of the candlestick is naturally mentioned here that we may not leave the tabernacle without light. The light indeed is emblematic of the light of him who is Light, and who enlightens his own transcendent dwelling-place (Rev. xxi. 23). It serves also to indicate the need of a minister of the tabernacle, and so to prepare the way for the office and array of the high priest.

## CHAP. XXVIII.—THE ATTIRE OF THE PRIESTS.

4. חֹשֶׁן *breast-piece*; r. *be fair* or graceful. It is perhaps connected with חֹצֶן *the breast*; r. *be strong, firm.* אֵפוֹד *ephod,* a jacket or shoulder-piece; r. *draw on,* over, or round. מְעִיל *robe,* a second tunic, without sleeves, worn under the ephod, reaching to the knees; r. *cover* or *extend.* מִצְנֶפֶת *mitre, tiara;* r. *wind.* אַבְנֵט *girdle;* r. *bind.*

17. אֹדֶם σάρδιον, a stone of a red color, the *sardius* or carnelian פִּטְדָה τοπάζιον, the topaz of Kush (Job xxvii. 19). It is generally of a yellow color; which agrees with von Bohlen's derivation from the Sanscrit *pita,* yellow. בָּרֶקֶת σμάραγδος; r. *flash.* It is akin to the emerald.

18. נֹפֶךְ ἄνθραξ, carbuncle or ruby. סַפִּיר σάπφειρος, *sapphire*; r. *scrape,* polish. יַהֲלֹם ἴασπις; r. *beat, strike.* Some make this the emerald. It may be the diamond, as others take it.

19. לֶשֶׁם λιγύριον, a kind of hyacinth. שְׁבוֹ ἀχάτης, agate, a compound of quartz, chalcedony, carnelian, jasper, and other ingredients. אַחְלָמָה ἀμέθυστος; r. *dream.* It was supposed to have the power of causing dreams.

20. תַּרְשִׁישׁ χρυσόλιθος. A gem of Tarshish or Tartessus in Spain. שֹׁהַם ὄνυξ, as the Sept. elsewhere gives. It is of a pale color, like the human nail. יָשְׁפֵה ἴασπις; r. *shine, be smooth.* A stone of a bright green color.

22. גַּבְלוּת a *bordering* or *connecting;* r. *border.* Others render it a twisting or wreathing.

30. אוּרִים *lights.* תֻּמִּים *perfections, rights.*

XXVIII. 1. And thou bring near for thee Aaron thy brother, and his sons with him, from among the sons of Israel, to act as priests unto me; Aaron, Nadab, and Abihu, Eleazer and Ithamar, Aaron's sons. 2. And thou shalt make holy garments for Aaron thy brother for glory and for beauty. 3. And thou shalt speak unto all the wise of heart, whom I have filled with the spirit of wisdom; and they shall make Aaron's garments, to consecrate him to act as priest unto me. 4. And these are the garments which they shall make; a breastplate, and an ephod, and a robe, and a chequered coat, a mitre and a girdle: and they shall make holy garments for Aaron thy brother, and for his sons to act as priests unto me. 5. And they shall take gold, and blue, and purple, and crimson, and fine linen. ¶ 43.

6. And they shall make the ephod of gold, blue, and purple, crimson and twined fine linen, with cunning work. 7. It shall have two shoulder-straps joining it; at the two edges thereof shall it be joined. 8. And the belt for fastening it, which is upon it, according to the work thereof, shall be of the same; of gold, of blue, and purple, and crimson, and twined fine linen. 9. And thou shalt take two onyx stones, and grave on them the names of the sons of Israel. 10. Six of their names on the one stone, and the names of the other six on the second stone, according to their birth. 11. With the work of an engraver in stone, the engravings of a signet, shalt thou grave the two stones with the names of the sons of Israel: enclosed in ouches of gold shalt thou make them. 12. And thou shalt put the two stones upon the shoulders of the ephod, to be stones of memorial for the sons of Israel: and Aaron shall

bear their names before the LORD upon his two shoulders for a memorial. § 66.

13. And thou shalt make ouches of gold. 14. And two chains of pure gold, attaching shalt thou make them, of wreathen work, and thou shalt fasten the wreathen chains on the ouches. § 67.

15. And thou shalt make the breastplate of judgment with cunning work; after the work of the ephod shalt thou make it: of gold, of blue, and purple, and crimson, and twined fine linen, shalt thou make it. 16. It shall be square, doubled; a span shall be its length, and a span shall be its breadth. 17. And thou shalt set in it settings of stone, four rows of stones; a row of sardius, topaz, and emerald, shall be the first row. 18. And the second row a carbuncle, a sapphire, and a diamond. 19. And the third row, a ligure, an agate, and an amethyst. 20. And the fourth row a chrysolite, and an onyx, and a jasper; they shall be mounted with gold in their settings. 21. And the stones shall be with the names of the sons of Israel, twelve, according to their names; with the engravings of a signet, each with its name, shall they be for the twelve tribes. 22. And thou shalt make upon the breastplate attaching chains of wreathen work of pure gold. 23. And thou shalt make upon the breastplate two rings of gold, and put the two rings on the two ends of the breastplate. 24. And thou shalt put the two cords of gold in the two rings on the ends of the breastplate. 25. And the other two ends of the two cords thou shalt fasten on the two ouches, and put them on the shoulders of the ephod, in front of it. 26. And thou shalt make two rings of gold, and put them upon the two ends of the breastplate, on the border thereof which is on the side of the ephod inward. 27. And thou shalt make two rings of gold, and put them on the shoulder-straps of the ephod beneath,

in the front of it, over against the joining thereof, above the belt of the ephod. 28. And they shall bind the breastplate by its rings to the rings of the ephod with a lace of blue, to be upon the belt of the ephod, that the breastplate be not loosed from the ephod. 29. And Aaron shall bear the names of the sons of Israel in the breastplate of judgment upon his heart, when he goeth into the holy place, for a memorial before the LORD continually. 30. And thou shall put in the breastplate the Urim and the Tummin: and they shall be upon Aaron's heart when he goeth in before the Lord: and Aaron shall bear the judgment of the sons of Israel upon his heart before the LORD continually. § 68.

31. And thou shalt make the robe of the ephod all of blue. 32. And there shall be a hole for the head in the midst thereof: it shall have a binding round the hole of it of woven work, as it were the hole of a habergeon, that it be not rent. 33. And thou shalt make upon the hem of it pomegranates of blue, and purple, and crimson, round about the hem thereof; and bells of gold between them round about. 34. A bell of gold and a pomegranate, a bell of gold and a pomegranate, upon the hem of the robe round about. 35. And it shall be upon Aaron to minister: and his sound shall be heard when he goeth into the holy place before the LORD, and when he cometh out; and he shall not die. § 69.

36. And thou shalt make a plate of pure gold, and grave upon it with the engravings of a signet, HOLINESS TO THE LORD. 37. And thou shalt put it on a lace of blue, and it shall be upon the mitre; upon the forefront of the mitre shall it be. 38. And it shall be upon Aaron's forehead, and Aaron shall bear the iniquity of the holy things, which the sons of Israel shall hallow in all their holy gifts: and it shall be upon his forehead continually, that they may be accepted before the LORD.

39. And thou shalt weave in figures the coat of linen, and
thou shalt make a mitre of linen, and thou shalt make a girdle
of needlework.

40. And for Aaron's sons thou shalt make coats, and thou
shalt make for them girdles, and bonnets shalt thou make for
them for glory and beauty. 41. And thou shalt put them
upon Aaron thy brother, and his sons with him; and thou
shalt anoint them, and fill their hand, and sanctify them, and
they shall be priests unto me. 42. And make for them linen
breeches to cover the flesh of nakedness; from the loins even
unto the thighs shall they be. 43. And they shall be upon
Aaron and upon his sons when they go into the tent of meetings, or when they draw nigh to the altar to minister in the holy place; and they shall not bear iniquity or die: a statute for ever to him and to his seed after him. § 70.

As soon as we arrive at the altar we feel the need of the priest who is to officiate thereat. The priest stands at the middle point between God and man in this description. Hitherto we have come forth from God to man. With the priest we shall presently return from man to God. From God the priest comes to man, authorized to invite the sinner to return with penitence, confession, and faith to God, and to make the propitiatory sacrifice for all who return. From man he returns to God, having made propitiation, to make prevailing intercession for all whom he represents. His generic character then is to be the mediator between God and man, authorized on the one hand, and accepted on the other. His specific difference is, that, inasmuch as man is sinful, he has to make the expiation that satisfies for sin, and renders his mediation effectual. The present chapter enjoins the calling and clothing of Aaron and his sons in official robes. The garments of the priests are so minutely specified, not because the outer covering is of any importance in itself, provided it be only decent and comely, but because it is intended to be symbolic of the various duties which the priest has to perform. This design comes out again and again in the description, and gives an instructive significance to matters which would otherwise have been left to the taste of the individual. Teaching by figures was peculiarly appropriate in the infantile state of the world, when men had their very ideas yet to form, and oral instruction and literary education were open to a very few.

1–5. The call to the priesthood, and the general enumeration of the priestly garments. *And thou.* Moses has been hitherto the plenipotentiary of heaven, including all offices and powers in himself. To him, then, all commands are issued. *Bring near for thee.* For thy part bring near unto me. *From among the sons of Israel,* who are all in a larger sense, "unto me a kingdom of priests and a holy nation" (xix. 6). *To be priests unto me.* The term כֹּהֵן (Kohen) is sometimes applied to a civil officer, bearing the same relation to the king that the priest does to the King of kings (2 Sam. viii. 18, xx. 26; 1 Kings. iv. 8; 1 Chron. xviii. 17). Hence it originally means a mediator, advocate, or intercessor appointed by the sovereign. The element of sin in the case of man involves the office of expiation in an efficacious mediator, and this is the priest, strictly so called. 2. *Holy garments.* Holy because divinely prescribed, and having a holy significance. They figured the righteousness which is the outward garb of a soul loyal to God. *For glory and for beauty.* Glory is the outshining of intrinsic excellence. Beauty is that pleasing characteristic which distinguishes the glorious from the shameful. For evil has its sensible outgoing of shame and ugliness. The inward cannot but have its corresponding outward show to an all-penetrating eye. The highest of all excellence is moral rectitude, the glory and beauty of which are shadowed forth by the priestly garments. 3. *The wise of heart.* The heart is the term for the whole mental faculties in the metaphorical usage of Hebrew speech. *The spirit of wisdom* here is that pre-eminent mechanical skill which is competent to conceive and realize the design in hand. 4, 5. Six parts of the sacerdotal attire are here enumerated, three of which are peculiar to the high priest — the breastplate, the ephod, and the robe. The other three are common with him to the other priests — the chequered coat, the mitre, and the girdle, with this difference, that in place of the mitre, the common priest has the bonnet or turban (vs. 40). The number three is conspicuous here, as in the structure of the tabernacle. The doubling of this number in the high priest's attire indicates his pre-eminence in priestly rank. The materials of which they are to consist are the same that were used in making the inner curtains of the sanctuary.

6–14. *The ephod.* The materials and workmanship of the ephod and the curtains of the mishkan are the same, with the exception of the cherubim. 7, 8. A patient consideration of the description of the ephod leads to the conclusion that it was a shoulder-piece (ἐπωμίς Sept.) or single lappet covering the back and reaching under the arm. This was kept in its place by two contrivances: First, *two shoulder-straps* extending from the upper part behind were attached to the side pieces under the arms that came out in front immediately above the waistband: Secondly, *the belt* along the lower part of the ephod went round the waist, and so fastened it on. The Rabbins, indeed, and many commentators after them, hold that there were two lappets, each a cubit in length, one in front and one behind, connected by two shoulder-straps. But this is against the text, and against Josephus, who expressly states that the ephod left the breast uncovered (Antiq. iii. 7, 5). The lappet, straps, and belt were all of the same materials, and apparently of the same piece. The gold was beaten into thin plates, and cut into wires, in order to be interwoven with the blue, and purple, and scarlet, and fine linen (xxxix. 3). 9–12. *Two onyx stones* are to be set in ouches of gold on the shoulders of the ephod. The names of the sons of Israel are to be engraven, six on each stone, *according to their birth.* The names of the elder six sons, according to Josephus, were on the right shoulder, and those of the other six on the left. The probable arrangement is, Reuben, Simon, Levi, Judah, Dan, Naphtali; Gad, Asher, Issakar, Zebulun, Joseph, Benjamin. These stones are to be *stones of memorial for the sons of Israel before the Lord.* The engraven names, like all writings, perpetuate the remembrance of the persons or things named. This, therefore, intimates that the descendants of Israel are on the memory of the high priest when he appears before the Lord. And the direction concerning these names indicates that in all this the God of mercy has Israel in perpetual remembrance. The office of the high priest has a twofold aspect, as he is the plenipotentiary of heaven to man, and as he is the propitiator of heaven for man. The badge of official authority was carried on the shoulder. Hence the ephod with its onyx stones shadows forth, on the one hand, the authority of the high priest as appointed of God to his high office. On the other hand, the bearing of the names on the shoulder indicates the propitiatory power of the high priest's office. The shoulder is the seat of bearing power. And bearing the names of the sons of Israel is a forcible Hebrew symbol for saving them by an interposition, which prevails in virtue of a proper atonement. By a familiar expansion of the figures, the high priest appears as the shepherd (Gen. xlix. 24) who bears the lambs on his shoulders. He thus becomes the significant type of the great High Priest, whose everlasting arms are underneath his people. The onyx stones are two, simply because the shoulders are two on which the people are borne. The names are in a group upon these stones, to indicate that the one atonement is made for the whole body of the faithful.

13, 14. These two verses stand by themselves in the original text, and form the transition from the description of the ephod to that of the breastplate. The *ouches of gold* seem to be those in which the onyx stones are set. *Attaching.* The word גַּבְלֻת is very obscure. The meaning, "twisted," now generally given to it, is implied in the following word. It appears to refer to the use made of the chains. They were formed not of rings, but of gold threads twisted in the manner of a cord. These are fastened on the ouches, and serve to suspend the breastpiece, and form a close connection between it and the onyx stones.

15–30. The breastplate of judgment, λογεῖον τῆς κρίσεως (vs. 30) is not a plate strictly so called, but a piece of figured stuff like the ephod; which, when doubled, formed a square of a span, or about nine inches each way. 17. *Thou shalt set it in settings of stone.* The twelve stones were to be set in gold (vs. 20). The settings may have been separate, but it is much more likely that they were connected in a square frame of gold, which was attached to the variegated cloth of the breastplate, as the settings of the onyx stones to the shoulder-straps of the ephod. The names of the twelve sons of Israel were to be engraven on these stones. The probable equivalents of the Hebrew names of these stones are given in the version. It is of no importance to ascertain the precise nature of each stone, as the particular name engraven on each is not specified. It suffices to know that the characters of the tribes were as different as those of the stones. 22–25. The wreathen or twisted chains before mentioned in connection with the ephod (vs. 15) are here introduced in their relation to the breastplate. They are hooked on two rings attached to the upper corners of the breastplate, while their other ends are fastened, as already stated, to the ouches on the shoulders of the ephod. 26–28. The breastplate, thus suspended, is to be kept in its place by a lace tying a ring on each of its two lower corners to a corresponding ring on each of the lower ends of the shoulder-straps above the belt of the ephod. 26. The two rings of the breastplate are to be placed *on the border of it, on the farther* or lower *side of the ephod, inward;* that is, on the side next the ephod. 27. The two rings of the ephod are to match them *underneath* on the ends of the shoulder-straps, which are continued down to the belt, *in the front of it*, on the borders of it which come under the arms to meet the breastpiece, which overlaps it, and covers the space left in front. *Over against the joining thereof*, the joining of the shoulder-strap with the side and with the belt of the ephod.

29. The breastplate itself, filling up the space of a span on the breast between the two shoulder-straps, and attached thereto above and below, is to be regarded as the complement of the ephod. As the breastpiece was two spans or a cubit deep, so Josephus informs us (iii. 7, 5) that the ephod was of the depth of a cubit, and so extended as far below the belt behind as the breastplate itself before. Being part of a common whole, they share in a common significance. The names on the breastplate, in common with those on the ephod, serve for a memorial of Israel before the Lord (vs. 12). As the heart, in its ethical sense, is the seat of intellectual and moral faculty, the breastplate on the heart is the emblem of oracular and judicial utterance. Hence it is called the breastplate of judgment, and in the Sept. λογεῖον τῆς κρίσεως, the oracle of judgment. In this respect the high priest appears as the authoritative and inspired spokesman of him who is the God of truth and the Judge of all the earth. On the other hand, the bearing of the names of the sons of Israel on his heart is a symbol of intercession, the second half of the priestly mediation for the children of God. As each name is now on a separate stone, so every individual believer in Him who has made the all-covering atonement has a special place in that all-prevailing intercession which is continually going on at the throne of grace.

30. The Urim and the Tummim. *And thou shalt put into the breastplate.* The breastpiece itself is a piece of elaborately finished cloth (vs. 15). The symmetrical set of precious stones mounted in gold, whether separate or in a common frame, had to be constructed apart, and then placed *within the compass of* (אֶל) the breastplate, and attached to it in the ordinary way. This is expressed, not before, but now, in the words above quoted. This being so, the Urim and Tummim are the twelve precious stones mounted in gold, which are now put in the breastplate. *And they shall be upon Aaron's heart when he goeth in before the Lord.* These significant stones shall be on the breast of the high priest when he goes in to intercede, or essays to consult the Lord for Israel or a son of Israel.

*And Aaron shall bear the judgment of the sons of Israel upon his heart before the Lord continually.* A judgment is a decision or sentence according to law or right. Now the right of those who are actually guilty, and therefore obnoxious to the penalty of the law, resides not in themselves, but in their high priest, who gives satisfaction for the offence, and fulfils the requirements of the law on their behalf. Hence Aaron is said to bear the judgment of the sons of Israel when he prosecutes their cause before the Lord on the merits of his official compliance with the law in their stead. And he is said to bear the judgment of *the sons of Israel* when the Urim and Tummim are upon his heart, simply because these words are a significant name for the set of precious stones on which their names are engraven. The precious stones, distinct from, yet bearing the names of, the sons of Israel, appear to stand for him who has been already described as "the Stone of Israel" (Gen. xlix. 24), or more precisely to point out certain of his leading qualities, either in their unity, as the onyx on the shoulder, or in their diversity, as the twelve stones on the breastplate. These qualities are expressed by the terms the Urim and the Tummim, the lights and the rights, rendered by the Sept. τὴν δήλωσιν καὶ τὴν ἀλήθειαν. Hence the importance of this highly significant emblem for determining the spiritual meaning of the breastplate. Now the two leading qualities of a precious stone are brilliance and hardness. For the latter some may incline to substitute perfection, purity, or freedom from any flaw. The stones of the breastplate, then, are naturally called the lights in respect of their brilliance, and the rights (perfections or purities) in respect of their hardness (or perfection). These two qualities in the stone represent the light and the right that are in the high priest for the enlightenment and the reconciliation of those who come to God by him. He exercises the functions of teaching and sacrificing, as the type and shadow of a greater than himself. The Lord above is the great Illuminator of the darkened soul by his quickening Spirit (Gen. i. 3, viii. 3, xii. 7, xlviii. 15), and at the same time the great Vindicator from the evil consequent on sin (Gen. xlviii. 16) by a righteousness not then fully manifested to the infant church. The deep import of the Urim and the Tummim, however, already dawned upon the early believer, when he witnessed the high priest clothed with the divinely-instituted breastplate, making an offering on the altar, accepted by fire, for the sins of the people, and returning oracular answers from God to the reverent inquirer; and when he felt within himself the new-born emotions of faith and repentance towards God, and of that peace of conscience which arises from the confidence that an atonement has been made and accepted on his behalf. It pleased the Lord to indicate the light and right which he vouchsafed to his people by the precious stones on the breastplate of the high priest; but it was not his pleasure that these should reside in the stones as a charm in an amulet. Hence, though it was ordained that the high priest should be clothed in the ephod and breastplate when the Lord was consulted through him, yet the divine response was not always either withheld in the absence of the breastplate, or granted when it was present. The Lord had various ways of communicating knowledge to the high priest, by an audible voice, and by other means which we cannot precisely define. But we have no ground whatever for the fancy that he conveyed verbal messages to the high priest by illuminating or raising up certain letters on the stones. The four letters, ח, ט, צ, ק, do not occur on the stones. And besides, no possible advantage can arise from this gratuitous conjecture, as there is no scarcity of possible ways in which the oracular response may have been given. Here it becomes us to observe the rational, intelligible, and open meaning of this most significant part of the sacerdotal attire. There is nothing concealed: no idolatrous, mystical, or magical object or image, such as the Teraphim (Spencer, Legg. Ritual, iii. 3, 2), or three ancient stones, one for the affirmative, one for the negative, and a third for neither (Michaelis, Mos. R. i. 52), or diamond dice (Züllig); nothing like the golden figure of the Goddess of Truth (Thmei) worn by the chief judge of Egypt (Diod. Sic., i. 48, 75); but simply a series of precious stones worn openly on the breast, with the names of the twelve sons of Israel engraven in plain letters on them for a memorial. These are called Urim and Tummim, lights and rights, in reference to the high functions of prophetic revelation and priestly intercession which were exercised by the high priest for the benefit of the people.

31–35. The robe of the ephod. This phrase implies that the robe belonged to the ephod; and hence the three pieces — the breastplate, the ephod, and the robe — were regarded as one whole. The robe is to be entirely of blue. It is a close-fitting garment, having an aperture for the head, and slits, we must understand, for the arms. It was without seam, being entirely woven, even to the hem or binding round the neck. It reached to the knee, being longer than the ephod, and shorter than the checkered coat. 33–35. Upon the skirt of it were to be pomegranates of blue, and purple, and crimson, alternating with bells of gold. Aaron is to wear this robe when he ministers; and thus his sound shall be heard when he goeth into the holy place and when he cometh out, that he die not. This robe is a type of that which preserves from death. Now we know that disobedience is the cause of death, and of course obedience is the safeguard against it (Gen. xvi. 17). The robe, then, is a symbol of that righteousness which is the only security of eternal life. Without this robe, then, the high priest may not appear in the presence of God, on pain of death. The sound manifests to Aaron and to all concerned that the mail of proof has been put on, and the dread of death is removed. It is not probable that the people in general were so near as to hear the tinkling of these bells, and therefore we cannot suppose that the actual hearing of the sound during the ministration of the high priest within the sanctuary was intended to convey any intimation to them. This view of the robe confirms the import of the ephod and breastplate that are connected with it. The conjoint indication of the threefold whole is, that the high priest is appointed by God to bear the sins of the people, to intercede on their behalf, to reveal to them the truth of God, and to appear in a perfect righteousness as their representative.

36–38. The crown of holiness (xxxix. 30). Before proceeding to the parts of the priestly attire which are common to all priests, the significant crown of holiness is to be added to what has gone before. This consists of a plate of pure gold, attached to the mitre by a lace of blue, so that it may rest on the forehead. On this plate is engraven the phrase, HOLINESS TO THE LORD. By the names of the sons of Israel on the precious stones Aaron was marked out as the representative of the people. By the sentence on the diadem he is signalized as the representative of God. In him is typified that intrinsic holiness on account of which alone the people can be accepted. By this holiness alone can he be qualified to undertake the cause of the people, and so "bear the iniquity of their holy things," that they may be accepted before the Lord. It is notable that in the significance of the ephod and the breastplate the bearing of the people is mentioned, and in the explanation of the crown the bearing of their sins is brought forward. The reason of this seems to be that in the former case the power and wisdom of the mediator are regarded, in the latter his holiness is made prominent. It is also worthy of remark that in the ephod the priestly office is obvious, in the breastplate the prophetic comes into view, and in the crown of holiness the kingly makes its appearance, while at the same time the priestly discloses itself throughout.

39. In one verse the three pieces of dress that are common to all the priests are summarily described. The coat of linen is to be checkered or figured in the loom. It was worn above the shirt, provided with sleeves, and reaching to the feet. It was probably an emblem of moral purity. The *mitre* was of the same material, and seems to have been wrapped round the head like a turban. On the front of it was attached the golden plate described in the previous verses. The *bonnet* was used by the ordinary priest in place of the mitre. The *girdle* was also of linen, embroidered with the needle. Josephus says that it was four fingers wide, wound twice round the body, and tied in front, the ends hanging down to the feet. Maimonides asserts that it was three fingers wide and thirty-two cubits long. It forms a very ornamental part of Eastern dress.

40–43. The dress of the other priests consisted of coats, girdles, and bonnets. *For glory and beauty* (vs. 2). Garments of splendid appearance and pleasing to the eye become the incomparable dignity of the priestly office. 41. The chapter now closes, as it began, with directions to put these garments upon Aaron and his sons, to annoint them, to fill their hand, and sanctify them, that they may minister to the Lord in the priests' office. The filling of the hands is the placing of the prescribed sacrifices in their hands, in the offering of which they are not only sanctified for, but instituted into, their office. The Levitical priests had to offer for themselves, as they were but fallen men, like their fellow-worshippers, and therefore but types and shadows of a true and perfect priest to come. 42. The breeches are mentioned apart because they do not belong to the official dress of the priest, but are prescribed for the sake of decency. The organs of excretion are called the flesh of nakedness, because their exposure is the exposure of a defilement connected with decay and death, and indicative of that moral defilement which brought death into the world of mankind. These parts are to be specially concealed in those who are to be types of moral purity when they approach the tent of meeting or the altar. The "statute for ever" may be regarded as applying to the whole of the regulations concerning dress.

Tradition records that the old garments of the priests were unravelled and made into wicks for the lamps at the feast of tabernacles.

### CHAP. XXIX.—THE CONSECRATION OF THE PRIESTS.

24. תְּנוּפָה *a wave-offering;* r. wave to and fro.
27. תְּרוּמָה *a heave-offering;* r. be high.

XXIX. 1. And this is the thing that thou shalt do unto
them to hallow them to act as priests unto me: take one young
bullock and two rams without blemish. 2. And unleavened
bread, and unleavened cakes tempered with oil, and unleavened
wafers anointed with oil; of wheaten flour shalt thou make
them. 3. And thou shalt put them into one basket, and
bring them in the basket, with the bullock and the two rams.
4. And Aaron and his sons thou shalt bring unto the door of

the tent of meeting; and shall wash them with water. 5.
And thou shalt take the garments, and clothe Aaron with the
coat and the robe of the ephod and the ephod and the breast-
plate; and gird him with the belt of the ephod. 6. And thou
shalt set the mitre upon his head, and put the holy crown
upon the mitre. 7. And thou shalt take the anointing oil and
pour it upon his head and anoint him. 8. And his sons thou
shalt bring, and clothe them with coats. 9. And thou shalt
gird them with girdles, Aaron and his sons, and bind on them
bonnets: and the priestly office shall be theirs for a perpetual
statute: and thou shalt fill the hand of Aaron and the hand
of his sons. 10. And thou shalt bring the bullock before the
tent of meeting; and Aaron and his sons shall put their hands
upon the head of the bullock. 11. And thou shalt kill the
bullock before the LORD, at the door of the tent of meeting.
12. And thou shalt take of the blood of the bullock and put it
upon the horns of the altar with thy finger, and pour all the
blood at the bottom of the altar. 13. And thou shalt take all
the fat that covereth the inwards, and the caul above the liver,
and the two kidneys, and the fat that is upon them, and burn
them upon the altar. 14. And the flesh of the bullock, and
his skin and his dung, shalt thou burn with fire without the
camp: it is a sin offering. 15. And thou shalt take the one
ram; and Aaron and his sons shall lay their hands upon the
head of the ram. 16. And thou shalt slay the ram, and thou
shalt take his blood and sprinkle upon the altar round about.
17. And thou shalt cut the ram in pieces, and wash his
inwards and his legs, and put them on his pieces and on his
head. 18. And thou shalt burn the whole ram on the altar:
it is a burnt-offering unto the LORD, a sweet savor, an offering
by fire unto the LORD. 19. And thou shalt take the other
ram; and Aaron and his sons shall lay their hands upon the

head of the ram. 20. And thou shalt kill the ram and take of his blood, and put it upon the tip of the right ear of Aaron, and upon the tip of the right ear of his sons, and upon the thumb of their right hand and upon the great toe of their right foot; and thou shalt sprinkle the blood upon the altar round about. 21. And thou shalt take of the blood that is upon the altar, and of the anointing oil, and sprinkle it upon Aaron and upon his garments, and upon his sons and upon his sons' garments with him; and he shall be hallowed and his garments, and his sons and his sons' garments with him. 22. And thou shalt take of the ram the fat and the rump, and the fat that covereth the inwards, and the caul of the liver, and the two kidneys, and the fat that is upon them, and the right shoulder; for it is the ram of consecration. 23. And one loaf of bread and one cake of oiled bread and one wafer, out of the basket of unleavened bread that is before the LORD. 24. And thou shalt put all in the hands of Aaron and in the hands of his sons; and thou shalt wave them for a wave-offering before the LORD. 25. And thou shalt take them out of their hands, and burn them upon the altar for a burnt-offering, for a sweet savor before the LORD: it is an offering by fire unto the LORD. 26. And thou shalt take the breast of the ram of consecration which is Aaron's and wave it for a wave-offering before the LORD: and it shall be thy part. 27. And thou shalt hallow the breast of the wave-offering, and the shoulder of the heave-offering, which is waved and which is heaved up, of the ram of consecration, of that which is to Aaron and to his sons. 28. And it shall be Aaron's and his sons' by statute for ever from the sons of Israel; for it is a heave-offering: and a heave-offering shall it be from the sons of Israel of the sacrifices of their peace-offerings, their heave-offering unto the LORD.

29. And the holy garments of Aaron shall be for his sons

after him, to annoint them therein and to fill their hands in them. 30. Seven days shall the priest after him of his sons put them on, when he cometh into the tent of meeting to minister in the sanctuary. 31. And thou shalt take the ram of consecration, and seethe his flesh in a holy place. 32. And Aaron and his sons shall eat the flesh of the ram, and the bread that is in the basket, at the door of the tent of meeting. 33. And they shall eat those things wherewith atonement was made, to fill their hands and hallow them: and a stranger shall not eat thereof, for they are holy. 34. And if there remain any of the flesh of consecration and of the bread until the morning, then thou shalt burn the remainder with fire: it shall not be eaten, for it is holy. 35. And thus shalt thou do unto Aaron and to his sons, according to all that I have commanded thee: seven days shalt thou fill their hand. 36. And thou shalt offer every day a bullock of sin-offering for atonement: and thou shalt purge the altar, when thou makest atonement upon it, and thou shalt anoint it to hallow it. 37. Seven days shalt thou make atonement upon the altar, and hallow it: and the altar shall be most holy; whatsoever toucheth the altar shall be holy. § 71.

38. And this is that which thou shalt offer upon the altar; two lambs of the first year day by day continually. 39. The one lamb thou shalt offer in the morning and the other lamb thou shalt offer between the evenings. 40. And a tenth deal of flour mingled with the fourth of a hin of beaten oil, and for a drink-offering the fourth of a hin of wine for the one lamb. 41. And the other lamb thou shalt offer between the evenings, and shalt do thereto according to the meat-offering of the morning and according to the drink-offering thereof, for a sweet savor, an offering by fire unto the Lord. 42. A continual burnt-offering throughout your generations at the door of

the tent of meeting before the Lord, where I will meet you to speak there unto thee. 43. And there I will meet with the sons of Israel; and it shall be hallowed by my glory. 44. And I will hallow the tent of meeting and the altar: and Aaron and his sons will I hallow to act as priests to me. 45. And I will dwell among the sons of Israel and will be their God. 46. And they shall know that I am the Lord their God, that brought them forth out of the land of Misraim, that I might dwell among them: I am the Lord their God. ¶ 44.

Having given specific directions concerning the official attire of the priests, the sacred writer proceeds to settle the mode of their consecration or solemn induction into office.

1–28. The form of consecration. In this solemn process Moses, by special appointment of heaven, is to act the part of priest and consecrator, and so lay the foundation of the Aaronic priesthood. To consecrate the priests is *to hallow them to act as priests* unto the Lord. It consists of three chief parts: (1) anointing them; (2) making atonement for them by sacrifice; (3) causing them to perform a part of their office, in earnest and in token of the performance of the whole thenceforward with full authority. All this is preceded by three preliminary arrangments. 1–3. First, the bringing forward of the articles for sacrifice. The offering consists in its fullest form of three parts — the animal or proper sacrifice, in which the blood that makes atonement was shed, the meat-offering, and the drink-offering. In these two the thanksgiving and self-devotion of the offerer are jointly expressed; and hence the meat-offering only is sometimes employed, as in the present instance, to denote this state of mind. The three animals for sacrifice are a young bullock and two rams. *Without blemish.* This outward freedom from fault is symbolic of that intrinsic integrity or perfection which must belong to the real sacrifice for sin. Three kinds of bread made of wheaten flour are employed for the meat-offering — bread baked in the usual manner; cakes mingled with oil, a kind of short bread, perforated, as its name indicates; and wafers with oil spread upon them. These indicate the fulness and variety of the feelings and duties acknowledged. They are all *unleavened,* in token of the sincerity of the worshipper. They are put into one basket as being one offering, and are brought forward with the bullock and the rams.

The second preliminary is the bringing forward of Aaron and his sons, the parties to be set apart for office. *Unto the door of the tent of meeting.* The tent has been already described (xxvi. 7–15). It was stretched over the tabernacle. It is called the tent of meeting, because it is the appointed place of meeting with God on the part of the high priest, and also on that of every stated assembly of the people on solemn occasions (vs. 42, 43; see on xii. 3). *At the door of the tent* means in a circle, the circumference of which touches the door, be the same more or less, according to the number constituting the meeting. It is obvious that a door ten cubits wide and a gate to the court of twenty cubits will allow a wide scope for the phrase *at the door of the tent of meeting. And shalt wash them with water.* At the time when this direction would be carried into execution the laver (xxx. 17–21) would have been constructed, and placed between the altar and the door of the tent (xl. 11, 12), say twenty-five feet from each. Hence Aaron and his sons were at the door of the tent of meeting when they were twenty-five feet from the entrance. The washing with water is one of the figures for personal cleansing or sanctification, while the sprinkling with blood shed at the altar was typical of legal cleansing or justification.

5, 6. The investiture is the third preliminary. The coat is first put on over the shirt, then the robe, then the ephod and breastplate, with the belt of the ephod, and lastly the mitre, with the crown of holiness, on the head. We have already seen the typical significance of the articles of dress. Aaron being now present in his official attire, and accompanied with the offerings, the consecration or solemn ordination is to take place.

7. The first part of the proper ordination is the anointing. The composition of the anointing oil is afterwards prescribed (xxx. 22–25). The mode of application is pouring upon the head. He thus becomes a mashiach, a representative of the great Messiah. The anointing denotes qualification for office by the enlightening and sanctifying operation of the Spirit of the Lord.

8, 9. The sons of Aaron are now brought forward. Their investiture is summed up in the direction to clothe them with coats. And then girdles are put on Aaron and his sons. It appears from this that the girdle was put over the belt of the ephod. The bonnets are bound on their heads, and must therefore be furnished with ties for this purpose. *The priestly office shall be theirs for a perpetual statute.* The priesthood, in its virtue and effect, is absolutely perpetual. In its present form, it lasts as long as the Levitical economy. *And thou shalt fill the hand.* After the qualification comes naturally the institution, described as the filling of the hands with the instruments of office, that they may be used in some initial service. But in proceeding to this we meet with the propitiation or atoning sacrifice, by which they become *recti in curia*, right in point of law.

10–28. The second part is the removal of legal disqualification by a series of sacrifices. The first is the sin-offering (vs. 10–14). Here is the direct recognition of sin in the intended officials, and therefore of the need of an atonement. The bullock is to be brought before the tent of meeting. Aaron and his sons are to put their hands on its head, in token that their sins are laid on it. This symbolic action takes place in all the offerings (vs. 15, 19). Moses is to slay the animal in the presence of the Lord. He is to sprinkle of the blood upon the horns of the altar, and pour the rest at its base. It is the blood, which is the life, that makes atonement. All the fat covering the inwards, the caul or midriff, the kidneys and their fat, are to be burnt upon the altar. The fat is the best, and this is to be consumed on the altar, as a satisfaction to justice beyond the mere privation of life. The remainder of the sin-offering is to be carried without the camp, as an unclean thing, and there consumed with fire, to indicate that that in which sin resides must be given over to destruction. Such is the awful, yet hopeful significance of the sin-offering.

15–18. Next is the burnt-offering. The victim is in this case wholly burnt on the altar, to denote that a full propitiation is to be made for guilt. The blood of the one ram is to be sprinkled on the altar round about. Its body is then to be cut in pieces, perhaps into quarters, the inwards and legs to be washed, and laid upon the pieces and the head on the altar. The burnt-offering is as old as Noah's day (Gen. viii. 20). The offering of the whole victim on the altar gives prominence to the idea of a complete substitution of one for another. It is *a sweet savor*, because it scents the air with the flavor of savory meat, and thereby vividly expresses how pleasing to the Almighty is the satisfaction to justice which opens the way to remission and restoration. It is *an offering by fire*, because this brings to view the utter destruction that awaits everything tainted with sin

19–28. The third is the ram of consecration. Touching the body with the blood figures the application of that which expiates to the person purged from guilt. The ear is the organ of hearing, and therefore understanding and willing. The hands and the feet are the two great organs of nearer and more distant outward act. All these channels of true obedience needed propitiation. The sprinkling of the blood upon the altar noted to whom the expiation was made. 21. This was followed by a remarkable sprinkling of the persons and garments of the priests with both the blood upon the altar and the anointing oil, to symbolize at the same time the outward and legal and the inward and moral purification which was essential to the priestly office.

22–25. The filling of the hands here begins. This simple but significant act is the third and crowning part of the induction of the priests into office. The fat and fatty parts of the ram, with one of each kind of cakes in the basket, are taken by Moses. *The rump.* This is the tail of the sheep, which in the broad-tailed species often weighed twenty pounds, consisting chiefly of fat, and was so valuable that a little cart was sometimes placed under it to preserve the fat, and relieve the animal. 24. All these are to be *put in the hands* of Aaron and his sons. From a comparison of the present passage with others in the trial of jealousy and the institute of the Nazarite (Num. v. 18, vi. 19), it appears that to put an offering into the hands of the offerer is to cause him thereby to take a part in the offering and in all its consequences. The significance of this taking in hand depends on the nature of the offering in question. Here it is the ram filling the hand (vs. 22). Aaron and his sons, then, here take the first step in offering, and are thereby initiated in the priestly office. But Moses is further directed to *wave them for a wave-offering*, while they are in the hands of the priests. This seems to be accomplished by Moses placing his hands beneath those of the priests, and conveying to them a motion to and fro. Waving is explained by Maimonides and Rashi to be a going and coming; that is, a going towards the altar in token of dedication to the Lord, and a coming again towards the priest in token of transference to the priest as his share. This, however, does not suit the present case, in which the things waved are afterwards consumed on the altar. Later rabbins describe it as a movement towards the four quarters of heaven, to denote a consecration to the omnipresent God. But the horizontal movement probably indicates equality of rank, while heaving, a vertical movement, points to superiority and inferiority of rank. On this supposition, while either movement may denote an active part in the sacred service, waving may shadow forth the communion of the worshippers with one another, and heaving the communion of the worshipper with the Being worshipped. In the present case, the waving will indicate the communion of Aaron and his sons with Moses in the act of sacrifice. After the waving Moses is to take the things waved out of their hands and burn them upon the altar. As the ram is here parenthetically called "the ram of filling" of the hand, it is manifest that this is the first act of that official initiation which is continued through the seven days of consecration (vs. 35).

26–28. The part of the sacrifice usually assigned to the priest. The first victim offered on this occasion is a sin-offering, the second a burnt-offering. After sin has been expiated, and complete satisfaction made, reconciliation and communion with God naturally follow. Hence the third victim, the ram of consecration, is of the nature of a peace-offering, in which the worshipper, still acknowledging his need of atonement, yet advances to the end of all propitiation — peace with God, communion with him, and all the joy of salvation. Hence the peace-offering included a feast upon a sacrifice, shadowing forth the communion of the worshippers with God. The priests were partakers in this communion; and accordingly the wave-breast was assigned to them, and the heave-shoulder to him who officiated on the occasion (Lev. vii. 32–34). Here then, the breast of the ram of consecration is assigned to Moses, who for the present sums up the whole priesthood in himself. He is to wave it for a wave-offering, in token of his communion with the offerers in the blessings of peace and privilege. 27. He is to *hallow*, or set apart to a sacred use, the shoulder of the heave-offering. The heave-shoulder was to be the share of him who transacted the deed of atonement and fellowship with God, in offering up the fat of the peace-offering unto the Lord (Lev. vii. 33). It was taken or heaved up in token of its being offered to God, by whom it is assigned to his representative among men. 28. This is the heave-offering out of the peace-offerings of the sons of Israel, by a perpetual statute (xxv. 2).

29–37. Additional directions concerning the ordination of the high priest. The successor of Aaron shall put on the official dress of his father at his consecration, and wear it during the seven days of institution. 31–34. The solemn feast of the consecration. The flesh of the ram of consecration is *to be seethed in a holy place*, namely in some part of the court of the tabernacle. Aaron and his sons are then to eat it, with the bread in the basket, at the door of the tent of meeting. These are the remainder of the things *wherewith atonement was made to fill their hands*, and set them apart for their sacred service. They are therefore holy, and to be used only by the priests, who are holy. For the same reason, any part that remains till the morning is to be consumed with fire. 35–37. The filling of their hand is to continue seven days. Seven is the number of sacredness, and is therefore connected with this most holy transaction. Nothing can transcend the moment of that which typifies the atonement between erring man and his Maker. Every day *a bullock of sin-offering for atonement* is to ascend the altar, which is to be itself purged thereby. It is also to be anointed, and thus completely hallowed. *Whatsoever toucheth* the altar shall be holy. This is capable of two meanings. He that is to touch the altar must be holy. Or that which in the way of offering toucheth the altar, which is not only the medium of propitiation, *but is now made most holy*, becomes thereby holy, as the altar sanctifies the gift (Matt. xxiii. 19). Both are true; but the latter seems most in keeping with the context here and in xxx. 29.

38–46. The continual burnt-offering, and the resulting communion of God with his people. When the order of the priesthood has been instituted the daily sacrifice can be celebrated. *Two lambs of the first year*, the one in the morning, the other between the evenings (xii. 6). 40, 41. The meat-offering is to be the tenth of an ephah of flour mingled with the fourth of a hin of beaten oil. The omer, or tenth of the ephah, was above three pints, or the daily allowance of one person. A handful of the flour and oil was offered on the altar, and the remainder fell to the priest (Lev. ii. 2, 3). The fourth of a hin, about one pint (xii. 36). The drink-offering is to be the fourth of a hin of wine. It was poured out about the altar in the holy place (Num. xxviii. 7; Joseph. Antiq. iii. 9, 4).

42–46. The continual burnt-offering is to be presented at the door of the tent of meeting. The altar was probably thirty-three and a third cubits, or about fifty feet from the door. The tent of meeting is so called, because there the Lord will meet with Moses to speak with him. After the sacrifice of propitiation comes the reconciliation and communion with God, which is here simply and beautifully expressed by his meeting and conversing with Moses, the representative of the people. 43. The intercourse is extended to the sons of Israel, of course through the high priest. The place of meeting is to be hallowed by the glory of the Divine presence (vs. 44). The tent of meeting, the altar, and the priests, are to partake alike of this sacred character. 45, 46. God will dwell among them and be their God, and by all their past experience shall the people know that he is *the Lord their God*, the self-existent Author of all being, who is Eternal and Almighty, and who has deigned to have mercy on them, and adopt them to be his people; and in pursuance of this gracious determination has *brought them forth out of the land of Mizraim*, that he might dwell among them. To this glad announcement of his grace, he sets the seal of promise and assurance by adding, *I am the Lord their God.* These specifications of the tabernacle service are no mere dry detail, but a record of heavenly life and promise.

## CHAP. XXX.—THE REMAINING ARTICLES FOR THE TABERNACLE.

23. מֹר *Myrrh*, an aromatic plant of Arabia. מֹר דְּרוֹר flowing or liquid myrrh; r. *flow*. קִנָּמוֹן *κιννάμωμον*, Cinnamon is of the best quality in Ceylon; r. perhaps קָנֶה *reed*. קָנֶה *καλαμος* grows in Arabia and India.

24. קִדָּה of the same class with קְצִיעָה *cassia;* r. *split*.

84. נָטָף *στακτή*, a gum spontaneously distilling from the myrrh plant. Others take it to be storax, a plant growing in Syria, Arabia, and other countries, which yields a fragrant gum; r. *drop*. שְׁחֵלֶת *ὄνυξ*, onycha,

the crustaceous covering of the shells of the trochus and conus; r. *scrape off.* חֶלְבְּנָה χαλβάνη, the gum of the stagonitis growing in Arabia, Syria, and Abyssinia; r. *fat* or *milky.* לְבֹנָה λίβανος, frankincense, the native place of which is Arabia Felix; r. *be white.*

XXX. 1. And thou shalt make an altar to burn incense
upon; of shittah wood shalt thou make it. 2. A cubit shall
be the length thereof, and a cubit the breadth thereof: square
shall it be; and two cubits shall be the height thereof: its
horns shall be of the same. 3. And thou shalt overlay it with
pure gold, its top, and its sides round about, and its horns:
and thou shalt make for it a crown of gold around about. 4.
And two golden rings shalt thou make for it under the crown
of it on the two flanks thereof; on the two sides of it shalt
thou make them: and they shall be places for the staves to
bear it withal. 5. And thou shalt make the staves of shittah-
wood, and overlay them with gold. 6. And thou shalt set it
before the vail that is by the ark of the testimony, before the
mercy-seat that is over the testimony, where I will meet with
thee. 7. And Aaron shall burn thereon incense of spices:
every morning, when he dresseth the lamps, shall he burn it.
8. And when Aaron setteth up the lamps between the evenings,
he shall burn it: a perpetual incense before the LORD through-
out your generations. 9. Ye shall burn upon it no strange
incense, nor burnt-offering, nor meat-offering; neither shall ye
pour drink-offering thereon. 10. And Aaron shall make an
atonement upon the horns of it once in a year; with the blood
of the sin-offering of atonement once in the year shall he make
atonement upon it throughout your generations: it is most
holy unto the Lord. 21. ¶ ¶ ¶ 45.

11. And the LORD spake unto Moses, saying, 12. When
thou takest the sum of the sons of Israel who are numbered,

then shall they give each a ransom for his soul unto the LORD, when they are numbered; and there shall be no plague among them when they are numbered. 13. This they shall give, every one that passeth among the numbered, half a shekel after the shekel of the sanctuary; the shekel is twenty gerahs; half a shekel is the offering unto the Lord. 14. Every one that passeth among the numbered, from twenty years old and above, shall give the offering unto the LORD. 15. The rich shall not give more and the poor shall not give less than half a shekel, when they give the offering unto the LORD to make atonement for their souls. 16. And thou shalt take the money of atonement from the sons of Israel, and shalt give it for the service of the tent of meeting; and it shall be a memorial for the sons of Israel before the LORD to make atonement for your souls. ¶ 46.

17. And the LORD spake unto Moses, saying, 18. Thou shalt also make a laver of brass, and its stand of brass, to wash withal: and thou shalt set it between the tent of meeting and the altar; and thou shalt put water therein. 19. And Aaron and his sons shall wash thereout their hands and their feet. 20. When they go into the tent of meeting, they shall wash with water, and shall not die: or when they come near to the altar to minister, to burn an offering by fire unto the Lord. 21. So they shall wash their hands and their feet, and not die: and it shall be to them a statute for ever, to him and to his seed throughout their generations. ¶ 47.

22. And the LORD spake unto Moses, saying, 23. And thou take for thee principal spices, of pure myrrh five hundred shekels, and of sweet cinnamon half so much, two hundred and fifty, and of sweet calamus two hundred and fifty, 24. And of cassia five hundred, after the shekel of the sanctuary, and of olive oil a hin. 25. And thou shalt make it an oil of

holy ointment, a perfume compounded after the art of the perfumer: it shall be a holy anointing oil. 26. And thou shalt anoint with it the tent of meeting and the ark of the testimony, 27. And the table and all its vessels, and the candlestick and its vessels, and the altar of incense, 28. And the altar of burnt-offering and all its vessels, and the laver and its base. 29. And thou shalt hallow them, and they shall be most holy: whatsoever toucheth them shall be holy. 30. And Aaron and his sons thou shalt anoint, and hallow them to act as priests unto me. 31. And thou shalt speak unto the sons of Israel, saying, This shall be a holy anointing oil unto me throughout your generations. 32. Upon man's flesh shall it not be poured; nor shall ye make any like it in its proportion: holy is it, holy shall it be unto you. 33. Whosoever compoundeth any like it, or whosoever putteth of it upon a stranger, shall even be cut off from his people. § 72.

34. And the LORD said unto Moses, Take unto thee spices, stacte, and onycha, and galbanum; spices with pure frankincense: part by part shall there be. 35. And thou shalt make it an incense, a perfume, the work of the perfumer, salted, pure, and holy. 36. And thou shalt beat of it fine, and put of it before the testimony in the tent of meeting where I will meet with thee: it shall be unto you most holy. 37. And the incense which thou shalt make in its proportion ye shall not make for yourselves; it shall be for you holy unto the LORD. 38. Whosoever shall make like unto it to smell thereto shall even be cut off from his people.

We have already hinted at the order observed in this specification of the tabernacle and its appurtenances. The author of this remarkable document proceeds from God to man; from the centre, the ark of the testimony and the holy of holies, to the circumference, the altar of sacrifice and the court (xxv.–xxvii). He next determines the official attire, mode of consecration, and stated functions of the priests (xxviii., xxix). And then in a closing chapter he returns with the high priest from man to God, from the altar of sacrifice to the altar of incense, adding certain things of essential moment that occur on this blessed return. The starting-point is the altar of propitiation, then the laver of purification, and lastly the altar of praise, including confession, adoration, prayer, and thanksgiving. Parallel with the two latter are the ointment of sanctification, with which all things are to be hallowed, and the incense of supplication, which is to be presented before the mercy-seat. The progress and regress here are the prophecy and the history of salvation. First God comes forth to man with the mighty purpose of mercy in his heart and on his lips for four thousand years. Then the great High Priest makes atonement, and returns to the Father to send forth the Spirit of sanctification, and to make intercession for all who accept his mediation. So the awakened sinner finds the atonement for sin and the cleansing of the heart to be on the way to the Father.

1–10. The altar of incense. It is called *an altar*, a place of slaughtering for sacrifice, though no such offering was to be made on it, to intimate that all acceptable worship or service is only through an atonement previously made. It therefore presupposes, and is itself a monument of, the altar of burnt-offering. *To burn incense upon.* Incense in regard to the priest is only the merit of obedience for another, and to burn it is to make intercession for that other. In regard to the general worshipper, the offering of incense symbolizes every act of prayer, thanksgiving, or obedience, which is accepted through the intercession of the high priest. For the propitiation has already been made on the altar of sacrifice, and the sanctification has been shadowed forth by the laver. And the redeemed and regenerate man, now filled with the spirit of adoption, loves to speak and to walk with his Heavenly Father. 1–5. The altar is made of the same wood as the other parts of the tabernacle. It is overlaid with gold, and so is in keeping with the table, and stands in close relation with the candlestick and the ark of the covenant. It is adorned with a crown of gold, like the table and the ark. It is furnished with rings and staves, with which it may be moved from place to place. 6. It is to be placed *before the vail* that hangs before the ark of the testimony, *before the mercy-seat*, with which it stands in intimate correspondence of meaning. Both presuppose an atonement made and accepted; and over the mercy-seat is the presence of God merciful and gracious, and at the altar of incense is the high priest presenting the ransomed people, that they and their service may be accepted, Hence the addition, *where I will meet with thee.* In accordance with this intimate connection, the altar of incense was probably placed close to the vail. In this way the candlestick, the altar, and the table would stand at the middle points of the inner side of the holy place, and the altar would be in closest proximity with the mercy-seat. 7–10. Incense of spices is to be burned on it morning and evening continually. *No strange incense*, none but that prepared by divine appointment (vs. 34–38), no burnt-offering, meat-offering, or drink-offering is to be burnt on it. Once every year Aaron is to make atonement upon the horns of it by sprinkling upon it with his finger seven times the blood of the sin-offering of atonement, to cleanse it and to hallow it from the uncleanness of the sons of Israel (Lev. xvi. 19). This was directed to be done also when a sin-offering was to be presented for the high priest or the congregation (Lev. iv. 7, 18). *It is most holy unto the Lord.* This character is ascribed to the inner sanctuary (xxvi. 33), to the altar of burnt-offering (xxix. 37), to all the furniture of the tabernacle when anointed (xxx. 29), to all the offerings that were appropriated to the priests, and to the place in which they were to be eaten (Num. xviii. 9, 10). In the first of these instances it distinguishes the most holy from the holy place: in the others it expresses emphatically the exclusive holiness of that which belongs to God.

11–16. A regulation is here introduced concerning those who are to be enrolled as the host of the Lord (Num. i. 3). They are to *give each a ransom for his soul unto the Lord when they are numbered.* Here is the constantly recurring intimation that all were guilty before God. They cannot, therefore, be received into his service as the host of the Lord without a ransom. A plague must fall on the unransomed soul that was enrolled in the sacred list. The ransom money is a bekah, or half shekel. This is directed to be *after the shekel of the sanctuary.* The standard is fixed at twenty gerahs. We have not the means of ascertaining the value of the coins before the captivity. But the approximate value of the shekel was 2s. 3d. (xxi. 32). The *shekel of the sanctuary* may be one of full weight in contrast with that of commerce, which may have been of less weight. We have here the following table of coins or weights:

Gerah, or *bean*.
Beka (Gen. xxiv. 22), or *half* shekel, = 10 gerahs.
Shekel, or *weight*, = 20 gerahs.

Every one from twenty years old and upwards passed among the numbered or registered host, and paid the half shekel. The rich and the poor give alike, because their souls are of equal value, and the beka is the money of atonement for each. The offering is to be for the service of the tent of meeting (xxxviii. 27–31).

17–21. The laver was to be made of brass, and its stand of the same material (xxxviii. 8). Its place was between the altar and the door of the tabernacle. If the interval between the door of the tabernacle and the gate of the court (see on xxvii. 19) were fifty cubits, or seventy-five feet, the altar and the laver may have divided this into three equal spaces of twenty-five feet. The Talmud supposes the laver to have been placed a little south of the middle line of the court. This will depend very much on the degree of importance attached to the laver. If it be merely a means of cleanliness, it may be set aside. But if its use be a symbol of sanctification, it will stand in the same line with the altar. Its purpose is washing, that Aaron and his sons may *wash thereout their hands and their feet.* The phrase *thereout* indicates that water was taken out of the laver into a smaller vessel for washing. The washing itself indicates that the priests were unclean, not only by mingling with the people, but by their own inherent sinfulness. The feet and hands with which they go and minister are to be cleansed, lest they die. Death is the penalty of sin, and therefore this outward cleansing is an emblem of that inward purity which must characterize him who is to make atonement for the sins of the people. This cleansing is a perpetual statute. This is in keeping with its intrinsic importance as the symbol of sanctification.

22–33. The holy anointing oil. This is to be composed of five ingredients: five hundred shekels of pure myrrh, two hundred and fifty of sweet cinnamon, two hundred and fifty of sweet calamus, and five hundred of cassia, and a hin, about three quarts, of olive oil. It is said to be compounded after the art of the perfumer. It is probable, therefore, as the Rabbins suppose, that the three spices were soaked in water, and boiled, and their essence extracted and mingled with the myrrh and oil. 26–30. With the anointing oil are to be anointed the tent of meeting, the ark of the testimony, the table, the candlestick, and the altar of incense, the altar of burnt-offering, the laver, and all their appurtenances. Being thus anointed, they are hallowed, and are accounted most holy (vs. 10). Aaron and his sons are to be anointed and consecrated to their priestly office. 31–33. This is to be a standing oil for anointing, not to be used for common purposes, not to be imitated in ordinary compounds, on pain of excommunication (Gen. xvii. 14). The anointing oil is an impressive symbol of sanctifying grace. It is analogous to the water of the laver, which cleanses. The latter points to the quality required; the former to the end contemplated. That which is dedicated to God must be cleansed from stain.

34–38. The incense. This also contains five simples — stacte, onycha, galbanum, frankincense, and salt. Stacte is the natural dropping of some sweet-scented plant, probably the storax. Onycha is probably the operculum, claw, or lid of the shell of a strombus, or other fish, emitting a scent, which, if not agreeable in itself, enhances the sweet odor of the other ingredients combined with it. Galbanum is the gum of a species of ferula (μετώπιον Dioscor.) or stagonite (Pliny), of a sharp bitter taste, fitted to add to the strength and duration of the other components. Frankincense is the odoriferous resin of a plant that grew in Arabia Felix and India, which was frequently used in religious offerings. *Pure*, free from adulteration. *Part by part shall there be*, each prepared apart from the others, or an equal part of each shall enter into the compound. 35. *An incense* for burning on the golden altar. *A perfume* diffusing an agreeable fragrance. *The work of the perfumer*, prepared according to the rules of a well-known art. *Salted*, as every meat-offering was. Salt is the emblem of incorruptibility. *Pure*, free from foreign admixture. *Holy*, dedicated to the holy use for which its purity fits it. 36. *Beat of it fine*, reduce it to a powder, that it may burn freely. *And put of it before the testimony*, on the altar of incense, which stood close to the veil that separated the holy from the most holy place, containing the ark of the testimony. *In the tent of meeting, where I will meet with thee.* Where the Lord meets with the representative of the people, there is the place of conference, and therefore of prayer, adoration, confession, and inquiry on the one hand; and on the other hand of hearing, granting, accepting, and answering. Incense is accordingly the emblem of prayer and praise. 37, 38. This incense is not to be applied to any ordinary use, or imitated, on pain of excision.

### CHAP. XXXI.—THE MASTER OF THE WORK.

1. בְּצַלְאֵל Betsalel. This is usually explained, *in the shadow of God.* אוּרִי Uri, *light.*

6. אָהֳלִיאָב Oholiab, *tent-father.* אֲחִיסָמָךְ Achisamak, *help-brother.*

10. שְׂרָד *separation*, distinction, official distinction; r. *separate, escape, remain.*

XXXI. 1. And the Lord spake unto Moses, saying, 2. See,
I have called by name Bezalel, son of Uri, son of Hur, of the
tribe of Judah: 3. And filled him with the spirit of God, in
wisdom, and in understanding, and in knowledge, and in all
workmanship, 4. To devise designs; to work in gold, in silver,
and in brass, 5. And in cutting of stones for setting, and in
carving of wood; to work in all workmanship. 6. And I, behold
I have given unto him Aholiab, son of Ahisamak, of the tribe
of Dan; and in the heart of every wise-hearted one I have put
wisdom; and they shall make all that I have commanded thee:
7. The tent of meeting, and the ark of the testimony, and the
mercy-seat that is thereupon, and all the vessels of the tent;
8. And the table and its vessels, and the pure candlestick and
all its vessels, and the altar of incense, 9. And the altar of
burnt-offering and all its vessels, and the laver and its stand;
10. And the garments of office, and the holy garments for
Aaron the priest, and the garments of his sons to serve as
priests; 11. And the anointing oil, and the sweet incense for
the holy place: according to all that I have commanded thee
shall they do. ¶ 47.

12. And the Lord spake unto Moses, saying, 13. And thou speak unto the sons of Israel, saying, Verily my Sabbaths ye shall keep; for it is a sign between me and you for your generations to know that I am the Lord that halloweth you. 14. And ye shall keep the Sabbath, for it is holy unto you: he that defileth it shall surely be put to death; for whosoever doeth any work therein, that soul shall be cut off from among his people. 15. Six days shall work be done; and in the seventh is a Sabbath of rest, holy to the Lord: whosoever doeth any work on the Sabbath-day shall surely be put to death. 16. And the sons of Israel shall keep the Sabbath, to observe the Sabbath in their generations for a perpetual covenant. 17. It is a sign between me and the sons of Israel for ever: for in six days the Lord made heaven and earth, and on the seventh day he rested and was refreshed. § 74.

18. And he gave unto Moses, when he made an end of speaking with him upon mount Sinai, the two tables of testimony, tables of stone, written with the finger of God.

The seventh chapter completes the specifications by naming the chief workman, with his second, and assigning to him the execution of all the works. This is followed by an injunction concerning the Sabbath; and then the scene is closed by handing over to Moses the two tables of the law written with the finger of God.

1–11. The calling of Bezalel. *I have called by name*, appointed to office by naming the man. *Bezalel.* The order of descent is Judah, Parez, Hezron, Kaleb, Hur, Uri, Bezalel (1 Chron. ii. 1–20). Hence Bezalel belongs to the seventh generation after Jacob, and it is evident that he was now at man's estate, and may have been the father of a family. For Kaleb, his great grandfather, is at least three generations before Kaleb the son of Jephunneh, the companion of Joshua, and probably of the same generation with Bezalel. Hur, the son of Kaleb, belongs to the fourth generation from Judah, and is therefore parallel with Moses and Aaron, who are in the third from Levi. 3. *Filled him with the spirit of God.* His natural powers are hereby exalted for the works he has to perform. *Wisdom* to devise, *understanding* to apprehend, *knowledge* to explain, and *workmanship* to make expert. 4, 5. *To devise designs,* from a mere verbal explanation. *To work* in the various materials employed in the tabernacle. 6. A companion and deputy is provided in Aholiab of the tribe of Dan, whose qualifications are described in xxxviii. 23. And all the wise-hearted men are required to take part in the work. 7–11. The various works to be executed are now enumerated. 10. *And the garments of office.* The phrase thus rendered occurs only in three other places (xxxv. 19, xxxix. 1, 41), in two of which it is followed by the words, " to minister in the sanctuary." It appears to denote, not the cloths for covering the furniture (Num. iv. 6–14), as they were not strictly for ministering in the sanctuary, nor the inner curtains of the sanctuary, as they are previously mentioned in xxxix. 40, but the special parts of official array worn by the high priest to distinguish him from the others.

12–17. The keeping of the Sabbath is here reinforced, because it might be supposed that so holy a work as the construction of the tabernacle might supersede the weekly rest. *Verily my Sabbaths ye shall keep.* They are by no means to be remitted, even on this extraordinary occasion. *It is a sign between me and you.* As the Sabbath was a divine institution commemorative of that creation in which the progenitor of the human race came into being, the observance of it by any remnant of the human family was a token that, amidst the general apostasy, they had retained or returned to their allegiance to the God of their being. *For your generations.* The commemorative rest is to continue as long as the intelligent race whose origin it celebrates. *To know that I am the Lord that halloweth you.* The people called to his favor and hallowed to his service know themselves and are known by others to be his by the Sabbath which they receive, understand, and sacredly observe. 14, 15. The civil penalty of death, as well as the hierarchical one of excision from the people of God, is attached to its desecration. 16, 17. The perpetuity of its obligation, and the significance of its observance are then reiterated. In referring to its origin the sacred historian employs the remarkable expression, " on the seventh day he rested and was refreshed." The " refreshment " must be understood in a sense worthy of him who " fainteth not neither is weary." It includes, at all events, the pure delight arising from the consciousness of a design accomplished, and from the contemplation of the intrinsic excellence of the work.

18. At the end of the communication made to Moses, the two tables of stone on which were written the ten commandments by the finger of God. To receive these he was summoned to appear before the Lord on the mount (xxiv. 12). *The two tables* were, when placed side by side, somewhat less than two and a half cubits by one and a half, if they were to lie beside each other on the bottom of the ark (xxv. 10). If they were each a cubit square they might easily contain on the four surfaces which they present, the six hundred and twenty letters contained in the Decalogue, and could be readily carried by Moses. *Of testimony.* The ten words contain the testimony of the Lord regarding the relation of the people to him and their consequent obligations (xxv. 16). *Tables of stone.* Stone was the native material for a monumental inscription. It was in constant use for the purpose among the ancients. *Written with the finger of God.* As these ten words were proclaimed by the voice, so they are here said to be written by the finger, of God. But as they heard on that dread occasion "the voice of words, but saw no similitude," so the engraving on stone implies no visible finger of God, but only the putting forth of his power for the production of an authentic and permanent copy of the moral law.

## XIV. THE FIRST BREACH OF THE COVENANT.—Ex. xxxii.-xxxiv.

### CHAP. XXXII.—THE ACT OF APOSTASY.

XXXII. 1. And the people saw that Moses delayed to come down out of the mount, and the people gathered unto Aaron, and said unto him, Up, make us gods, who shall go before us: for this Moses, the man that brought us up out of the land of Mizraim, we know not what is become of him. 2. And Aaron said unto them, Pluck off the gold rings which are in the ears of your wives, your sons, and your daughters, and bring them unto me. 3. And all the people plucked off the gold rings which were in their ears, and brought them unto Aaron. 4. And he took them from their hand, and formed it with a graving tool, and made it a molten calf: and they said, These be thy gods, O Israel, who brought thee up out of the land of Mizraim. 5. And Aaron saw it, and built an altar before it: and Aaron proclaimed and said, A feast to the Lord to-morrow. 6. And they arose early on the morrow, and offered burnt-offerings and brought peace-offerings: and the people sat down to eat and to drink, and rose up to play. ¶ 48.

7. And the Lord spake unto Moses, Go, get thee down; for thy people, which thou broughtest out of the land of Mizraim have done corruptly. 8. They have turned aside quickly out of the way which I have commanded them: they have made them a molten calf, and bowed down to it and sacrificed unto it, and said, These be thy gods, O Israel, who have brought thee up out of the land of Mizraim. 9. And the Lord said unto Moses, I have seen this people, and behold it is a stiff-necked people. 10. And now let me alone, and my wrath shall wax hot against them, and I will consume them; and I will make of thee a great nation. 11. And Moses besought the Lord his God, and said, Why, O Lord, doth thy wrath wax hot against thy people, which thou hast brought out of the land of Mizraim with great power and with a mighty hand? 12. Why should Mizraim speak, saying, For evil he has brought them out, to slay them in the mountains, and to consume them from the face of the ground? Turn from thy hot wrath, and relent from the evil against thy people. 13. Remember Abraham, Isaac, and Israel, thy servants, to whom thou swarest by thyself, and spakest unto them, I will multiply your seed as the stars of heaven; and all this land of which I have spoken will I give unto your seed, and they shall inherit it forever. 14. And the Lord relented from the evil which he had said he would do unto his people. ¶ 49.

15. And Moses turned and went down from the mount, and
the two tables of the testimony in his hand: the tables were
written on both their sides; on this side and on that were they
written. 16. And the tables were the work of God; and the
writing was the writing of God, graven on the tables. 17.
And Joshua heard the voice of the people as they shouted;
and he said unto Moses, The voice of war is in the camp. 18.
And he said, It is not the voice of the cry for mastery, nor the
voice of the cry for weakness; the voice of them that sing do I
hear. 19. And it came to pass when he came nigh unto the
camp, then he saw the calf and the dances, and Moses's anger
waxed hot, and he cast the tables out of his hands, and brake
them beneath the mount. 20. And he took the calf which
they had made, and burned it in the fire, and ground it to
powder, and strawed it upon the water, and made the sons of
Israel drink of it. 21. And Moses said unto Aaron, What hath
this people done unto thee, that thou hast brought a great sin
upon them. 22. And Aaron said, Let not my lord's anger
wax hot; thou knowest the people, that they are set on evil.
23. And they said unto me, Make us gods, who shall go
before us; for this Moses, the man that brought us up out of
the land of Mizraim, we know not what is become of him. 24.
And I said unto them, Whosoever hath gold, pluck it off; and
they gave it me: and I cast it into the fire, and this calf
came out. 25. And Moses saw the people that they were broken
loose, for Aaron had cast them loose, for a hissing among their
adversaries. 26. And Moses stood in the gate of the camp,
and said, Whoever is for the Lord, come unto me; and all the
sons of Levi gathered unto him. 27. And he said unto them,
Thus saith the LORD God of Israel, Put every man his sword
on his thigh, pass and return from gate to gate in the camp,
and slay every man his brother, and every man his friend,

and every man his neighbor. 28. And the sons of Levi did according to the word of Moses: and there fell of the people that day about three thousand men. 29. And Moses said, Fill your hand to-day unto the LORD, that every man may be upon his son and upon his brother, and he may bestow upon you to-day a blessing

30. And it came to pass on the morrow, that Moses said unto the people, Ye have sinned a great sin: and now I will go to the LORD; mayhap I shall make an atonement for your sin. 31. And Moses returned unto the LORD, and said, Ah, this people have sinned a great sin, and made them gods of gold. 32. And now, if thou wilt forgive their sin——; and if not, blot me now out of thy book which thou hast written. 33. And the LORD said unto Moses, Whosoever hath sinned against me, him will I blot out of my book. 34. And now go lead the people to the place of which I have spoken unto thee; behold my angel shall go before thee: and in the day of my visitation I will visit their sin upon them. 35. And the Lord smote the people, because they made the calf which Aaron made. § 75.

Moses had now been forty days, or little short of six weeks, absent from the people. This was to him a period of adoration, inquiry, and instruction, and to the people of patience and probation. The awful voice of the Lord proclaiming in articulate words the ten commandments from the pillar of fire on Mount Sinai had struck upon their ears. They had been so awe-stricken with the scene that they besought their leader to hear himself the words of the Lord and communicate them to them, promising instant and unreserved obedience. The pillar of cloud and fire into which Moses had been received was still conspicuous on the mount. But still they had become familiar with the sublime spectacle, and the time of their leader's absence seemed long. The general mass of them at length gives way to impatience, and Aaron himself, yielding to their importunity, makes them a golden calf as a sensible representation of the God whom they still so grossly misapprehended. This was a direct violation of the second precept at least of that Decalogue which had received their voluntary assent under circumstanees of so great solemnity, though they seem still to have intended to acknowledge and adhere to the Lord their God. This untoward event warns us against the hasty conclusion that a whole people bowing before God in a moment of intense feeling have there and then passed from a fallen to a renewed state, rendered a unanimous homage to the God of mercy and salvation, learned the whole scheme of theological truth, or acquired the habit of intelligent and uniform obedience to the law of eternal rectitude. There has been in all an incipient intention of allegiance to the Lord of heaven, but only in some had this been the outgoing of a renewed heart, and only in a few has it been so strong as uniformly to resist the wayward impulses and lingering habits of the old nature. Even Aaron is carried away by the general movement. The few true hearts are weak and mute. This breach is well calculated to impress us with the fact that the true Saviour is yet to come, and that we are still in the time of types and shadows.

1–6. The image worship. *Moses delayed*, literally, put the expectants to shame by his non-appearance, a word very expressive of the state of mind into which the people had got towards the end of the forty days. *Make us gods.* The plural form is here carried in the syntax, and is therefore retained in the translation, though the one great object of worship is understood, as when we use the phrase, "the powers above." The idol which Aaron forms is accordingly a single figure. *Who shall go before us?* This implies an impatience of the unaccountable delay, which in their yet unsubdued dispositions they could not brook. They must away to that land of promise which presented in their imagination so bright a contrast to the bleak and barren wilderness in which they lay encamped. *This Moses*, with the wand and hand of power, had been to them a tangible proof of the divine presence, precluding the necessity of a visible symbol. But they *know not what is become of him.* He seems to have deserted them. At all events, he has been so long absent, that they seem to have lost confidence in him and respect for him. 2, 3. Aaron demands of them, as part of the material for making the idol, the rings of gold which were in their ears, apparently to make them feel their personal responsibility for the step which they required him to take. They hesitated not to comply. 4. *He took* the gold trinkets, *formed it*, the idol, with a graving tool, and made it a molten calf. The sacred historian takes no pleasure in this transaction, and therefore gives us only a brief and general account of it. It is probable that the idol was a piece of wood carved into shape, and then overlaid with the gold which was obtained by melting down the ear-rings; and so it became a molten calf. The people accept this as the similitude of God, who brought them out of Egypt. The model after which it was formed was no doubt the bull (either Mnevis of Heliopolis, representing the sun, or Apis of Memphis, representing Osiris), worshipped, as the people were well aware, by the Egyptians. 5, 6. Aaron, seeing their disposition, proceeds to erect an altar and proclaim a feast to the Lord on the morrow. The intention is to worship the Lord, though in an unworthy manner. The next day finds them early engaged in bringing burnt-offerings and peace-offerings. Of the latter it was the custom to partake, and after the festal repast *they rose up to play*. This phrase includes the wanton license which they had been accustomed to witness in the abominable rites of the heathen.

7–14. This religious revel had taken place on the fortieth day of Moses's abode on the mount. He had received the two tables from the Lord (xxxi. 18), and was therefore prepared to descend, when he was surprised with the order, "Go, get thee down, for thy people, which thou broughtest out of the land of Mizraim, have done corruptly." In the abhorrence which their idolatrous and licentious worship created, they are called the people of Moses, and their deliverance is ascribed to him. The crime they had committed is then briefly and emphatically described. 9, 10. After a pause, in which he has time to recover somewhat from his consternation of mind, the Lord calls upon Moses, who was no doubt preparing to make supplication on their behalf, to let him alone, that he may consume this stiff-necked people in the fire of his just wrath, and make of Moses a great nation. 11. This strong and natural expression of righteous indignation does not, however, forbid, but rather calls forth the beseeching expostulation of Moses. He urges three reasons why the Lord should forego the demands of justice in regard to the people. First, they were his own people. whom he had delivered from Egypt by great power; secondly, the glory of his wisdom and goodness would be tarnished in Egypt; and thirdly, his promises to their fathers would be neglected. Moses makes, and could make, no appeal to any mitigating circumstance in the people themselves. He rises, therefore, at once above all this to the purpose of God in bringing them out of Egypt, which was not to destroy, but to save, and that not themselves only, but by them the whole race ultimately; then to the lesson which was to be read to Egypt, and which would be unread if Israel were destroyed; and lastly, to the faith which was to be kept with the fathers who had received the promises. 14. At the intercession of Moses, the Lord relents. He by whom all events are foreseen, cannot be taken by surprise or waver in his purpose. His indignation at moral evil is simply the burning feeling of its intrinsic demerit, and of the requital which justice demands. His repentance is merely his relenting from the rigid enforcement of justice, in accordance with his determined purpose to dispense his mercy to returning penitents of the tempted and fallen race of man.

15–29. After this agitating scene, Moses turns hastily to descend from the mount. It is carefully noted that the two tables of the testimony were in his hand; their preciousness is indicated by the words of immutable truth which were inscribed on both sides of them; their sacredness by the remembrance that both the forming of the tables and the writing upon them was the immediate work of God. 17, 18. Joshua has been waiting for Moses, apparently outside the cloud of the divine presence. He is therefore ignorant of what is going on in the camp. He supposes it at first to be the sound of war. After listening further, Moses remarks that it is not the cry of the conqueror or the conquered, but of those who are making merry. 19, 20. The scene which was presented when they drew nigh to the camp aroused the regretful indignation of Moses. He felt that the solemn covenant with God had been shamefully violated. He cast down the tables containing the holy and gracious conditions of this covenant, and broke them before their eyes (Deut. ix. 17).

This act expressed with a terrible distinctness the consequence of their infatuated crime. He burned the calf, ground it to powder, and strowed it on the water, in the brook from which alone they were supplied with drink (Deut. ii. 21). The stock of the idol, being probably of wood, was burned, and, with the gold, reduced to a powder.

It is not likely that the gold was calcined by a chemical process. The drinking of the water mingled with the ashes of their idol was well calculated to remind them both that an idol is nothing in the world, and that they must all reap the bitter fruits of their common infatuation. 21–24. Moses now expostulates with Aaron for his highly inexcusable part in this crime. *What hath the people done unto thee?* What force had they put upon him? What was the necessity under which he had acted? Aaron's defence is that the people were set on evil, and that he yielded to their will. It is plain that he was guilty of a weak and timid compliance with what he knew to be wrong. And we are informed elsewhere that Moses made special intercession for him (Deut. ix. 20). 25–29. Moses now turns from Aaron to the people, whom he perceives to be *cast loose* from all right feeling and reverence for God, thrown into a state of reckless disorder and helpless anarchy, and exposed as an object of contempt to their adversaries. His sudden reappearance among them, his stern decisiveness, in marked contrast with the yielding feebleness of Aaron, the remembrance of the miracles which he was enabled to perform, the significant acts of breaking the tables of covenant and destroying the symbol of their guilt, had arrested their wild carousal and paralyzed their force of resistance. At this critical moment he summons to him all that are on the Lord's side, and commands them to gird on the sword, and, without respect of kindred, slay every man that stands out in his rebellion. The sons of Levi, moved, among other considerations, by a clearer insight and a deeper feeling of what is right, and it may be by their relationship to Moses, range themselves by his side, take the sword of execution, and three thousand of the people (doubtless the turbulent and rebellious) fall by their hands. 29. *Fill your hand to-day unto the Lord.* Take your part in that which is due to the Lord, *that every man may be upon* or against his nearest relative among the rebels against the Most High. In a moment of wide-spread treason against the Supreme Governor, to whom allegiance has been sworn, it behooves the few bold and loyal men to strike promptly and resolutely for the cause of truth and order. Such faithfulness in the day of treachery wins the blessing from that Sovereign whom there is no possibility of either deceiving or resisting. It need not seem strange that the Levites met with no effectual resistance in their stern vindication of the law. A great number of the people must have disapproved, though in silence, of the idolatrous proceeding. Many more were totally indifferent, though they suffered themselves to be led by the few turbulent and perverse spirits. All these would shrink away conscience-stricken before the eye, the hand, and the word of Moses. Only a few grovelling souls that lusted after the abominations of the idol-worship in Egypt would remain to fall under the swords of those whose ancestor was so prompt to avenge the adultery of Shekem (Gen. xxxiv. 25).

30–35. Moses turns from the now trembling people with the promise that he would intercede for them with the Lord. It is true that the Lord had relented from his fierce wrath. But Moses had meanwhile witnessed the deplorable revolt of the people. And though instant perdition was stayed, yet he felt that they were not yet fully pardoned or altogether restored to favor. His mode of intercession is brief, but forcible. He confesses the enormity of their sin, and then says, *And now, if thou wilt forgive their sin.* This is an impassioned form of entreaty. It leaves the consequence unuttered, in the urgency and inexpressible earnestness of desire. We may imagine the unspoken issue to be, that Moses would count life a blessing. For he immediately adds, *And if not, blot me now out of thy book which thou hast written.* He feels at the moment that life would be insupportable if his people were unforgiven. The book here spoken of is the book of life. It was even then the custom of every city in a literary community to keep a list of the burgesses. The Israelites were familiar with the custom of keeping a register of families (Gen. v. 1). The shoterim or "officers" were employed in keeping these and other registers (vs. 6). Hence Moses uses a familiar figure in speaking of God's book (Ps. lxix. 29; Dan. xii. 1). 33, 34. The Lord directs Moses to go and lead the people to the land of promise. He promises that *his angel* shall go before him. The angel here spoken of is that mediating angel of whom we read in Gen. xiv. 7, and Ex. xxiii. 20, who possesses the attributes and exercises the prerogatives of the Most High. But at the same time he adds, *In the day of my visitation I will visit their sin upon them.* The fulness of their iniquity was not yet come, though it is foreseen. The intercessor has prevailed, but he has not yet heard the sentence of full remission. 35. No further account of this plague or of its nature is given. *They made the calf which Aaron made.* Those who cause a thing to be made are chargeable with the making of it.

CHAP. XXXIII.—THE INTERCESSION OF MOSES.

XXXIII. 1. And the LORD spake unto Moses, depart and go
up hence, thou and the people which thou hast brought out of
the land of Mizraim, unto the land which I sware unto Abra-
ham, Isaac, and Jacob, saying, Unto thy seed will I give it.
2. And I will send an angel before thee, and I will drive out
the Kenaanite, the Amorite, and the Hittite, and the Perizzite,
the Hivite, and the Jebusite: 3. Unto a land flowing with
milk and honey; for I will not go up in the midst of thee,
because thou art a stiff-necked people, lest I consume thee
in the way. 4. And the people heard this evil saying, and
mourned; and no man put on his bravery. 5. And the LORD
said unto Moses, say unto the sons of Israel, Ye are a stiff-
necked people: in one moment, were I to go up in the midst
of thee, I should destroy thee: and now put off thy bravery
from thee, and I shall know what to do unto thee. 6. And
the sons of Israel stripped off their bravery afar from the
mount Horeb.

7. And Moses took the tent and pitched it for him without
the camp, afar off from the camp, and called it the tent of meet-
ing: and it came to pass that every one that sought the LORD,
went out unto the tent of meeting which was without the camp.
8. And it came to pass that when Moses went out unto the
tent all the people rose up, and stood every man at his tent
door; and they looked after Moses until he went into the tent.
9. And it came to pass as Moses went into the tent the pillar
of cloud came down, and stood at the door of the tent: and he

spake with Moses. 10. And all the people saw the pillar of cloud stand at the tent door: and all the people arose and bowed down, every man in his tent door. 11. And the LORD spake unto Moses face to face, as a man speaketh unto his friend: and he returned to the camp, and his minister Joshua, son of Nun, a young man, moved not out of the tent. ¶ 50.

12. And Moses said unto the LORD, Behold, thou sayest unto me, Bring up this people, and thou hast not let me know whom thou wilt send with me: and thou hast said, I know thee by name, and thou hast also found grace in mine eyes. 13. And now, if now I have found grace in thine eyes, shew me now thy way, and let me know thee, that I may find grace in thine eyes; and observe that this nation is thy people. 14. And he said, My presence shall go, and I will give thee rest. 15. And he said unto him, If thy presence go not, carry us not up hence. 16. And wherein shall it be known indeed that I and thy people have found grace in thine eyes, if not in thy going with us? and I and thy people shall be distinguished from all the people that is upon the face of the ground. ¶ 51.

17. And the Lord said unto Moses, This thing also that thou hast spoken will I do; for thou hast found grace in mine eyes, and I know thee by name. 18. And he said, Show me now thy glory. 19. And he said, I will make all my goodness to pass before thee, and I will proclaim the name of the LORD before thee: and I will be gracious to whom I will be gracious, and show mercy to whom I will show mercy. 20. And he said, Thou canst not see my face; for no man shall see me and live. 21. And the LORD said, Lo, there is a place by me, and thou shalt stand upon the rock. 22. And it shall come to pass, while my glory passeth by, that I will put thee in a clift of the rock: and I will cover thee with my hand while I pass by. 23. And I will take away my hand, and thou shalt see my back; but my face shall not be seen ¶ 52.

Moses receives a commission to conduct the people to the land destined for them, with the promise of the divine aid, but without the divine presence amidst them. He accordingly removes the tent where the Lord met him out of the camp. He entreats the Lord to go with him and shew him his glory.

1–6. The commission to Moses again refers to the people "whom thou hast brought up out of the land of Mizraim." The Lord does not yet choose to acknowledge them as his own. They have been separated by a new transgression, and they have not yet returned with penitence or borne any fruit meet for repentance. Nevertheless, his promise stands sure. He will send his angel (xxxii. 34) before them. But he will not go in the midst of them, as he had been hitherto doing and intended to do (xxv. 8), lest he should consume them in their perversity. 4–6. This unfavorable message affects the people with sorrow, and they begin to lay aside all gaiety in dress. While they are in this state of feeling the Lord sends a message to them by Moses requiring them to put off their bravery of apparel, that he may know what to do with them. This was a strong affirmation of their perversity. *In one moment, were I to go up.* If I were to go into the midst of thee, I must in that moment consume thee. But there is a hint of mercy in the following words sufficient to encourage them in their incipient repentance. *Afar from the mount Horeb*, retiring from the presence of the Lord to their tents.

7–11. *And Moses took the tent.* The tent here is not the sanctuary or sacred tent of the Lord, which was not yet constructed, nor any temporary dwelling of the Lord, as he only appeared hitherto in the pillar of cloud and fire, but simply the tent or pavilion of Moses, in which he officially abode. This he now pitched outside the camp at some distance, and called it the tent of meeting, because, like the tabernacle, it was the place where God met with him. The object of this removal was to maintain intercourse with the Lord, when he would no longer manifest himself amidst the people who had broken the covenant. Moses had not transgressed, and was still in fellowship with God. He will avail himself of this privilege to bring about a renewal of friendly relations between God and the people. The separation had also the effect of setting before the eyes of the people not only the continued followship of Moses with God, but also their own present estrangement from him. And now any one who sought the Lord for counsel, judgment, or aid, went out to the tent of meeting. 8. The people stood up with reverent interest to behold Moses going from the camp to the tent of meeting to discharge his official functions. 9. When Moses was in the tent the pillar of cloud came down and stood at the tent door, to manifest in the most solemn manner that God was with Moses. The wondering people bowed down with devout reverence when they beheld the supernatural signs of the divine presence. 11. The Lord spake with Moses, not by a voice from heaven but in the pillar standing at his door, *face to face, as a man speaketh with his friend.* He beheld not the divine essence (vs. 20), but such a vision of his face as is possible for a man to behold and live. When Moses was absent from the tent, Joshua his minister took his place.

12–16. The mind of Moses is in a state of anxious inquiry, and he now comes before the Lord to have all his pressing perplexities solved *Behold.* This is a matter of intense moment to me. *Thou sayest unto me, Bring up this people.* I feel the weight of this charge more than ever, in consequence of this breach of the newly-made and willingly-accepted covenant. This has interrupted the happy relation in which the people stood to thee. I do not yet fully comprehend the new relation in which they are to stand. (1.) Thou speakest of an angel who is to go before us. *And thou hast not let me know whom thou wilt send with me.* Who is this angel? Let me have some personal knowledge of him, that my mind may be at ease. *Thou hast said, I know thee by name, and thou hast also found grace in mine eyes.* Moses is personally known to God as one whom he has accepted and appointed to be the leader of his people. He therefore humbly prays to be informed how this angel stands to God and to himself. Much peace and comfort will result to him from this knowledge. (2.) The way in which this people are henceforth to be dealt with he desires to understand. They have been heedless and perverse. They may be so again. He wants to penetrate more thoroughly into the great principle on which their salvation rests with certainty amidst the uncertainty of their wills. *Shew me thy way* of salvation, of deliverance and guidance for this people to the promised end. *And let me know thee.* For all is in thee — the angel guide, the certain way. *That I may find grace in thine eyes,* present, constant, everlasting grace. (3.) Another word of thine has perplexed me. Thou callest the people mine, whom I have brought up. But observe that *this nation is thy people.* That is the plain undeniable truth, far transcending my merely ministerial part in their redemption. I beseech thee to look at this, and acknowledge it. Such is this wondrous prayer of faith springing up from the heart of Moses.

14–16. A single clear and cheering sentence encourages Moses. *My presence shall go, I will give thee rest.* My face or presence is of the same import as myself. Hence it is simply added, I will give thee rest. The angel, then, is the angel of his presence (Isa. lxiii. 9), in whom is his name (xxiii. 20), that is, the Lord himself in angelic office and presence. Moses seizes on the precious word. *If thy presence go not, carry us not up hence.* It is not a mere angel, but Jehovah, the angel of the covenant (Mal. iii. 1), whom he desires to have with him. This is the only incontestable evidence that they had found favor with God. *I and thy people.* He now associates himself with the people, and the people with God. The presence of the Lord distinguishes them from all the people on the whole earth.

17–23. The Lord now fully concedes the earnest request of Moses. He will go with them. He acknowledges them to be his people. The only other thing that remained on the mind of Moses was the "way" of the Lord regarding mercy and truth, righteousness and peace. To show mercy and yet do justly; to magnify grace and holiness at the same time; to bestow a perpetuity of blessing on a people wavering now and again into disobedience, was a problem that seemed to task the highest intelligence, to transcend the ordinary ways of providence, and call into exercise some inner and higher reaches of the Eternal mind. Moved by a wish to do his duty with intelligence, Moses ardently desires some insight into this profound mystery, and he feels that it touches the very centre of the divine nature, and involves the sublimest manifestations of his glory. Hence his last and grandest petition. *Show me now thy glory*, is the fitting close to his prevailing intercession. It is also granted, as far as man is capable here of receiving such a boon. 19. *All my goodness.* The goodness of God, his moral character, is the perfection of his glory. *The name of the Lord.* The name is the manifest and revealed nature. The Lord is Jehovah, the Creator of all things, the Keeper of covenant, the Performer of promise. *I will have been gracious to whom I will be gracious.* Here is discriminating and determinate grace. It is discriminating; some are taken and others left. It is determinate; the chosen are kept from the evil forever. This sentence is reiterated in other words. It solves some of Moses's difficulties. Whatever may befall, a remnant will be saved. 20. *Thou canst not see my face.* This separate sentence is emphatic and essential. My face is my direct, immediate, intrinsic self. The essential power of God is irresistible; the essential wisdom inscrutable to the creature. The essential holiness of the Almighty and All-wise is insupportable to that which is tainted with guilt. Hence man shall not see him and live. 21–23. *My back* is my averted, mediate, extrinsic self, visible to man in my works, my word, and my personal manifestations to my people. The place near the Lord where Moses was to stand, the clift of the rock in which he was to be put, the hand which was to cover him while the Lord in his glory passed by, and to be taken away that he might see the Lord when his face was averted, are the simple elements of a real scene, in which the Lord conveyed to the sense and the reason of Moses the deep things of his glorious grace in a manner which was exactly adapted to the capacity of the inquirer. Whether the clift of the rock was the grotto under the ruined mosque on the top of Jebel Musa it is not worth while to inquire.

### CHAP. XXXIV.—THE COVENANT RENEWED.

XXXIV. 1. And the Lord said unto Moses, Hew thee two tables of stone like the former: and I will write upon the tables the words that were on the former tables, which thou brakest. 2. And be ready in the morning: and come up in the morning unto Mount Sinai, and present thyself there to me on the top of the mount. 3. And no man shall come up with thee, nor let any man be seen in all the mount: nor let the flocks or herds feed before this mount. 4. And he hewed two tables of stone like the former, and Moses rose up early in the morning, and went up into mount Sinai, as the Lord commanded him: and he took in his hand the two tables of stone.

5. And the LORD came down in the cloud, and stood with
him there: and he proclaimed the name of the LORD. 6. And
the Lord passed by before his face, and proclaimed, the LORD,
the LORD God, merciful and gracious, long-suffering and abun-
dant in mercy and truth: 7. Keeping mercy for thousands,
forgiving iniquity and transgression and sin: and he will by
no means acquit the guilty, visiting the iniquity of the fathers
upon the sons and upon the sons' sons, unto the third and to
the fourth generation. 8. And Moses made haste, and bended
towards the earth and bowed down. 9. And he said, If now I
have found grace in thine eyes, O Lord, let the Lord now go
in the midst of us: for it is a stiff-necked people; and thou
wilt pardon our iniquity and our sin, and take us for thine
inheritance. 10. And he said, Lo, I make a covenant; before
all thy people I will do marvels, which have not been enacted
in all the earth nor in all the nations: and all the people
among which thou art shall see the work of the LORD; for it is
a terrible thing that I will do with thee.

11. Observe thou that which I command thee this day: lo, I
drive out before thee, the Amorite, and the Kenaanite, and the
Hittite, and the Perizzite, and the Hivite, and the Jebusite.
12. Take heed to thyself, lest thou make a covenant with the
inhabitants of the land whither thou goest, lest it be a snare
in the midst of thee. 13. For ye shall destroy their altars,
and break their pillars, and cut down their statues. 14. For
thou shalt bow down to no other God: for the LORD, whose
name is Jealous, is a jealous God. 15. Lest thou make a cov-
enant with the inhabitant of the land, and they go a whoring
after their gods, and sacrifice unto their gods, and one call thee,
and thou eat of his sacrifice; 16. And thou take of their

daughters unto thy sons, and their daughters go a whoring after their gods, and make thy sons go a whoring after their gods. 17. Molten gods thou shalt not make thee. 18. The feast of unleavened bread shalt thou keep: seven days thou shalt eat unleavened bread, as I commanded thee in the set time of the month Abib: for in the month Abib thou camest out of Mizraim. 19. All that openeth the womb is mine; and all thy cattle, the firstling of ox or sheep, that is a male. 20. And the firstling of an ass thou shalt redeem with a lamb; and if thou redeem it not, then shalt thou break its neck: all the first-born of thy sons thou shalt redeem, and none shall appear before me empty. 21. Six days thou shalt labor, and on the seventh day thou shalt rest: in ploughing and in reaping time thou shalt rest. 22. And thou shalt keep the feast of weeks, of the first fruits of wheat harvest, and the feast of ingathering at the turn of the year. 23. Three times in the year shall all your males appear before the Lord, the LORD God of Israel. 24. For I will dispossess the nations before thee, and enlarge thy border: and no man shall desire thy land, when thou goest up to appear before the LORD thy God three times in the year. 25. Thou shalt not offer the blood of thy sacrifice with leaven: and the sacrifice of the passover feast shall not be left unto the morning. 26. The first of the first-fruits of thy ground thou shalt bring unto the house of the LORD thy God: thou shalt not seethe a kid in its mother's milk.

§ 53.

27. And the LORD said unto Moses, Write thou these words: for after the tenor of these words I have made a covenant with thee and with Israel. 28. And he was there with the LORD forty days and forty nights; he ate not bread nor drank water: and he wrote upon the tables the words of the covenant, the ten words.

29. And it came to pass when Moses went down from Mount
Sinai, that the two tables of testimony were in Moses's hand
when he went down from the mount; and Moses knew not
that the skin of his face shone when he talked with him. 30.
And Aaron and all the sons of Israel saw Moses, and lo, the
skin of his face shone: and they were afraid to come nigh him.
31. And Moses called them, and Aaron and all the princes in
the assembly returned to him: and Moses talked with them.
32. And afterward all the sons of Israel came nigh: and he
commanded them all that the LORD had spoken with him in
Mount Sinai. 33. And Moses ceased from speaking with
them, and he put a vail upon his face. 34. And when Moses
went in before the LORD to speak with him, he took the vail
off, until he came out: and he came out and spake unto the
sons of Israel that which he was commanded. 35. And the
sons of Israel saw the face of Moses, that the skin of Moses's
face shone: and Moses put the vail upon his face again, until
he went in to speak with him.

The order is now given to Moses to return to the mount, when the Lord proclaims himself the God of mercy and justice, and renews the covenant, with certain injunctions suitable to the occasion.

1–4. *Hew thee.* The former tables were made by God himself. As they had been broken by Moses in the outburst of his righteous indignation against the idolatry of the people, the Lord directs him to prepare a second set of tables, on which he promises to write a second copy of the law. 3. *And no man shall come up with thee.* On the former occasion the elders, with Aaron, Nadab, and Abihu, accompanied him a certain way up the mount, and Joshua, apparently, to the edge of the cloud that was on the top. But no man went with him into the cloud, and, as in the case of the lawgiving (xix. 12), neither the people nor the cattle were permitted to appear on the mount.

5–10. When Moses went up with the new tables the Lord vouchsafes to come down and meet with him. In fulfilment of his promise he proclaims before him the name of the Lord. *The Lord*, the Creator and Covenant-keeper. This name is here rendered emphatic by being repeated. *God*, the Eternal and Almighty. Then follow seven significant characteristics, three pairs referring to his mercy, and a single one affirming his justice. *Merciful and gracious*, disposed to relieve suffering and dispense happiness. *Long-suffering and abundant in mercy and truth*, having long patience and much kindness and truthfulness in store for the penitent. The former pair speaks of the general tendency, the latter of the long duration and vast plenitude of the divine compassion and constancy. This serves to calm the solicitude of Moses, brooding in sadness on the recent perversity of the people. *Keeping mercy for thousands, forgiving iniquity and transgression and sin.* This speaks at length not of disposition or its amount, but of the certain and final application of mercy and forgiveness to all generations of those who seek it with penitence. Sin is moral aberration; transgression involves breach of trust; and iniquity implies perversity of conduct. The last appears the most aggravated; yet all these forms of sin he may and will forgive the returning penitent. Yet at the same time the proclamation runs, *he will by no means acquit.* And as a special case of the unalterable principle of rectitude, he visits the iniquity of the impenitent, even though it descend to the son from the father (xx. 5). In the case of those forgiven, the guilt that cannot be acquitted falls on the head of a voluntary and accepted substitute. The perplexity of Moses is now so far solved, that he sees mercy secured and perpetuated in some to all generations, while others will obstinately refuse it and inevitably perish. He can now repose in tranquil confidence on the purpose of him who keeps mercy for a thousand generations of them that love him (xx. 6). This purpose determines the perpetuity of the church on earth, though many from time to time fall away. He does not tell us, he could not convey in words, what he saw when the Lord passed by. But he records for our comfort the sublime proclamation which he heard, containing the substance of that revelation which was then made to him of the glory of God. Filled with wonder and solemn awe, he made haste, bent his head and bowed his body in profoundest reverence.

9, 10. Moses now repeats his already effectual intercession. *O Lord.* He addresses God now as the moral Governor and Judge, to whom it pertains to dispense pardon. *For it is a stiff-necked people.* The *for* here applies not to the first clause only, but to the whole sentence following. It is a stiff-necked people whom thou wilt pardon and make thine inheritance. Therefore, go with us. *Our iniquity and our sin.* Moses here identifies himself with the people, and entreats forgiveness for the common guilt of all. His conduct in this whole transaction is actuated by motives purely benign. 10. The covenant is now restored. It is to be celebrated by marvels of unparalleled power. *Enacted*, effected by no less than creative power. The whole people will behold the work of the Lord, which will be terrible in its judgments upon the adversaries.

11–26. Here a series of admonitions suitable to the occasion is repeated and enforced. 11–16. No treaty is to be made with the old inhabitants of the land, as it would involve a compliance, or a temptation to comply, with their idolatrous customs (xxiii. 23, 24). The list of nations here given differs from that in iii. 8, by giving the first place to the Amorites, with whom the people are to come first in contact (xxiii. 23). *Lest it be a snare in the midst of thee*, insinuating a new kind of apostasy from thy own God. *Their pillars*, the monumental stones connected with their idols. *Their statues*, the wooden posts or rudely carved figures of Astarte, the female moon-deity of the Kenaanites. *Whose name is Jealous.* The figure of marriage, applied to the covenant relation of God and his people (xx. 5), is now carried a step further. The worship of idols or false gods is described as fornication or adultery, a term peculiarly appropriate to rites that were grossly licentious in themselves, as well as acts of high treason against the only true God. Intermarriage with these votaries of idolatry and uncleanness is expressly forbidden.

17–26. Molten gods (xx. 23) are again emphatically prohibited. The feast of unleavened bread (xii.), the sanctification of the first-born (xiii.), the observance of the Sabbath (xvi.), the other annual festivals (xxiii. 10–19) are then called to mind, and their observance reinforced. As they are connected with leading events in the national history, and are eminently characteristic of the national worship, they are well fitted to awaken the gratitude and keep alive the faith of the ransomed people. 24. A promise is given that their lands will not be coveted or seized when they are gone to appear at the great festivals before the Lord. 25, 26. Certain minute but significant directions are here reiterated. Leaven, as the emblem of moral corruption, is to be absent from their offerings. The passover lamb, as the type of atonement, is to be all-necessary, as well as all-sufficient for its immediate use. The first of the first-fruits is to be dedicated to the Lord, as the beginning and earnest of all that we have. The mother's milk, that which is given with maternal kindness for nourishment, is not to be coldly turned into a means of destruction. These four secondary regulations, constantly whispering in our ears that the service of God must be sincere, prompt, entire, and tender, are well calculated to cultivate in the soul a growing abhorrence of idolatry, with all its inherent and attendant abominations.

27, 28. *Write thou these words*, evidently the record of this interview and all that was said on the occasion; as he wrote the book of the original covenant (xxiv. 4–7). These are to be on record, as the special conditions of the civil part of the covenant. *Forty days and forty nights.* The descendants of Israel left Egypt on the fifteenth of the first month (xii.) On the first of the third month (xix. 1) they reached the Wilderness of Sinai, and probably on the sixth the law was proclaimed on the mount. On the seventh the covenant was ratified, and Moses and the elders ascended some part of the mount (xxiv. 4). The seventh day after, apparently, and in that case on the fourteenth of the third month, Moses was called and entered into the cloud. Forty days after, or on the twenty-third of the fourth month, he descends to witness the festival in honor of the golden calf. The Talmud, however, places this act of apostacy on the 17th of Tammuz, and therein agrees with many interpreters, who include the six days during which Moses waited before he was summoned into the cloud surrounding the divine presence in the forty days of his abode on the mount. On the day after (xxxii. 30) Moses makes intercession for the people, removes the official tent from the camp, and receives a favorable answer from the Lord. The next day, apparently (xxxiv. 2), is the first of the second forty days spent on the mount. Allowing twenty-nine days and thirty days for the next two months, we arrive at the fifth of the sixth month, as the day on which he may have descended the second time. Here, again, Jewish tradition assumes that he ascended on the first of the sixth month and came down on the tenth of the seventh, which is the day of atonement. But there seems to be no reason for allowing an interval of at least thirty-six days to elapse between the first descent and the second ascent. Nor is there anything suitable in the people afflicting their souls on the day of Moses's return from the mount; and there is certainly no allusion to the day of atonement in the narrative. And further, only five months and a half are left for the construction of the tabernacle, which was finished within the first year. Josephus assigns seven months for this undertaking, which is a short enough period. If Moses came down on the fifth of the sixth month, we have nearly seven months, and if his descent was six days earlier, or on the last day of the fifth month, we have precisely seven months for the construction of the tabernacle and all its appurtenances. *And he wrote* From the first verse we learn that it was God himself who wrote the ten words on the two tables which Moses had prepared (Deut. x. 4).

29–35. The glory on the face of Moses. *Moses knew not.* He was not conscious of this appearance in himself, which was obvious to others. *That the skin of his face shone*, sent forth rays of light. The original word signifies to spring forth as horns, and hence the Vulgate has *esse cornutam*, and the painters have drawn Moses with horns. The Lord had passed by him. He had even stood with him and *talked with him.* So much of his glory had shone upon the senses and the face of Moses as mortal man was able to bear. 30. This extraordinary lustre struck Aaron and the people with wonder and apprehension. They were afraid to come nigh him, as one who still bore the conspicuous marks of his long converse with God. 31, 32. When he called them, however, Aaron and the princes of the assembly approached, and he conversed with them. The people then drew nigh, and he gave them in command all that the Lord had communicated to him. 33–35. When his discourse was finished *he put a vail on his face.* When his public and official part was performed, he vails the dazzling lustre of his face, not only in modest reserve, but also for the convenience and comfort of private intercourse. When, however, he went in before the Lord, he withdrew the vail until he had received his commands and delivered them to the people. Hence it was his custom to resume the vail until he went in to speak with the Lord. The place of communication was, we may suppose, the separate tent of meeting, until the tabernacle was erected. The awe-struck multitude had here a conspicuous sign before their eyes that Moses was the veritable servant of the Most High God, the prime minister of the old covenant. The shrinking of their gaze from this borrowed splendor demonstrated to them that they were not yet prepared for the higher manifestations of the divine glory itself. The vail on the face of Moses, like the vail before the mercy-seat, taught them that the present economy was adapted to the weakness of their spiritual vision; while so much of the brightness shone through as to satisfy their present needs and capacities, and give them a foreglance and earnest of what awaited them in the advancing stages of their spiritual training (2 Cor. iii. 7–18).

Thus ends this sudden outbreak of idolatry and sad interruption of spiritual prosperity in a new and unexpected display of the divine mercy vouchsafed on the intercession of Moses to the chastened and repentant people. The breach being healed, and the covenant restored with even additional splendor, the construction of the tabernacle will now proceed.

## XV. THE TABERNACLE MADE AND SET UP.—Ex. xxxv.-xl.

### CHAP. XXXV.—PREPARATIONS FOR MAKING THE TABERNACLE.

22. חָח *hook, clasp, ring;* used for female ornament, and for an instrument in the nose of a bull for controlling it. נֶזֶם a nose or *ear-ring* (Gen. xxiv. 47; xxxv. 4); r. *bind* or *lace.* טַבַּעַת a finger-*ring;* r. *dip.* כּוּמָז *little ball, bead, necklace of beads.*

XXXV. 1. And Moses gathered all the assembly of the sons of Israel, and said unto them, These are the words which the Lord commanded us to do. 2. Six days shall work be done, and on the seventh day shall be for you a holy Sabbath of rest to the Lord: whosoever doeth work therein shall die. 3. Ye shall not kindle a fire in all your dwellings on the Sabbath day. ¶ 54.

4. And Moses spake unto all the assembly of the sons of Israel, saying, This is the word which the Lord hath com-

manded, saying, 5. Take from among you an offering unto the Lord; whosoever is willing of heart shall bring it, an offering of the Lord: gold and silver and brass; 6. And blue and purple and crimson; and fine linen and goats' hair; 7. And rams' skins dyed red, and badgers' skins; and shittah wood; 8. And oil for the light; and spices for the anointing oil, and for the incense of perfumes; 9. And onyx stones and stones for setting, for the ephod and for the breastplate. 10. And every one wise of heart among you shall come and make all that the Lord hath commanded. 11. The tabernacle, its tent and its covering; its taches and its boards, its bars, its pillars, and its sockets; 12. The ark and its staves, the mercy-seat, and the vail of covering; 13. The table and its staves, and all its vessels, and the shew-bread; 14. And the candlestick for the light, and its vessels and its lamps, and the oil for the lights; 15. And the altar of incense and its staves, and the anointing oil and the incense of perfumes, and the cover for the door at the entrance of the tabernacle; 16. The altar of burnt-offering and the brazen grate for it, its staves and all its vessels; the laver and its stand; 17. The hangings of the court, its pillars and their sockets, and the cover for the door of the court; 18. The pins of the tabernacle and the pins of the court and their cords; 19. The garments of office to minister in the sanctuary, the holy garments for Aaron the priest, and the garments of his sons to serve as priests.

20. And all the assembly of the sons of Israel went forth from the presence of Moses. 21. And they came, every man whom his heart stirred up; and every one whom his spirit made willing brought the Lord's offering for the work of the tent of meeting and for all its service and for the holy garments. 22. And they came the men with the women: all the willing of heart brought clasps and ear-rings and rings and necklaces,

all jewels of gold; and every man made a wave-offering of gold unto the LORD. 23. And every man with whom was found blue and purple and crimson, and fine linen and goats' hair, and rams' skins dyed red, and badgers' skins, brought *them*. 24. Every one making an offering of silver and brass brought the offering of the LORD: and every one with whom was found shittah wood for any work of the service brought it. 25. And every woman wise of heart span with her hands: and they brought yarn, blue and purple and crimson, and fine linen. 26. And all the women whose heart stirred them up with wisdom span the goats' hair. 27. And the rulers brought onyx stones and stones for setting, for the ephod and for the breastplate; 28. And spice and oil, for the light and for the anointing oil and for the incense of perfumes. 29. Every man and woman whose heart made them willing to bring for all the work which the LORD commanded to do by the hand of Moses, the sons of Israel brought a free-will offering unto the LORD. ¶ 55.

30. And Moses said unto the sons of Israel, See, the Lord hath called by name Bezalel, son of Uri, son of Hur, of the tribe of Judah. 31. And filled him with the spirit of God in wisdom, in understanding, and in knowledge, and in all workmanship; 32. And to devise designs, to work in gold and in silver and in brass; 33. And in cutting of stone for setting and in carving of wood, to make every work of design. 34. And he hath put it in his heart to teach, both in him and in Aholiab, son of Ahisamak, of the tribe of Dan. 35. Them hath he filled with wisdom of heart to do all the work of the artificer, and the designer, and the embroiderer in blue and in purple and in crimson and in fine linen, and of the weaver; who do every work and devise designs.

Of the remaining six chapters, the first records the offerings and other preparations for the tabernacle ; the next four, the progress from the beginning to the end of the work ; and the last, the actual erection and inauguration of the house of God. There is little to remark on these chapters, as they are mainly a detail of the execution of that of which the plan is contained in chapters xxv.–xxxi.

1–3. A preliminary injunction concerning the Sabbath. Moses begins where the directions concerning the sanctuary close (xxxi. 12–17). The special precept of this passage is, " Ye shall not kindle a fire in all your dwellings on the Sabbath day." This precludes smith-work and cooking. For domestic comfort, fire was not a thing of necessity or mercy in the Peninsular of Sinai. In colder regions it is otherwise ; and there the law of necessity or mercy regulates the observance of the Sabbath.

4–19. The materials required of the people, and the articles to be made for the sanctuary are here specified. The former are repeated from xxv. 1–7. 10. The *wise of heart* are those who possess the natural gift or the acquired training for the various mechanical arts. 11–19. The whole apparatus of the sanctuary is here enumerated from the previous directions (xxv. 30). The garments of office are repeated from xxxi. 10.

20–29. The contribution of the people. *The Lord's offering* (תְּרוּמָה, xxv. 2), that which is lifted up in token of dedication to the Lord (xxix. 24, 27). 22. *The man with the woman.* Both sexes join in this free-will offering. The *jewels of gold* are apparently the offerings of the women. *Every man made a wave-offering.* While each female presented her own gold trinket of whatever kind, the men seem to have made a joint contribution of gold. This may account for the phrase " made a wave-offering " (xxix. 24). 25. *Span with her hands.* This was a feminine employment. *Blue and purple and crimson.* This implies that the dyeing preceded the spinning. As the fine linen is distinguished from the colored stuffs, it is probable that they were of wool (Num. xix. 6 ; Heb. ix. 19). 29. *The sons of Israel.* This verse proves that the phrase may extend, when the occasion requires, to the female as well as the male descendants of Israel.

30–35. The calling of Bezalel and Aholiab is announced to the people (xxxi. 1–6).

### CHAP. XXXVI.—THE TABERNACLE MADE.

XXXVI. 1. And Bezalel and Aholiab, and every wise-hearted man in whom the LORD put wisdom and understanding to know how to do every work of the service of the sanctuary, shall do according to all that the LORD hath commanded. 2. And
Moses called Bezalel and Aholiab and every wise-hearted man, in whose heart the LORD had put wisdom, every one whom his heart stirred up to draw near to the work to do it. 3. And
they received of Moses all the offering which the sons of Israel had brought for the work of the service of the sanctuary to do it: and they brought unto him yet a free offering from morning to morning. 4. Then came all the wise men that were doing the work of the sanctuary, every man from his work which he was doing. 5. And they spake unto Moses, saying,
The people are bringing much more than enough for the service of the work, which the Lord commanded to make. 6.
And Moses commanded, and they issued a proclamation in the camp, saying, Let not man or woman make any more work for the offering of the sanctuary. And the people were restrained from bringing. 7. And their work was sufficient for all the work to make it, and more. § 77.

8. And all the wise of heart among them that were doing the work of the tabernacle made ten curtains of twined fine linen, and blue and purple and crimson: with cherubim of cunning work made he them. 9. The length of one curtain
was eight and twenty cubits, and the breadth of one curtain four cubits: the curtains had all one measure. 10. And he
coupled five curtains one unto another; and five curtains he coupled one unto another. 11. And he made loops of blue on
the selvedge of the first curtain at the end in the coupling: so he made in the selvedge of the last curtain in the second

coupling. 12. Fifty loops made he in the first curtain; and fifty loops made he in the edge of the curtain that was in the second coupling; the loops matching one another. 13. And he made fifty taches of gold, and coupled the curtains one to another with the taches; and the tabernacle became one. ¶ 56.

14. And he made curtains of goats' hair for a tent over the tabernacle; eleven curtains made he them. 15. The length of one curtain was thirty cubits, and four cubits the breadth of one curtain; the eleven curtains had one measure. 16. And he coupled five curtains by themselves, and six curtains by themselves. 17. And he made fifty loops on the selvedge of the last curtain in the coupling; and fifty loops made he on the selvedge of the curtain in the second coupling. 18. And he made fifty taches of brass to couple the tent that it might be one. 19. And he made a covering for the tent of rams' skins dyed red, and a covering of badgers' skins from above. § 78.

20. And he made boards for the tabernacle of shittah wood standing up. 21. Ten cubits was the length of a board, and a cubit and a half the breadth of one board. 22. Two tenons were to one board, set alike one to another: thus he made for all the boards of the tabernacle. 23. And he made the boards for the tabernacle, twenty boards on the south side southward. 24. And forty sockets of silver made he under the twenty boards; two sockets under one board for its two tenons, and two sockets under another board for its two tenons. 25. And for the other side of the tabernacle northwards he made twenty boards. 26. And their forty sockets of silver; two sockets under one board, and two sockets under another board. 27. And for the rear of the tabernacle westward he made six boards. 28. And two boards made he for the corners of the tabernacle in the rear. 29. And they were doubled beneath, and together they were complete at the top

for the one ring; thus he did for the two of them for the two
corners. 30. And there were eight boards, and their sockets
of silver were sixteen sockets; two sockets each under the one
board. 31. And he made bars of shittah wood, five for the
boards of the one side of the tabernacle, 32. And five bars
for the boards of the other side of the tabernacle, and five bars
for the boards of the tabernacle to the rear westward. 33.
And he made the middle bar to shoot in the middle of the
boards from end to end. 34. And he overlaid the boards with
gold, and made their rings of gold to be places for the bars:
and he overlaid the bars with gold.

35. And he made the vail of blue and purple and crimson,
and twined fine linen: of cunning work made he it, with cher-
ubim. 36. And he made for it four pillars of shittah, and
overlaid them with gold, and their hooks were of gold: and
he cast for them four sockets of silver. 37. And he made a
cover for the door of the tent of blue and purple and crimson,
and twined fine linen, wrought with needlework. 38. And
its five pillars and their hooks, and he overlaid their chap-
iters and their rods with gold; and their five sockets were
of brass. ¶ 57.

The commencement of the work and the construction of the tabernacle are recorded in this chapter, which after the first section corresponds with chapter xxvi.

1–7. The materials for the work handed over to the workmen. *And Bezalel ..... shall do* (וְעָשָׂה). This verse is properly the close of the address of Moses to the people, and should have stood at the end of the previous chapter. 2. He now addresses Bezalel, Aholiab, and their men. 3–7. The people bring enough, and more than, enough for the work, until they are required to desist. As the spinning and weaving must have begun almost simultaneously with the labors of the other workmen, they were bringing in wrought materials for some months after the works began.

8–38. The construction of the tabernacle is here minutely reported. The full detail into which the sacred writer enters indicates the paramount importance attached to the work. The narrative begins with the tabernacle itself, which is the largest piece of the work. But we may suppose that other sets of workmen were engaged on the furniture, the court, and the priestly dresses. It was necessary also that the tabernacle should be ready for the sacred utensils as soon as they were prepared. The sections of this chapter after the first correspond nearly with those of chapter xxvi.

## CHAP. XXXVII.—THE FURNITURE IN THE TABERNACLE.

XXXVII. 1. And Bezalel made the ark of shittah wood;
two cubits and a half the length of it, a cubit and a half
the breadth of it, and a cubit and a half the height of it. 2.
And he overlaid it with pure gold within and without; and
made for it a crown of gold round about. 3. And he cast
for it four rings of gold upon its four feet: and two rings
were on the one side of it, and two rings on the other side
of it. 4. And he made staves of shittah wood, and overlaid
them with gold. 5. And he put the staves in the rings on
the sides of the ark, to bear the ark. 6. And he made a
mercy-seat of pure gold; two cubits and a half the length of
it, and a cubit and half the breadth of it. 7. And he made
two cherubim of gold; of beaten work made he them, on the
two ends of the mercy-seat. 8. One cherub on the one end,
and another cherub on the other end; out of the mercy-seat
made he the cherubim on its two ends. 9. And the cherubim
were spreading out two wings above, covering the mercy-seat
with their wings, and their faces each to the other; toward the
mercy-seat were the faces of the cherubim. ¶ 58.

10. And he made the table of shittah wood; two cubits the
length of it, and a cubit the breadth of it, and a cubit and a

half the height of it. 11. And he overlaid it with pure gold, and made for it a crown of gold round about. 12. And he made for it a border of a hand breadth round about, and made a crown of gold for the border thereof round about. 13. And he cast for it four rings of gold; and put the rings on the four corners of its four feet. 14. Over against the border were the rings, the places for the staves to bear the table. 15. And he made the staves of shittah wood, and overlaid them with gold, to bear the table. 16. And he made the vessels which are upon the table, its dishes, and its bowls, and its flagons, and its cups, to pour out withal, of pure gold. ¶ 59.

17. And he made the candlestick of pure gold: of beaten work made he the candlestick; its block and its shaft, its cups its knops and its flowers, were of the same. 18. And six branches coming out of its sides; three branches of the candlestick out of the one side, and three branches of the candlestick out of the other side: 19. Three almond-shaped cups in one branch, a knop and a flower; and three almond-shaped cups in another branch, a knop and a flower: so for the six branches coming out of the candlestick. 20. And in the candlestick were four almond-shaped cups, its knops and its flowers. 21. And a knop under two branches of the same, and a knop under two branches of the same, and a knop under two branches of the same, for the six branches coming out of it. 22. Their knops and their branches were of the same; all of it was one beaten piece of pure gold. 23. And he made its seven lamps, and its snuffers and its snuff-dishes of pure gold. 24. Of a talent of pure gold made he it and all its vessels. ¶ 60.

25. And he made the altar of incense of shittah wood; a cubit the length of it, and a cubit the breadth of it, being square, and two cubits the height of it; its horns were of the

same. 26. And he overlaid it with pure gold, its top and its sides round about and its horns; and he made for it a crown of gold round about. 27. And two rings of gold made he for it under the crown of it, on the two flanks thereof, on the two sides of it, for places for the staves to bear it withal. 28. And he made the staves of shittah wood, and overlaid them with gold. 29. And he made the holy anointing oil, and the pure incense of perfumes, the work of the perfumer. § 79.

This chapter records the making of the ark and mercy-seat, the table, the candlestick, and the altar of incense. These are all the internal furniture of the tabernacle. It corresponds to chapter xxv., wanting the first nine verses, and to vs. 1–5, and 22–25 of chapter xxx. The last section is here summed up in a single verse.

3. *And he cast ..... upon its four feet.* The sense is pregnant here. It is understood that the rings, when cast, are put upon the feet of the ark. So in xxxviii. 5.

### CHAP. XXXVIII.—THE COURT AND ITS FURNITURE.

XXXVIII. 1. And he made the altar of burnt-offering of shittah wood; five cubits the length of it, and five cubits the breadth of it, being square, and three cubits the height of it. 2. And he made the horns of it on the four corners thereof, the horns thereof of the same; and he overlaid it with brass. 3. And he made all the vessels of the altar, the boxes, and the shovels, and the basins, and the flesh-hooks, and the fire-pans; all its vessels made he of brass. 4. And he made for the altar a grate of net-work of brass, under its border beneath unto the half of it. 5. And he cast four rings in the four ends of the grate of brass, to be places for the staves. 6. And he made the staves of shittah wood, and overlaid them with brass. 7. And he put the staves in the rings on the sides of the altar to bear it withal: hollow, of boards, made he it. § 80.

8. And he made the laver of brass, and its stand of brass, of the mirrors of the women who attended at the door of the tent of meeting. § 81.

9. And he made the court; for the south side southward, the hanging of the court of fine linen twined a hundred cubits. 10. Their pillars twenty, and their sockets of brass twenty; the hooks of the pillars and their rods of silver. 11. And for the north side a hundred cubits, their pillars twenty and their sockets of brass twenty; the hooks of the pillars and their rods of silver. 12. And for the west side the hangings were fifty cubits, their pillars ten and their sockets ten; the hooks of the pillars and their rods of silver. 13. And for the east side, eastward, fifty cubits. 14. The hangings fifteen cubits for the wing; their pillars three and their sockets three. 15. And for the other wing on this side, and on that side of the court gate, the hangings were fifteen cubits; their pillars three and their sockets three. 16. All the hangings of the court round about were of fine linen twined. 17. And the sockets for the pillars were of brass, the hooks of the pillars and their rods of silver, and the overlaying of their chapiters of silver: and all the pillars of the court were joined with rods of silver. 18. And the covering of the court gate was wrought with needlework of blue and purple and crimson, and fine linen twined: and twenty cubits was the length, and the height in the breadth five cubits, matching the hangings of the court. 19. And their pillars four, and their sockets of brass four; their hooks of silver, and the overlaying of their chapiters and their rods of silver. 20. And all the pins for the tabernacle and for the court round about were of brass. 23. § § § 82.

21. These are the accounts of the tabernacle, the tabernacle of the testimony, that was counted at the word of Moses, the service of the Levites by the hand of Ithamar, son of Aaron

the priest. 22. And Bezalel, son of Uri, son of Hur, of the tribe of Judah, made all that the Lord commanded Moses. 23. And with him Aholiab, son of Ahisamak, of the tribe of Dan, an artificer and designer, and an embroiderer in blue and in purple and in crimson and in fine linen. 24. All the gold that was used for the work in all the work of the sanctuary, even the gold of the offering, was nine and twenty talents, and seven hundred and thirty shekels, by the shekel of the sanctuary. 25. And the silver of those who were numbered of the assembly was a hundred talents, and a thousand and seven hundred and five and seventy shekels, by the shekel of the sanctuary. 26. A beka for the poll, the half shekel by the shekel of the sanctuary, for every one passing into the numbered from twenty years old and upward, for six hundred thousand and three thousand and five hundred and fifty. 27. And the hundred talents of silver went for casting the sockets of the sanctuary and the sockets of the vail; a hundred sockets for a hundred talents, a talent for a socket. 28. And of the thousand and seven hundred and five and seventy shekels made he hooks for the pillars, and overlaid their chapiters, and rodded them. 29. And the brass of the wave-offering was seventy talents and two thousand and four hundred shekels. 30. And with it he made the sockets for the door of the tent of meeting, and the brazen altar and the brazen grate for it, and all the vessels of the altar; 31. And the sockets of the court round about and the sockets of the court gate; and all the pins of the tabernacle and all the pins of the court round about.

This chapter describes the construction of the altar of burnt-offering, the laver and the court in which they were placed, and ends with an account of the metals employed in the work.

1–20 correspond with chapter xxvii. 1–8, xxx. 18, and xxvii. 9–18.

21–31. This passage refers to xxx. 11–16, and xxvii. 19. It is an account of the metals required for the sanctuary. *That was counted* refers directly to the tabernacle, concerning which the account was kept. *By the hand of Moses*, at his order. *The service of.* This reckoning was the business of the Levites under the superintendence of Ithamar. 25–26. *The silver of those that were numbered of the assembly.* The order given in xxx. 11–16, including the payment of a beka for every male from twenty years old and upwards, had been so far executed, probably on the day of atonement. The sum of the class numbered is six hundred and three thousand five hundred and fifty. This was an important part of the service of the Levites (vs. 21). This census was completed by the examination of the documents and the drawing up of an authenticated register about half a year after, of which we have an account in the first chapters of Numbers. 27, 28. From these verses it appears that a talent was equal to 3000 shekels. Reckoning the shekel at 220 grains, we find that the gold amounts to nearly 3350 pounds troy weight, the silver to nearly 11,526 pounds, and the brass to nearly 8112 pounds.

The Israelites had left Egypt the year in which they made this contribution for the construction of the tabernacle. Though many of them were employed in servile labors, yet the people as a whole must have been possessed of considerable wealth. To this the Egyptians made a considerable accession at their departure. The sum here contributed is moderate in comparison with the enormous treasures amassed by the Assyrians, the Babylonians, the Arabians, and the Egyptians themselves.

## CHAP. XXXIX.—THE PRIESTLY GARMENTS.

XXXIX. 1. And of the blue and the purple and the crimson they made garments of office to minister in the sanctuary: and they made the holy garments for Aaron, as the LORD commanded Moses. ¶ 61.

2. And he made the ephod of gold, of blue and purple and crimson, and fine linen twined. 3. And they beat out thin

plates of gold, and cut threads to work in amid the blue and the purple and the crimson, and the fine linen twined, with cunning work. 4. Shoulder-straps made they for it, joining it; at the two edges thereof was it joined. 5. And the belt for fastening it, that was upon it, was of the same, according to the work thereof; gold, blue and purple and crimson, and fine linen; as the LORD commanded Moses. § 83.

6. And they wrought onyx stones enclosed in ouches of gold, engraven, like the engravings of a signet, with the names of the sons of Israel. 7. And he put them on the shoulders of the ephod, to be stones of memorial for the sons of Israel; as the LORD commanded Moses. ¶ 62.

8. And he made the breastplate of cunning work, like the work of the ephod; of gold, blue and purple and crimson, and twined fine linen. 9. It was square; double made they the breastplate; a span its length, and a span its breadth, being doubled. 10. And they set in it four rows of stone, a row of sardius, topaz, and emerald, the first row. 11. And the second row, a carbuncle, a sapphire, and a diamond. 12. And the third row, a ligure, an agate, and an amethyst. 13. And the fourth row a chrysolite, an onyx, and a jasper, enclosed in ouches of gold in their settings. 14. And the stones were engraven with the names of the sons of Israel; these are twelve, according to their names, with the engravings of a signet, each with its name, for the twelve tribes. 15. And they made on the breastplate attaching chains of wreathen work, of pure gold. 16. And they made two ouches of gold, and two rings of gold, and put the two rings on the two ends of the breastplate. 17. And they put the two cords of gold upon the two rings on the two ends of the breastplate. 18. And the two ends of the two cords they fastened in the two ouches, and put them on the shoulders of the ephod in front of it. 19. And

they made two rings of gold, and put them on the two ends of the breastplate, on the border of it which was on the further side of the ephod inward. 20. And they made two rings of gold, and put them on the two shoulder-straps of the ephod beneath in the front of it, over against the joining thereof, above the belt of the ephod. 21. And they bound the breastplate by its rings unto the rings of the ephod with a lace of blue to be upon the belt of the ephod, that the breastplate be not loosed from the ephod; as the LORD commanded Moses. ¶ 63.

22. And he made the robe of the ephod of woven work, all of blue. 23. And the hole of the robe was in the midst of it, as the hole of a habergeon; a binding was on the hole of it around, that it might not be rent. 24. And they made upon the hem of the robe pomegranates of blue and purple and crimson, twined. 25. And they made bells of pure gold, and put the bells between the pomegranates, upon the hem of the robe around between the pomegranates. 26. A bell and a pomegranate, a bell and a pomegranate, on the hem of the robe around, to minister therein; as the LORD commanded Moses. § 84.

27. And they made the coats of fine linen, of woven work, for Aaron and for his sons; 28. And the mitre of fine linen, and the goodly bonnets of fine linen, and the linen breeches of fine linen twined; 29. And the girdle of fine linen twined, and blue and purple and crimson, of needlework; as the LORD commanded Moses. § 85.

30. And they made the plate of the holy crown of pure gold, and wrote upon it a writing, like the engravings of a signet, HOLINESS TO THE LORD. 31 And they put upon it a lace of blue to fasten it on the mitre above; as the LORD commanded Moses. § 86.

32. Then was finished all the service of the tabernacle of the
tent of meeting: and the sons of Israel did according to all
that the Lord commanded Moses, so did they. ¶ 64.

33. And they brought the tabernacle to Moses, the tent, and
all its vessels; its taches, its boards, it bars, and its pillars and
its sockets; 34. And the covering of rams' skins dyed red, and
the covering of badgers' skins, and the vail of covering; 35.
The ark of the testimony and the staves thereof, and the mercy-
seat; 36. The table, all its vessels, and the shew-bread; 37. The
pure candlestick, the lamps thereof, the lamps of the ordering,
and all its vessels, and the oil for the light; 38. And the altar
of gold, and the anointing oil, and the incense of perfumes,
and the cover for the tent door; 39. The altar of brass, and
its grate of brass, its staves and all its vessels, the laver and
its stand; 40. The hangings of the court, its pillars and its
sockets, and the cover for the court gate, its cords and its pins;
and all the vessels of the service of the tabernacle for the tent
of meeting: 41. The garments of office to minister in the
sanctuary; the holy garments for Aaron the priest, and the
garments of his sons to serve as priests therein. 42. Accord-
ing to all that the Lord commanded Moses, so did the sons of
Israel all the service. 43. And Moses saw all the work, and,
lo, they had done it as the Lord had commanded, so had they
done: and Moses blessed them. ¶ 65.

This chapter contains the making of the priestly attire, the ephod, the breastplate, the robe, the coats, the mitre and bonnet, the girdle, and the plate of the holy crown; and the presenting of the whole to Moses for inspection and approval.

1–32. The articles of dress are here, no doubt, arranged in the order of manufacture.

33–43. The finished articles are enumerated in detail. 36. *And the shew-bread.* This is included here as an accompaniment of the table, for which all the requisite materials were provided. 37. So "the oil for the light" was ready. 38. The anointing oil and the incense of perfumes had also been compounded by the perfumer. 43. This verse reminds us of Gen. i. 31. *And Moses blessed them*, in token of his approval of the manner in which they had executed the work.

## CHAP. XL.—THE TABERNACLE SET UP.

XL. 1. And the LORD spake unto Moses, saying, 2. On the
first day of the first month shalt thou set up the tabernacle of
the tent of meeting. 3. And thou shalt put therein the ark of
the testimony, and cover the ark with the vail. 4. And thou
shalt bring in the table and arrange the order thereof; and thou
shalt bring in the candlestick and set up the lamps thereof.
5. And thou shalt set the altar of gold for incense before the
ark of the testimony, and put the hanging of the door to the
tabernacle. 6. And thou shalt set the altar of burnt offering
before the door of the tabernacle of the tent of meeting. 7.
And thou shalt set the laver between the tent of meeting and
the altar, and put water therein. 8. And thou shalt set up
the court around, and put the cover at the court gate. 9.
And thou shalt take the anointing oil, and anoint the taber-
nacle and all that is therein; and shalt hallow it and all its
vessels, and it shall be holy. 10. And thou shalt anoint the
altar of burnt-offering and all its vessels; and thou shalt hallow
the altar, and the altar shall be most holy. 11. And thou
shalt anoint the laver and its stand, and hallow it. 12. And
thou shalt bring Aaron and his sons unto the door of the tent
of meeting, and wash them with water. 13. And thou shalt
clothe Aaron with the holy garments; and shalt anoint him
and hallow him, and he shall serve me as priest. 14. And
thou shalt bring his sons and clothe them with coats; 15. And

thou shalt anoint them, as thou didst anoint their father, and
they shall serve me as priests; and their anointing shall be to
them a perpetual priesthood for their generations. 16. And
Moses did according to all that the LORD commanded him,
so did he. § 87.

17. And it came to pass in the first month in the second
year, on the first day of the month, that the tabernacle was set
up. 18. And Moses set up the tabernacle, and fastened its
sockets, and set on the boards thereof, and put in the bars
thereof, and set up its pillars. 19. And he spread the tent
over the tabernacle, and put the covering of the tent upon it
above; as the LORD commanded Moses. § 88.

20. And he took and put the testimony in the ark, and set
the staves on the ark; and put the mercy-seat upon the ark
above. 21. And he brought the ark into the tabernacle, and
put on the vail of covering, and covered the ark of testimony;
as the LORD commanded Moses. § 89.

22. And he set the table in the tent of meeting on the side
of the tabernacle northward, without the vail. 23. And he
laid in order upon it the bread before the Lord; as the LORD
commanded Moses. § 90.

24. And he set the candlestick in the tent of meeting over
against the table, on the side of the tabernacle southward. 25.
And he set up the lamps before the LORD; as the LORD com-
manded Moses. § 91.

26. And he set the altar of gold in the tent of meeting before
the vail; 27. And burnt on it incense of perfumes; as the
LORD commanded Moses. § 92.

28. And he put the cover of the door on the tabernacle.
29. And the altar of burnt-offering set he at the door of the
tabernacle of the tent of meeting; and offered upon it the
burnt-offering and the meat-offering; as the LORD commanded
Moses. § 93.

30. And he set the laver between the tent of meeting and
the altar, and put water therein for washing. 31. And Moses
and Aaron and his sons shall wash their hands and there feet
thereout; 32. When they go into the tent of meeting, and
when they draw near to the altar, they wash; as the Lord
commanded Moses. § 94.

33. And he set up the court around the tabernacle and the
altar; and put on the cover of the court gate: and Moses
finished the work. ¶ 56.

34. And the cloud covered the tent of meeting; and the
glory of the Lord filled the tabernacle. 35. And Moses was
not able to enter the tent of meeting, because the cloud abode
thereon, and the glory of the Lord filled the tabernacle. 36.
And when the cloud was lifted up from over the tabernacle
the sons of Israel set out in all their journeys. 37. And if
the cloud was not lifted up, then they did not set out till the
day when it was lifted up. 38. For the cloud of the Lord was
upon the tabernacle by day, and the fire was on it by night, in
the eyes of all the house of Israel in all their journeys.

This chapter contains the setting up of the tabernacle, including the commencement of the prescribed services, and the manifestation of the divine presence and grace in the sanctuary.

1–16. The command is issued for the rearing of the tabernacle, and the anointing of it, and all its vessels and ministers. 9–15. This anointing is to signify the hallowing or setting of them apart to a holy use. Everything here has been tainted with the presence of sin. The sinner must be sanctified in order to be received again into the fellowship of his Maker. The great agent of sanctification is the Holy Spirit. His purifying work is here typified by the anointing with oil.

17–22. We have then an orderly detail of the execution of the first part of this command. 17–19. The date of the rearing of the tabernacle is the first day of the first month of the second year (see on xxxiv. 28). 20, 21. After the rearing of the tabernacle, the testimony, that is, the two tables of stone with the ten commandments engraven on them, is placed in the ark, and the ark with the mercy-seat in the most holy place. 22, 23. The table is placed on the north side of the holy place, probably at the middle of the wall. The shew-bread is set in order upon it. 24, 25. The candlestick occupies the corresponding place on the south side. Its lamps are set on. 26, 27. The altar of gold is placed before the vail at the middle points. The incense is kindled upon it. 28, 29. The altar of brass in the middle between the two sides, say twenty-five feet from the gate of the court. The burnt-offering and the meat-offering are offered upon it. 30–32. The laver we may suppose to be twenty-five feet from the altar, and from the door of the tent of meeting. *Shall wash*, will have washed whenever they proceed to the altar or the sanctuary. 32. *Wash.* This expresses the rule and custom of those engaged in the service of the tabernacle. 33. The whole is completed by the erection of the court. We observe in the rearing up of the tabernacle that every part of the ritual service is declared to be commenced as the corresponding part of the furniture is put in its place — the bread laid on the table, the lighted lamps set on the candlestick, the incense kindled on the altar of gold, and the appropriate offerings made on the altar of brass. This may mean either that these acts were done on the instant or in due course of events. In the absence of any reason to the contrary we may presume the former to be the fact. In this case the setting up of the service corresponds with the history of salvation. The ark, with its enclosed testimony, mercy-seat, and overshadowing cherubim, indicates the purpose of salvation in the mind of the present Deity. The bread, the light, and the incense shadow forth the actual blessings and privileges of the saved on account of the atonement yet to be made. The altar of brass and the laver are the emblems of atonement and renewal eventually accomplished in the history of mankind. The process for the individual is now reversed. When the burnt-offering and meat-offering have ascended the altar the atonement has been typically made and accepted. When the priest cleanses himself at the laver the internal holiness is symbolized. Then follows the intercession, represented by the incense on the golden altar. After that the full communion of holiness and blessing. And lastly, the union with God is sealed for ever.

34–38. Then follows an event of solemn import, which is best expressed in the simple language of the text. *Moses was not able.* In the first overwhelming display of the divine glory the tabernacle was not to be approached by man. The after proceedings, however, are not here recorded. We have to wait for them till we reach the subsequent books. This manifestation of the divine glory indicates the acceptance of the tabernacle and of the worship that is now commenced in it. 36. *When the cloud was lifted up.* This intimates that from this time forward the cloud continued resting on the tabernacle. The lifting of it up was the signal of departure. The cloud by day and the fire by night were conspicuous before the eyes of "all the house of Israel in all their journeys." Young and old, male and female, the numbered and marshalled host and the wandering clans tending their flocks and herds, were alike spectators of this wondrous sign of the divine presence, of the central encampment of their race, and of their perfect security under the divine protection. With this beautiful thought and cheering fact the sacred writer closes his account of an act which is the consummation of the exodus. Some circumstances antecedent to the rearing of the tabernacle, and many inseparably connected with it, have yet to be recorded. But the fine taste of the narrator taught him that the descent of the divine glory upon the erected tabernacle was the fitting conclusion of this stage of his unparalleled narrative.

The nations of the earth are no longer visibly one on the momentous question of allegiance to God. The holy nation has publicly come out from the world. The great body of mankind has become gradually more and more estranged from the true and living God. Four hundred and thirty years ago, Abraham has been called to separate himself from his father's home and land in preparation for this sad event. And now, when the process of human ungodliness is come to a head, a little nation sprung from him stands forth as a witness for God, a light in the midst of darkness, and a salt that is yet to preserve the earth. This little people is itself the type and germ of all coming stages of the kingdom of God on earth. Cradled in persecution, it yet escapes to the wilderness, and is fed with manna from the sky and water from the rock, by the omnipotent word of God. Its conscience is awakened by the promulgation of the moral law, and then led from the despair of guilt to the calmness of peace with God through the symbolic propitiation of the tabernacle. In the infancy of its mind it is wisely and kindly trained by the use of appropriate symbols to grasp the transcendent thoughts of mercy and truth, of righteousness and peace, of atonement, of redemption and regeneration. The roots of bitterness again and again burst through the soil and shoot up into a baneful luxuriance. Nevertheless, the planting of the Lord has taken root, and has been growing and gathering strength again after many storms and amidst many thorns through all the course of time. If Genesis tells of that first disobedience that brought death into the world of mankind, Exodus speaks with cheering hope of that suffering but surviving obedience that brings eternal life to the returning penitent. These two books, then, contain the pith and marrow of the ancient gospel; Leviticus and Numbers being subsidiary, and Deuteronomy a recapitulation. From the death of Joseph, the last event in Genesis, to the rearing of the tabernacle, is an interval of about one hundred and forty years, as may be gathered from the following table:

| Event. | Age of Father. | Date of Event. | Interval. | Date of Death. |
|---|---|---|---|---|
| Abraham called, at the age of 175 | -- | 2078 | | 2183 |
| | | | 30 | |
| Birth of Isaac, | 180 | 2108 | | 2288 |
| | | | 60 | |
| Birth of Jacob, | 147 | 2168 | | 2315 |
| | | | 91 | |
| Birth of Joseph, | 110 | 2259 | | 2369 |
| | | | 39 | |
| Jacob's descent into Egypt, | -- | 2298 | | |
| | | | 71 | |
| Death of Joseph, | -- | 2369 | | |
| | | | 59 | |
| Birth of Moses, | -- | 2428 | | |
| | | | 80 | |
| Exodus, | -- | 2508 | | |
| From call of Abraham to exodus, | -- | -- | 430 | |